In Season

cooking with vegetables and fruits

Sarah Raven

photography by Jonathan Buckley

foreword by Dan Barber

UNIVERSE

Foreword 7
Introduction 10

January | February
Cabbages 14   Chicories 22   Citrus 30
Evergreen herbs 40   Winter salad greens 50

March | April
Cauliflower 58   Purple sprouting broccoli, calabrese,
and spring greens 62   Rhubarb 66   Spinach 72
Spring herbs 80   Watercress and wild garlic 92

May | June
Asparagus 98   Fava beans 104   Crunchy lettuces 110
Globe artichokes 116   New/waxy potatoes 122
Peas 128   Radishes 134   Samphire and
elderflowers 138   Strawberries 144

July | August
Apricots, peaches, and nectarines 154   Beets 160
Blackcurrants, white currants, and redcurrants 166
Cherries 174   Zucchini 180   Cucumbers 192
Edible flowers 198   Green beans 204
Gooseberries 212   High-summer herbs 218
Melons 234   New summer carrots 238   Onions,
shallots, and garlic 242   Plums and greengages
254   Raspberries, tayberries, and loganberries 260
Tomatoes 266

September | October
Apples 288   Eggplants 296   Cranberry beans 302
Fennel 308   Celery 312   Chili peppers 316   Damson
plums, sloes, rowans, blackberries, mulberries, and
elderberries 320   Figs and grapes 328   Maincrop/
floury potatoes 334   Mushrooms 342   Nuts 348
Pears 358   Sweet peppers 366   Pumpkins and winter
squashes 372   Quinces and medlars 378   Corn 382

November | December
Brussels sprouts 388   Chard 392   Kale 398
Leeks 404   Pomegranates and cranberries 410
Winter root vegetables 420

Index 444

Foreword

I've never met Sarah Raven. I came close a few years ago, when she gave a talk here at Stone Barns Center for Food & Agriculture in Pocantico Hills, New York. The anticipation of her visit nearly turned the place inside out.

I remember walking past the dooryard garden that day and wondering why it looked so especially immaculate, and why our vegetable farmer, Jack Algiere, a Paul Bunyan-esque character of immense talent, had, for the first time since I've known him, cropped his beard and combed his hair.

"Big day," I heard Andrew, our normally laconic waiter say as he zipped passed me into the restaurant. Since waiters don't run to work, ever, I wondered aloud: "What's going on?"

That's when Philippe Gouze, our general manager and gardening guru slid up next to me and placed his hand on my arm. "Sarah Raven," he said. "Is coming. Today." The last time Philippe had held my arm for effect, the restaurant was under construction and the new kitchen had just caught fire.

"Unbelievable!" I said to Philippe, "Very exciting!"

Sarah Raven? I had no idea who she was. In the kitchen the cooks were going about their business, but off in the corner, a young cook we call Linguini (after the hapless skinny hero of *Ratatouille*) was bent so far over a platter of artfully arranged salad greens he practically disappeared behind the counter.

"Linguini," I shouted. "What the hell?"

He picked his head up, blinking. "Chef?"

"What are you doing?"

"Um, because we're supposed to have some salads for the guests after Ms. Raven's talk…"

"You know about Sarah Raven?" I asked quietly, coming over to him.

"Ah, yup, yes, well, because my mother is a big, big fan." I stared at him. "*The Cutting Garden*? I grew up with it on our coffee table. She's like the greatest flower gardener in the world." I must have looked angry. "Sorry chef, because I took it upon myself to pick some greens from the greenhouse this morning. Because I thought she'd like to see what we're all about?"

I've spent the last several years learning what Sarah Raven is all about, and what I've discovered continues to impress and fascinate. At age thirty, she received a medical degree (having already earned a history degree, and given birth to a daughter), but when she gave birth to her second daughter, at home in Sussex (in front of the fire, of course), she decided that practicing medicine wouldn't allow her to be the mother she wanted to be. So she became a florist (unable to find books on growing flowers for cutting, she wrote her own), then a professional gardener (winning the Garden Writers' Guild Award for Best Gardening Book), then a teacher, which, naturally, segued into a cooking school. Did I mention she's also a television host for the BBC?

You might think Sarah Raven's got it in her genes, and you'd be partially right: her father was a lecturer of classics at Cambridge and a part-time botanist—in other words, he was an old-school, Renaissance version of his daughter.

But in Raven's case, that's selling her short. She's more earth mother for the twenty-first century than a throwback to traditional mores. In my mind this book offers a peek at the future of cooking. Flip though the July and August chapters and you'll see the kind of dishes—zucchini and lemon salad, barbequed carrots, plums with bread and butter pudding—that draw you in not just with their hard-to-resist flavors, but because they give you the feeling that you are a part of something much greater than a good recipe. You feel instantly that the summer roasted soil is everywhere around, and that the days disappear into a blissful haze of marketing and gardening, cooking and eating.

You won't stand in awe of any dish in this book—that's not the point here—the plating is as direct and as unpretentious as the woman behind the stove. What you will feel is that the world of Sarah Raven and Co. is vibrant, joyful, and pleasantly disarrayed.

After you spend some time with this book, you'll likely imagine a Sunday afternoon in the kitchen with kids playing, dogs shedding, chairs in need of upholstering, and even a garden in need of weeding. You'll sit back and say, "Oh, this is real," and because of that, and Sarah's can-do approach, you'll want to mimic her in every way you can.

Food is the medium here, but the message amounts to a philosophy of life. She may teach us a thing or two about cooking, but the real lesson is learning how to eat.

Dan Barber

Introduction

This book is all about the pleasures that fruit and vegetables can give you; its aim is to put them at the center of every meal. It's also a practical guide to all that is wonderful in the edible plant kingdom, with more than 450 recipes using the vegetable garden—or a good farmers' market or grocery store—as both their source and inspiration. It's not a vegetarian book—although it contains plenty of recipes that have nothing but vegetables in them.

For many of us over the past 150 years, meat has dominated our diet. In the nineteenth century the invention of the refrigerated ship meant that meat could be brought fresh from anywhere in the world, and it became increasingly cheap. The development of factory farming and the efficient networks of the global economy have meant that daily meat has become a possibility for everyone. In one way, that's a good thing, but a consequence has been that it is now as if a meal is no good unless it is built around a slab of flesh, which is a sad and reduced place to have arrived at.

Meat is hungry for resources. It uses land in the most profligate ways; it requires far more calories to produce meat than it eventually delivers. And, of course, it uses large amounts of energy in being shipped around the world. That is not how it used to be. Meat was once considered precious, a regular, delicious, but occasional visitor to the plate. The mainstays of your diet were vegetables and fruit. In a way, this book is advocating a return to an older habit, where these foods can reclaim their rightful place, not as a stand-in or supporting part, but at center stage.

The world is thankfully turning in the right direction. Think of your average American grocery store twenty years ago. Its racks would have been dominated by apples, potatoes, carrots, floppy lettuce, and cabbage. Today, those things will still be there, but you'll find them among fennel, celeriac, figs, pomegranates, and a great array of mushrooms. Add to them the farmers' markets that are springing up all over the place, with their "limited editions" of red brussels sprouts, sweet tomatoes picked the night before, pumpkins and squash of all colors and sizes, and you will see that these are good times for fruit and vegetables.

Other parts of the world have kept faith with a more balanced approach in their cooking cultures. The Mediterranean has always been a wonderful source of inspiration for this way of eating. Traditionally, in France and even more so in Italy and Spain, where families would raise and slaughter their own animals, you'd eat meat or fish on holidays, but by no means every day. In these food cultures, vegetables are not the optional extras—"the trimmings"—but the daily foundation of food itself.

When I was a child in the 1970s, we often went on holiday to Asolo in the Veneto, a honey-colored town in the foothills of the Dolomites. Orchards and farmland ran up to its medieval walls, and all the produce of garden and field was on sale in the market square and under the shady stone arcades lining the streets. Day after day, under the shopping and cooking guidance of Angelica, the cook in the house where we stayed, we would feast on an abundance of unfamiliar ingredients: globe artichokes, herby salads, wild greens, borlotti beans, bitter chicory, sometimes with bread, sometimes with pasta, sometimes with rice, but rarely with meat.

At university, like so many before me and since, I read Elizabeth David over and over again, and I cooked with her books at hand in a tiny house I used to rent in the mountains of the Auvergne. Then, to support myself through medical school in London, I waitressed at the River Cafe, which has done so much to bring the Italian culinary tradition into the English mainstream. These influences molded me to a way of cooking that is based on really good ingredients and that focuses on taste rather than appearance. Fruit and vegetables lend themselves to simplicity; the less you do to them, the better. Food cooked this way is alive with the flavor of its raw ingredients.

A great bonus of eating local, seasonal food is that your diet will never be repetitive. As the seasons unfold, old favorites recur and new opportunities present themselves. And, for the most part, there's no need for it to have traveled from the other side of the world. In the winter, there are almost as many delicious possibilities as there are in summer.

I have poured enormous amounts of myself and my life into this book. I think of it as a compendium of everything I've loved in the garden and the kitchen over the last fifteen or twenty years. I'm hoping that you will cook your way through it, and that over the years you'll have a good time doing so. But I have a further ambition for you, too. If you're lucky enough to have access to any outdoor space, growing fruit and vegetables is a wonderful thing to do. It can't be claimed that growing your own food is not time-consuming, but it is, I think, a way to be happy, involving a little thinking, some physical work, and some creativity. Harvesting and cooking from the garden is one of my greatest pleasures in life.

Sarah Raven

January | February

Cabbages

When you are preparing cabbage, rip off the leaves one at a time and get rid of most of the central stem. It cooks at a different rate to the leaves, so chuck it away. With any green cabbage, if there's time, strip off the leaves a couple of hours before you want to eat, tear them into pieces, and float them in a sink of cold water. As with salad, this perks cabbage up and keeps it crisp. The plant cells absorb water by osmosis. The cell walls then bulge with the contained water. That's what gives them the crunch, which they retain when lightly cooked. Always cook cabbage with the lid off to keep it bright green.

Cabbage has a versatile flavor, which is delicious with butter and plenty of salt and pepper. For a simple lunch, have a plate of cabbage, yogurt, and some grated nutmeg. If on a diet, treat it like pasta: cut it up into fine spaghetti-like strands and serve it garnished with grated Parmesan cheese, or try it with finely grated ginger, or dry-roasted caraway, sunflower, or cumin seeds.

Cabbage is wonderful raw, either on its own or very finely sliced and mixed with carrot in a simple salad. Don't make it all slurpy like coleslaw, but dress it lightly with fruity olive oil, minced garlic, plenty of salt and pepper, and lemon juice. Greek restaurants often serve this and it's good to eat with grilled meat or fish as a contrast to the ubiquitous tomato, cucumber, and feta salad.

As well as green or white cabbage, at this time of year you must have a few meals of red. The virtues of red cabbage are its incredible color and its texture, which is firmer than green. It will take more cooking, so it is the ideal vegetable for rich, reduced, slow-cooked dishes like braised red cabbage and soup. With an added acid—vinegar or wine—the color fixes as a brilliant magenta. Without this, it can turn an unappetizing grey.

Fried cabbage
with juniper

A wonderfully healthy and delicious lunch. Have the cabbage on its own, or on top of a bowl of rice. For something more substantial, cut some seared steak, tuna, or lambs' liver into thin strips and toss them in.

Serves 4 to 6

1 small (or ½ large) savoy cabbage (about 1½ pounds)
1 tablespoon sesame seeds (you can mix in sunflower seeds too)
1 tablespoon juniper berries, crushed (optional)
2 garlic cloves, chopped
Sea salt
2 tablespoons peanut oil
1 red chili, seeds removed and thinly sliced (red is good for the color)
2 teaspoons toasted sesame oil
1 tablespoon finely chopped fresh ginger
1 tablespoon honey
Splash of Japanese soy sauce
Freshly ground pepper
Small bunch of cilantro, coarsely chopped

Cut the cabbage—savoy is best—into quarters and discard the hard white heart and leaf midribs before chopping it finely.

Toast the sesame seeds in a pan over low heat until they're golden brown. This will take about 5 minutes, but don't let them burn. Then put them to one side. Crush the juniper berries and garlic with the sea salt, using a mortar and pestle.

Heat a tablespoon of the peanut oil in a wok or large frying pan. Add the chili and cook for 1 minute over medium heat. Remove the chili from the oil, leaving the spicy oil in the pan, and add the sesame seeds. Add the rest of the peanut oil and the sesame oil to the same pan. Then add the cabbage, salt, juniper berries, and garlic. Turn up the heat. Stir every minute or so for 5 minutes and then add all the other ingredients except the cilantro. Stir for another couple of minutes and remove from the heat. The cabbage should still be crunchy. This tastes lovely with chopped cilantro over the top.

Savoy cabbage
and cilantro soup

This cabbage soup is based on a recipe by the Irish chef Denis Cotter. I often make my version for lunch in the winter, cooking it for a shorter time than he recommends. The cabbage is then crisp and bright. This soup has lots of different flavors, with a lovely after-bite.

Serves 6

1 to 2 medium onions
½ medium savoy cabbage
2 tablespoons olive oil
1 to 2 green chilis, finely chopped
4 garlic cloves, finely chopped
2-inch piece ginger, peeled and chopped
2 tablespoons coriander seeds, crushed
3½ cups good vegetable stock
1 (14-ounce) can coconut milk
Bunch of cilantro, chopped
Juice of 3 limes
Salt and pepper

Finely chop the onions and very finely shred the cabbage, either by hand or by using the finest slicing disc on a food processor.

Heat the oil in a pan, add the onions and cabbage, and cook them over moderate heat for a couple of minutes before adding the chilis, garlic, ginger, and coriander. Continue cooking for about 5 minutes, stirring regularly, until the onions and cabbage are tender but still have a bite to them.

Bring the stock to a boil in a separate pan and add it to the vegetables. Simmer for 5 minutes, then add the coconut milk, half of the cilantro, the lime juice, and finally salt and pepper.

Serve the soup with extra cilantro to taste.

Sweet-and-sour marinated cabbage

This pickle is northern European in origin and is good with warming, intense-tasting winter food. It goes well with smoked fish—trout or eel—and is ideal with a strong cheese. The key to this treatment is the fine shredding of the cabbage and the large quantities of fresh dill, and dill (or fennel) and mustard seed, in the marinade. This dish needs to be made at least the day before you want to eat it, so that the flavors of the seeds really come through.

Serves 6

½ **white cabbage**
½ **cup cider vinegar**
½ **cup superfine sugar**
Large bunch of dill, finely chopped
3 tablespoons good sunflower oil
1 garlic clove, chopped
2 teaspoons dill or fennel seeds
2 teaspoons mustard seeds
Salt and pepper

Cut the cabbage into quarters and remove the midrib, then slice the cabbage very finely. Use the green leaf only, not the stem.

Heat the vinegar in a small pan over low heat and then stir in the sugar until it has dissolved. Allow this to cool.

Add the fresh dill, oil, garlic, dill seeds and mustard seeds, salt and pepper to the sweet vinegar and dress the cabbage with this marinade.

Leave in a jar or covered container at least overnight for the flavors to develop. This keeps very well in a screw-topped jar in the fridge and is still excellent after 2 or 3 weeks.

Bea's stuffed cabbage leaves

This is Bea Csap's recipe. She is from Hungary and is our gardener here on the farm. The stuffed cabbage leaves are excellent eaten on their own, dipped into plain yogurt, or with sauerkraut. The sauerkraut is not essential but it adds another flavor.

Serves 8 to 10 (Yield: about 20 rolls)

1 cabbage
4 bay leaves
½ **cup white wine vinegar**
Bowl of iced water
6 ounces bacon, chopped
1 onion, chopped
2 garlic cloves, crushed
Bunch of chopped mixed herbs (such as marjoram, thyme, and dill)
1 teaspoon smoked paprika
¼ **teaspoon ground cumin seeds**
Salt and pepper
1¼ **pounds ground pork**
1¼ **pounds ground beef**
½ **cup cooked long-grain white rice**
1 egg
1 jar of sauerkraut (optional)
Small bunch of dill
2½ **cups chicken or vegetable stock**

Preheat the oven to 350°F.

Choose the bright green outer leaves of the cabbage and blanch them whole for 2 to 3 minutes in a large pot of boiling salted water containing 3 of the bay leaves and the vinegar. Plunge the leaves into ice-cold water to cool and then remove the thickest part of the midrib. This makes them easier to roll.

Fry the bacon in a shallow pan until it's cooked but not crisp, and put aside. In the same pan, add the onion to the bacon juices with the crushed garlic, chopped herbs, paprika, cumin, salt, and pepper.

Mix the raw pork and beef together with the cooked rice and the

bacon (if using sauerkraut, reserve a little of the bacon to add to that) and onion mixture, adding a beaten egg to bind it and seasoning with salt and pepper (you can quickly fry a teaspoonful of the mixture in a dash of oil to test the seasoning). Take a small handful of this mixture, place on a cabbage leaf, and then roll it up, starting from the stem end and tucking the edges inwards to make a neat roll.

If you're using sauerkraut, drain the jar, keeping the liquor to one side, and rinse under cold water in a sieve. Fluff it up and mix with the reserved bacon and a little more chopped dill. Place this mixture on the bottom of a casserole dish and arrange the cabbage rolls in quite a tight layer on top.

Cover with the stock plus a little of the sauerkraut liquor, add the remaining bay leaf and some more dill, and cook, covered, in the preheated oven for 1½ hours.

The ultimate minestrone

A great winter meal of a soup, based on a recipe from Marcella Hazan, the doyenne of Italian cookery writing.

Serves 4 to 6
- 3 tablespoons olive oil
- 1 tablespoon butter
- 2 onions, chopped
- ¼ pound pancetta
- 1 large or 2 small carrot(s), chopped
- 1 celery stick, chopped
- 2 zucchini, chopped
- ¼ medium red cabbage, shredded
- 1 pound shelled fresh cranberry beans or 1 (8-ounce) can cannellini beans
- 3 large fresh tomatoes, chopped, or 1 (8-ounce) can chopped tomatoes
- Salt and pepper
- 2 cups good chicken or vegetable stock
- ½ cup red wine
- Freshly grated Parmesan cheese, as a garnish
- Crusty bread, to serve

Put the oil, butter, onions, and pancetta into a large saucepan. Cook over medium heat until the onions are a deep gold. Add the chopped vegetables, the shredded cabbage, and the fresh cranberry beans. (If you are using canned beans, do not add them at this stage.)

Add the chopped tomatoes and seasoning, and stir well. Then add the stock and the red wine, making sure that the liquid covers the vegetables. Cover the pan and simmer gently for at least an hour. If using canned beans, add them after about 50 minutes.

When the liquid has significantly reduced and the soup looks rich and quite thick, taste and adjust the seasoning. Rest it for 10 minutes (the flavors are better when it is not scalding hot) and serve with freshly grated Parmesan and crusty bread.

Quick braised red cabbage

It is always said that the best red cabbage is cooked with low heat for a very long time. It's true that this deepens the flavor, but this simple recipe is delicious after just an hour of cooking. It's ideal with baked potatoes, game, roasted red meat, or carbonnade of beef or venison.

Serves 6 to 8
- 1 large red cabbage
- 3 tablespoons butter
- Olive oil
- 1 large onion, chopped
- 2 tart apples, peeled and roughly chopped
- ¼ cup malt vinegar, and more if necessary
- Grated zest of 1 large orange
- 2 heaping tablespoons soft brown sugar
- Handful of raisins (optional)
- ¾ cup walnuts (optional)
- Salt and pepper

Remove the core of the cabbage and slice it thinly or put it into a food processor using the finest slicing disc.

Put the butter and a splash of oil into a large pot, add the chopped onion, and wait for it to soften before adding the red cabbage. Keep stirring to coat the cabbage well, then add the roughly chopped apples, malt vinegar, orange zest, and soft brown sugar. Add the raisins and walnuts if you want to. Season with salt and pepper, and cook either over low heat or in a 375°F oven.

Check the cabbage regularly to make sure that it is not sticking and add more vinegar if necessary. Make this as sweet and sour as you like by adding more or less brown sugar and vinegar to taste.

The cabbage and apples will have softened after about an hour and should have cooked to a lovely glossy deep red, with nearly all the liquid absorbed. This freezes well.

Chicories

Chicories are an elegant and refined group of plants, at their most handsome in cold weather when other things are rooty, earthy, and rather cloddish. There are many different types and varieties: the crimson croquet ball of radicchio with its tightly packed leaves; the creamy-green and white pointed bullets of Belgian endive; the larger, looser wine-red leaves of Treviso radicchio; the bright yellow-green, stippled crimson Variegata del Castelfranco; and curly endive (or frisée).

Try to find several different chicories from a good market. They look beautiful and last well in a large shallow bowl in the middle of the table. They are all durable once harvested, slow to rot and relatively long-storing.

Chicories can be off-putting to the uninitiated, as they are bitter when raw, but when cooked they are delicious. To offset the bitterness of a raw chicory, try combining it with sweet flavors. You can chop up a few leaves and add them to a mixed leaf salad; they have a complex flavor that is good as the odd surprise. The taste of raw chicory goes well with the sweet sharpness of any citrus, and it's good with strong cheese.

I'm not so keen on curly endive, the large serrated, crinkly rosettes that possess a milder, less bitter flavor. Their texture is tough and they are hard work to eat—a bit like an organic Brillo pad—but you could add a few handfuls to your bitter leaf salad. Endive works well with crisp bacon or pancetta as one of the leaves in a classic French Grilled goat cheese salad (see page 54). I have never eaten Variegata del Castelfranco cooked, but the other varieties are very good roasted, grilled, sautéed, or even deep-fried as tempura.

Treviso and Belgian endive are more expensive. Belgian usually—and Treviso sometimes—are force grown in the dark, which makes them more tender and less bitter. Radicchio and Variegata del Castelfranco are usually field grown and therefore easier and cheaper to produce. Much of the chicory we buy is sold as the heart of the plant only with the outer leaves removed. Many northern Italian households eat chicory almost every day from autumn until the late spring, when a wider selection of vegetables come into season, and it fills a good section of any Italian winter market stall. Treviso may be difficult to find here, so grab it when you can (although radicchio is fine as a replacement).

With all these chicories, if you can't buy them, consider growing them. Radicchio, Variegata del Castelfranco, and Treviso are hardy, easy-to-grow, invaluable cold weather plants ideal for a year-round productive patch.

Braised endive

An excellent quick winter dish. It's delicious eaten on its own with crusty bread dipped in the lemony cream. It's also good with grilled, roasted, or barbecued pork or veal.

Serves 6
2 pounds Belgian endive
½ pound prosciutto, chopped
Salt and pepper
3 tablespoons unsalted butter
A little water or white wine
Juice of 1 lemon
1 cup heavy cream

Butter an ovenproof dish that has a lid. Arrange the whole endives in the dish, scattering over the chopped prosciutto. Season with salt and pepper, and dot with butter. Cover the dish with a sheet of parchment paper under the lid and bake in a low oven for 40 minutes, until the chicory is tender and lightly browned. Check it from time to time to make sure there is enough moisture and add a little water or white wine if necessary.

Once it's cooked, add the lemon juice and cream—swirling them around the chicory—and serve with more coarsely ground pepper.

Endive and blue cheese salad

A very English version of a classic French salad, using Stilton, not Roquefort. With good hunks of cheese and some bread, it's quite enough for lunch, or you can make a smaller plate as a first course.

Serves 6
4 heads Belgian endive
3 pears—any firm medium-ripe pear will do
Juice of 1 lemon
½ cup walnuts

For the dressing:
8 ounces Stilton, Cashel Blue, or any crumbly blue cheese
Juice and grated zest of 1 lemon
2 tablespoons light cream
2 tablespoons olive oil
Salt and pepper

Break the endive into individual leaves and peel the pears. Slice the pears lengthwise, removing the core. To prevent them from turning brown, quickly cover the cut surfaces of the chicory and pears with a squirt of lemon juice.

To make the dressing, blend two-thirds of the cheese with the lemon juice and zest, the cream, and the olive oil in a blender or food processor. Add salt and pepper to taste.

Toast the walnuts for 3 minutes in a hot oven or a dry frying pan and break them into smaller pieces.

Using your hands, toss the leaves and pear slices with the dressing. Garnish with the walnuts and the rest of the cheese crumbled over the top of the salad.

Endive and blood orange salad

Putting fruit in a salad may seem a bit retro but don't worry, this salad looks beautiful and is ideal as a light winter first course when you're heading towards a rich meaty entrée. A squeeze of lemon with the orange juice in the dressing sharpens it up and gives it the strength to stand up to the bitterness of the leaves. To make the salad more substantial, add roasted walnuts.

Serves 4 to 6

2 small heads Belgian endive
1 small head Treviso (if not
**   available, use all Belgian endive)**
Squeeze of lemon juice
2 blood oranges

For the dressing:

3 tablespoons olive oil
1 tablespoon walnut oil
Juice of ½ blood orange
Juice and grated zest of ½ lemon
Salt and pepper
1 heaping tablespoon walnuts,
**   roughly chopped (optional)**

If using small endives, you can peel away the leaves one by one and eat them just as they are, without slicing. If you can only find big heads, cut each frond in half lengthwise and squirt immediately with lemon juice. Meanwhile, toast the roughly chopped walnuts, if using them, for 3 minutes in a hot oven or dry-roast in a pan.

To end up with slices of orange free of white pith, cut a slice off both ends of the orange and then peel it as you would an apple: hold the orange with your non-preferred hand and, with a small serrated knife held with the blade pointing upwards, make short up-and-down sawing movements, going round and round the fruit until it is completely skinned. There should be no pith left on the orange. You can then follow each layer of skin down to the heart to cut the fruit into skinless segments, or slice the whole orange horizontally as thinly as you can, into cartwheels. Remove the pithy center of each segment.

Make the dressing by mixing the olive and walnut oils, orange juice, lemon juice and zest, salt, and pepper, making sure that it has a sharp enough taste. If you're using ordinary oranges—which have a sweeter flavor than blood oranges—add more lemon juice to make it good and tart. Garnish with the walnuts, if using them.

Treviso al forno with griddled polenta

I had this slow-cooked vegetable at a simple restaurant in a beautiful arcaded walkway in Asolo, in the Veneto region of Italy. Cooked chicory, and particularly Treviso, is on almost every menu there throughout the winter and this is one of the most adaptable ways to eat it. Treviso al forno— roasted in the oven— is delicious with almost anything: meat, fish, or just polenta and some grated Parmesan. If you can't get Treviso, use Belgian endive.

Serves 10 as a starter or a side dish
   6 heads Treviso or Belgian endive
   Extra virgin olive oil, plus a bit
      extra for drizzling
   Plenty of salt and pepper

For the polenta:
   1½ cups instant polenta
   3 tablespoons butter
   ½ cup grated Parmesan cheese,
      plus a bit extra to garnish

Preheat the oven to 375°F.
   Cut the endive in half lengthwise. Drizzle the halves with olive oil, season with salt and pepper, and bake them, covered, in the preheated oven for 30 minutes.
   To make the polenta, bring 6 cups salted water to a boil and then remove from the heat while you whisk in the polenta grains. Keep whisking until the mixture is quite smooth, and then put the pan back on the heat. It will start to bubble furiously, but keep stirring and turn the heat down.
   Cook the polenta for a few minutes until it is thick and creamy. Add the butter and Parmesan, and season well. This really benefits from lots of salt and pepper. If you prefer "wet" polenta, rather than grilled or panfried, add less polenta flour to the same amount of water, butter, and Parmesan, and keep it warm until you want to eat. It won't be stiff enough to grill.

To grill or panfry the polenta, turn it out on to a large shallow plate or dish (ideally, the depth of the polenta should be about ¾ inch). Allow it to cool completely while you cook the endive. When the polenta is cold, cut it into triangles or strips ready for cooking. Make sure the grill or cast-iron skillet is really hot. Cook the wedges of polenta for about 5 minutes on either side.
   Put a dollop of polenta (or one or two slices if grilled) and one or two halves of roasted endive on each plate. Drizzle with olive oil and garnish with coarsely grated Parmesan.

Treviso lasagne

I learned how to make this Treviso lasagne, or pasticcio, in the house of some Italian friends—Daniella, Luciano, and Silvia Piccolotto—just outside Asolo. The occasion was a bustling family affair, with several generations milling around in the kitchen. We ate it as a second course, after the antipasti and before the meat. It takes more preparation than everyday pasta, but does very well for a big family meal. We made our own pasta, rolling out the sheets until they were very thin, but you can, of course, use the ready-made variety.

This is one of my favorite winter meals. Add ½ pound chopped fried pancetta for a meatier dish.

Serves 8 to 10
- **1½ pounds Treviso or radicchio**
- **½ onion**
- **1 garlic clove**
- **6 tablespoons extra virgin olive oil, plus a little to grease the dish**
- **½ cup grated Parmesan cheese**
- **Salt and pepper**
- **8 ounces lasagne sheets— homemade or dried**
- **1 or 2 tablespoons butter**

For the béchamel sauce:
- **1 quart milk**
- **6 tablespoons butter**
- **½ cup all-purpose flour**
- **1 egg yolk**
- **1 cup mascarpone cheese**
- **Freshly grated nutmeg, to taste**
- **1 cup (or to taste) grated cheese, such as Cheddar, pecorino, or Parmesan**

Preheat the oven to 350°F.

Cut the Treviso or radicchio into ½-inch slices. Slice the onion and peel the garlic clove, crushing it with the side of a knife but leaving it whole.

Heat the olive oil in a deep saucepan and cook the onion and garlic over low heat until they are golden brown. Remove the garlic and add the radicchio to the pan, stirring continuously to avoid it catching. Once it's wilted and brown—after 2 to 3 minutes—take it off the heat and season.

To make the béchamel sauce, bring the milk to a boil and, in a separate pan, melt the butter. Stir the flour into the butter, allow it to cook for a couple of minutes, and then gradually add the hot milk. Add the egg yolk mixed with the mascarpone and plenty of nutmeg, stirring continuously as you add the ingredients. Season with plenty of salt and pepper.

Put one ladleful of the sauce to one side and mix the rest with the radicchio. Add almost all the grated cheese and stir until it melts.

If your pasta needs pre-cooking, boil the sheets in plenty of salted water and allow them to dry flat on a clean cloth. Lightly oil an ovenproof dish. Alternate the pasta with thin layers of the radicchio béchamel mixture in the dish. The layers of béchamel mixture should be quite thin so that the lovely bitterness of the radicchio is balanced with the flavor of the pasta.

Finish with the remaining béchamel, then the grated cheese, and finally dot the top with the extra butter and a bit of extra nutmeg. Cook the lasagne in the preheated oven for 35 to 40 minutes.

Radicchio and lemon pasta

This is a simple chicory and pasta dish, quick to prepare. It's also delicious cold the next day, by which time the radicchio has lost some of its bitterness.

Serves 4
- **¼ pound pancetta, chopped**
- **2 to 3 tablespoons extra virgin olive oil**
- **½ onion, chopped**
- **1 garlic clove, finely chopped**
- **8 ounces dried egg tagliatelle**
- **½ pound radicchio (or Treviso)**
- **3 tablespoons dry white wine**
- **3 tablespoons butter**
- **Grated zest of 1 lemon**
- **⅓ cup heavy cream**
- **Salt and pepper**
- **Handful of flat-leaf parsley, chopped**
- **Grated Parmesan cheese, to serve**

Bring a large pot of water to a boil. Put the chopped pancetta into a wide, shallow pan over moderate heat with half the olive oil. When the fat begins to run, add the chopped onion and garlic, and then cook with the pancetta for about 3 to 4 minutes, until the onion has softened.

Put the pasta into the pot of salted boiling water and cook until al dente.

Thinly slice the radicchio and add it to the onion mixture with the wine and sauté until the radicchio begins to wilt. Add the butter and lemon zest; pour in the cream and season well.

Add this to the drained pasta with the remaining olive oil and the chopped flat-leaf parsley. I love this pasta dish with a generous topping of Parmesan.

Citrus

In all but the warmest regions, citrus trees need to be indoors or in a greenhouse in the winter, and then put out in pots in a sheltered spot in the garden for the warmer months, but even so they won't produce enough fruit to cook. So having citrus in a garden cookbook is a bit of a cheat for those with cold winters, but it's now, in the winter, that the main citrus season reaches its peak, and they're hard to resist. Lemons, limes, oranges, and grapefruits make some of the best desserts at this time of year, when there isn't any native fruit to pick; and, of course, they are the essential ingredient in marmalade.

When there are lots of small cheap oranges, buy them to squeeze for juice. Tart blood oranges make the tastiest and they're around at the end of winter and for most of spring. What do you do with all the squeezed orange skins? You're not supposed to put them in the compost—they're too acid. We went to stay with friends last winter who had the answer. Dry them out for a day or two in a slow oven or on top of a radiator, until they desiccate, but don't burn them. Their waxy skins mean they make effective firelighters and as they burn, they fill the room with a good marmalade-y smell.

With all these recipes, you want to use unwaxed fruit, but it isn't always easy to find. Try to buy organic—the others may have preservative in the skin—and then dewax them (you can do this with lemons, limes, oranges, grapefruits, or clementines): drop the fruit whole into boiling water and swirl them around for a couple of minutes to melt the wax from the skin.

Amber marmalade

This is a delicious alternative to traditional English marmalade made with Seville oranges and it has a beautiful color.

Yield: about 7 or 8 pints
  3 grapefruits
  3 oranges
  3 large lemons
  About 5 pounds sugar

Wash the fruit and squeeze out the juice (an electric juicer is fantastic for this job, as it halves the time and makes the pithy membrane easier to remove). Pull out the thick white membrane and then slice the fruit thinly, keeping the pips.

Measure the fruit and juice and put them in a large bowl with three times their volume of water (about 1 gallon). Put the pith that you have removed, together with the pips, into a cheesecloth bag.

Pour the contents of the bowl into a preserving kettle or large pot, and tie the cheesecloth bag to the handle so that it hangs into the pot and steeps overnight. The next day, simmer, covered, over low heat for about half an hour, and then remove the lid and cook for a further hour or so, until the fruit is soft. Warm the sugar in a very low oven for about half an hour.

Remove the cheesecloth bag, squeezing out the liquid into the pot, and measure the fruit and juice. For every 2½ cups of juice add 2½ cups of sugar. Put the pot back on low heat and make sure that the sugar is completely dissolved before raising the heat and boiling rapidly until the gelling point is reached.

To test for the gelling point, put a saucer in the fridge to cool. When you think the marmalade might be ready, put a spoonful of the boiling jam on the saucer. Return the saucer to the fridge. Once it is cold, the jam should wrinkle when you push it with your finger.

Skim the scum from the surface with a spoon. Allow it to rest for at least 20 minutes—or the fruit peel will all float to the top. Stir once and pour into warm sterilized dry jars. Put a greaseproof disc on the top of each jar and cover immediately.

Marmalade ice cream with fresh oranges

Marmalade ice cream is one of the easiest you can make. We do it in our ice cream maker, but you don't need one. Just mix the marmalade with the cream, yogurt, and juice, pour it into a Tupperware container, and put it into your freezer. You don't even need to stir it.

This ice cream is rich, so eat it with these tart, nutmeg-flavored orange slices.

Serves 6 to 8
For the ice cream:
  12 ounces Seville marmalade
  1¼ cups heavy cream
  1¼ cups plain yogurt
  3 tablespoons orange juice

For the oranges:
  6 oranges
  1 heaping tablespoon Seville marmalade
  A little freshly grated nutmeg

To make the ice cream, put the marmalade, cream, yogurt, and orange juice into an ice cream machine and freeze/churn for 20 minutes. You might want to strain out a bit of the orange peel beforehand. Pack into plastic containers and freeze. Allow to rest 20 minutes in the fridge before serving the ice cream.

Meanwhile, peel the oranges, getting rid of every bit of pith (see page 26), and then cut them into segments. Collect as much of the juice as possible as you slice. Put the fruit and juice into a bowl and stir in the marmalade. Grate a little nutmeg over the bowl.

Tunisian orange and almond cake

This is an excellent cake to eat on its own or with baked fruit, such as rhubarb. It stores brilliantly.

Serves 8
½ cup slightly stale breadcrumbs
1 cup superfine sugar
¾ cup ground almonds
1½ teaspoons baking powder
1 cup (2 sticks) butter, melted
4 eggs
Finely grated zest of 1 large orange
Finely grated zest of 1 lemon
Whipped cream, thick Greek yogurt, or crème fraîche, to serve

For the syrup:
Juice of 1 orange
Juice of 1 lemon
½ cup sugar
2 cloves
1 cinnamon stick

Mix the breadcrumbs with the sugar, almonds, and baking powder in a food processor. Add the melted butter and eggs and beat well, then stir in the citrus zests. Pour into a greased and lined 8-inch cake pan. Put into a cold oven and set the heat to 375°F. Bake for 40 to 50 minutes, until the cake is a rich brown and a toothpick inserted into the center comes out clean. Allow to cool in the pan for 5 minutes, and then turn out on a plate.

While the cake is baking, make the syrup. Put all the ingredients into a pan and bring to a gentle boil, stirring until all the sugar has dissolved. Simmer for 3 minutes. Remove the cloves and cinnamon stick.

While the cake is still warm, pierce holes in it with a skewer and pour over the syrup. Leave to cool, spooning the excess syrup back over the cake until it is all soaked up.

Serve with whipped cream, thick Greek yogurt, or crème fraîche.

Orange pasta

This is a surprising mix of things for a pasta sauce, but I remember enjoying it in a small restaurant in Rome. In fact I liked it so much that we went back three times in a five-day visit, until I'd worked out how to make it.

Serves 4
8 ounces tagliatelle
¼ cup heavy cream
1 garlic clove, crushed and peeled but left whole
Juice and grated zest of 1 orange
Grated zest of ½ lemon
Salt and pepper
2 tablespoons brandy
3 tablespoons butter
5 ounces Parmesan cheese, grated, plus a little extra for garnishing

Cook the pasta in salted boiling water until just al dente.

While it is cooking, heat the cream with the garlic and bring to a boil for a minute. Remove the garlic and add the orange and lemon zest, some salt and plenty of pepper, then remove the pan from the heat to allow the cream to steep in these flavors for about 10 minutes.

Add the orange juice, brandy, butter, and Parmesan, and toss with the drained hot pasta.

Garnish with a little more Parmesan cheese and add salt and plenty of pepper.

Sicilian orange and lemon salad

British author and restaurateur Antonio Carluccio told me about this salad, which is perfect with smoked fish, and eel in particular. You can just eat the citrus salad straight as you would in Sicily, where the fruit is at its absolute best, or mix it in with watercress.

Serves 8
4 oranges (blood oranges are lovely)
2 lemons
2 grapefruits
2 bunches of watercress

For the dressing:
Juice of 1 lime
4 tablespoons extra virgin olive oil
Sprigs of mint
Salt and pepper

Peel the oranges, lemons, and grapefruits with a sharp serrated knife, removing all the white pith (see page 26). Cut out each segment from between the membranes and put into a ceramic bowl while you make the dressing. Whisk together the lime juice, olive oil, mint, salt, and pepper, and pour it over the fruit.

Put a couple of bunches of watercress in a separate bowl. The fruit and watercress are lovely eaten together, but when dressed the watercress collapses within minutes, so keep them apart until you eat, and then just put a handful of watercress with a couple of spoonfuls of the citrus salad on each plate.

Preserved lemons

This recipe comes from John and Mary Stratton of Stratta, who sell infused oils, flavored vinegars, and pickles at our farmers' market.

Preserved lemons are used in North African tagines and make a wonderful addition to any lamb, chicken, or fish stew. Just rinse one or two segments, chop them finely, and throw them in about half an hour before the end of cooking. Try adding them to fish baked in an envelope of parchment paper or slicing some and adding them to oven-roasted vegetables. They are also good for seasoning rice or couscous. Lemons preserved in this way allow you to eat the entire fruit, including the pith, but rinse off the salt before using them and don't add any more salt until you have tasted what you have cooked.

For 1 pint jar
   4 to 6 organic lemons, depending on size
   3 tablespoons sea salt
   Boiling water, to cover

Choose unwaxed lemons—ideally organic and with as few skin blemishes as possible, or dewax your lemons (see page 30). Scrub them clean and cut into quarters. Remove the pips and pack firmly in the preserving jar, separating the layers with a sprinkling of salt.

Top with any remaining salt and fill the jar with boiling water, turning it to expel any air bubbles. Close firmly and store for a month before using. This allows the fruit to mellow and mature. Once the jar has been opened it can be kept in the fridge with a layer of extra virgin olive oil floating on the surface to exclude the air.

Lemon cordial

You can use other citrus fruits for this cordial recipe. In Spain, you'll see a similar recipe made with clementines and it's delicious with limes.

Yield: Two 750ml wine bottles
   3 unwaxed lemons
   4 cups boiling water
   4 cups sugar
   2 tablespoons citric or tartaric acid

With a potato peeler, cut thick ribbons of rind from the fruit, leaving the white pith behind.

Put the rind into a heatproof bowl and pour over the boiling water. Stir in the sugar, keeping the water moving until the sugar has all dissolved.

Leave the mixture to cool and then add the juice from the lemons and the citric acid, and leave everything to steep overnight.

Next day, strain the rind away and bottle the cordial. Don't leave the rind in any longer or the cordial will become bitter.

Serve the cordial—just a little in the bottom of a glass—diluted with still or sparkling water.

This will store for about a month in the fridge, or you can pour it into clean plastic milk cartons and freeze it.

Homemade lemonade

You get a straightforward version of this—citron pressé—in every French and Italian café, where you add sugar to your own glass to taste, but I love this version of lemonade, which is frothed up in a blender with lots of ice.

Yield: a pitcher for 6
   10 lemons
   8 tablespoons superfine sugar
   4 tablespoons ice, plus some whole ice cubes, to serve
   20 mint or lemon balm leaves

Peel the lemons as instructed for oranges on page 26, making sure that you have removed all of the white bitter pith.

Then put the fruit in a blender with the sugar, ice, herbs, and 1 quart of water, and whiz for 2 minutes. (It makes a terrible noise!)

Put a few mint or lemon balm leaves, some whole ice cubes, and some lemon slices into a large pitcher and strain the lemonade into it. This lemonade doesn't store (see left for one that does) and should be drunk straightaway. You can make this sort of drink with any citrus fruit.

Penne with preserved lemon and avocado

This too is John and Mary Stratton's recipe and it is a deliciously different way in which to use Preserved lemons (see page 35). It makes the perfect weekday supper as it takes so little time to make. Cold, the next day— with a handful of mint, cilantro, and/or arugula—it also makes a great salad. My twin sister, Jane, said she wasn't tempted by the sound of this recipe when she read it. She is now a major convert.

Serves 4
  2 skinless organic chicken breasts
  1 cup white wine
  2 tablespoons butter
  8 ounces penne
  1 cup crème fraîche
  1 cup heavy cream
  1 large avocado
  2 tablespoons pine nuts, toasted
  **2 thinly sliced preserved
     lemon quarters**
  Salt and plenty of pepper

Preheat the oven to 350°F.
      Put the chicken breasts in an ovenproof dish with a little wine, dot them with butter, and then cover with foil. Cook the chicken in the oven for 20 minutes.
      Cook the pasta in salted boiling water until al dente. While it is cooking, heat the crème fraîche and heavy cream together in a small saucepan. Mash or cut up the avocado and cut the chicken into pieces.
      Drain the pasta and add the avocado and chicken along with the cream mixture, toasted pine nuts, and sliced preserved lemons. Stir gently to combine and season with salt and pepper.

Mrs. Root's lemon soufflé

This is an extremely lemony mousse— tart and delicious—that was often made for us by a wonderful woman, Mrs. Root or "Rootie", my mother's housekeeper, when we were children. She used to make it in a bain-marie, but this is a quicker and simpler version. Note that it contains uncooked egg.

Serves 8
  Grated zest and juice of 3 lemons
  **2 tablespoons (2 envelopes)
     unflavored gelatin**
  **3 large or 4 medium-sized eggs,
     separated**
  ½ cup superfine sugar
  1¼ cups heavy cream

In a small pan, mix the lemon zest and juice and the gelatin, warming it a little to dissolve it completely.
      Beat the egg yolks and superfine sugar until foamy, then add to the gelatin and lemon mixture.
      Whip the cream, then wash the beaters and beat the egg whites to form stiff peaks.
      Fold the egg yolk mixture and the whipped cream together, then gently fold in the egg whites.
      Pour it into a shallow bowl and leave it to set for 4 hours, or overnight, before serving.

Lemon posset

A quick and easy alternative to Mrs. Root's lemon soufflé from the Whitehouse Restaurant, run by my sister-in-law, Jane Stuart Smith, and Sarah Jones, in Lochaline on the west coast of Scotland.

They make this dessert through the year, serving it in champagne flutes and adding raspberries—picked wild—when they're in season.

Yield: 8 champagne flutes
3½ cups heavy cream
1¼ cups superfine sugar
Juice of 3 lemons and grated zest of 1 lemon

Bring the cream and sugar to a boil, stirring until the sugar has dissolved completely. Take this off the heat and whisk in the lemon juice and zest.

Pour into molds or glasses from a height. Allow them to cool and then refrigerate overnight.

Lemon and cumin cookies

These are lovely on their own, or with ice cream or cheese. This comes from *The African Kitchen*, a fantastic book by Josie Stow and Jan Baldwin.

Yield: 30 cookies
1½ cups superfine sugar
½ cup (1 stick) butter
2 egg yolks
Finely grated zest of 2 lemons and 4 tablespoons juice
2 teaspoons freshly ground cumin seeds
2¼ cups all-purpose flour
1 teaspoon baking soda

Preheat the oven to 350°F.

Cream the sugar and butter together until light and fluffy. Gradually beat in the egg yolks, lemon zest and juice, and cumin. Sift together the flour and baking soda, then fold into the butter mixture to form a soft dough.

Place the dough on a sheet of wax paper and roll into a cylinder about 2 inches in diameter, twisting the ends of the paper together and being very careful not to wrap any of the paper into the dough. Place the dough in the freezer for 1½ to 2 hours until it is hard.

Line a baking sheet with a piece of parchment paper. Unwrap the dough and cut into ¼-inch slices. Place these on the baking sheet, leaving a very generous space between them to allow for spreading.

Bake the cookies for 8 to10 minutes, or until just firm to the touch. Slide them onto a wire rack and leave to cool.

Lemon and mint ice cream

Teresa Wallace is my twin sister's mother-in-law and this is her lemon ice cream recipe. She is a wonderful and impatient cook, so she has a way with quick and easy tip-top recipes. This one is a cinch to make. The portions—once divided into six—may look a bit stingy, but it's rich, although light because of the egg whites. Note that this recipe uses uncooked eggs.

Serves 6
2 large eggs
¼ cup superfine sugar
½ cup heavy cream
Juice of 3 lemons
2 handfuls of mint leaves, very finely chopped

Separate the eggs and whisk the whites, adding the sugar when stiff. Whisk the egg yolks until they are foamy. Then whisk the cream until it is the same consistency as the egg whites. (If you whisk in this order you don't have to wash the beaters in between each ingredient.)

Fold the egg whites, yolks, and cream together. Gently stir in the lemon juice and chopped mint leaves. Put the mixture into a plastic container and freeze. There is no need to beat or churn.

Take it out of the freezer and put in the fridge about 20 minutes before serving.

Ceviche

The lovely flavor of fish with limes makes this one of the freshest-tasting salads. In the winter, eat it with crunchy salad leaves. I had it recently with Sicilian orange and lemon salad (see page 34) and it's also lovely in the summer with sliced tomato salad.

Serves 6

1¼ pounds fillets of salmon, skinned
1¼ pounds fillets of sole (or other mild white fish), skinned
A few scallops (optional)
1 shallot, very finely chopped
Zest of 1 lime and ½ cup lime juice (about 3 to 4 limes)
4 tablespoons white wine vinegar
Salt and pepper
Flat-leaf parsley, finely chopped
Generous handful of arugula leaves
4 tomatoes, chopped and skinned (if in season)
Extra virgin olive oil

Cut the skinned fish roughly into slivers ¼ inch wide and put into a bowl with the scallops (if using), shallot, lime zest and juice, vinegar, salt, and pepper, and leave for at least 3 hours, stirring from time to time. Drain well, mix in the parsley, and pile into a shallow dish.

Serve with a small salad of arugula leaves and skinned chopped tomatoes (if in season), combined with a little extra virgin olive oil, salt, and freshly ground pepper.

Pink grapefruit and Pimm's granita

This granita from Caroline Liddell and Robin Weir's book on ice cream is summer all over, so it doesn't really belong in a winter chapter, but grapefruits are at their best at this time of year. It is perfect when you want just a light sweet taste at the end of a meal.

Serves 6

½ cup sugar
8 tablespoons Pimm's No. 1
Juice of 4 to 5 pink grapefruits
1 tablespoon lemon juice
8 mint leaves
1 egg white

Heating them together, dissolve the sugar in the Pimm's (this takes a few minutes). Stir in the strained grapefruit and lemon juice and ½ cup water. Roll up the mint leaves and cut across the roll to make very thin strips. Add these to the liquid and chill in the fridge.

Break up the egg white gently with a fork, but do not whisk. Mix into the chilled liquid, pour into an ice cream maker, and freeze/churn until firm enough to serve, making sure the mint leaves are well distributed. Either pack into a plastic container for freezing or serve immediately.

If you don't have a machine, this sorbet can be made in the freezer. Pour the chilled mixture into a plastic container to give a depth of at least 1½ inches, cover with a lid, and put into the freezer. Check after about 1½ hours, by which time it should have frozen around the edge with a slushy center. Beat with a hand whisk, cover, and return to the freezer. Do this a couple more times, leaving about 1½ hours in between. After you have done this a third time, leave it in the freezer for at least 3 hours before serving. (This method can be used for most sorbets, and those that do not contain alcohol freeze more quickly.)

Mandarin sorbet

All citrus sorbets are delicious. You can also use this recipe to make blood orange sorbet, which looks and tastes good, or make it with clementines, but mandarin is the best of all.

Serves 4

10 unwaxed mandarins
¾ cup sugar
1 tablespoon fresh lemon juice

If you can't find unwaxed mandarins, drop the fruit into boiling water for a couple of minutes and dry them.

To make the sugar syrup, dissolve the sugar in ¾ cup water over low heat. Slowly bring to a boil. Boil for 2 to 3 minutes and then allow to cool. This stores very well in the fridge.

Pare away the zest with a potato peeler, add half of the zest to the syrup in a small saucepan, and simmer for a couple of minutes. Allow to cool completely and then strain off the liquid.

Squeeze the juice from the mandarins and combine it with the cold syrup, lemon juice, and reserved uncooked zest.

Pour into an ice cream machine. Freeze/churn for 20 to 25 minutes and pack into a plastic container. Freeze for several hours. If you don't have an ice cream machine, see left. Take the sorbet out of the freezer and put it in the fridge 20 minutes before serving.

Evergreen herbs

Rosemary, sage, thyme, and bay are stalwarts of the kitchen during the cold months. If you choose one edible plant to grow, whatever the size of your garden, rosemary has to be a contender. It's easy, will be happy in a pot indoors or out depending on the weather, is pickable fifty-two weeks of the year, and has a delicious taste, much better fresh than dried. There are three varieties of rosemary in my garden, each with a slightly different character and use. 'Sissinghurst Blue' is a shrubby variety with an unusually dark-blue flower. The bank outside the school is covered with a cascading, weeping form, 'Prostratus'. The plants, spaced two feet apart, have now merged into a beautiful, gnarled waterfall of dark green. Around one of the beds in the vegetable garden is 'Miss Jessopp's Upright'. This is ideal for edging, as its very vertical habit means it doesn't fill much horizontal space, and it's also the best for flower arranging.

There are five varieties of sage in my garden, but only three are good for cooking. The pretty, smoky-crimson-leaved Salvia officinalis 'Purpurea' and the variegated, S.o. 'Tricolor', don't have much flavor. For the kitchen you want to grow one of three: the straight S. officinalis, with its bright silvery leaves, is excellent for cooking, as is S. lavandulifolia, with much greener leaves. I also grow the large, round-leaved S.o. 'Berggarten'. This last variety is excellent for tempura (see page 46) as it has leaves twice the size of those of ordinary sage, with plenty of flesh to get your teeth into. All are fine growing in a pot. Like rosemary, sage is easy to grow and to propagate by cuttings. It thrives in an open sunny position with well-drained soil. You can also grow it from seed. Treated as an annual, it never gets woody and produces new fresh leaves at a brisker rate.

Thyme is another wonderful herb for cold weather picking and is easily grown from seed or cuttings. I love lemon thyme in all its forms and that seems to do best for me on my heavy soil. It is one of the finest flavorings for pastry (see page 131), makes wonderful herb butter (see page 84), and is a good addition to burgers and meatballs (see page 49) as well as tapenade (see page 49).

As with rosemary, sage, and thyme, there are so many dishes that need bay leaves. It's the crucial ingredient in a classic béchamel sauce and few stocks or stews are complete without it. The flavor is also superb in mashed potatoes (see page 336). It's tempting to throw in lots of leaves whenever you use bay, but one bay leaf is usually all you'll need. It may be evergreen where you live, so you can pick it all year, but if you don't have a plant, the leathery texture of the leaves makes it a good herb for drying. Even crinkly and old, they lose little flavor.

Rosemary and anchovy crusted lamb

This is a dish that looks impressive but requires little effort, though it is worth finding really good lamb. The rosemary, anchovies, and lemons give flavor to the crust. Eat this with a Potato and sage gratin (see page 48) and Fried cabbage with juniper (see page 17).

Serves 6

2 racks of lamb (2 to 3 cutlets per person)
Small bunch of thyme
2 sprigs of rosemary
1½ cups fresh breadcrumbs
2 garlic cloves, finely chopped
1 (2-ounce) can anchovy fillets
Grated zest of 1 lemon
Salt and pepper
Seasoned all-purpose flour
1 egg, beaten

For the sauce:
2 oranges
½ cup port
1 tablespoon redcurrant jelly

Cut away the chine bones from the lamb or ask your butcher to do it for you. Trim the lamb of all but a thin covering of the fat protecting the meat. Preheat the oven to 425°F.

In a food processor, pulse the herbs, breadcrumbs, garlic, and anchovy fillets until they are well combined and stir in the lemon zest. Season with a little salt and plenty of freshly ground pepper.

Dip the lamb into some seasoned flour, knock off the excess, and then, with a pastry brush, cover with a layer of beaten egg. Pat on a thick layer of the breadcrumb mixture, pressing it firmly onto the surface.

Bake the lamb in the preheated oven for 45 to 50 minutes, depending on the size of the joints. (If they are becoming too brown, just cover them lightly with a sheet of foil.) Allow to rest for 10 minutes before serving.

While the lamb is cooking, make the sauce. Peel the rind of the oranges with a potato peeler and then shred it into fine strips. Cut the oranges into segments and put in a small saucepan with the shredded rind, port, and redcurrant jelly, and bring to a simmer, making sure to whisk the jelly until it dissolves. Remove from the heat and keep warm until the lamb is ready.

Rosemary and pork farfalle

I love this meat pasta sauce and so do my children, particularly if I leave out the nonessential chili pepper and onion. It takes only 10 minutes to make and is one of our standard midweek suppers. It has an unusual taste—a mix of rosemary with toasted sesame oil—that you never forget once you've tried it.

Serves 2 to 3

1 onion, finely chopped (optional)
1 tablespoon olive oil
2 tablespoons toasted sesame oil
1 garlic clove, chopped
1 red chili, finely chopped (optional)
1¼ pounds lean ground pork, or pork tenderloin, sliced into thin strips
1 sprig of rosemary, the leaves stripped and finely chopped
½ cup hot water
Salt and pepper
8 ounces pasta (penne or farfalle)
Freshly grated Parmesan cheese, as a garnish

Put your pasta water on to boil and meanwhile, if you are using it, fry the onion in the olive oil and toasted sesame oil for a few minutes until soft. Add the garlic, chili if you are using it, pork, and rosemary, and cook them together quickly to brown the meat. Then add the hot water and leave to cook gently with the lid on for another 5 minutes. Add plenty of salt and pepper.

Cook the pasta until it is al dente. Drain it and mix with the sauce. Garnish with lots of grated Parmesan.

Patmos chickpeas

There is a taverna—Flisvos—on the Greek island of Patmos where I had these chickpeas once, and I still remember them. It's taken several years and countless visits by a friend, Sofka Zinovieff-Papadimitriou, who lives in Greece, to get this recipe out of the cook. The keys to its deliciousness are plenty of onion and rosemary and, most importantly, very long cooking.

The joy of chickpeas is that you can't overcook them; they always keep their shape. The dish is even better heated up the next day. Eat this as one of a group of Greek starters, such as Ithaca pie (see page 74), wild greens, fried calamari, and Saganaki (see page 273), as an accompaniment to meat or fish, or just with a big salad.

Serves 6 to 8
   16 ounces dried chickpeas
   4 onions, 2 left whole, 2 finely chopped
   Salt and pepper
   4 tablespoons olive oil (Greek cooking is always generous with the oil)
   2 tablespoons finely chopped rosemary
   ½ cup white wine

Soak the chickpeas in cold water overnight and then boil them with the 2 whole onions and no salt. As the scum comes to the top of the liquid, remove it. Continue simmering the chickpeas gently, for about 40 minutes, until soft. Strain and season, reserving a little of the liquid and the onions.

Preheat the oven to 300°F.

Gently fry the 2 finely chopped onions in the olive oil. Puree one-third of the chickpeas with the 2 boiled onions and a little of the reserved cooking liquid. I use an immersion blender.

Put the remaining two-thirds of the chickpeas with the fried onion in an ovenproof dish with a lid. Throw in the rosemary, salt, pepper, and white wine. Pour over the pureed onion and chickpea mix. Put into the preheated oven, covered, and cook slowly for about 2 hours. If the dish dries out, then just add a little of the reserved cooking juices.

You can use canned chickpeas, but the flavor and texture is not as good. If you're using canned, boil the onions separately for about 30 minutes. Mix with one-third of the chickpeas and follow the instructions as above, but cook them for only half the time.

Rosemary, olive, and lemon chicken

This is a simple meal-in-one-pot. It's a classic Greek dish, often made with oregano rather than rosemary, and it's also lovely with bay. Eat this with a mound of spinach or Horta (see page 395). You can also use this recipe to roast a whole chicken.

Serves 5 to 6
   1 chicken, cut into 8 portions
   Juice of 3 lemons
   Leaves of 4 sprigs of rosemary (or 1 heaping tablespoon), coarsely chopped, plus a sprig or two for adding whole
   Salt and pepper
   2 pounds waxy potatoes, peeled and quartered lengthwise
   15 kalamata black olives
   5 tablespoons extra virgin olive oil

Preheat the oven to 350°F.

Rinse the chicken pieces and pat them dry. Lay them out in a baking tray. Pour half the lemon juice over the chicken. Sprinkle with some of the chopped rosemary, salt, and pepper.

Cut the potatoes into segments and arrange around the chicken. Add the olives, pour on the rest of the lemon juice, and then sprinkle more rosemary over the potatoes. Using your hands, turn the potatoes to make sure they're coated well in the herbs and lemon juice.

Pour over the olive oil and add the sprigs of rosemary, plus a cup of water, and cook for 1½ hours in the preheated oven.

When the chicken is cooked, remove it and allow it to rest while you turn up the heat to crisp up the potatoes in a 425°F oven for 15 minutes.

Rosemary flat bread

You can make flat bread standing on your head. The dough takes under 5 minutes to combine and about an hour to rise. This makes it ideal for whipping up quickly if you've got people coming to supper.

This rosemary version is lovely for dipping into hummus (see pages 85 and 305), Saganaki (see page 273), or White gazpacho with grapes (see page 330). Alternatively, you can smother the breads in dill or fennel seeds as you put them in the oven to bake.

Yield: 6 medium-sized flat breads
1½ cups unbleached flour
½ teaspoon active dry yeast
⅔ cup lukewarm water
1 tablespoon extra virgin olive oil
Salt
Rosemary, coarsely chopped

Put the flour into a large bowl and add the yeast. Add the water, olive oil, and a pinch of salt, and start mixing it all together to form a rather sloppy dough: if your mix is too dry, add a little more water; if the mix is too wet, add a little more flour.

Once you have a ball of dough, take it out of the bowl and knead on a floured surface for 5 minutes until it is elastic but slightly tacky. Leave the dough to rest under a damp towel for an hour. It will rise until it has about doubled in size.

Preheat the oven to 350°F. Break off a ¾-inch-sized ball of dough and roll it out thinly on a floured surface. Repeat, until you have used all the dough. Brush each flat bread with olive oil. Sprinkle with a little salt and garnish with rosemary. Bake on baking trays for about 10 minutes, until the surface starts to bubble and turn a golden brown. Don't cook them too long or they'll turn into cardboard. Serve immediately.

Sage leaf tempura

Making tempura is easy. If you do it for just a few people who are happy to graze and chat, it's one of the greatest vegetable starters there is.

Use sage leaves as part of a winter garden tempura, with parsnips and Jerusalem artichokes, or in the summer with French beans and zucchini flowers. Sage leaves are ideal for tempura as the batter sticks well to their wrinkly texture. Leave the stems on so that you have something to hold onto while you eat.

This makes perfect picnic food (see Summer garden tempura on page 207). Sage leaf tempura is also good on its own with a glass of wine, and the delicious oily, smoky flavor goes well with liver or pounded and breaded pork cutlets. There is a wonderful recipe by Joyce Molyneaux (of the original Carved Angel restaurant in Dartmouth, England) for Pork scallops with thyme tapenade (see page 49) and these tempura sage leaves are an ideal accompaniment to that.

Serves 8 as a snack or a side dish
1¼ cups all-purpose flour
Plenty of sea salt and pepper
2 eggs
1½ cups iced sparkling water
  or cold beer
Peanut oil, for frying
30 to 40 sage leaves, depending
  on size and variety

Sift the flour into a bowl with the salt and pepper and make a well in the center. Add the eggs and, with a balloon whisk, mix in the cold water or beer to make a not-too-smooth batter. It should be the thickness of heavy cream. Keep this in the fridge until you need it. The coldness of the batter hitting the hot oil gives a lighter, airier texture to the tempura leaves.

Pour the oil into a deep fryer so that it reaches about one-third of the way up the side and have a lid or wire-mesh top on standby to prevent the oil spitting too much after you add each batch of leaves. Heat the oil until it reaches about 350°F. If you don't have an oil thermometer, it's easy to test. Drop a cube of bread into the oil. It should turn golden brown in less than a minute.

Dip the herb leaves into the batter and then into the hot oil, and cook until pale gold and crisp. Fish them out with tongs and dry them on paper towels. These are at their best eaten hot and served sprinkled with sea salt and ground pepper.

Potato and sage gratin

This is rich and absolutely delicious, and has a lovely flavor of sage. If you're worried about the amount of cream and milk, you can use a mixture of three-quarters good stock to a quarter cream.

Serves 6

4 or 5 large potatoes
1 cup milk
1¼ cups heavy cream
2 garlic cloves
6 tablespoons butter, plus a bit more for the dish
Salt and pepper
Freshly grated nutmeg
80 small sage leaves, coarsely chopped
4 ounces Gruyère cheese

Preheat the oven to 180°F.

Peel and thinly slice the potatoes. Mix the milk and cream together, then add the chopped garlic. Butter an ovenproof dish and arrange a layer of potato slices in the bottom. Season well and grate over some nutmeg. Cover this with a layer of sage and dot with butter.

Repeat the layers, seasoning as you go, until you have used up all the potatoes and sage leaves, and pour over the cream mixture. Cover with a layer of grated Gruyère and cook for about 1½ hours (at least: this dish takes ages to cook), until a deep gold on top. Test with a skewer to check that the potato is completely cooked. Cover the top if it is browning too quickly at any point. This freezes well.

Matthew's confit of chicken

My friend Matthew Rice is a devotee of the chicken, whether running around his garden or sitting on his plate. This is his recipe. Confit is best done with two chickens—cook too much for one meal, so that you can eat it from the fridge for the rest of the week. It is preserved in its own fat and lasts for days. Confit is a dish that requires long cooking, so buy a free-range bird. The bones of factory-farmed birds disintegrate easily and certainly won't stand up to the confit technique.

Serves 12

2 free-range organic chickens
4 handfuls of sea salt
40 garlic cloves, crushed a bit using a mortar and pestle to release their fragrance
20 fresh bay leaves
Lots of ground black pepper

Cut the chickens into pieces, taking off the breasts, wings, and legs, so that you're left with two limbless bare frames. With their skins on, rub the meat pieces with the salt, garlic, torn-up bay leaves, and pepper. Cover with plastic wrap and put in the fridge. If you can, wait a couple of days for the meat to pick up the flavors of the herbs. If you can't, it will be fine to use the next day.

Preheat the oven to 400°F.

Put the chicken frames in a roasting tray and cook in the preheated oven for 20 minutes, then reduce the oven to 300°F and cook the chicken more slowly for 2 hours, draining off the fat into a bowl as you go. You need to render all the fat, and it's a surprising amount. With some birds, the fat is scarce. If this is the case, add a lump of butter. Throw away the frames and put the fat somewhere cool.

Wash the chicken pieces so that they are free of salt, etc., and lay them in a clean earthenware or metal baking dish. Pour all the chicken fat over them and add a handful of fresh bay leaves. Cook very slowly at 300°F, uncovered, for 2 hours, or until the meat comes away from the bone easily. The pieces should be swimming in a shallow pool of fat. It sounds disgusting, but I promise it's not.

Eat the chicken there and then, or store it in the fridge. When you're ready to eat, warm it up thoroughly in a frying pan in a little of the fat. You won't really want anything else with it except a green salad and, perhaps, some mashed potatoes.

Pork scallops with thyme tapenade

I sometimes use thyme tapenade to spread over the pita bread for Fattoush (see page 273) and I love it with Joyce Molyneaux's wonderful bread-crumbed pork scallop recipe. She uses a straight olive tapenade, but it is even tastier with the thyme addition.

Serves 4
For the tapenade:
Small bunch of thyme
8 ounces olives (these must be really good ones—never buy the pitted kind)
2 to 3 canned anchovies in oil, drained
1 to 2 garlic cloves
2 tablespoons capers, rinsed
Olive oil

1¼ pounds pork tenderloin
2 eggs, beaten
2 handfuls of dried breadcrumbs
Olive oil, for frying

First, make the tapenade. Pull the leaves from the stalks of the thyme and pit the olives. Put all the ingredients into a blender and process for a few minutes. Add just enough olive oil in a stream to give you a thick, spreadable mixture. Put into small sterilized jars and cover.

This will make more tapenade than you need. You will have enough left over to fill a small jar, which will keep for about 3 months in the fridge.

Now for the pork. Cut the tenderloin at a slant across the grain into 12 slices. Spread one side of each slice with the tapenade. Dip the slices into the beaten egg and coat in the breadcrumbs. Leave in the fridge for about half an hour to firm up.

Heat some oil in a pan and fry the pork scallops for 5 minutes on either side until nicely browned.

Lamb burgers with thyme and rosemary

Ground lean lamb shoulder, trimmed of excess fat, is excellent for this recipe as the meat is sweet and tender. Serve with a large bowl of yogurt, a crisp green salad, and some flat bread (see page 46).

Yield: 6 burgers or 12 canapés
2 small shallots
1¼ pounds lean ground lamb
1 teaspoon chopped fresh rosemary
1 tablespoon chopped fresh thyme
1 to 2 garlic cloves, crushed and chopped
½ red chili (optional)
1½-inch piece of ginger, grated
1 small egg, beaten
Salt and pepper
Seasoned all-purpose flour
2 to 3 ounces feta cheese
Olive oil

Chop the shallots and add to the ground lamb in a large bowl. Chop the herbs, garlic, and chili (if using). Add these and the ginger to the bowl, along with the beaten egg, and season well.

Generously sprinkle a large board with seasoned flour and have some more to one side for dusting your hands. Take a small handful of the lamb mixture and shape into a 2- to 3-inch round, about 1 inch thick. Put a small chunk of feta in the middle of the lamb and place another round of lamb, the same size, on top. Press down lightly, using some extra seasoned flour to help shape a lamb burger about 3½ inches across. You can make these burgers as large or as small as you like—half this size makes a great little canapé.

Heat some oil in a frying pan or oil a barbecue grill and cook the lamb over medium heat for about 3 minutes on each side. Alternatively, you can sear them quickly over high heat and then finish them off on an oiled baking tray in a moderate oven for about 8 minutes.

Winter salad greens

The antioxidants in freshly picked salad leaves are one of the best guarantees against ill health, but try to avoid eating ready-washed packets, which have often been drenched in chlorine. There are many cut-and-come-again salad leaves and loose-leaf lettuce varieties that may grow and produce well through the winter. Mizuna, mibuna, arugula, garden cress, mâche or corn salad, purslane, and any of the leafy mustards all make a delicious and interesting winter salad.

Arugula is good on its own and so is watercress, but mixing different punchy-flavored leaves makes a delicious salad too. Add a bit of chervil or parsley, both good cold-weather soft green herbs, as well as some gentler leaves—lettuce or mâche—as background. With a boring supermarket lettuce, you need to make more of the dressing, but with tasty winter leaves, you don't always need to add the sharpness of vinegar or the fruitiness of oil.

If you like the idea of such a varied salad, try eating it without dressing. I love grabbing a good fistful of undressed salad from a central bowl and putting it on my plate to eat with my hands. You can then tear up or break in half a long spiky leaf of mizuna or a shred of horseradish-hot Red Giant mustard, trying the flavors one by one. Without dressing, you don't get covered in oil and you can just sit and graze. Any leaves you don't eat you can put back into a sealed plastic bag for the next meal. Without dressing or air, they last for days in the bottom of a fridge.

Whether you've bought the leaves or picked them, chuck the whole lot in a sink or bowl of cold water for a couple of hours before you eat. The salad benefits from a good long soak and stays perkier for longer. Drain and dry them gently—so as not to bruise the leaves. If you must leave them for any length of time, cover the bowl with a cold damp cloth or put them into a large plastic bag, secure the top, and put them in the bottom of the fridge.

If you want your salad dressed, make the dressing in the bottom of the bowl. If you fancy something punchy, try shallot (see page 248) or garlic dressing (see page 54) but, on the whole, a simple dressing works best with the strong flavors of these winter leaves.

For a big bowl of salad to feed eight, use a generous splash (measured, about four tablespoons) of a good olive oil, the juice and grated zest of a half lemon, and a generous twist of pepper. Drop the herbs in on top of the dressing, and then the leaves. Finally, sprinkle sea salt—lots of it, salty salads are delicious—over the leaves, and toss well before serving.

Duck breast and peppery-leaf salad

Use a mix of leaves for this warm salad—Red Giant mustard, arugula, mizuna, or watercress. Smoked duck breasts make this salad even easier to prepare.

Serves 6 as a starter
- **3 duck breasts**
- **1 tablespoon fennel seeds**
- **Grated zest of 2 oranges**
- **Pinch of sea salt**
- **6 small handfuls of mixed salad leaves**

For the dressing:
- **2 tablespoons sesame oil**
- **1 tablespoon honey**
- **2 teaspoons Hoisin or plum sauce (see page 257)**
- **Juice of ½ lemon**
- **Splash of sherry**

Preheat the oven to 350°F.

For perfectly cooked duck breasts—crisp on the outside and pink and juicy on the inside—make a criss-cross pattern with a serrated knife on the skin and rub in a mixture of fennel seed, orange zest, and salt. Fry the breasts, skin side down, in a dry pan and cook on medium heat until nearly all the fat is rendered—melted from beneath the skin—and the skin is golden brown. This will take about 10 minutes. Pour off the excess fat at least once and save it. It's delicious for cooking roast potatoes.

Transfer the breasts, in the same pan if you can, to the preheated oven for 8 minutes. Remove them from the oven; wrap them loosely on a plate with foil and leave to rest for at least 10 minutes. This is vital. It allows the flesh to relax and makes it deliciously tender.

While the duck is resting, mix the ingredients for the dressing. Slice the breasts thinly and add them to the salad just before you need them. Drizzle the dressing over the top.

Grilled goat cheese salad

You'll find this as a standard dish on the set menu of simple French restaurants. Mix as many leaves into the salad as you can get your hands on—a few fronds of frisée, any chicory, Belgian endive, and dandelion to give some bitterness, as well as some milder-tasting leaves.

Serves 6
- ¼ pound pancetta, chopped
- 1 garlic clove, crushed (not sliced)
- 1 small French baguette
- 2 tablespoons honey
- 8 ounces small aged goat cheese, with rind, rather than the fresh variety
- 6 sprigs of thyme
- 3 small handfuls of mixed mild salad leaves
- 3 small handfuls of bitter leaves, such as dandelion, any chicory, and frisée
- 20 to 30 slow-roasted cherry tomatoes, if in season (see page 278)
- 2 tablespoons pine nuts, toasted

For the dressing:
- 1 garlic clove, finely chopped
- 1 tablespoon red wine vinegar or balsamic vinegar
- 4 tablespoons olive oil
- 1 teaspoon Dijon mustard
- Salt and pepper

Fry the pancetta, with the garlic. Remove the pancetta once it begins to brown and let it cool. Discard the garlic. Slice the French baguette into ½-inch-thick ovals and toast these on one side. Heat the honey.

Cut the goat cheese into thick slices and put one per piece of bread on the untoasted side. Season and drizzle over the warm honey. Put a sprig of thyme on the top and put the bread under the broiler until the cheese begins to melt.

Tear up the salad leaves and make the dressing, combining all the ingredients and whisking with a fork. Dress the leaves and put on individual plates. Garnish the tomatoes, if you're using them, with the pancetta and pine nuts, and then add the toasted goat cheese.

Winter flower and toasted seed salad

It's surprising how many edible flowers there are to pick, even in winter, but check they're not poisonous before you gather them. Winter-flowering pansies are all edible and, if picked regularly, happily flower for me even in the coldest months, and in the south primroses appear in late winter on sunny banks. With the warmer winters, chervil and arugula—and even parsley—may start to flower. Pick a good handful of any of these for your salad. For a nutty taste, garnish with some dry-toasted seeds.

Serves 8

- **3 heaping tablespoons of mixed seeds, such as pumpkin, sunflower, poppy, and sesame**
- **30 or so mixed flowers**
- **8 handfuls of leaves (at least 3 or 4 different varieties)**
- **4 tablespoons good olive oil**
- **Juice and grated zest of ½ lemon**
- **2 handfuls of any soft green herb (such as mint, parsley, cilantro, or chervil)**
- **Plenty of salt and pepper**

Toast the seeds in a frying pan for 2 to 3 minutes with no oil, shaking them a couple of times as you do. You can toast them in the oven for a few minutes until they turn golden brown (or silver in the case of mustard seeds), but if they are hidden away in the oven, I tend to burn them.

Toss all the other salad ingredients together at the last moment, when you want to eat. Your hands are best for the job. Throw the toasted seeds over the top.

Fillet of beef with arugula

Thinly sliced raw fillet of beef, as used in the Italian dishes of carpaccio and carne all'albese, are excellent with the pepperiness of arugula. There are several types of arugula, but the two that you will see most often are wild and salad arugula.

Serves 8

- **1½ pounds fillet of beef as a first course, or 2½ pounds as a main course**
- **3 tablespoons extra virgin olive oil**
- **Salt and coarsely crushed pepper**
- **A few coriander seeds, coarsely ground**
- **6 handfuls of arugula (wild or salad)**
- **Parmesan cheese, shaved**
- **4 lemons, halved**

Put the unsliced fillet into the freezer for 2 hours. This makes it easier to cut into very thin slices.

Slice the beef into slivers and put each slice in between two layers of wax paper or plastic wrap. Beat out as thinly as you can without breaking the flesh. Lay the slices out on a flat plate and drizzle with olive oil. Garnish the slices with the pepper and coriander.

Mix the arugula with a little olive oil, salt, and more pepper and put a mound of leaves in the middle of the beef. Garnish with a few generous shavings of Parmesan. Serve with half a lemon on the side of each plate for your guests to squeeze over the meat. Don't do this in advance, as the acidity will discolor the meat.

Arugula, beet, and feta salad

I've been making this salad for years and it remains a stalwart. I sometimes mix mizuna in with the arugula if I don't have enough of that. Even in winter, you may be able to find fresh uncooked beets; but, if not, go for the vacuum-packed kind. Try to avoid the ones pickled in vinegar.

To make a refreshing summer lunch, the beets can be replaced with cubes of watermelon or, in the autumn, cubes of roasted squash. Roasted pumpkin seeds (see page 372) then make a delicious addition, along with a sweet balsamic sauce (see page 191).

Serves 8 to 10

- **4 medium-sized beets (or 8 small), cooked and cut into chunks**
- **8 handfuls of arugula**
- **2 handfuls of mint**
- **8 ounces feta cheese, crumbled**

For the dressing:

- **3 tablespoons extra virgin olive oil**
- **Juice and grated zest of 1 lemon**
- **Salt and pepper**

Leaving their skins on, simmer the beets in a pan until they're tender (20 to 30 minutes, depending on size). Let them cool slightly and rub off the skins, using your fingers. Cut them into chunks and allow them to cool. Combine the dressing ingredients.

Put all the other ingredients together in a salad bowl, reserving several mint leaves. Pour over the dressing, toss well, and garnish with the reserved mint leaves just before serving.

Cauliflower

A white cauliflower is a beautiful thing and quintessentially a cold climate plant. That's where many of the best recipes for it come from. Cauliflower is widely used in Indian cooking, but it's rare to see it featuring in Italian, Spanish, or even French food.

Cauliflower is available all year, but at its best in the spring and autumn. It's in the early spring—in March, the so-called famine month—that I find I use them most from my garden. Sown in late summer, the plants grow well through the winter, free from the usual brassica scourges of caterpillars and white fly, and they plump up at just the moment when there's very little else to pick.

The best variety I've grown is 'All Year Round' but, as with all cauliflower, when its curds are fattening up you have to watch it. They can be still a bit small one day, and already shot and starting to run up to flower just a few days later. Keep checking and you'll cut it at the perfect moment.

I also love 'Limelight' and 'Romanesco' in lime-green, which you'll see in good markets and which are also relatively easy to grow. Both mature quite quickly in early autumn from a late spring sowing. There is also orange cauliflower and rich purple ones like the very old winter-hardy 'Purple Cape', worth buying or growing if you can find the seed.

With all these fantastic-colored cauliflowers, steam them and serve them just dusted with freshly ground cumin, or deep-fry them, but don't hide them with sauce. Alternatively, cut them up into small florets for eating raw as part of a plate of crudités, dipped into a spring bagna cauda, or creamy anchovy dip (see page 422).

If you're in the mood, there's little better than a still slightly crunchy cauliflower cheese. You can add bacon or a scattering of crisped-up ham, or smother it in a fluffy soufflé top (see page 61), which elevates it beyond family supper food.

As long as the florets are small, cauliflower is delicious raw. One of my favorite salads for this time of year is cauliflower in yogurt, lime juice, and toasted poppy seeds. Very fresh raw cauliflower takes on a creamy taste.

Vegetable korma

This is a dish for using up almost whatever you have in your vegetable basket, but cauliflower makes a good base. It's the perfect quick-and-easy weekday supper. Serve it with rice and one of your summer- or autumn-made chutneys.

Serves 6

- **1 onion, finely chopped**
- **2 tablespoons vegetable oil**
- **1 teaspoon good curry powder**
- **2 (14-ounce) cans coconut milk**
- **1 cauliflower, chopped**
- **2 carrots, chopped**
- **1 parsnip, chopped**
- **2 good handfuls of chard or spinach, chopped**
- **Green beans (good, but not essential)**
- **Bunch of cilantro, roughly chopped**
- **Salt and pepper**

Fry the onion in the oil gently until soft. Add the curry powder and fry again for another minute or two. Then add the coconut milk and vegetables, except the beans, if you are using them.

Cook for about 10 minutes, until the vegetables are tender but not soft. If using beans, add them a couple of minutes before the end, as they take almost no cooking. Take off the heat and add the cilantro. Season to taste.

Cauliflower cheese with Lord Dalrymple's top

This is a delicious Edwardian dish that was included in my aunt Fortune Stanley's 1974 cookery book, *English Country House Cooking*. With a crunchy salad of bitter leaves—chicory, dandelion, and arugula—it is perfect for a main course.

Serves 4

- **1 large cauliflower**
- **¾ cup (1½ sticks) butter, plus a little more to grease the dish**
- **3 tablespoons all-purpose flour**
- **6 tablespoons light cream**
- **8 ounces strong Cheddar cheese**
- **Salt and pepper**
- **1 tablespoon mustard**
- **6 eggs, separated**

Preheat the oven to 350°F.

Divide the cauliflower into chunks and steam it for 3 to 4 minutes. Put the cauliflower in the bottom of a buttered soufflé dish.

Melt the butter, add the flour, and stir over low heat for 1 to 2 minutes. Add the cream and cheese. Season and add the mustard, and cook for 3 to 4 minutes, stirring continuously, until the mixture thickens to the consistency of heavy cream. Take off the heat and stir in the egg yolks.

Whisk the egg whites and fold in. Pour the soufflé mixture over the cauliflower and bake in the preheated oven for about 15 minutes, until the top is risen and turned brown.

Cauliflower soup

This is a creamy, gentle soup, with a lovely hint of almond.

Serves 6 to 8

- **1 medium-sized cauliflower**
- **1 to 2 tablespoons butter**
- **1 large onion, chopped**
- **1 garlic clove, roughly chopped**
- **¼ cup ground almonds**
- **4 cups good chicken or vegetable stock**
- **2 bay leaves**
- **2 cups milk**
- **Salt and pepper**
- **Freshly grated nutmeg**
- **Cayenne pepper**
- **Sliced almonds, toasted**

Break the cauliflower florets into roughly even-sized pieces. Melt the butter in a frying pan and sweat the onion—without allowing it to color—over low heat for 5 minutes.

Add the garlic, cauliflower, and ground almonds, and stir well. Pour in the stock, add the bay leaves, bring to a boil, and simmer, covered, for 10 minutes, until tender.

When slightly cooled, remove the bay leaves, puree in a food processor, and put back into a clean pan. Add enough of the milk to give the consistency you want, grate in a little nutmeg, season carefully, and bring to simmering point. Do not boil.

Serve dusted with cayenne pepper and scattered with toasted almonds.

Purple sprouting broccoli, calabrese, and spring greens

Purple sprouting broccoli, like rhubarb, appears when the garden and field harvest is sparse. It's iron-rich, packed with vitamins A, B, and C, and delicious—somehow you know from the way that it tastes that it's good for you.

I grow three types of sprouting broccoli. The earliest is 'White Eye', a tasty, greeny-white variety, less prolific than its purple cousins. Next comes purple 'Rudolph', another early cropper that I start to pick in February. I harvest these for a couple of months, picking little and often to encourage them to keep cropping. Pick the large central head first, which will then be followed by a profusion of tender side shoots. I also grow a mid- to late season variety, 'Red Arrow', which produces for us in earnest from late March until May.

Ideally, pick your stems not long before you eat them. This is one of the quickest brassicas to flop. If you need to keep them, seal them in a plastic bag in the fridge. Picked or bought very fresh, you can steam finger-thick shoots and eat every scrap. But if you have chunkier stalks, don't discard them. When you're preparing them, press your thumbnail into the stalk. If it goes in easily, it's tender enough to eat; if not, peel the outer skin with a potato peeler, but don't chop the stalk off.

Lay the purple sprouting broccoli stems out in a single layer in a pan on the stove, with about three inches of boiling salted water. Steam or boil hard, uncovered, for a couple of minutes and then test with the tip of a knife. I love the idea—described by Lynda Brown in her brilliant book *The Cook's Garden*—of dipping the smallest shoots, like asparagus, into a soft-boiled egg.

Also try eating purple sprouting broccoli like asparagus with hollandaise sauce (see page 233). Tie ten thin shoots, trimmed right down, into neat little bundles with string. Stand them upright in 3 inches of salted boiling water for about seven to eight minutes, until the stems are soft but the heads not collapsing. Put a bundle on each plate, season, and add a dollop of hollandaise.

Many of these recipes can also be made with calabrese broccoli but the flavor of purple sprouting is stronger and more interesting. It's more akin to that of spring greens.

At this time of year, there are also brussels sprout tops. Freshly picked, these are delicious sautéed, or steamed and dressed in a drizzle of olive oil or melted butter.

Broccoli with lemon and hazelnuts

This is almost too easy to call a recipe, but it's one of my favorite ways of eating purple sprouting broccoli. Serve this as a first course. People are always a bit surprised at the elevation of broccoli to a course on its own like asparagus, but they are soon converted.

Serves 4
   1 pound purple sprouting broccoli
   About ½ cup (1 stick) butter
   Juice and grated zest of ½ lemon
   Salt and pepper
   ½ cup hazelnuts, halved and toasted

Trim the broccoli and steam until just tender but retaining a good bite.

Warm the butter and add the lemon juice and zest.

Arrange the broccoli stems on a large shallow dish or on individual plates (both warmed) and pour over the hot butter.

Season well with salt and pepper, and scatter over the toasted hazelnuts.

Purple sprouting broccoli pasta

This is a very familiar recipe, but so good that it would be a shame to leave it out. You can make this sauce with purple sprouting broccoli or the chunkier, greener calabrese.

Serves 4
   1 (7-ounce) can anchovies in olive oil
   1 garlic clove, chopped
   1 red chili, chopped (optional)
   12 ounces penne or farfalle
   1 pound purple sprouting broccoli or calabrese
   Drizzle of olive oil
   Black pepper
   Lots of grated Parmesan cheese

Pour the can of anchovies with its oil into a frying pan over low heat. The anchovies will gradually dissolve in the oil, in 2 to 3 minutes. Add the garlic and chili (if using), and fry for another minute or two. Be careful not to let the garlic brown. Take the pan off the heat.

Meanwhile, cook the pasta in salted boiling water until al dente.

Trim the purple sprouting broccoli, retaining much of the stem as well as the heads. If the stems are tough, pare off the outer layer and then cut the stems into chunks. If using calabrese, separate the heads into small florets, breaking them off the main stem.

Steam the broccoli for about 5 minutes, until soft. Puree one half, leaving the other in little chunks. Toss all together with the anchovies. Add a little olive oil and pepper to taste. Stir this into the pasta and add lots of Parmesan.

Broccoli soup with Gorgonzola

This is a classic soup, even better with Gorgonzola than Stilton.

Serves 4
   1 pound purple sprouting broccoli or calabrese
   2 tablespoons butter
   1 onion, roughly chopped
   2 small potatoes, cut into chunks
   2 garlic cloves, roughly chopped
   5 cups hot chicken stock
   1 tablespoon lemon juice
   ¾ cup milk
   4 ounces Gorgonzola cheese
   Salt and pepper
   3 tablespoons heavy cream (optional)

Trim the purple sprouting broccoli, retaining much of the stem as well as the heads. If the stems are tough, pare off the outer layer and then cut the stems into chunks. If using calabrese, separate the heads into small florets, breaking them off the main stem.

Melt the butter in a large saucepan and put in the onion, chopped potatoes, and garlic. Cook for 5 minutes without allowing to brown and add the broccoli. Stir well to combine and pour in the hot stock and lemon juice. Cover and simmer for 10 to 15 minutes, until tender.

When the mixture has cooled a little, puree in a food processor and, if you want a very smooth soup, push it through a food mill or sieve into a clean pan.

Add the milk—more or less than the quantity given above, depending on how thick you like it. Then add the crumbled cheese and season carefully (Gorgonzola is salty).

Reheat gently without bringing to a boil and add the cream, if using.

Double pepper broccoli

This is good as a vegetable side dish or, with rice, as a light supper. This recipe can be made with cavolo nero kale, but blanch it before adding to the wok.

Serves 4 to 6
  1¼ pounds purple sprouting
    broccoli or calabrese
  1 sweet red pepper
  2 tablespoons peanut oil
  1 tablespoon black mustard seeds
  1 teaspoon dried chili, crumbled
  3 tablespoons good chicken or
    vegetable stock
  Salt

Trim the purple sprouting broccoli, retaining much of the stem as well as the heads. If the stems are tough, pare off the outer layer and then cut the stems into chunks. If using calabrese, separate the heads into small florets, breaking them off the main stem.

Deseed the pepper and then cut it into strips.

Heat the oil in a wok or deep frying pan and add the mustard seeds. Add the crumbled dried chili and, when the mustard seeds begin to pop, add the broccoli and stir to combine. Add the strips of pepper and stock, and stir again.

Cover the pan, turn down the heat, and cook for about 4 to 5 minutes, or until the broccoli is tender but crisp. If any liquid remains in the pan, raise the heat and boil it off. Season with salt before serving.

Spring greens risotto

This is a good, simple garden risotto. It is excellent with roast chicken.

Serves 4 as a side dish
  ½ pound spring greens
  1 tablespoon extra virgin olive oil
  2 tablespoons unsalted butter
  1 small onion, finely chopped
  ½ red chili, finely chopped
  1 cup Arborio rice
  2 garlic cloves, chopped
  Salt and pepper
  ½ cup red or white wine
  About 3 cups good chicken stock
  Plenty of grated Parmesan
    cheese, plus more as a garnish

Remove the stems from the spring greens, roll the leaves into cigar shapes, and cut these across to produce long ribbons. Steam or blanch for 2 to 3 minutes. Drain.

Heat the oil and 1 tablespoon of the butter in a heavy pan and add the onion. Sweat the onion and chili until the onion begins to look translucent. To prevent it from coloring, cook it over low heat under a piece of parchment paper.

Add the rice, garlic, salt, pepper, and spring greens, and stir well. Add half of the wine and let it bubble up and evaporate.

In a separate pan, bring the stock to a boil. Add the hot stock to the rice by the ladleful, stirring constantly between additions and waiting until the stock has been absorbed before adding the next ladleful.

After about 20 minutes, test to see if the rice is cooked (it should still have a bite). Adjust the seasoning if necessary. Remove from the heat and beat in the remaining butter, wine, and Parmesan. Serve with a bowl of extra Parmesan.

Rhubarb

Rhubarb is a miraculous plant. It is harvested when the garden and fields are at their barest. It is increasingly hailed as a superfood, rich in antioxidants, as well as being an excellent gentle purgative. It's also incredibly easy to grow, being one of the rare productive plants that will put up with shade and continue to produce despite almost total neglect. In fact, rhubarb is so extremely persistent that when archaeologists and historians spot it in the middle of nowhere, they assume people must have lived there once. There may be no architectural remains, but a good clump of rhubarb is a sure sign that the ground was once cultivated.

From early in the year, you'll find forced rhubarb—stems that have been grown with heat in the dark and are the sweetest and most tender. Exposure to light encourages them to become more fibrous and the taste to become sharp. Wakefield in West Yorkshire is still the heart of rhubarb forcing country in the UK and has been for over a hundred years. There it's picked by candlelight, which is less intense than day or electric light, and so less likely to affect the newly emergent stems.

By the middle of spring, field-grown rhubarb becomes available—a cheaper and still delicious thing. This has emerged naturally under its own steam and will need a little more cooking and sugar, but it's still invaluable for making delicious desserts.

I grow lots of rhubarb, cultivating three different varieties to give me maximum picking time. I start with 'Timperley Early', which has the least flavor, but in my garden is ready from mid-March if covered. Then I move on to mid-season 'Stockbridge Arrow', and finish with the late 'Queen Victoria', which produces right into June.

If you want to blanch your plants for extra sweetness, allow the crown—the heart of the plant—to die back in the autumn and clear away any debris once the leaves are brown and withered. When the weather starts to get milder in the spring, water the plants well first and then cover the crowns with straw and a tall rhubarb forcing pot. A bucket is usually too short, but a chimney pot or narrow trash can can work well. Use bubble wrap or straw to clad the outside. This helps protect against frost, which will split the stems, making them translucent and not good to eat. Six to eight weeks is the usual forcing time. The stalks grow quickly once they get going, so after six weeks inspect every couple of days.

To pick the stems, pull them gently from the base, taking care not to break the secondary stems nestled right at the heart of the plant. To store, slice off the leaves, and put the stems in a plastic bag. Otherwise, they wilt quickly.

Rhubarb syllabub

This old English pudding is one of my favorite spring desserts. It's easy and quick to make, as well as being light, frothy, and delicious.

Serves 6 to 8
- **Juice and grated zest of 1 orange**
- **½ cup superfine sugar**
- **6 stems of young pink rhubarb (about 1 pound)**
- **2 cardamom pods**
- **2 star anise**

For the syllabub:
- **1¼ cups heavy cream**
- **Grated zest and juice of 1 large lemon**
- **3 to 4 tablespoons Grand Marnier, dry sherry, or white wine**
- **½ cup superfine sugar**

Preheat the oven to 375°F.

Warm the orange juice in a pan and dissolve the sugar in it.

Cut the rhubarb into sections the length of your thumb and cook in the orange juice with the zest, cardamom, and star anise for 10 minutes. Then cool the fruit.

To make a syrupy juice, lift out the rhubarb pieces and boil the juice until it thickens.

To make the syllabub, put the cream, lemon zest and juice, alcohol, and sugar into a bowl and beat for several minutes, until the mixture becomes thick and light.

Remove the cardamom pods and star anise from the rhubarb. Put the rhubarb into individual glasses, spoon the syllabub mixture over the top, and chill for a couple of hours.

Rhubarb sorbet

A wonderfully light sorbet with a really punchy taste. It's a good way of using up rhubarb when there's too much to keep up with in the garden.

Serves 6 to 8
For the sugar syrup:
- **2½ cups sugar**

- **1½ pounds rhubarb**
- **Juice of 1 orange**
- **1 teaspoon vanilla extract**
- **Juice of 1 to 2 lemons**

To make the sugar syrup, dissolve the sugar in 2½ cups water over low heat. Slowly bring to a boil. Boil for 2 to 3 minutes and then allow to cool. This stores very well in the fridge. Cut the rhubarb into short lengths and put them into a saucepan with the orange juice. Simmer, covered, until the rhubarb is tender, then put to one side to cool.

Add the sugar syrup to the rhubarb and blend in a food processor until smooth. Add the vanilla and lemon juice to taste, and freeze/churn in an ice cream machine until nearly frozen. (Or pour into a plastic container with a lid, freeze, and, after about 1½ hours, beat with a hand mixer or food processor. Put the mixture back into the freezer and repeat the process again a couple of times at intervals until frozen.)

Transfer to the fridge about 20 minutes before serving. You need to eat this within a couple of months.

Rhubarb upside-down cake

This treacly and delicious cake looks and tastes fantastic.

Serves 6 to 8
- **1 pound rhubarb**
- **½ cup soft brown sugar**
- **¼ cup (½ stick) butter**
- **Grated zest of 1 orange**
- **½ cup (1 stick) butter**
- **¾ cup superfine sugar**
- **3 eggs**
- **1¼ cups all-purpose flour**
- **1 teaspoon baking powder**
- **½ teaspoon salt**
- **1 tablespoon milk**
- **Sliced almonds, toasted**
- **Confectioners' sugar, for dusting**
- **Crème fraîche and Demerara or raw cane sugar, to serve**

Preheat the oven to 350°F.

Cut the rhubarb at an angle into slices about 2 inches long. Melt the brown sugar with the butter in a 10-inch cast-iron skillet. Add the orange zest and remove from the heat. Cover the base of the pan with the rhubarb.

Cream the butter and sugar. Gradually add the eggs, one at a time, while still beating. Sift the flour, baking powder, and salt, and fold into the mixture. Add the milk and mix well. Spread the mixture over the rhubarb with a spatula.

Bake in the preheated oven for about 30 minutes, until the cake mixture is firm to the touch. Leave to cool for about 20 minutes in the pan and then invert onto a large flat serving plate.

Sprinkle with the toasted almonds and dust with confectioners' sugar. Serve warm with crème fraîche.

To reheat, put on a large baking sheet, sprinkle with Demerara sugar, and bake for 15 to 20 minutes in an oven preheated to 350°F.

Rhubarb tart

A lovely tart with a fresh and sharp flavor.

Serves 4 to 6
For the shortbread crust:
1 cup all-purpose flour
¼ cup superfine sugar
6 tablespoons unsalted butter,
    very cold
1 egg yolk
A little iced water

3 eggs
1 cup heavy cream
¼ cup sugar
Grated zest of 1 orange
A few saffron strands
1 pound rhubarb, cut into roughly
    1-inch lengths
½ cup toasted sliced almonds

Make the crust by processing the flour and sugar together for a minute or so. Chop the cold butter into chunks and add to the flour and sugar. Pulse carefully until the mixture resembles breadcrumbs, remove, and put into a mixing bowl.

Mix the egg yolk with a little iced cold water, add to the bowl, and mix until the pastry comes together in a soft ball. Roll out on a floured surface and use to line an 8-inch tart pan, then chill for half an hour in the fridge.

Preheat the oven to 375°F. Prick the unbaked crust with a fork, cover with a round of parchment paper or foil, and weight this down with some baking beans or rice. Bake the crust blind for about 15 minutes.

Take it out of the oven, but leave the oven on, and remove the beans or rice and the paper or foil. Put it back in the oven to cook for another 10 minutes. Let it cool slightly.

Lightly beat the eggs and mix with the cream, sugar, orange zest, and saffron. Cut the rhubarb into lengths and arrange in circles in the pan.

Pour over the cream mixture and bake in the oven for 15 minutes, then lower the temperature to 350°F and continue to bake for about 10 minutes, until the filling is firm and beginning to color.

Allow to cool and garnish with the toasted almonds.

Poached rhubarb with ginger ice cream

This recipe is delicious with the sweet, tender early stems of rhubarb.

Serves 10
For the ice cream:
2½ cups milk
½ cup superfine sugar
Few drops of vanilla extract
8 ounces sweetened condensed
    milk
Pinch of salt
2 cups heavy cream
6 pieces of stem ginger (or
    candied ginger in syrup), finely
    chopped
2 tablespoons ginger syrup

Juice and grated zest of 3 oranges
2 tablespoons muscovado or dark
    brown sugar
3 star anise
6 rhubarb stems (about 1¾
    pounds)
1½-inch piece of ginger, peeled
    and thinly sliced

First, make the ice cream. Heat the milk with the sugar and vanilla, and bring just to the boiling point. Remove from the heat and cool. Add the condensed milk, salt, cream, chopped stem ginger, and its syrup.

If you have an ice cream maker, freeze/churn the mixture for 20 minutes; if you don't, put it into a plastic container and freeze, breaking up the ice particles a couple of times with a fork at 2-hour intervals.

Preheat the oven to 375°F.

Warm the orange juice in a pan and melt the sugar, then add the star anise. Cut the rhubarb into sections the length of your thumb and lay them in a shallow heatproof dish, almost touching. Pour the warm liquid over the rhubarb and scatter over the orange zest and ginger.

Cover and bake for about 10 minutes. Serve with a couple of scoops of the ice cream.

Spinach

If you were a castaway on a temperate desert island, it would make sense to take a packet of spinach seed. With so many different ways to eat spinach, you'd be slow to get bored. The young leaves are as good raw as cooked; it is lovely wilted in a little water, butter, or olive oil, and just as delicious slow cooked in an Italian pasticcio or spanakopitta—Greek spinach pie (see page 74). Spinach makes good soup, good pasta, and good risotto. Like potatoes, it goes with everything.

It's always been said to be particularly good for you, very rich in iron and easily absorbed. Pregnant women were told to eat it by the wheelbarrow-load to avoid anemia; it was the source of Popeye's strength. In fact, spinach is rich in iron, but not in a form from which we can benefit; it is excreted from our bodies almost totally unabsorbed. However, spinach is an excellent source of vitamin A and folic acid. Spinach can protect against cancer of the prostate, breast, stomach, colon, lung, skin, and cervix. Consumers of spinach also gain protection against osteoporosis, heart disease, and arthritis.

Spinach is easy to grow and, as nonorganic spinach is usually covered in more chemicals than most other vegetables, growing your own is a good idea. It does best in the garden in the spring and autumn. The northern European variety 'Giant of Winter' is hardier than the rest here, and is said to crop all the way through our coldest months, but it doesn't come near Swiss chard's winter productivity. 'Trinidad', on the other hand, is slower to bolt in the summer and suits a hot climate. Most spinach varieties are happiest and harvested for the longest period in cool temperatures, moderate light levels, and plenty of rain.

My favorite variety is 'Dominant', with good mildew and disease resistance, and fantastic texture and taste. When I visited chef Raymond Blanc's vegetable garden at Le Manoir aux Quat' Saisons in Oxford, I was glad to hear 'Dominant' had come out tops in their taste trials, as it had done for me at Perch Hill. It is now the only variety we grow.

So-called perpetual spinach is a leafy kind of beet, and will produce right through the winter, if not the entire year. It's tougher than spinach, easier to grow, slower to bolt, coarser in texture and taste, but still well worth it.

Spinach freezes well, so when you have plenty in the garden, freeze it for later. Remove the stems and tear the leaves into ribbons. Blanch for two minutes, plunge into ice-cold water, and squeeze with your hands or twist in a clean towel to get it really dry before freezing in batches. When cooked, it reduces in volume by about three-quarters.

Spinach and lentil soup

Spinach is excellent with lentils, chickpeas, or almost any bean. This is a delicious warm winter soup—very filling and perfect for a weekend lunch.

Serves 6
- ½ pound spinach
- 1 cup red lentils
- 2 tablespoons olive oil
- 1 tablespoon ground cumin
- 1 tablespoon ground coriander seeds
- 1 tablespoon ground turmeric
- 1 teaspoon ground cloves
- 1 teaspoon ground cinnamon
- 1 onion, finely chopped
- 4 garlic cloves, finely chopped
- 5 tomatoes, skinned and chopped, or 1 (14-ounce) can chopped tomatoes
- 1 teaspoon tomato paste
- 1 (8-ounce) can coconut milk
- Large bunch of cilantro, roughly chopped
- Lemon juice, to taste

Remove the stems from the spinach and finely chop the leaves.

Cook the lentils in 6 cups of water. Bring to a boil and simmer for 15 to 20 minutes, until just tender.

Heat the oil in a frying pan and stir-fry all the spices. Add the onion and garlic, and sweat until soft.

Add the spices and onions to the lentils in their cooking liquid, and then add the tomatoes, tomato paste, and coconut milk. Cook for a further 15 minutes.

Add the spinach and cook just enough to wilt. Take off the heat and add the cilantro and lemon juice to taste, then season.

Ithaca pie

This is a local Ithacan version of spanakopitta that we ate in a small taverna in Stavros. It was cooked with spinach mixed with horta—wild greens picked from the hillside. A combination of spinach, kale, chard, dill, and mint gives almost the same rich and varied taste, but if you don't like the hint of bitterness, just use spinach, parsley, mint, and dill. Serve this with a finely chopped cabbage and grated carrot salad, dressed with good Greek olive oil, salt, and lemon juice.

Serves 12 to 15
For the filling:
- 2 pounds spinach, chard, kale (one, or a mixture of all, of these greens)
- Large bunch of dill, finely chopped
- 4 tablespoons finely chopped mint
- 4 tablespoons finely chopped parsley
- 1 onion, finely chopped
- 2 garlic cloves, finely chopped
- 1 cup olive oil
- 4 scallions, finely chopped
- 2 leeks, finely chopped
- ½ cup long-grain rice
- 6 ounces feta (optional)
- Salt and pepper

For the crust:
- 5 cups all-purpose flour
- 1 teaspoon salt
- 1¾ cups (3½ sticks) unsalted butter
- 3 eggs, beaten
- Ice-cold water
- 1 tablespoon sesame seeds

Remove tough stalks from the spinach, chard, and kale. Coarsely chop the leaves and add the finely chopped herbs. Sauté the onion and garlic in a little oil in a large pan and add all the greens, including the scallions and leeks. Mix well with most of the remaining oil. Add the uncooked rice and take off the heat. Season well.

To make the crust, sift the flour with the salt and rub in the butter or pulse in a food processor until it has the consistency of breadcrumbs. Add enough beaten eggs and iced water to bring the dough together in a ball. Wrap it in plastic and leave it in the fridge for at least 30 minutes.

Preheat the oven to 350°F. Divide the dough in two, allow it to warm up for a minute or so, and roll it out—on a floured surface—as thinly as you possibly can.

Roll one piece around a rolling pin to carry it and put it in the base of a baking pan about 16 by 20 inches and 1½ inches deep. It is important that there's plenty of extra pastry hanging over the side of the pan.

Add the filling and then crumble over the feta, if you are using it. Cover with the other layer of pastry. Then crimp the two layers together by brushing with a little water and pinching around the edge.

Brush a little oil over the top, scatter with a few sesame seeds, and prick the surface with a knife. Bake the pie in the preheated oven for just over an hour.

This is delicious once it has cooled a little and is perhaps even better eaten cold the next day. It's also excellent for feeding lots of people on a picnic.

Spinach and Gruyère tart

There are many delicious spinach tarts, but this very simple one is the best I have tried. Serve with a salad.

Serves 4 to 6
For the crust:
   3 cups all-purpose flour
   ½ teaspoon salt
   1 cup (2 sticks) unsalted butter
   1 egg, beaten
   Ice-cold water

   ½ pound spinach
   ¼ pound sorrel
   ¾ cup heavy cream
   ½ cup milk
   3 eggs
   1 teaspoon Dijon mustard
   Freshly grated nutmeg
   ½ teaspoon cayenne pepper
   7 ounces Gruyère cheese, grated
   Salt and pepper
   ½ cup pine nuts

To make the crust, sift the flour with the salt and rub in the butter or pulse in a food processor until it has the consistency of breadcrumbs. Add enough beaten egg and iced water to bring the dough together in a ball. Wrap it in plastic and leave in the fridge for at least 30 minutes.

Preheat the oven to 400°F. Roll out the chilled dough and use to line an 8-inch tart pan. Prick the bottom of the tart with a fork, cover with a round of parchment paper or foil, and weight this down with some baking beans or rice.

Bake the crust blind for about 15 to 20 minutes. Take it out of the oven (leaving the oven on but turning the temperature down to 350°F) and let it cool slightly, then remove the beans or rice and the paper or foil.

Pick over the leaves, removing any tough ribs. Cook until tender and drain thoroughly. To remove excess liquid, squeeze the leaves out with your hands or twist them gently in a clean tea towel. Chop the greens very roughly.

Mix the cream, milk, and eggs together and add the mustard, grated nutmeg, cayenne, and cheese. Season with salt and pepper.

Spread out the greens on the crust. Scatter over the pine nuts and pour over the cream mixture.

Cook the tart for 30 to 35 minutes and serve warm.

Spinach and sorrel frittata

Frittatas make easy, quick, substantial family food. I love this with a combination of spinach and sorrel, but spinach also works well on its own.

Serves 4
   1 pound spinach
   1 garlic clove, finely chopped
   1 egg white
   2 ounces Parmesan cheese, finely grated, plus more as a garnish
   1 cup breadcrumbs
   Freshly grated nutmeg, to taste
   1 tablespoon spring herbs (parsley, chives, or fennel), finely chopped
   Salt and pepper
   1 tablespoon all-purpose flour
   Really rich tomato sauce (see page 277)

Remove any large stems from the spinach and finely chop the leaves. Steam or cook them in a little salted water until tender. Squeeze out the water. Combine the spinach with the garlic, egg white, Parmesan, breadcrumbs, nutmeg, herbs, salt, and pepper.

Shape the mixture into small dumplings the size of whole walnuts. Roll each lightly in flour, just to coat. The easiest way to cook these is to steam them. You can then do two layers at once. Lay them out, spaced an inch apart, in a steamer lined with layers of perforated parchment paper, with a little butter or olive oil on the sheets to prevent the dumplings from sticking. Put the lid on and steam for 10 minutes.

Serve with melted butter or plenty of Really rich tomato sauce (see page 277), and garnish with grated Parmesan.

Creamed spinach

There are many recipes for creamed spinach, but this one is quick, light, and simple.

Serves 4 as a side dish
1 pound spinach
1 tablespoon olive oil
2 tablespoons butter
4 shallots, chopped
2 garlic cloves, chopped
¼ cup heavy cream
A little freshly grated nutmeg
Salt and pepper

Wash the spinach leaves well and dry them off in a salad spinner. Steam the spinach for 3 minutes and roughly chop.

In a deep frying pan, heat the oil and butter together, add the shallots and garlic, and gently sweat until they have softened and become translucent. Add the chopped spinach, raising the heat slightly to bubble away any excess liquid from the spinach. Lower the heat again and add the cream, grated nutmeg, salt, and pepper, and stir to heat through. Serve immediately.

Spinach with split peas or lentils

Fave e foglie, as it is called in Italy, is a classic Roman dish. It is delicious yet virtuous-feeling, and is best eaten when just warm. You can use fava beans, lentils, or split peas, but I prefer lentils. Chard or wild greens, such as nettles or chicory, can be substituted for spinach.

Serves 6 as a starter
1 cup lentils (preferably Puy lentils)
or split peas
1 cup white wine
2 bay leaves
2 whole garlic cloves
Small bunch of thyme
1 celery stalk
Extra virgin olive oil
Salt and pepper
Large bunch of flat-leaf parsley,
coarsely chopped
1 pound spinach or chard
Juice and grated zest of 1 lemon
2 tablespoons capers, rinsed

Boil the lentils or split peas with the wine, bay leaves, garlic, thyme, and celery stalk (left whole), with enough water to cover. Cook for about 20 minutes, until just tender. Remove the bay, thyme, garlic, and celery. Drain the lentils, pour over a little olive oil, and season while still hot. Allow to cool a little and then add the parsley.

Steam the spinach or chard leaves. Dress with a little olive oil mixed with the lemon juice and zest. Season with salt and pepper.

On each plate, serve a large spoonful of lentils, topped with a few capers, alongside a mound of leaves.

Sag aloo

Our own version of the Indian classic. Serve with a meat curry and rice.

Serves 4
1 pound new potatoes
¾ pound young spinach leaves
1 teaspoon mustard seeds
1 tablespoon sunflower oil
1 teaspoon cumin seeds, toasted
and ground
½ teaspoon chili powder
1 large onion, chopped
3 garlic cloves, chopped
2-inch piece of ginger, peeled
and chopped
1 cup vegetable stock or water
1 teaspoon garam masala
1 tablespoon olive oil
Salt and pepper
Plain yogurt, as a garnish

Peel the potatoes and cut them into 1-inch chunks. Blanch the spinach or steam it for 2 to 3 minutes. Drain well and chop it coarsely.

Put the mustard seeds in a heavy-bottomed pan with the sunflower oil and fry until the seeds begin to pop. Add the ground cumin and chili powder, and cook for a minute or two. Add the onions, garlic, and ginger, and cook gently for a further 4 to 5 minutes.

Stir in the chopped potatoes and 1 cup of the stock with some salt and pepper. Cook for 8 to 10 minutes and then add the chopped spinach.

Cover the pan and cook until the potatoes are just tender. If it needs more liquid during the cooking, add the remaining stock or water. Take off the heat, stir in the garam masala with the olive oil, and adjust the seasoning.

This is lovely served warm with plenty of plain yogurt.

Baby spinach, pancetta, and roasted almond salad

Raw baby spinach makes one of the most mild and tender salad leaves.

Serves 4
For the croutons:
2 to 3 thick slices whole wheat bread
Sunflower oil, for frying

3 ounces pancetta, very thinly sliced (but not chopped)
¼ cup almonds
½ pound baby spinach
Good handful of small sorrel leaves, stems removed
2 large avocados (optional)
2 ounces Parmesan cheese

For the dressing:
2 teaspoons Dijon mustard
1 teaspoon superfine sugar
1½ teaspoons red wine vinegar
½ cup sunflower oil
3 tablespoons extra virgin olive oil
Salt and pepper

Preheat the oven to 350°F.

First make the croutons: cut the slices of bread into large cubes. Heat some sunflower oil in a small frying pan and, when the oil is really hot, cook the bread cubes until golden and crisp. Dry on paper towels and season while hot.

Put the pancetta slices on an oiled baking sheet and bake in the preheated oven for about 10 to 15 minutes, until crisp.

Halve and toast the almonds in a frying pan for a few minutes, tossing them once or twice as they cook.

To make the dressing: whisk the mustard, sugar, and vinegar together in a jug, using a hand mixer. Gradually add the two oils in a stream while whisking and season carefully with salt and pepper.

Put the spinach and sorrel leaves in a large shallow bowl and toss in just enough of the dressing to coat the leaves.

Peel the avocados if you are using them, slice into large pieces, and season. Pare the Parmesan with a potato peeler.

Add the croutons, sorrel, avocado, Parmesan, and herbs to the spinach, combining gently, and add the pancetta slices and almonds. Drizzle more dressing over the top.

Spinach malfatta

These light dumplings are just as good, and easier to prepare than spinach ravioli.

Serves 4
1 pound spinach
1 garlic clove, finely chopped
1 egg white
2 ounces Parmesan cheese, finely grated, plus more as a garnish
1 cup breadcrumbs
Freshly grated nutmeg, to taste
1 tablespoon spring herbs (parsley, chives, or fennel), finely chopped
Salt and pepper
1 tablespoon all-purpose flour
Really rich tomato sauce (see page 277)

Remove any large stems from the spinach and finely chop the leaves. Steam or cook them in a little salted water until tender. Squeeze out the water. Combine the spinach with the garlic, egg white, Parmesan, breadcrumbs, nutmeg, herbs, salt, and pepper.

Shape the mixture into small dumplings the size of whole walnuts. Roll each lightly in flour, just to coat. The easiest way to cook these is to steam them. You can then do two layers at once. Lay them out, spaced an inch apart, in a steamer lined with layers of perforated parchment paper, with a little butter or olive oil on the sheets to prevent the dumplings from sticking. Put the lid on and steam for 10 minutes.

Serve with melted butter or plenty of Really rich tomato sauce (see page 277), and garnish with grated Parmesan.

Spring herbs

Herbs are productive plants that everyone can grow. They take up little space, are happy in a pot on a windowsill or patio, and are bountiful for months at a stretch. A handful of leaves, finely chopped, is often all that's required to transform a dish.

There are four stalwarts that are the first to emerge in early spring—chives, fennel, sorrel, and lovage. These join parsley and chervil—both hardy biennials—that grow outside for most of the cold months. By spring, you'll also have cilantro, which is best sown in the early spring or late summer. It runs up to flower too quickly in the hotter months, but grows well in these cool bright days. Combine a few leaves of each of these herbs (using lovage sparingly) and make a Spring salsa verde or Green mayonnaise (see page 83).

The first young leaves of all these herbs are also delicious chopped or torn and scattered over a salad. This is my favorite way of eating lovage—just a sprinkling, as it has a strong smoky celery taste. Once the leaves of lovage grow beyond the size of a child's hand, they're too strong to use raw, but are invaluable as flavoring in stews (see Hungarian goulash on page 88) and stocks. Lovage makes an ornamental plant when fully grown, so why not grow it?

If you keep picking chives, cilantro, fennel, and sorrel little and often, they'll remain succulent and tasty for longer. Left unpicked for weeks, they'll flower and then seed, and lose their flavor. Cilantro is a short-lived annual and will need resowing, but the rest just need to be cut to the ground and fed with a potash-rich feed around mid-June. They'll have sprouted again within a couple of weeks and will be there to harvest for the rest of the summer and into the fall.

Pick your herbs as and when you want them, but if you need to store them, wash the leaves and wrap them in paper towels. Put them, still wrapped, in a plastic bag at the bottom of the fridge and most will last ten days. You can also freeze herbs in ice cubes: finely chop them, mix them in a little water, and fill the trays. You can add these cubes to soups and stews. Herb butters are also ideal if you have too much of any one herb. Take a handful of any soft herb and mix it with soft unsalted or lightly salted butter in a food processor. Place the herb butter on a length of plastic wrap, roll it into a cylinder, and freeze. Cut it off in discs with a warmed knife to melt over a steak or a bowl of vegetables.

The flavor of all these herbs comes from oils in the leaves. Parsley and lovage will take some cooking and still retain their flavor, but with chives, chervil, sorrel, fennel, and cilantro, the rule is "less is more" for cooking times. Add them just before taking the pan off the heat.

Spring salsa verde

A herb dressing that is wonderful with globe artichokes, chicken, fish, beef, or lamb.

Serves 8 to10
- 1 large bunch of flat-leaf parsley
- 1 large bunch of mixed herbs (chives, fennel, chervil, cilantro, sorrel, and just one or two leaves of lovage or winter savory)
- 4 cornichon pickles, rinsed
- 20 to 30 small capers, rinsed
- 1 cup olive oil
- Juice of ½ lemon
- Salt and pepper

Chop the herbs coarsely.

Add the cornichons and capers with the olive oil and lemon juice. Chop briefly in a food processor or by hand so that you have a coarse-textured sauce. Season to taste.

Green mayonnaise

I love green herb mayonnaise, particularly in spring, when the first chives and sorrel give a sharpness to the taste. It is lovely to eat with salmon, prawns, and boiled potatoes or cold chicken and ham.

There are a few things worth knowing about mayonnaise: the ingredients must be at the same temperature, so take your eggs out of the fridge a couple of hours before you start. To thin any mayonnaise, whisk in a little boiling water. Mayonnaise can be very successfully made in a food processor, but you will need to make a bigger quantity than that made by this recipe (at least 4 eggs).

Serves 8 to 10
- 1 good handful of mixed green herbs (half parsley, with the other half made up from one or all of chives, fennel, chervil, and sorrel)
- 1 egg yolk
- 1 whole egg
- 2 tablespoons lemon juice
- 1 garlic clove
- 1¼ cups sunflower oil (or ¼ cup olive oil and 1 cup sunflower oil)
- Salt and pepper

Finely chop your herbs by hand or in a food processor. Add the egg yolk, whole egg, lemon juice, and garlic, and whisk for a few seconds. While beating with a whisk or with the motor running, add the oil in a slow stream and the mayonnaise will thicken. Season well.

If your mayonnaise curdles, you can rescue it by putting another beaten egg yolk into a jug or bowl and, while whisking continuously, pouring the rogue mayonnaise into this in a thin stream.

Mayonnaise will keep in the fridge for at least 5 days, stored in an airtight container.

Herb dumplings

Dumplings—not too big—can be the making of a stew. If they're flavored with herbs, so much the better. Parsley, chives, and lovage all make delicious flavored dumplings.

Yield: 12 small dumplings
- 1¼ cups all-purpose flour
- 3 tablespoons baking powder
- 3 heaping tablespoons chopped fresh herbs
- Salt and pepper
- ¾ cup milk
- 3 tablespoons vegetable oil

Sift the dry ingredients together in a bowl and add the chopped herbs. Season with salt and freshly ground pepper and stir in the milk and oil. Flour your hands and shape the mixture into small balls. Add these to a casserole for the last 20 minutes of the cooking time. Make sure they sit on top of the stew and are not submerged.

Continue to cook your casserole, covered. About 10 minutes before the end, if cooking in the oven, remove the lid and allow the dumplings to brown a little on top. If cooking on the stove, take the lid off and place the casserole in a 400°F oven for the final 10 minutes.

Spring herb and wild greens pasta

This Provençal pasta dish is never quite the same each time you make it, as it depends on what you can find growing at the time. Young dandelions, purslane, and any other wild salad greens are good additions. In spring, when the young shoots are tender, a discreet amount of winter savory is also good, but basil, cultivated marjoram flower buds and leaves, lemon balm, rocket, hyssop, parsley, sorrel, celery leaves, and scallions are all possible candidates.

Serves 4
   Pinch of salt
   2 to 3 tablespoons chopped fresh herbs and salad greens, plus a small handful of herbs as a garnish
   2¼ cups pasta flour, plus more for dusting
   2 eggs plus 1 egg yolk, beaten
   1 tablespoon olive oil
   Extra virgin olive oil or unsalted butter
   Grated Parmesan cheese

Pound together the salt, herbs, and greens, either using a mortar and pestle or in a food processor, to form a paste.

Put the 2¼ cups of flour into a mixing bowl and make a well in the center. Pour the herb mixture and the eggs into the well and stir with a fork, moving outwards to bring in the flour gradually and adding, if necessary, a splash of warm water or more flour to form a soft but sticky dough.

Flour a work surface well and turn the dough onto it. Knead repeatedly and turn it in the flour. Push with the heel of your hand to stretch it, fold it, turn it in the flour, and repeat. The greens will release their liquid and absorb more flour.

When the dough feels silky and no longer sticky, form it into a ball, cover it with a towel, and leave it to rest for 1 hour.

Scrape the work surface clean, flour it again, and roll out the dough as thin as you can. Cut it into strips about 1½ inches wide and cut the strips across into squares.

Bring a large pot filled with salted water to a boil. Add the oil. Toss the squares loosely in your hands (or in a sieve) to rid them of excess flour and drop them in the boiling water. When the water returns to a boil, adjust the heat to maintain a gentle boil and cook, stirring regularly, until tender, for about 12 to 15 minutes.

Drain and serve in warmed soup plates. Garnish with extra virgin olive oil or unsalted butter, the remaining herbs, and plenty of grated Parmesan.

Chervil butter

With mixed leaves, anchovy, and capers, this is more than just a herb butter. It is wonderful with fresh tuna, lamb, or pork chops.

Serves 6 to 8
   3 sprigs of chervil
   A few spinach leaves
   A few watercress leaves
   ½ cup (1 stick) unsalted butter
   1 teaspoon capers
   1 garlic clove
   1 anchovy fillet
   2 teaspoons lemon juice
   Salt and pepper

Blanch the herbs by dropping them into boiling water for 30 seconds and then refresh them in very cold water. Dry them on paper towels or twist them gently in a clean towel.

Put the herbs, butter, capers, garlic, anchovy, and lemon juice into a food processor, and blend until smooth. Season and put the mixture on a sheet of plastic wrap. Roll up into a tube shape and then roll in the plastic. Put in the fridge or freezer until firm and then wrap in another layer of plastic or wax paper.

With a knife dipped into boiling water, cut slices from the roll when you need them for meat or fish.

Smoked salmon pâté with chervil

A light and delicious pâté, which is excellent on white or brown bread. I particularly love chervil with salmon, but later in the year I make this with chives or dill. All three are delicious.

Serves 8

6 ounces smoked salmon
16 ounces cream cheese
1 cup heavy cream
¼ cup (½ stick) unsalted butter, softened
Lemon juice to taste, plus slices of lemon as a garnish
1 teaspoon cayenne pepper
2 tablespoons chopped fresh chervil, chives, or dill
Black pepper
Sliced bread for toast

Put the salmon, cream cheese, and cream into a food processor. Whiz briefly.

Add the butter, lemon juice, cayenne pepper, herbs, and black pepper. Process until the mixture forms a paste consistency. Check the seasoning and adjust if necessary.

Pack into a pâté dish and put in the fridge for an hour or two to set.

Serve with warm toast and a slice of lemon.

Hummus with cilantro

I love hummus anyway, but with the extra brightness of cilantro this is one of my favorite lunches. Eat it with flat bread (see page 46) or chunks of cucumber, radish, cauliflower, fennel, carrots, and celery for a healthy and delicious meal.

Serves 6

¾ cup dried chickpeas
1 head garlic
1 tablespoon tahini
1 cup yogurt, preferably the thick Greek kind
Handful of fresh cilantro, chopped
Salt and pepper

Soak the chickpeas overnight.

Preheat the oven to 350°F. Drain the chickpeas and pour over more water to cover generously, bring to a boil, cover, and cook for about 30 minutes, until tender but still intact.

Meanwhile, roast the head of garlic in the oven for about 20 minutes, until the cloves feel very soft.

Drain the chickpeas, reserving a little of the liquid, and allow to cool for 5 to 10 minutes before putting into a food processor with the tahini, yogurt, chopped cilantro, and salt and pepper to taste.

Crush the roasted garlic cloves to release the sweet soft garlic pulp and add as much or as little as you like to the hummus.

Pork tenderloin with cilantro

A pork dish with a bright and sparky flavor. It's very quick to make and an ideal midweek supper. Eat it with rice or, even better, Spinach with split peas or lentils (see page 78).

Serves 2

12-ounce pork tenderloin
1 onion
2 tablespoons butter
1 tablespoon olive oil
2 teaspoons coriander seeds, crushed
¼ pound cremini or button mushrooms, halved
1 large garlic clove, crushed and chopped
¼ cup ginger wine or sweet white wine
1 heaping teaspoon soft brown sugar
1 tablespoon lemon juice
1 cup crème fraîche
Salt and pepper
A few sprigs of cilantro, chopped

Trim the tenderloin and slice it across into ¾- to 1-inch-thick slices.

Slice the onion and sauté in the butter and oil with the crushed coriander seeds for a few minutes until translucent. Lift out with a slotted spoon, put to one side, and keep warm.

Sauté the mushrooms in the same pan for 2 to 3 minutes with the garlic and add them to the onion.

If necessary, heat a little more oil in the pan and add the pork. Turn it in the butter and oil for 3 to 4 minutes and return the vegetables to the pan.

Add the ginger wine or wine, brown sugar, and lemon juice, and allow it all to bubble for about 5 to 6 minutes, until the liquid begins to go syrupy.

Add the crème fraîche, season with salt and pepper, and finally stir in the chopped cilantro.

Alastair Little's stuffed chicken with cilantro pesto

This dish, named for the famous London chef, is excellent for a spring or summer lunch, eaten outside or, even better, for a picnic. You can make it the day before, and the taste will intensify as the chicken sits in the cilantro juices. It can be eaten with new potatoes and green salad or sliced for sandwiches.

Serves 6
For the cilantro pesto:
2 large bunches of cilantro leaves
Large bunch of flat-leaf parsley
2 large garlic cloves
12 chive stalks
5 ounces Parmesan cheese
½ cup pine nuts
Salt and pepper
1 cup extra virgin olive oil, plus more for drizzling

1 (3-pound) chicken, boned, plus 2 large boneless chicken breasts, ideally free-range
4 thin slices pancetta
Large bunch of tarragon
Sprig of lemon thyme
2 garlic cloves
½ cup dry white wine
1 tablespoon olive oil
Salt and pepper
Cilantro and flat-leaf parsley leaves, as a garnish
Lemon wedges

First, make the pesto. Take the stems off the cilantro and the parsley. Peel and chop the garlic. Cut up the chives thinly. Grate the Parmesan by hand or with the grating disc of a food processor. Add the garlic and pine nuts to the Parmesan, and process to incorporate. Add the cilantro, chives, and parsley, and process until combined. Season carefully with salt and pepper. Add the olive oil to the mixture in the processor by adding it in a thin stream while the motor is running.

Preheat the oven to 400°F. Spread half of the pesto on the inside of the flattened chicken. Wrap the chicken breasts in 2 of the pancetta slices and place these centrally on the pesto-rubbed chicken. Spread the remaining pesto on top of them and wrap the boned bird up around these to form a rolled shape.

I've eaten this with my friend Caroline Owen-Lloyd. She sews the chicken up at this stage, using a darning needle and string—separated into strands so that you can thread it. This keeps most of the stuffing in.

Put the herbs and unpeeled garlic in an ovenproof dish (or loaf pan) into which the rolled chicken will fit snugly and pour in the wine.

Brush the breasts of the bird with the olive oil and season with salt and pepper. Put the remaining pancetta slices on top and cover loosely with foil.

Roast for 1½ hours, removing the foil and basting after 1 hour. Baste again 20 minutes later.

Remove from the tin, place on a board, and wrap in tin foil to rest for 10 minutes, then carve into slices about an inch thick.

Drizzle with a little extra virgin olive oil and garnish with fresh cilantro and flat-leaf parsley. Serve with wedges of lemon.

Lettuce and lovage soup

The flavor of lovage is at its best when it's young and fresh, as it is when it first appears—as a perennial herb—in early spring. With this soup, the smokiness of the lovage offsets the mildness of the cooked lettuce. It's delicious.

Serves 6
6 Little Gem or other small lettuces
Handful of young lovage leaves
2 tablespoons butter
4 scallions, chopped
2 tablespoons all-purpose flour
2 cups milk
2 cups good vegetable stock
Freshly grated nutmeg
Salt and pepper
Cream or Greek yogurt

Pull the lettuce apart and steam with the lovage until just tender. Allow to cool for 5 minutes and then puree in a food processor.

Melt the butter in a saucepan and sweat the scallions without allowing them to brown. Stir in the flour and allow it to cook but not brown. Add the milk and stock bit by bit, whisking all the time. Simmer for a couple of minutes and then add the lettuce mixture. Season well with nutmeg, salt, and pepper.

Eat this hot or cold with a dollop of cream or Greek yogurt.

Hungarian goulash with lovage

I had this dish at the twenty-first birthday party of my friend Caroline Frapwell, and still remember it! It is excellent party food, and the flavor improves if you cook it the day before. If there are no dumplings, serve with rice and steamed broccoli.

Serves 6 to 8

  1 large onion, chopped
  2 tablespoons sunflower oil
  1 red pepper, cut into strips
  12 ounces button mushrooms, whole or halved
  1 garlic clove, chopped
  1¼ pounds pork fillet
  Flour
  Salt and pepper
  ½ teaspoon cayenne pepper
  2 teaspoons paprika
  1 bay leaf
  4 tablespoons finely chopped lovage
  1½ cups good vegetable stock
  1 (14-ounce) can chopped tomatoes
  3 tablespoons tomato paste
  1 cup crème fraîche
  Large bunch of flat-leaf parsley, finely chopped

Fry the onion in a little oil in a casserole dish until soft. Add the red pepper and mushrooms, and cook for 5 minutes. Then add the garlic and set aside.

Cut the pork into strips. Season the flour with salt and pepper. Roll the pork in the flour and fry in a little sunflower oil to seal. Add to the casserole dish.

Add the spices, bay leaf, and some of the lovage, followed by the stock, canned tomatoes, and tomato paste. Cook gently, covered, for at least 2 hours. You can add Herb dumplings for the last half hour (see page 83). Allow the goulash to cool a little and then add the crème fraîche with plenty of parsley and more lovage.

Jane's Thai chicken curry

There are a great many Thai chicken curry recipes, but I like this one from my sister Jane as it includes lots of vegetables and tastes delicious. Cilantro—added in large quantities at the end—is central to its flavor.

Serves 6

  4 medium-sized to large organic skinless, boneless chicken breasts
  About ½ thumb-size piece of ginger, coarsely chopped
  Stick of lemongrass, cut into 3
  1 pound mixed vegetables (to include, depending on the time of year, fava beans, peas, green beans, scallions, zucchini, Swiss chard, spinach, cabbage, or cavolo nero kale)
  Dash or two of olive oil
  1 to 2 tablespoons Thai red or green curry paste (or to taste)
  1 (14-ounce) can coconut milk
  Juice of 2 limes
  Dash of soy sauce
  Dash of Thai fish sauce
  Large bunch of cilantro, coarsely chopped

You can cook this in the oven or on the stovetop. If you are using the oven, preheat to 350°F.

Put the chicken breasts in a saucepan—halve them if they are really large. Just cover with water. Add the ginger and lemongrass and poach for 10 minutes. Strain, reserving the liquid. Cut the chicken breasts into walnut-sized pieces.

Cut the vegetables into chunks, not too small. Fry them gently in olive oil in a wide-based saucepan for 10 minutes, turning regularly. Add the chicken to the pan.

In another small pan, fry the curry paste for 3 minutes in a little olive oil. Add the coconut milk and lime juice to taste, and heat for 5 minutes. Pour the sauce over the chicken and vegetables, and cook in the preheated oven or on the stovetop for 20 minutes. Add a splash each of soy and fish sauce, and serve garnished with lots of cilantro. Serve with rice. (The liquid you have reserved can be eaten separately, like miso soup, or used as stock for risotto.)

Parsley soup

A wonderfully clean-tasting, fresh spring soup.

Serves 6
- **2 leeks**
- **2 potatoes**
- **Handful of curly or flat-leaf parsley, leaves and stems**
- **1 onion, sliced**
- **1 tablespoon butter**
- **3½ cups good stock**
- **Salt and pepper**
- **¾ cup milk**
- **¼ cup light cream (optional)**
- **Deep-fried parsley (see page 90), as a garnish**

Rinse the leeks and slice them, making sure that you use at least some of the green tops. Peel and chop the potatoes. Separate the tops from the stems of the parsley and then chop up the stems.

Fry the onion in the butter and, when soft, add the potatoes, parsley stems, and sliced leeks. Cook for about 5 minutes without allowing the vegetables to color.

Add the stock and cook for about 10 minutes, until the potatoes are tender. Allow to cool for a few minutes. Mince the parsley leaves in a food processor or chop them by hand and add to the mixture. Puree and season carefully.

Return to the rinsed pan and add the milk. Reheat, adding the cream, if using, but without allowing the soup to boil. Garnish with deep-fried parsley.

Parsley sauce

This is a béchamel sauce with lots of parsley. Parsley sauce is, of course, traditional with fish and new potatoes, but it's also the best thing to eat with a clove-flavored ham, baked potatoes, and carrots.

Serves 8
- **4 cups milk**
- **1 onion, stuck with a few cloves**
- **A few black peppercorns**
- **2 bay leaves**
- **6 tablespoons butter**
- **½ cup all-purpose flour**
- **Large bunch of curly or flat-leaf parsley, stems removed, finely chopped**
- **Plenty of salt and pepper**

Bring the milk to a boil with the clove-studded onion, peppercorns, and bay leaves.

In a separate pan, melt the butter and stir in the flour, allowing it to cook for a couple of minutes. Then gradually add the strained hot milk. Add the parsley, stirring continuously. Season with salt and pepper.

Deep-fried parsley

The spring alternative to deep-fried kale, with a softer, gentler, and more fragrant taste. Eat it with an aperitif, or scatter it on top of almost any soup. Curly-leaved parsley is better for this than the flat-leafed form.

Serves 8 to 10
- **½ pound curly-leaf parsley, stems and any coarse midribs removed**
- **Peanut oil, for deep-frying**
- **1 teaspoon soft brown sugar**
- **2 good pinches of sea salt, finely crumbled**
- **2 tablespoons crushed cashew nuts or sliced almonds (optional)**

Wash the parsley and dry thoroughly in a clean towel or salad spinner.

Heat some oil for deep-frying to 325°F. Use a deep-fat fryer if you have one. If you don't have a fryer, use a large saucepan, but fill it only one-third full of oil and fry in small batches to keep the temperature constant.

Drop a handful of parsley into the oil. Fry for just a few seconds, remove with a slotted spoon, and drain on paper towels. Repeat with the rest of the parsley.

Scatter the soft brown sugar and salt over the top, adding crushed cashew nuts or sliced toasted almonds if you like.

Serve the parsley right away. It tastes nicest when it's hot.

Warm chickpea and parsley salad

All you need is a pile of crunchy lettuce on the side of this lovely spring salad.

Serves 4
- **½ pound chickpeas**
- **½ onion, stuck with a couple of cloves**
- **½ carrot**
- **2 bay leaves**
- **Sprig of thyme**
- **2 tablespoons extra virgin olive oil**
- **Sea salt and black pepper**
- **Very large handful of chopped parsley**
- **1 sweet white onion, thinly sliced**
- **2 garlic cloves, finely chopped**
- **Lemon juice (optional)**

Soak the chickpeas in cold water to cover overnight.

Drain and pour over fresh water, covering the chickpeas well. Add the onion, carrot, bay, and thyme. Bring to a boil and cook, covered, for about 30 minutes, or until tender but still intact. Check from time to time that there is enough water, and add more if necessary. Remove the onion, carrot, and herbs and drain the chickpeas.

Pour over the extra virgin olive oil while the chickpeas are still hot, season with plenty of sea salt and black pepper, and stir in the chopped parsley, sliced onion, and finely chopped garlic. Add lemon juice if you want a sharper taste.

Jane Grigson's sorrel sauce with fish

The best ever sauce to eat with fish by the great British cookery writer. Serve it with a whole turbot or use it to transform an ordinary salmon steak.

Serves 4 to 6
1 (3- to 3½-pound) whole fish or several fillets
1 cup white wine
1 onion, sliced
1 garlic clove, coarsely chopped

For the sauce:
2 handfuls of sorrel leaves
1 cup heavy cream
Salt and pepper

Cook your fish in a 350°F oven in the white wine, along with the onion and garlic, until done.

Prepare your sorrel puree. Sorrel cooks very quickly, wilting down to virtually nothing in the pan and turning a drab olive color. (To keep its freshness and color, you only want it to touch the heat.) Remove the central leaf midrib and chop it finely.

Bring the cream to a boil, add the sorrel, and immediately take the pan off the heat.

Add 4 tablespoons of the fish juices and season to taste.

Sorrel soup

Another spring classic. We tried many sorrel soups, and this simple recipe made the tastiest.

Serves 6
1 tablespoon unsalted butter
1 tablespoon olive oil
3 shallots, finely chopped
2 leeks, finely chopped
½ pound potatoes, chopped
4 cups good vegetable stock
½ pound sorrel, ribs and stems removed, and sliced
½ cup cream
Salt and pepper

Warm the butter and olive oil in a pan, and sweat the shallots and the leeks without allowing them to brown.

Add the potatoes and stir in the stock. Simmer the vegetables, covered, for about 25 minutes. Add the sorrel for the last 2 minutes. Take off the heat and puree in a blender. Add the cream and season well.

Warm before serving, but do not allow to boil. Thin the soup with a little milk or stock, if necessary.

Potato gratin with sorrel

The flavor of sorrel is excellent with potatoes, which absorb some of its citrus taste. This is delicious with salmon or chicken.

Serves 4 to 6
2 to 3 tablespoons unsalted butter, plus more to grease the dish
2¼ pounds potatoes
½ pound young sorrel leaves
½ pound onions
Salt
¾ cup heavy cream

Preheat the oven to 350°F and butter a 2-quart gratin or shallow casserole dish.

Peel the potatoes and slice them lengthwise as thinly as possible—a mandoline is useful for this. Remove the stem from the sorrel, roll it up tightly, and cut across to make thin strips. Thinly slice the onions.

Melt a tablespoon of the butter in a sauté pan over low heat. Add the sorrel, sprinkle with a little salt, and cook for a minute, stirring with a wooden spoon, until the sorrel just begins to wilt. Add the cream and simmer for a minute. Remove from the heat.

Put the potatoes and onions in a saucepan. Add a good pinch of salt, and pour over just enough water to cover them. Bring to a boil, cooking for 8 to 10 minutes, shaking the pan regularly to make sure they don't stick to the bottom. Take off the heat and drain. Pour a layer into the gratin dish, spread some sorrel mixture evenly over the top, and repeat.

Place in the preheated oven and bake for about an hour.

Watercress and wild garlic

Watercress makes a particularly delicious salad. It has the pepperiness of mature arugula, but not the bitter overlay. It's also very good for you, with a high concentration of vitamin C, as well as beta-carotene and vitamin A equivalents. These are important antioxidants, needed for healthy skin and eyes.

Watercress doesn't like either cold or hot, preferring a temperature somewhere in between, so it flourishes in the spring and we traditionally eat most of it at Easter. It seems to have a spring detox association, at a time when we crave strong acerbic flavors.

Buy it when it's looking perky and emerald-green, and when you get it home slice off the ends of the stalks, pick the rest over, rinse it, and put it in a plastic bag. Squeeze out the air and then store it in the salad drawer at the bottom of the fridge for up to a couple of days.

Like watercress, wild garlic or ramps are good for you. They are particularly effective in reducing high blood pressure and cholesterol levels. Where I live, walk into a damp part of almost any wood in late spring, and you're greeted by an amazing carpet of wild garlic. It flowers at the same time as bluebells, which colonize drier ground. The smell is particularly strong when the flowers fade and the plants run to seed.

You can dig up and eat the bulbs, but they can give me an upset stomach, so I stick to the leaves. Just a few leaves—picked when young and quite finely chopped—will give an extra punch. Use them as a base for pesto to eat with starchy potatoes or pasta (see page 95). The leaves are best blanched first.

Watercress soup

A peppery, fresh, and delicious soup.

Serves 4
- **1 tablespoon sunflower oil**
- **1 tablespoon butter**
- **1 onion, chopped**
- **1 large potato, peeled**
- **1 pound watercress, plus a few sprigs for decoration**
- **1½ cups vegetable or chicken stock**
- **Salt and pepper**
- **1¼ cups milk**
- **Lemon juice**
- **Dollop of cream**

Heat the oil and butter and sweat the onion in this gently, until translucent.

Add the potato and cook for 3 or 4 minutes, without allowing it to brown.

Take the leaves from the stalks of the watercress and then chop up the stalks roughly.

Add these to the pot and then add the stock. Season, cover the pot, and simmer gently until the potatoes are tender.

Chop the watercress leaves coarsely and add them to the pot. Pull off the heat and allow to cool a little before transferring to a food processor to blend.

Return the soup to the rinsed pot and add enough milk to give a creamy consistency. Bring to the simmering point.

Remove from the heat, add a little lemon juice to taste, and season. Serve with a dollop of cream and sprigs of watercress.

Fried watercress

A tasty base on which to put baked fish, fish cakes, and grilled chicken. The leaves are just wilted, but the stalks retain their crunch and tasty hot flavor.

Serves 4 as a base for an entrée or 2 as a side dish
- **¼ pound watercress**
- **1 teaspoon hazelnut (or other nut oil)**
- **2 garlic cloves, crushed and chopped**
- **Sea salt**

Wash the watercress thoroughly and dry in a salad spinner.

Heat the nut oil in a nonstick frying pan, add the garlic, and cook for a few seconds.

Throw in the watercress and turn in the oil and garlic for not more than a few seconds.

Remove from the heat and toss with plenty of sea salt.

Watercress hollandaise

This delicious peppery sauce is fantastic with any fish or chicken.

Serves 6 to 8
- **3 tablespoons white wine vinegar**
- **6 black peppercorns**
- **1 bay leaf**
- **3 egg yolks**
- **6 tablespoons unsalted butter, cut into small chunks**
- **Salt and pepper**
- **2 bunches of watercress**
- **1 tablespoon vegetable stock or white wine**

Boil the vinegar with 1 tablespoon of water, the peppercorns, and bay leaf, until it is reduced to 1 tablespoon, and allow to cool.

Fill a wide shallow pan halfway with water and bring to the simmering point. Put the yolks in a heatproof bowl, sit this in the pan of water, and whisk well. Add the butter bit by bit, whisking all the time. Gradually as it warms, the mixture will become thick and shiny. Remove from the heat and stir in the cooled reduced vinegar, salt, and pepper (see page 233 for more hollandaise tips).

Take the leaves from the watercress and puree them with a tablespoon of stock or white wine in a food processor (or use an immersion blender if you are making a small quantity).

Stir this into the warm hollandaise.

Watercress and smoked trout salad with horseradish

You can throw this simple spring salad together quickly. The watercress and horseradish are ideal with the rich, oily fish.

Serves 4
  4 leeks
  Bunch of chives, chopped
  ½ pound watercress
  4 smoked trout fillets

For the dressing:
  **2 tablespoons freshly grated
    horseradish**
  1 tablespoon Dijon mustard
  2 tablespoons white wine vinegar
  ½ cup peanut oil
  Salt and pepper

Cut the leeks into quarters lengthwise, wash, and boil or steam for 8 to 10 minutes. Drain well.

Make a dressing by mixing together the grated horseradish, mustard, vinegar, and 1 tablespoon of water, then add the peanut oil. Season well.

Add the dressing to the leeks and leave for a few minutes. Add the chopped chives.

Lift the leeks out of the dressing and put them into a large platter, toss the watercress in the dressing, and add to the dish. Finish with the smoked trout.

Wild garlic pesto

I make lots of this in the spring, using it as pasta sauce and to stuff baked potatoes (see page 339). It freezes well for use right through the year, but if freezing leave out the cultivated bulb garlic.

Yield: 1 large jar
  **2 handfuls (about ¼ pound) of wild
    garlic leaves with flowers or
    ramps**
  **¾ cup extra virgin olive oil, plus a
    bit more for sealing**
  **3 tablespoons pine nuts or
    walnuts**
  2 garlic cloves
  **2 ounces Parmesan cheese,
    grated**
  Salt and pepper

Blanch the wild garlic leaves or ramps in boiling water for about 10 seconds. Refresh in cold water and pat dry on kitchen paper.

Put the wild garlic or ramps, olive oil, and pine nuts or walnuts, together with the garlic cloves, into a food processor and blend to a puree. Transfer to a bowl and mix in the grated Parmesan. Season carefully and put into a sterilized jar.

Pour over a little extra olive oil to seal and cover tightly.

Wild garlic soup

A traditional spring soup from the south of France where wild garlic thrives.

Serves 4
  **About 50 wild garlic leaves or
    ramps, plus a few garlic flowers
    if you have them**
  2 cups milk
  1 tablespoon butter
  2 shallots, finely chopped
  ½ red chili, finely chopped
  **¼ pound potatoes, peeled and
    chopped**
  4 to 6 garlic cloves, chopped
  ¾ cup light cream
  Salt and pepper

Blanch the wild garlic leaves or ramps for a few seconds in boiling water. Refresh in cold water, drain, and dry.

Bring the milk to a boiling point, take off the heat, and add the wild garlic leaves or ramps. Leave to infuse until cold.

Heat the butter and sweat the shallots and chili without allowing them to color. Add the potatoes and the garlic cloves, and add in the butter. Add the milk mixture and cook until the potatoes are tender.

Puree in a food processor and return to the pot. Add the cream and season with salt and pepper. Reheat without boiling.

Serve the soup with chopped garlic flowers.

May | June

Asparagus

I've never met anyone who doesn't relish asparagus. Freshly picked, it's the caviar of the productive plant world, with a powerful and unique taste. There is endless debate as to how you should cook it. Some say just lay it flat in a pan; others swear by cooking the stems upright in a tall, narrow steamer, with the boiling water coming up to about a third of their height. Cooked in either of these ways, asparagus is perfect after seven or eight minutes. Then there are those who say you get the best flavor if you toss it in olive oil, sprinkle it with salt and pepper, and roast it for fifteen to twenty minutes, and even a few who vote for cooking it in a cast-iron skillet or on the barbecue grill, scattering over pecorino or Parmesan as you eat. I don't think it makes much difference. If you've got very fresh asparagus, it's magnificent however you cook it.

It's the fresh-as-a-daisy factor, picking it that day or in a pinch the day before that really makes the difference. After a day, both the texture and taste deteriorate. The newly emerged stems are full of sugars, which gradually convert to starch after picking, and the flavor will acquire a slightly bitter undertone.

If you live in an asparagus area, you can get hold of just-picked bundles from beside the road. If you don't, and you have the space, this is one of the most life-enhancing plants to grow. It may only produce spears for six to eight weeks each year, but over that time, you will have several truly delicious meals a week.

All asparagus needs is some salt and, perhaps, lemon butter or hollandaise. Last spring I had a supper with British cookery expert Hugh Fearnley-Whittingstall of a few spears of asparagus served with a soft-boiled egg instead of the customary bread soldiers. That was as good as it gets.

Asparagus is a long-lived perennial and with a bit of planning you can put in a few plants of several forms, all ready for harvest at slightly different times. 'Connover's Colossal' is the earliest to produce for me. Next in line are 'Franklim', and 'Gijnlim,' a new Dutch variety; both produce lots of spears with famously good flavor in mid-May once they have settled in. I also have 'Dariana', a highly recommended French midseason form to be harvested in May. The last is 'Martha Washington,' which produces lots of long spears into early June here.

The unblanched green spears have a stronger yet sweeter flavor than the white so popular in Italy and France. The latter is achieved by mounding soil up around the spears, so that they grow in the dark. This makes for a more tender spear and a subtler flavor, ideal for canning. I'd rather eat them strong and fresh.

Asparagus with almonds

This is simple and delicious, the perfect May first course.

Serves 4
   2 pounds asparagus
   About 4 tablespoons (½ stick) butter
   Juice of ½ lemon and grated zest of 1 lemon
   Plenty of sliced almonds, toasted
   Flaky sea salt

Break off the tough or bendy bottom ends of the asparagus. Cook your asparagus in loose bundles, standing the stems upright in the pan or steaming them lying on their side.

Meanwhile, melt the butter. Once it is melted, add the lemon juice.

Remove the asparagus from the pan as soon as the thickest bit of the stalk is only just cooked and still has a bite to it. Drain and lay the spears out on a warm serving plate. Pour over the lemon and butter mix, and garnish with the lemon zest, almonds, and salt.

Asparagus omelette

We eat this all the time in late spring. It's the perfect midweek supper, and lovely eaten with slices of brown toast or some small minty new potatoes.

Serves 2
   ½ pound asparagus
   3 tablespoons olive oil
   4 eggs
   1 tablespoon cold unsalted butter, cut in small pieces
   Salt and pepper

Break off the tough or bendy bottom ends of the asparagus. If the stems are quite thick, pare off a thin layer of stalk at the stem end with a potato peeler. Cut the spear end at an angle into 2 or 3 slices and the stalks into smaller slices, as they take longer to cook. Drop these into a pan of boiling water for 1 minute. Drain and dry.

Heat some oil in a pan and sauté the asparagus for half a minute or so, then remove from the pan.

Break the eggs into a bowl, add the butter, salt, and pepper, and beat with a fork. Add the asparagus. Season well.

In an omelette pan set over high heat, swirl the oil around until it's practically smoking, and pour in the egg mixture, shaking the pan to distribute it. As soon as you see it beginning to cook, lift the edge of the omelette, allowing more of the uncooked egg to reach the hot base of the pan. When it begins to set, roll the omelette over and over itself into a loose tube shape and tip it onto a warm serving plate.

Asparagus pasta with lemon

Simple lemon pasta is always delicious, and with the addition of asparagus it's magnificent.

Serves 4
   ½ pound asparagus
   12 ounces penne or egg tagliatelle
   Salt and pepper
   3 tablespoons unsalted butter
   ⅓ cup heavy cream
   Grated zest and juice of 1 lemon
   2 tablespoons extra virgin olive oil
   1 tablespoon finely chopped flat-leaf parsley, to serve
   Grated Parmesan cheese

Break off the tough or bendy bottom ends of the asparagus. If the stems are quite thick, pare off a thin layer of stalk at the stem end with a potato peeler. Cut the stalks at an angle, leaving the tips whole. Steam or boil the asparagus for 7 to 8 minutes, until tender but still crisp. Rinse in cold water and drain.

Cook the pasta in a pot of salted boiling water until al dente.

While you're cooking the pasta, warm the butter and cream in a pan over low heat and simmer for a couple of minutes. Add the cooked asparagus and the lemon zest and juice. Take off the heat and leave for 5 minutes for the flavors to blend.

When the pasta is cooked, drain all but a tablespoon of the cooking liquid, add the olive oil, and combine with the asparagus and lemon sauce.

Stir, season, and serve with plenty of chopped flat-leaf parsley scattered on top and a bowl of grated Parmesan on the side.

Primavera risotto

A Venetian classic that always looks as good as it tastes, with the first tender mini beans, asparagus, and snow peas of the season.

Serves 4 to 5
- **About 1 pound selection of new vegetables, such as asparagus, fava beans, peas, and snow peas**
- **About 6 cups good vegetable or chicken stock**
- **6 tablespoons unsalted butter**
- **1 large onion, chopped**
- **2½ cups Arborio or Carnaroli rice**
- **1 to 1½ cups white wine**
- **4 ounces grated Parmesan cheese, plus more as a garnish**

Blanch the vegetables for 2 minutes in a large pan of boiling vegetable or chicken stock. To stop them cooking, plunge them into cold water and put to one side. Reserve the stock and keep it warm.

Melt half the butter in a heavy-bottomed pan and fry the onion, without allowing it to color, for about 5 to 6 minutes. Add the rice and stir to coat it with the butter. Add the wine, letting it bubble up and evaporate.

Gradually add the hot stock, a ladleful at a time, stirring continuously. Allow each ladleful of stock to be absorbed before adding the next. The rice will reach the al dente stage after about 18 minutes. If you like your risotto softer, cook for another 5 minutes.

Take off the heat and beat in the remaining butter. Add the blanched vegetables and the Parmesan, and heat through.

Check the seasoning and serve immediately with a bowl of grated Parmesan on the side.

Salad of asparagus, fava beans, arugula, and peas

A wonderful fresh, delicate salad using young spring vegetables. When they're small and very fresh, asparagus spears are delicious just briefly blanched.

Serves 4
- **Bunch of new asparagus**
- **Handful of pea pods**
- **Handful of small fava beans**
- **Bunch of arugula (or for a milder flavor, spinach)**
- **Salt**
- **2 tablespoons extra virgin olive oil**
- **A little chopped flat-leaf parsley**
- **A few slivers of pecorino cheese**
- **Balsamic vinegar**

Break off the tips of the asparagus and blanch for 2 minutes. Remove any coarse bits from the asparagus stalks with a potato peeler and slice thinly at an angle. Blanch these too.

Shell the peas and blanch for 2 minutes. Do the same with the fava beans and, if they're larger than a thumbnail, remove their pale inner skins, revealing the bright green beans inside.

Dress the arugula with salt and olive oil and put to one side.

Lightly dress the fava beans, peas, and asparagus with olive oil and salt, and pile on a plate.

Put the arugula on the top and toss a little, adding the parsley, curls of pecorino, and a drizzle of the balsamic vinegar.

Fava beans

I think fava beans should be eaten when they are about the size of a thumbnail, but they're often twice that size when you buy them— leathery-skinned and starchy. So it's really worthwhile growing your own, as you can then eat them at every stage. In Italy and France, you'll be served the pods cooked whole, when they are an inch or so long. In Italy, you'll eat the beans raw, when they're small, with pecorino cheese. The saltiness of the cheese is perfect with the young beans, washed down with plenty of red wine.

When the beans themselves have reached the size of a quarter, they're better cooked, and bigger than that, they're best cooked and skinned. Pop out the bright green beans from their inner skins by pinching between your thumb and forefinger. Put them into a bowl and dress them (while still warm) with lemon juice and a good fruity olive oil. They're also delicious at this mature stage when pureed with a little olive oil and herbs (see page 109) and piled on crostini.

Fava bean tips—the top section of the young plant—are also quite tasty. Chop them up small and wilt them into a Primavera risotto (see page 102), or make a pasta with the beans and their tips, mixed with pancetta, crème fraîche, and some grated Parmesan cheese. If you have a glut of beans, freeze them while still small. Blanch them in boiling water for 2 minutes. Drain and plunge them into ice-cold water and freeze.

For me, the best all-round, early-autumn- or late-winter-sown fava bean is 'Super Aquadulce Claudia', and if you're going for only one variety, it should probably be this. It has good flavor, is highly prolific, and is hardy. I also love 'Stereo', a variety for spring sowing. This produces large numbers of petite pods containing small tender greenish-white beans. It's my favorite variety as far as flavor goes. 'The Sutton' is another worthwhile small variety that only reaches eighteen inches and yet produces a good crop of beans. It's ideal for small, exposed gardens. 'Red Epicure' is an unusual form, producing lovely rich crimson beans with good flavor. The color fades on cooking, so eat them small and raw. I usually grow this for its color, but it's not a heavy producer.

It's worth knowing that two pounds of fava beans in their pods give a little over two-thirds of a pound or one to one-and-a-half cups of shelled beans.

Fava beans with olive tapenade

Here is a quick and delicious way of cooking beans if you've had a surfeit. This dish has a strong taste that's good with roast chicken or Quick tomato tart (see page 279), or even just warm crusty bread. It keeps well for a day or two in the fridge.

Serves 6
   1 pound fava beans, shelled weight

For the olive tapenade:
   1 tablespoon good olive oil
   Handful of flat-leaf parsley, chopped
   1 garlic clove
   Handful of mint, chopped
   1 can anchovies in oil, drained
   3 tablespoons black olives, pitted
   1 tablespoon capers
   Juice and grated zest of 1 lemon

Cook the fava beans for 5 to 8 minutes, depending on size, until they're just tender. Immediately cool them under cold running water for a few seconds to stop them cooking and drain again.

To make the tapenade, put all the ingredients into a food processor and whiz for 30 seconds, no more, so that the herbs don't turn to mush.

Pour this over the cooked beans when they're still warm.

Spring vegetable soup

This is a lovely fresh light soup that—with all the baby vegetables—looks as good as it tastes.

Serves 6 to 8
   3 or 4 scallions
   ½ pound new potatoes
   2 tablespoons olive oil
   3 or 4 baby artichokes, halved, with the chokes removed and thinly sliced
   ½ pound Swiss chard or spinach, thinly chopped
   1 bunch of chervil or parsley
   1 garlic clove, crushed and chopped
   2 quarts good vegetable stock
   Salt and pepper
   ½ pound fava beans, shelled weight
   Grated Parmesan cheese
   Crusty bread

Thinly slice the scallions. Peel the new potatoes and chop them into small chunks. Heat the oil and gently sauté the scallions. Add the artichoke heart slices, potatoes, chard, herbs, and garlic, and cook for a further few minutes.

Add the stock and a little salt and bring to a boil. Simmer, covered, for about 15 to 20 minutes.

Add the fava beans and cook for about 5 minutes, until they are tender but still intact.

Serve with plenty of grated Parmesan and crusty bread.

Warm fava bean salad

A very simple salad of fava beans with a handful of herbs.

Serves 6
   ¾ pound fava beans, shelled weight
   1 tablespoon chopped mint
   2 tablespoons chopped chervil
   ½ teaspoon chopped tarragon
   2 scallions, finely chopped
   2 tablespoons tarragon or white wine vinegar
   ⅓ cup extra virgin olive oil
   Salt and pepper
   1 tablespoon chopped parsley

Bring a pot of water to a boil and cook the fava beans for about 5 minutes, depending on their size, until tender. Drain and immediately cool them under cold running water for a few seconds to stop their cooking. If the beans are large, skin them (see page 104); but, if they're tiny, don't bother.

Make a dressing by adding all the herbs except the parsley to the scallions and vinegar in a bowl and whisking in all but 1 tablespoon of the olive oil.

Heat the remaining olive oil and toss in the cooked fava beans just to warm them through before tipping into a serving bowl.

Toss the beans in the dressing. Season. Garnish with the parsley.

Tagliolini with fava beans and beurre blanc

This recipe is at its very best when the beans are still tender and small.

Serves 4
   4 tablespoons white wine
   4 tablespoons white wine vinegar
   1 heaping tablespoon finely chopped shallots
   Salt and pepper
   ½ cup (1 stick) cold unsalted butter, diced
   ½ pound fava beans, shelled weight
   12 ounces tagliolini or fine spaghetti
   ⅓ cup chopped fried pancetta or prosciutto
   2 tablespoons finely chopped summer savory or thyme
   Grated Parmesan cheese

To make the beurre blanc, reduce the wine, vinegar, shallots, salt, and pepper in a small saucepan until you have only a tablespoon of liquid left. Whisk in the cold butter bit by bit over a very low heat, until thick and creamy. Season to taste. Keep it warm in a bain-marie.

Bring a large pot of water to a boil. Cook the beans in the water for 4 minutes. Remove them, reserving some of the cooking liquid, and cool them quickly in a sieve under cold running water.

Pop some of the bright green beans out of their skin by pinching them with your thumb and forefinger. Discard the skins and puree half the beans with a tablespoon of the cooking water.

Cook the pasta in salted boiling water until just al dente, leaving a tablespoon or two of the cooking liquid in the pot. Add the bean puree, pancetta or prosciutto, and the beurre blanc, and stir. Season carefully.

Lastly throw in the remaining beans and stir. Serve sprinkled with savory or thyme and Parmesan.

Young fava beans in cream

Soft, comforting, and delicious, this is one of my favorite ways of eating fava beans. It's good with chicken and new potatoes, and makes a delicious sauce for fettuccine.

Serves 8 as a side dish
   1⅓ pounds small fava beans, shelled weight
   2 tablespoons butter
   ½ tablespoon all-purpose flour
   1 cup heavy cream or crème fraîche
   Salt and pepper
   1 garlic clove, finely chopped
   Good bunch of fresh summer savory
   6 slices bacon or thinly sliced pancetta
   Small bunch of parsley, chopped

Use young small fava beans if you can. Cook them for 5 minutes and, if they are large, skin them as described on page 104.

Melt the butter in a shallow pan and add a little flour. Then pour in the cream and add salt, garlic, and summer savory. Bring to a boil and put aside to steep for 10 minutes.

Fry or roast the bacon or pancetta until crisp and break into small pieces.

Add the fava beans to the flavored cream and then boil, uncovered, for 5 minutes. Remove the summer savory. Add more salt and pepper to taste, and scatter with the broken-up bacon or pancetta and chopped parsley.

Fava bean crostini

Once fava beans get big and leathery, or they've been in the freezer for more than two or three months, don't eat them on their own. Turn them into a sort of lemony hummus, delicious dolloped on crostini, or dipped into with pieces of toasted pita bread, with fresh shredded mint scattered over the top.

Serves 6 to 8
For the crostini:
   Fresh good-quality white bread (a baguette works well)
   Extra virgin olive oil
   2 garlic cloves, peeled and cut in half
   Salt

   ⅓ pound fava beans, shelled weight
   3 tablespoons extra virgin olive oil
   Juice and grated zest of 1 lemon
   Handful of finely chopped mint, plus more as a garnish
   Salt and pepper
   A few slivers of pecorino cheese

To make the crostini, cut the bread into finger-thick slices and drizzle the olive oil over them, then toast them on a medium-hot barbecue grill or griddle pan until brown and crisp. Lightly scrape one side with the cut side of the garlic and sprinkle with salt.

Boil the fava beans for 5 minutes or so, until they're tender. If you have time, squeeze them out of their skins. Puree them with most of the olive oil, the lemon juice and zest, mint, and plenty of salt and pepper. Without their skins, the beans make a smoother puree.

Spread the crostini with the topping and sprinkle with olive oil, slivers of salty pecorino, and a scattering of mint.

Crunchy lettuces

A crunchy, sweet lettuce is essential for a good summer salad. Soft-textured, strong-flavored leaves—arugula, young mustard greens, and watercress—are fine in the winter and spring, but once it starts getting hot, you want crispy leaves that you can break in half.

There are plenty of salads with crunchy lettuce at their heart. I love a Caesar salad with grilled chicken (see page 112) and Niçoise salad (see page 210), but perhaps best of all is the perfect green salad. For this, it's worth remembering several things. First, buy or grow a good lettuce. It's hard to beat romaine or the looser 'Little Gem' since both are widely available. Steer well clear of commercially grown iceberg lettuce that has zero (or worse, a chemical) flavor.

In my trials here at Perch Hill, there are four front-runners in the crunchy lettuce brigade. The American variety 'Black Seeded Simpson' came out on top this year, with a lovely sweet taste, huge hearts the size of a savoy cabbage—it needs to be spaced eighteen inches apart—and every leaf having that all-important crunch. 'Reine de Glace' is another front-runner, as good cooked as raw. It's lovely in a salad and its crunchy stem also stands up well to cooking, with a hint of bitterness to its flavor. You can also never go wrong with 'Cos Lobjoits'.

All lettuces benefit from being broken up and submerged in a sink of cold water for a couple of hours. This perks up any floppy leaves. Then it's important to dry them well. Add good-quality olive oil to lemon juice or red wine vinegar, stir, and pour over the leaves at the last minute. As an alternative to an oil-and-vinegar dressing, try coating lettuce hearts in garlic-flavored butter or oil, still hot from the pan (see page 112).

You can do more with crunchy lettuce than just make a salad. Use it as you would Belgian endive in the winter, as a scoop for Hummus with cilantro (see page 85), or as a wrap for spicy ground meat. It's also good with lovage in soup (see page 87) and as a vegetable. I love it sautéed with bacon and peas, or with the stems still crunchy but the leaves wilted in a lamb fricassee (see page 115).

Caesar salad

The combination of lettuce, anchovies, and Parmesan is quite delicious. Serve it with grilled chicken breast or slices of smoked chicken. With these amounts you will have extra dressing to use later.

Serves 6
   **1 to 1½ cups homemade
      mayonnaise (see page 124)**
   2 garlic cloves
   20 anchovy fillets
   **Sunflower or peanut oil, for deep-
      frying**
   **3 slices white or brown bread, cut
      into large cubes**
   Salt and pepper
   **2 tablespoons grated Parmesan
      cheese**
   1 head romaine lettuce
   2 handfuls of arugula
   **5 or 6 slices pancetta, cut into
      strips and fried till crispy**

Put the mayonnaise, garlic, and half the anchovy fillets into a food processor and blend until smooth. If the mayonnaise is too thick, thin by whisking in a little hot water. Chop the rest of the anchovy fillets and fold these into the mixture.

   Fill a small saucepan one-third full of oil and heat. Drop in one bread cube and if it immediately sizzles, put in half the pieces of bread. Lift them out when they are crisp and golden, and put them on paper towels to drain. Fry the second batch and season well. While they are hot, sprinkle with some of the Parmesan. Keep warm.

   Tear the larger romaine leaves into pieces and mix them with the arugula. Toss with just enough of the dressing to coat the leaves, scatter with the remaining Parmesan, and throw in the croutons and crisp pancetta.

Lettuce hearts with hot butter dressing

Children who don't like lettuce often love it prepared this way. Roughly chopped chives and radishes are good with this. You can also serve crunchy lettuce hearts dressed with olive oil quickly heated with a clove of garlic, a squeeze of lemon, and some finely chopped red chili.

Serves 4
   **4 small crisp lettuce hearts, such
      as romaine or Reine de Glace**
   5 tablespoons unsalted butter
   **Sea salt and freshly ground
      black pepper**

Discard the outer darker-green leaves and quarter the lettuces lengthwise, and wash and dry them.

   Warm the butter in a small pan. Arrange the lettuce in a shallow bowl.

   Just before serving, pour over the hot butter with plenty of sea salt and black pepper.

Sauté of peas and lettuce

Serve this as a side dish with chicken or fish, or eat it as a meal on its own with a bowl of rice.

Serves 4 to 6
   5 tablespoons unsalted butter
   A little superfine sugar
   Salt and pepper
   1 pound fresh peas, shelled weight
   1 garlic clove, finely chopped
   6 thin slices pancetta or
      prosciutto, cut into strips
   2 small romaine lettuces, torn or
      sliced
   Bunch of parsley, finely chopped

Heat 2 cups of water with 1 tablespoon of the butter, a little sugar, and a good pinch of salt. Bring it to a boil and plunge in the peas for 3 to 5 minutes, depending on the size, and then drain and refresh under cold running water.

In a sauté pan, heat the rest of the butter and gently fry the garlic without allowing it to brown. Add the pancetta or prosciutto, lettuce, and peas, and cook together for just 2 minutes.

Season with salt and freshly ground pepper, and serve with a bit of butter and plenty of parsley.

Lamb fricassee with romaine lettuce, and lemon juice

Scatter plenty of toasted almonds and herbs over the top of this wonderful Greek classic, and eat with rice and a Grated carrot and poppy seed salad (see page 430).

Serves 4 to 6
   2 pounds boned lamb shoulder
   3 tablespoons olive oil
   1 large onion, or bunch of
      scallions, finely chopped
   Salt and pepper
   1 cup dry white wine
   1 cup chicken stock
   1 large head romaine lettuce,
      cut into ribbons
   Handful of dill, flat-leaf parsley, or
      mint, roughly chopped
   2 tablespoons sliced almonds,
      toasted

For the egg and lemon sauce:
   2 large eggs
   Juice of 2 lemons

Trim the fat from the lamb and cut it into bite-sized chunks. Sauté the meat gently in the olive oil in a large saucepan with the onion for about 10 minutes. Add salt and pepper, the wine, and the stock. Cover and simmer gently for about 1½ hours, or until the meat is tender. Add a little water if it becomes too dry.

Add the lettuce and three-quarters of the herbs right at the end, cooking them only very briefly (1 to 2 minutes), so that they remain slightly crisp and green.

Just before you eat, make the egg and lemon sauce by whisking the eggs with the lemon juice. Remove from the heat and stir this into the stew, beating vigorously. This will thicken the sauce.

Garnish with the remaining herbs and toasted almonds.

Globe artichokes

I love the unique acrid smell when you're cooking artichokes. You walk into the room and you know what you're having for supper. If you're feeding lots of people, start cooking early, as they take ages. Cook four or five at a time in two huge pans. Find a lid or a plate that is just too small to cover the pan and use it as a weight to prevent those at the top from floating and thus taking longer to cook. Put half a lemon in the water for a brighter green color and cook them for thirty to forty minutes, depending on size. They will start to smell strongly when nearly done. Test them by pulling off one of the bottom leaves. If it comes off easily, the artichoke is ready.

If you've grown your own artichokes, it's always worth soaking them in very salty water for an hour or so before cooking. The insect life nestling among the leaves will then float to the top. If you're buying them, only go for the ones that are fresh greeny-grey, with no dryness at the leaf tips. Also hold them up by the stem and jiggle them about; if they're really fresh, they don't flop around and when you cut the stem, it slices easily in one go. If the stems are tough and stringy—needing a serrated knife to cut them—they won't be quite as soft and tender.

You can prolong your picking season with artichokes, which are perennials in warmer climates, by growing a few different varieties that crop in succession. This is an imprecise science, but I find that the beautiful, neat 'Violetta' crops first, followed by 'Green Globe' and then the hugely fat-hearted French 'Gros de Laon'. This one has been bred for its hearts alone and if that's the bit you like best, seek it out.

The best way to introduce artichokes into your garden is from plants begged from a friend with a good variety. You can grow artichokes from seed, but they don't always come true. To build up more, you can start taking offsets—side chunks of root—from the mother plant in her second spring.

Artichokes have an extraordinarily sweet aftertaste and so make any wine taste strange. In Italy, you'll usually be offered a glass of water to have with them, not wine.

Globe artichokes with Angelica's sauce

My favorite recipe in the book—it reminds me of Angelica, the cook in the house my parents used to rent in Asolo, in the foothills of the Dolomites. I love the whole big production of eating artichokes: pulling the leaves off and dipping them into the rich sauce, until you get to the soft heart, which you dunk and eat all at once.

Serves 6 to 8
1 to 2 small artichokes per person
Salt

For the sauce:
4 eggs, hard-boiled and shelled
1 very large bunch of soft green herbs (half flat-leaf parsley and the rest a mixture of chives, fennel, dill, and/or cilantro, or any one of these)
2 cans anchovy fillets, drained and finely chopped
About 1 cup extra virgin olive oil
3 tablespoons red wine vinegar
Black pepper

Cook your artichokes in boiling salted water for about 40 minutes. Drain them in the sink, upside down, for 5 minutes and, when they've cooled a bit, give each a squeeze to get rid of any remaining water.

You can roughly chop the ingredients for the sauce in a food processor, but you want a coarse texture, not a puree, so it's best done by hand. I break up the eggs roughly with the back of a fork and chop the herbs and anchovies with a sharp knife. Mix everything together with the oil and vinegar in a large bowl. You won't need much salt because of the anchovies, but add plenty of pepper.

Give everyone an artichoke on a plate with enough room for a good dollop of sauce.

You'll need a large bowl on the table for the discarded leaves (these make great mulch for the garden).

Grilled mini globe artichokes

A recipe for young tender artichokes when they first appear in the spring or, if you're growing them, the small side ones that form on the stem below the main large king. This is also an excellent recipe for using just the hearts later in the year, when the artichokes have gotten too big and tough. You can eat them on their own, as a meze with a few fresh herbs chopped over the top, or make them into a lovely first course with some slabs of buffalo mozzarella and slices of a good sweet-tasting tomato such as Brandywine.

Serves 4
8 small artichokes (buy those with the longest stems, or pick with at least a 1½-inch stalk)
1⅔ cups white wine
⅓ cup extra virgin olive oil
2 garlic cloves, peeled, but left whole
Sprigs of thyme

Strip down the artichoke by removing the outer, tougher leaves until you get to the soft white ones. Then cut the top off the whole thing and pare off the stringy outer third of the long stem with a sharp knife. Cut the artichokes in half and, with a spoon, scrape out the choke—the nascent flower—if it has started to form. Drop them straight into a bowl of water acidulated with the lemon juice.

When they're all prepared, poach them gently for 20 minutes in equal quantities of white wine and olive oil, with the garlic and thyme added to the cooking liquid.

Grill them now, or the artichokes are delicious eaten just poached and still warm. Or you can store them in olive oil in the fridge for grilling later. They will last a couple of weeks there.

Raw globe artichoke heart salad

If you ever find artichokes cheap, or you have a glut in the garden, this is a wonderfully glamorous and wasteful recipe. You eat slivers of just the heart, raw and marinated in lemon juice with garlic, parsley, and olive oil. Restaurateur Antonio Carluccio showed me this dish, which can be out of the garden and on the plate in 10 minutes. I like that. Again, this is best with young, tender early artichokes or small ones from a side stem.

You need:
2 artichokes per person
Juice of 1 lemon
Extra virgin olive oil
Garlic, very finely chopped
Plenty of flat-leaf parsley,
    finely chopped
Salt and pepper

Pick or buy your artichokes with long stems as these, as well as the hearts, are delicious if you skin them and you then double your salad.

Prepare the artichokes as for Grilled mini globe artichokes (see page 118).

Slice the artichoke hearts lengthwise into fine slivers and lay the slices out on a flat plate. Squeeze the lemon juice over them and then add some olive oil, a little garlic, a good pinch of finely chopped parsley, and salt and pepper.

You can eat them right away, or alternatively leave them marinating for a couple of hours, which will make them more tender.

Globe artichoke heart tempura

My friend Matthew Rice, who grows groves of globe artichokes, gave this recipe to me. You prepare the artichokes in the same way as you do when eating them raw, but rather than marinating them, you blanch them and dip them in tempura batter. This brings out the incredible nutty flavor of the artichokes, and they're even more delicious dipped in a Green mayonnaise (see page 83). You can use artichokes of any size, but the bigger the hearts, the better.

Serves 6 as a starter
6 large globe artichokes
Juice of ½ lemon
Olive oil, for deep-frying

For the tempura batter:
2¼ cups all-purpose flour
Plenty of sea salt and
    black pepper
2 eggs
1¾ cups iced water or cold beer

Prepare slices of artichoke heart by stripping all the leaves and scraping out the choke (the fluff within the heart). Slice the heart into ¾-inch strips and drop immediately into a bowl of water acidulated with the lemon juice.

To make the batter, sift the flour into a bowl with the salt and pepper and make a dip in the center. Add the eggs and, with a balloon whisk, mix in the iced water or beer to make a not-too-smooth batter. It should be the thickness of heavy cream. Keep this in the fridge until you need it.

Pour the oil into a deep pan so that it reaches one-third of the way up the side. Heat the oil until it reaches about 325°F. If you don't have an oil thermometer, it is easy to test: just drop a cube of bread into the oil, and it should turn golden brown in less than a minute.

Dry and dip the slices of artichoke heart into the batter and then put them into the hot oil until they turn pale gold and crisp. Dry them on paper towels.

These are at their best eaten hot, sprinkled with sea salt and ground black pepper. If you have enough of them, you can eat globe artichokes like this on their own, but I love mixing them with other shapes and flavors, so I add other early summer herbs and vegetables, sage and basil leaves, and snow peas (all fried in a tempura batter), as well as some baby carrots and radishes, straight from the garden, to eat raw as a contrast to the hot crunchy tempura.

Globe artichoke tart

This recipe uses the young leaves and hearts of small artichokes, or just the artichoke hearts when they have reached full size. You can make one large tart or several tartlets.

Serves 4 to 6 as a starter
   5 new small globe artichokes or 5 artichoke hearts
   ⅓ cup olive oil
   ½ cup dry white wine
   ½ cup vegetable stock or water
   3 garlic cloves, unpeeled
   A few parsley stalks
   1 (1-pound) package puff pastry or phyllo dough
   1 (8-ounce) tub ricotta cheese
   1 large egg, beaten
   1 tablespoon milk
   Salt and pepper
   3 ounces Parmesan cheese, grated

Trim and cut away only the outer leaves of the artichokes (see Grilled mini globe artichokes, page 118), and put them into a heavy-bottomed pan. Cover with equal parts of olive oil, white wine, and stock or water. Put in the garlic cloves and parsley, and bring to a boil. Cover and simmer gently for about 30 to 40 minutes. Then remove the lid and cook further to reduce the liquid until it is thickened.

Preheat the oven to 400°F.

Roll out the puff pastry as thinly as you can and use to line a 9-inch tart pan. Fan out and separate the artichokes, or cut the hearts into thin slices and spread them in a layer over the pastry.

Mix the ricotta with the beaten egg and milk to thin the mixture. Season well. Spread this in a thin layer over the artichokes and scatter over the Parmesan.

Put into the preheated oven and bake for about 15 minutes, until the pastry is cooked. Then reduce the oven setting to 350°F and cook for a further 10 minutes.

Braised globe artichokes

This is a wonderfully luxurious way of eating artichokes as a side vegetable. The sweet flavor of the artichokes is excellent with chicken or fish.

Serves 4
   6 young artichokes
   4 tablespoons olive oil
   2 garlic cloves, peeled and chopped
   Handful of freshly picked herbs, such as summer savory, parsley, mint, and/or marjoram, all finely chopped
   1 red chili, chopped and deseeded (optional)
   ⅓ cup white wine or vermouth
   Salt and pepper

This is good with fresh young artichokes (see Grilled mini globe artichokes, page 118).

Heat the olive oil in a pan large enough to allow the hearts to lie next to each other, stem upwards. Add the artichokes to the heated oil and allow to cook until slightly brown. Add the chopped garlic, let it color a little, and then add half the herbs, turning the artichokes in the mix.

Add a little chili, if you are using it, and the wine or vermouth. Cook gently for 20 to 30 minutes, until the artichokes are soft when they are tested with a knife.

Add the remaining herbs and season.

New/waxy potatoes

You can buy what look like new potatoes in the winter, but they will have been long lifted and cold-stored. It's only in the summer that they have that memorable sweetness. The sugars quickly convert to starch on storing, so the real bonus of growing your own is that you can eat them within minutes of lifting them from the soil.

Potatoes divide in their consistency between floury ('Maris Piper' and 'Desiree') and waxy ('International Kidney', 'Charlotte', 'Belle de Fontenay', 'Ratte', and the late-season 'Pink Fir Apple'). The floury ones—those with a high water content—are good for chips, baked potatoes, roasting, and mashing. The flesh collapses when cooked, creating a rough surface that crisps up well in oil, while the insides become fluffy. Floury potatoes tend to be harvested towards the end of the year (see pages 334-41). Waxy potatoes, on the other hand, have a low water content and so hold up well to boiling and slicing, making them ideal in salads, and for sautéing and dauphinoise. Most of these are earlies, although a few come later in the summer for eating in the autumn.

The best way to eat really fresh new potatoes is simply to boil them in salty water with mint and serve them with a bit of butter, some mayonnaise, or a drizzle of extra virgin olive oil. Alternatively, try garnishing them with finely chopped summer savory and soft summer thyme, including the herb flowers. There are some lovely new potato combinations for salads, and do also try eating them parboiled and then roasted in a hot oven for an hour in good olive oil.

Opinions vary as to whether you should leave the skins on new potatoes or peel them. I cook them in the skins—to improve their flavor—but remove them before eating. The skins may be good for you, but I think they spoil the softness and sweetness of the potato flesh.

New potatoes are easy to grow and you don't even need a garden to do so. I grow my earliest potatoes in empty compost bags. Roll the plastic down to halfway and in early spring, fill the bags halfway with soil mixed with a few handfuls of manure and bury a couple of seed potatoes. Put the sacks somewhere light but frost-free and the potatoes will start to sprout. As the tops grow, roll up the bag's plastic and add a little soil to cover them. They'll have reached the top of the bag in May and lots of tasty baby potatoes will be ready. Turn the whole thing upside down or, if you want to eat them bit by bit, cut a slit in the side of the bag and rummage around.

New potatoes in saffron dressing

These are lovely either warm or cold, and look and taste magnificent.

Serves 4

1 pound new potatoes
⅓ cup light olive oil
3 tablespoons sherry
A few strands of good-quality saffron
1 garlic clove
½ red chili, finely chopped
½ teaspoon paprika (optional)
1 tablespoon Dijon mustard
3 tablespoons white wine vinegar
Salt and pepper

Cook the potatoes in boiling salted water for about 15 minutes, depending on size, and peel.

Warm the oil and sherry in a small pan and put in the strands of saffron to infuse for a few minutes.

Combine the remaining ingredients in a food processor, adding the oil mixture slowly in a thin drizzle until it makes a fairly thick emulsion.

Pour over the cooked potatoes and season.

Potato salad with capers and anchovies

My all-time favorite potato salad for a picnic or big summer lunch, best served with a bowl of Red onion marmalade (see page 249). All you need is a green salad. Chive flowers look and taste good with potatoes.

Serves 4

1½ pounds small waxy potatoes
1 medium-sized red onion, halved and very thinly sliced (optional)
2 tablespoons capers, rinsed and roughly chopped
1 can anchovies, drained and roughly chopped
Good handful of herbs (all or some of dill, basil, thyme, cilantro, parsley, fennel, chives, and mint), roughly chopped

For the homemade mayonnaise:

1 whole egg and 1 extra yolk
1 level teaspoon mustard powder
1 garlic clove (optional)
Good pinch of salt and pepper
¾ cup sunflower oil
½ cup olive oil
Lemon juice or white wine vinegar, to taste

Cook the potatoes in salted boiling water for about 15 minutes, until they're just done. Drain them in a colander and leave them to cool.

Meanwhile, make the mayonnaise. Put the egg and yolk, mustard powder, garlic (if using), salt, and pepper into a blender or bowl. Whisk until frothy. Add the sunflower oil and then the olive oil in a stream, while still blending or whisking, until the mixture thickens. Add the lemon juice or vinegar to taste and season.

If the mayonnaise curdles at any point, start the whole process again with a third egg yolk, whisking it in a clean bowl and adding the curdled mixture in a slow stream while processing or whisking. This makes just under 1½ cups and can be stored in the fridge for a few days. If you want to lighten the mayonnaise, you can mix it with an equal volume of plain yogurt.

Peel the potatoes and put them with the red onion (if you're including it), capers. and anchovies into a salad bowl. Add the mayonnaise and mix together gently. Garnish with the herbs.

Chorizo with potatoes

Originally a Nigella Lawson recipe championed by Nigel Slater in his book *Real Food*, this is a quick, cheap, and easy dish, perfect for a midweek supper. Morcilla sausage (Spanish black pudding) makes an interesting addition. Just replace ¼ pound of the chorizo with ¼ pound of morcilla. The morcilla will break up during the cooking, thereby enriching the sauce. This dish can be either a soupy or a dryish stew.

The quantities below will make it veer towards dryness—if you prefer, add just a little more water with the potatoes.

It is delicious served with crusty bread and a green salad. Cucumber raita (see page 196) also makes a tasty, tangy accompaniment.

Serves 4
- **1 tablespoon oil**
- **1 small to medium-sized onion, finely chopped**
- **¼ pound bacon or pancetta**
- **¾ pound semi-dried chorizo**
- **3 garlic cloves, finely chopped**
- **1 bay leaf**
- **⅔ cup dry sherry**
- **1½ pounds small waxy potatoes**
- **Boiling water**
- **Salt and pepper**
- **Chopped fresh cilantro**

Preheat the oven to 400°F.

Put the oil in a wide rather than deep pan that can go in the oven and put on the stovetop over medium to low heat. Add the onion and cook for 5 minutes or so, until it begins to soften.

While these are cooking, cut the bacon or pancetta into strips and skin and slice the chorizo into fat coins (if using morcilla, skin it but leave it whole, as it will disintegrate during cooking).

Add the garlic to the pan and cook, stirring, for another couple of minutes. Add the sausage and cook for 5 minutes, stirring regularly. Then add the bay leaf and sherry, and stir. Slice the potatoes in half or quarters, depending on the size, and add to the pot. Then pour over boiling water to cover, but not too much—don't worry about the odd potato sticking out. Stir and simmer for 10 minutes, and check the seasoning.

Put the dish, uncovered, in the preheated oven and cook for 30 to 40 minutes. Check it halfway through that time to make sure it hasn't dried out too much, and give it a stir.

Ladle into bowls, and garnish with some chopped cilantro.

Green beans with new potatoes

The squeaky texture of fresh green beans combines beautifully with the softness of potatoes, and there are many ways of using these two in a salad. You can toss them both in a little truffle oil and add a few arugula leaves, or serve them like this with a nut oil, toasted almonds, and lots of dill.

Serves 6
- **1 pound new potatoes**
- **1 pound green beans**
- **1 tablespoon walnut or hazelnut oil**
- **4 tablespoons chopped dill**
- **1 garlic clove, finely chopped**
- **1 cup sour cream**
- **1 teaspoon superfine sugar**
- **Salt and pepper**
- **2 tablespoons sliced or slivered almonds, toasted**

Cook the new potatoes in boiling salted water, then cut them in half and peel if you want to. Next, cook the beans for 4 minutes (the beans must be crisp).

Drain the beans and potatoes, plunge the beans into cold water, and drain again. Pour the oil over both while they are still warm. Toss to coat.

Combine the chopped dill and garlic with the sour cream, sugar, and seasoning, and carefully fold into the potatoes and beans. Garnish with the almonds.

Smashed roast new potatoes with garlic and rosemary

My children call out for this as soon as they see new potatoes coming in from the garden.

Serves 6

1 head garlic
2 pounds new potatoes
Boiling water
Sea salt and black pepper
¼ cup (½ stick) butter
1 tablespoon finely chopped rosemary
3 tablespoons olive oil
Grated pecorino (optional)

Preheat the oven to 400°F.

Put the head of garlic on a piece of foil and roast in the preheated oven for about 40 minutes, until soft.

Meanwhile, scrub the potatoes and put them into a saucepan. Pour over boiling water, add salt, and cook them for 15 minutes.

Melt the butter in a small saucepan. Drain the potatoes and smash them roughly. Squeeze out the soft garlic from the cloves and add it to the melted butter with the finely chopped rosemary.

Toss the smashed potatoes in the garlic butter mixture and season well. Drizzle with the olive oil.

Place in an ovenproof dish and roast until golden brown and crisp on the top. Garnish with freshly grated pecorino (if using).

New potato salad with quail eggs and black pudding

An interesting and robust summer salad that is ideal as a first course or as a light lunch. If no quail eggs are available, you can use organic hen eggs, quartered.

Serves 6 to 8
For the dressing:

2 tablespoons olive or sunflower oil
Lemon juice, to taste
1 teaspoon superfine sugar
Salt and pepper

2 pounds new potatoes, scrubbed
½ red onion, finely chopped
½ red chili, finely chopped
12 quail eggs or hen eggs
Celery salt
½ pound black pudding (or boudin noir or chorizo)
Sunflower oil, for frying
2 good handfuls of arugula leaves
Black pepper
Bunch of flat-leaf parsley, finely chopped

Whisk together all the ingredients for the dressing.

Bring a pot of salted water to a boil and cook the potatoes for about 15 minutes, until tender but not soft. Drain and pour a little of the dressing on the potatoes and add the finely chopped onion and chili. Boil the eggs for about 3 minutes and plunge into cold water. Peel and dust the eggs with a little celery salt and quarter them if using hen eggs.

Cut the black pudding or chorizo into slices, and then cut these in half and fry them in a little sunflower oil. Put to one side and keep warm.

Arrange the arugula in a large shallow bowl. Toss the potatoes and black pudding or chorizo in the dressing and season with pepper. Place on the arugula and scatter over the eggs and plenty of parsley.

Peas

Peas eaten raw, straight from pods just picked from the plant, are as good as it comes. They taste completely different from store-bought fresh peas—sweet, tender, and delicious. If you have a party in the summer, pick a bowlful of pods and leave them around for people to shell and eat.

As soon as you harvest them, peas start to lose sugar as it converts to starch. If you can't eat the peas within hours, they are best quickly blanched (two minutes in boiling water) and frozen, rather than left in the fridge. I've tried several different varieties and, after two or three days, they taste more like a lentil than a pea—dense in texture and starchy in taste.

Young fresh peas are so sweet that all they need is a sprig of mint in the cooking water and a bit of butter when you eat them. If you're growing peas, don't forget to pick and eat lots of pea tips—the growth tips and side shoots, one to one-and-a half inches long—covering the plant as it climbs. These are fantastic, called "green gold" by the Japanese. They have the sweetness of peas, with the succulence of the heart of a romaine lettuce. Add them to a crunchy-leaved salad, quick-fry them in a stir-fry, wilt them over a risotto (see page 131), or, if you have plenty, blanch and eat them as a vegetable.

There are various types of peas to choose from and they're easy to grow. I sow mine like radishes into a rain gutter pipe (see page 134). Sowing under cover ensures rapid and good germination, as well as giving some protection from mice and pigeons, both of which can be a scourge outside.

You can grow straightforward peas, such as the heavy-producing 'Hurst Green Shaft', or go for snow pea varieties, which you eat as flat unfilled pods, before the peas have formed. I grow the purple-podded snow pea 'Carouby de Mausanne', which looks magnificent, but the pods are only good when small. There are, of course, also sugar snaps—succulent pods filled with peas, which you eat in their entirety.

Sugar snaps and snow peas are heavy producers over a short season, so grow only a few plants or you'll be overwhelmed. If the pods are left on the plant to fatten up and toughen, they become much less good. Their quick growth curve makes them difficult to keep up with, but it also makes them ideal varieties for pea tips. Inevitably, stealing many of the growing tips will compromise the harvest of shelling peas. That's a shame with slower-growing forms, but it is a real blessing with these.

Pea puree

A simple and delicious puree that is at its sweetest and best with the peas that are just picked, although frozen peas are also fine. Don't overpuree the peas; in fact, they are nicer with two-thirds pureed and one-third left barely blitzed, to retain some texture. The puree is lovely with chicken or any roast meat.

Serves 4
- **1 pound shelled peas, fresh or frozen**
- **½ teaspoon sugar**
- **Small bunch of mint leaves, finely chopped, plus 1 sprig left whole**
- **1 tablespoon butter**
- **½ cup light cream**
- **Salt and pepper**

Put the peas into boiling salted water with the sugar and the sprig of mint. With frozen peas, cook for only a minute or so; with fresh peas, cook for 4 to 5 minutes, until just tender but still with a bite, and then drain, removing the mint.

Puree most of the peas in a food processor or roughly mash by hand with the butter and cream.

Season with pepper and garnish with finely chopped mint.

Crushed peas

This is a recipe by Raymond Blanc from Le Manoir aux Quat' Saisons, in which peas are flavored with marjoram, lemon, and olive oil. It's perfect with lamb, fish, or chicken.

Serves 4
- **1¼ pounds fresh shelled or thawed frozen peas**
- **⅓ cup extra virgin olive oil**
- **2 tablespoons finely chopped marjoram**
- **2 tablespoons finely chopped fresh mint**
- **Salt and white pepper**
- **Juice of ½ lemon**

Crush the peas in a food processor, using the pulse button. Do not puree them, as it is important to retain much of the texture.

Transfer the peas to a medium saucepan and stir in the olive oil, chopped herbs, plenty of salt, and a pinch of white pepper.

Cook the crushed peas on medium heat with the lid on for 4 minutes. Stir in the lemon juice, then taste and correct the seasoning if you need to.

Peas with cucumber and mint

The taste and texture of peas mixed with crunchy—just cooked—cucumbers are good with chicken and fish.

Serves 4
- **1 pound shelled peas**
- **½ large cucumber, skinned and with the seeds removed**
- **2 tablespoons butter or 2 tablespoons olive oil**
- **Bunch of scallions, chopped**
- **2 tablespoons dry sherry**
- **1 cup crème fraîche**
- **1 teaspoon superfine sugar**
- **2 tablespoons chopped mint**

Add the peas to a pan of boiling water and cook until just tender. Drain and plunge into cold water.

Cut the cucumber at an angle into ¼-inch slices.

Heat the butter or olive oil in a sauté pan and add the scallions, cucumber, and dry sherry, and bubble up for a couple of minutes.

Add the peas, crème fraîche, sugar, and chopped mint. Just warm through and serve.

Pea and ricotta tart with thyme pastry

My great friends Aurea Carpenter and Andrew Palmer first cooked me this Alastair Little recipe about 15 years ago, and I've cooked it every summer since. Eat it with a tomato salad.

Serves 4 to 6
For the thyme pastry crust:
½ cup all-purpose flour
Pinch of salt
¼ cup (½ stick) cold butter, cut into chunks
4 tablespoons cold lard or vegetable shortening, cut into chunks
1 heaping tablespoon finely chopped thyme

For the filling:
¾ pound shelled peas
8 ounces ricotta cheese
¾ cup crème fraîche
2 eggs
Salt and pepper
3 tablespoons coarsely chopped mixed herbs (basil, mint, and chives)
5 tablespoons grated Parmesan cheese

First, make the crust. Sift the flour and salt and rub in the butter and lard or process until the mixture resembles breadcrumbs. Put into a mixing bowl, and add the thyme and just enough cold water to bring the pastry together in a ball. Roll out the pastry and use to line a 9-inch tart pan. Rest it in the fridge for 30 minutes.

Preheat the oven to 400°F. Prick the bottom of the crust with a fork, cover with a round of parchment paper or foil, and weight this down with some baking beans or rice. Bake the crust blind for about 20 to 25 minutes. Take it out of the oven, reducing the oven setting to 350°F, and let it cool slightly, then remove the beans or rice and the lining paper.

Boil the peas for 3 minutes, drain, plunge into cold water, and put to one side.

To make the filling, mix the ricotta with the crème fraîche and the eggs, and season well. Stir in the chopped herbs and Parmesan.

Put the peas into the crust and pour over the mixture. Bake in the oven for 25 minutes. Serve warm.

Mint and pea tip risotto

Another quick garden supper for when peas and mint are at their most abundant and best.

Serves 6 to 8
½ pound shelled peas
Handful of fresh mint leaves, stalks removed, plus more to garnish
6 tablespoons unsalted butter
About 2 tablespoons olive oil
1 onion, finely chopped
2 garlic cloves, finely chopped
2½ cups Arborio or Carnaroli rice
1 to 1½ cups white wine
About 6 cups hot vegetable or chicken stock
6 ounces Parmesan cheese, grated, plus more as a garnish
Handful of pea tips, sugar snaps, or snow peas

Cook the peas with most of the mint. If they're home-grown, pick them at the last minute so that they retain their sweetness. Once soft, pulse them quickly in a food processor to a rough puree. Keep the puree warm.

Melt half the butter with the olive oil in a heavy-bottomed pan and fry the onion, without allowing it to color, for about 5 to 6 minutes. Then add the garlic and rice, and turn to coat these with the butter and oil. Add the wine, letting it bubble up and evaporate.

Gradually add the hot stock, a ladleful at a time, stirring continuously. Allow each addition of stock to be absorbed before adding the next. It will reach al dente stage after 18 minutes.

Take off the heat and beat in the remaining butter. Add the mint and pea puree and most of the Parmesan.

Blanch the sugar snaps/snow peas for 2 minutes, add them and the pea tips to the risotto, and warm through, stirring for a couple of minutes. Add more finely chopped mint and serve with more Parmesan.

Chilled pea soup with roasted garlic

This adaptation of Nigella Lawson's recipe is one of my favorite early summer soups. It's also delicious with frozen peas, just thawed in the hot stock and blended.

Serves 4 to 6
1 head garlic
1 quart good vegetable stock
2 tablespoons olive oil
1 small bunch of scallions, chopped
2 pounds shelled peas, fresh or frozen
Bunch of mint
½ cup light cream
Salt and pepper

Preheat the oven to 350°F and roast the whole head of garlic for half an hour until sweet and caramel-like inside (see page 253). Scrape the garlic flesh from the skin and put to one side.

Heat the stock.

In a large saucepan, heat the olive oil and cook the scallions in it gently, until softened but not browned. Add the peas and mint, and cook for a few minutes. Add the hot stock and cook until the peas are just tender. Remove the mint and drain the peas, reserving the stock.

Puree the peas with the garlic and a little of the stock, and return to a large mixing bowl. Add enough of the reserved stock to give the consistency you want (the soup will thicken slightly when it is chilled) and add the light cream. Season.

Cover the bowl and chill for at least 2 hours before serving.

Pea and pancetta farfalle

A classic pasta dish that will be loved by both children and adults alike.

Serves 4
10 slices bacon or pancetta
1 large onion, finely chopped
1 tablespoon olive oil
2 tablespoons butter
12 ounces farfalle
Salt and pepper
1 garlic clove, finely chopped
1 pound fresh shelled peas or frozen peas (cooked for 2 minutes in boiling water)
1 cup crème fraîche
Freshly grated nutmeg
Good handful of grated Parmesan cheese

Roast or fry the bacon or pancetta until it is crisp. Let it cool for a couple of minutes and then cut it into ¾- to 1-inch lengths with scissors.

Cook the onion very gently in the olive oil and butter for 6 to 8 minutes.

Meanwhile, cook your pasta in salted boiling water until al dente.

Add the garlic to the onion and cook for another minute or two before adding the crisp bacon or pancetta and peas.

Add the crème fraîche, and seasoning and nutmeg to taste, and stir around in the pan for a couple of minutes.

Combine the sauce and the pasta. Add plenty of Parmesan.

Squid, pea, and chorizo stew

My sister Jane gave me this recipe. In the summer serve it with rice and a green salad. It's also good in the winter made with frozen peas, eaten with crusty bread and Cucumber raita (see page 196).

Serves 6
½ pound chorizo, skinned
1 medium-sized onion, finely chopped
3 tablespoons olive oil
1 (29–ounce) can tomato puree
½ cup red wine
¾ pound squid, cleaned
½ pound fresh shelled or thawed frozen peas
Bunch of parsley, finely chopped

Cut the chorizo into discs and then cut these in half if you don't want them to be too chunky.

Fry the onion in the oil over low heat for 6 to 8 minutes.

Add the chorizo and cook for about 5 minutes, until the fat runs. Add the tomato puree and red wine. Reduce the sauce for 10 minutes over low heat.

Cut the squid into rings and cut up the tentacles a bit. Add to the stew and cook for about 10 to 15 minutes, until the squid is tender.

Add the peas about 5 minutes before the end of the cooking time.

Serve sprinkled with the parsley.

Radishes

There is a brilliant way of growing radishes in which you don't even need a garden, and you'll be picking them at least a month earlier than if they were growing outside. Sow the seeds, spaced one inch apart, in plastic rain gutters. You don't need to drill holes for drainage: just fill the pipe with compost and keep the compost moist. Put it somewhere warm. The seeds don't need light until they germinate, which they will do within a few days.

As soon as they show green leaves, put the pipe outside or on a windowsill or patio, or in the garden, and wait a month. You'll then have perfect plump crunchy radishes. We are quite efficient about this now and try always to have at least one pipe going. Radishes are almost always better fresh and home-grown. All too often the store-bought ones are a bit flaccid, and don't possess the all-important crunch.

There are various long, winter-hardy tap-rooted radishes that are good grated in salad, but my favorites are the jawbreaker-sized spring and summer forms. The best variety is the round, pink and white 'Cherry Belle', which knocks the socks off the widely available 'French Breakfast'. 'Cherry Belle' is hot, but not too hot, with an excellent texture. I also grow 'Sparkler', which is slower than any other variety to form a woolly heart. Even quite big, these still make lovely eating and are ideal for cooking, sliced in half or braised whole with other summer vegetables (see page 137).

To eat them raw, just wash the roots and have them with sea salt. To help the salt stick, smear the radishes in some softened unsalted butter or some ice-cold water before dipping them. This is a great nibble with a glass of wine before dinner, with some quail eggs and celery salt and a big bowl of just-picked peas.

If you grow your own radishes, you can also eat the leaves. Picked small and fresh, they have a good peppery flavor and make a punchy addition to any mixed leaf salad. When the leaves are larger, they get a bit coarse and hairy, but you can still use them, cut into ribbons and wilted, for extra flavor in a stir-fry, and they make a surprisingly delicious pasta sauce (see page 137).

Early summer crudités on ice with aioli

Fill a large flat bowl with ice and pile on all the youngest, most tender vegetables you can buy or pick. Serve them with aioli and perhaps some crème fraîche with a handful of dill. The ice will keep the vegetables fresh and crunchy and the whole thing looks and tastes fantastic. This makes great simple party food, ideal for serving lots of people.

Serves 6
For the aioli:
   2 garlic cloves
   Sea salt
   1 whole egg plus 1 extra yolk
   ½ teaspoon mustard powder
   Pepper
   2 tablespoons balsamic vinegar
   1 cup oil (I usually use two-thirds sunflower, one-third olive oil)

   Crushed ice
   Mixture of early summer vegetables, such as radishes, baby carrots, peas, and purple-podded snow peas

To make the aioli, crush the garlic with a pinch of sea salt, using a pestle and mortar. Put the egg and yolk into the bowl and add mustard, pepper, and half the vinegar.

   Whisk these together with a hand mixer or in a food processor, then carefully add the oil in a stream while stirring continuously, until the oil emulsifies and makes a thick, smooth mayonnaise. Adjust the seasoning and stir in more vinegar to taste.

   Fill a large, shallow bowl halfway with ice and lay out the vegetables on top, with a bowl of aioli in the middle.

Glazed summer vegetables

Serve this delicious mix of mini early summer vegetables with meat or fish.

Serves 8 to 10
   1 pound small new potatoes, scrubbed
   1 pound small new carrots
   1 pound large radishes
   1 pound small new turnips
   3 or 4 garlic cloves, peeled
   Sprigs of fresh thyme
   ⅓ cup olive oil
   2 tablespoons unsalted butter
   Salt and pepper

Cut the potatoes in half lengthwise and trim the tops of the carrots, radishes, and turnips to about ½ inch, but keep the roots whole.

   Combine the vegetables, garlic, and thyme in a heavy-bottomed pan and coat with the olive oil. Add 1¼ cups water and bring to a boil. Cover the pan with a sheet of parchment paper and then the lid, and simmer, stirring occasionally, for about 15 minutes, until all the vegetables are tender. Transfer the vegetables to a serving dish and keep warm.

   Remove the thyme and boil the remaining juices for a minute or two to emulsify the oil. Take off the heat and add the butter, stir well, and pour over the vegetables.

   Season well.

Radish top pasta

If you grow your own radishes, try this peppery pasta sauce, particularly when some of the radishes are too big and woolly to be good raw.

Serves 4
   About 25 radishes with their leaves
   Salt and pepper
   12 ounces pasta
   3 tablespoons extra virgin olive oil
   1 onion, chopped
   1 garlic clove, finely chopped
   2 tablespoons pine nuts, toasted
   3 ounces grated Parmesan cheese, plus more to serve
   Bunch of flat-leaf parsley, chopped

Cut the tops off the radishes and wash and dry them. Slice the radishes and chop their leaves.

   Bring a large pot of salted water to a boil and add the pasta.

   Meanwhile, heat the oil in a pan and sweat the onion for 3 to 4 minutes. Add the garlic, pine nuts, radish tops, and the sliced radishes, and cook until the tops wilt and soften.

   Remove from the heat, season, and keep warm.

   When the pasta is al dente, drain, leaving a couple of tablespoons of the pasta water in the pan. Add the radishes and the Parmesan, and stir them together.

   Serve the pasta with a bowl of more Parmesan and plenty of flat-leaf parsley.

Samphire and elderflowers

I love picking wild food. To engage with a particular place in the moment is absorbing, and any delicious things you find to eat are a bonus. During March and April, I look for watercress and wild garlic (see page 92) and wild sorrel (see page 80). In May and June, it's samphire and elderflowers. Later in the year, I never miss the blackberries and sloes (see page 320) and mushrooms (see page 342).

Samphire, often marketed as sea beans or glasswort, grows on coastal mud flats around much of my coastline and you tend to find it in vast carpets as far as the eye can see. It's best picked as it first emerges in early summer, when the fronds are about six inches long. It forms a bushy plant, which you can pull up by the roots, or snip off at the base with scissors so that it will shoot again. It needs to be washed several times, and picked over so as to discard the base of the stalks, but that's quick and easy to do. You can increasingly find it in nicer grocery stores.

Samphire is good for you: rich in vitamins and with excellent digestive and anti-flatulent properties. It was given to sailors to protect them against scurvy. It's not only healthy but also delicious. If it is young, you can eat it raw with a dressing, or sauté it quickly in butter with lime juice, parsley, garlic, salt, and pepper. I love it eaten like asparagus as a first course, just simply boiled for about ten minutes in plenty of water, and then topped with melted butter. It's also fantastic with fish, meat, or chicken. As the plants grow, the stems develop a tougher interior structure. Samphire is still delicious at this stage, but once it is cooked, you need to pull the exterior flesh off with your teeth as you eat it.

Elderflowers are also at their best in May and June. Pick the flowers in full sun, ideally a few days after they first come out. Every flower in the spray will then be open and rich in pollen, and will therefore have the cleanest, freshest flavor. Once the petals have gone flat white and lost the creamy hue, the pollen has dropped and the flavor is less strong. Don't pick the flowers once they have begun to brown, as the flavor takes on a nasty hint of cat's pee.

Use them to make the classic cordial, or make flower fritters by dipping them in batter and dusting them with confectioners' sugar to eat with a squirt of lemon juice. The unusual flavor of elderflowers combines well with sharp tastes, so mix them with lemon, rhubarb, blackcurrants, or the first of the gooseberries.

Samphire with fresh peas and young fava beans

One up from straight samphire, this makes an excellent first course. Wild samphire needs thorough rinsing as it can be very muddy.

Serves 8 to 10 as a starter
  2 pounds samphire
  6 tablespoons unsalted butter
  1 teaspoon superfine sugar
  1 pound fresh peas, shelled weight
  1 pound small fava beans
  1 garlic clove, chopped
  6 thin slices pancetta or prosciutto, cut into strips
  Black pepper

Rinse the samphire in a colander under cold running water. Heat 2½ cups water with 1 tablespoon of butter and the sugar. Bring to a boil, plunge in the samphire, and cook for 10 minutes. Add the peas and fava beans, and cook for another 3 to 5 minutes, depending on size. Drain and refresh under cold running water.

Melt all but a bit of the remaining butter in a frying pan and gently fry the garlic without allowing it to brown. Add the pancetta or prosciutto, samphire, peas, and fava beans, and cook together for just 2 minutes.

Season with pepper and serve with the reserved butter. You don't need salt as samphire is so naturally salty.

Samphire sauce

This makes a good accompaniment to any fish, but is particularly good with cold salmon and trout.

Serves 6
  2 to 3 big handfuls of young and tender samphire fronds
  3 tablespoons extra virgin olive oil
  Salt and pepper
  1 cup crème fraîche
  Grated lemon zest and juice to taste

Rinse the samphire thoroughly in a colander under cold running water. Chop very roughly, put into a food processor, and pulse to a puree. Slowly add the oil and season.

Put the samphire puree into a bowl and then fold in the crème fraîche, lemon zest, and a little lemon juice to taste.

Elderflower cordial

This excellent, not-too-sweet version of the classic cordial will keep for a very long time.

Yield: Two 750ml bottles
- **3 pounds sugar**
- **Flowers from 15 to 20 elderflower heads**
- **2 oranges, thinly sliced**
- **2 lemons, thinly sliced**
- **2 limes, thinly sliced**
- **1 ounce citric acid**

Put 5 cups water and the sugar in a saucepan, and dissolve the sugar completely before bringing to a boil. Add the flowers and return the water to a boil. Remove from the heat immediately.

Thinly slice the fruit into a large bowl or jug. Add the acid and pour over the hot syrup and flowers. Stir well and cover loosely. Leave for 24 hours.

Strain into warm sterilized bottles and seal. This keeps for a couple of months in the fridge. If you make plenty, pour some into plastic bottles and freeze. It will last for years.

Elderflower fritters

I first made these from Roger Phillips's book on wild food. They are lovely on their own and fantastic with Elderflower and gooseberry ice cream (see page 143).

Serves 6 to 8
- **¾ cup all-purpose flour**
- **Pinch of salt**
- **1 egg, lightly beaten**
- **⅔ cup lukewarm water**
- **12 elderflower heads, unwashed but picked over**
- **Peanut oil, for deep-frying**
- **Confectioners' sugar, for sprinkling**

Sift the flour with the salt into a bowl. Make a well in the center and add the egg. Whisk while adding the water, until you have a smooth batter. Hold the flower heads by their stalks and dip them into the batter. Deep-fry them in very hot oil, about 325°F, until golden, and drain on paper towels. Trim the excess stalk and serve warm, sprinkled with sugar.

Elderflower and gooseberry jam

This is one of the most delicious jams—typically British, and a taste that reminds one immediately of summer.

Yield: 10 to12 jars
- **6 pounds gooseberries**
- **6 pounds sugar**
- **1 tablespoon butter**
- **A few elderflower heads, tied in a cheesecloth bag**

Remove the stem and blossom ends of the gooseberries and put them into a preserving pot with 5 cups of water. Warm the sugar in a bowl in a very low oven for about half an hour.

Simmer the fruit gently, with the cheesecloth bag of elderflower heads tied to the handle or the pot, until the fruit is soft. Pour in the warm sugar, stirring to make sure that it is dissolved.

Add the butter, raise the heat, and boil rapidly until the gelling point is reached (see page 170).

Pour into clean, warm jars, cover with wax discs, and seal.

Elderflower and gooseberry sauce

A wonderful sauce for oily fish, such as mackerel, also very good with goose.

Serves 4 to 6
1 pound gooseberries
½ cup white wine
2 to 3 elderflower heads
⅛ to ¼ cup sugar, depending on how sharp you like the sauce
¼ cup (½ stick) butter
Freshly grated nutmeg

Remove the stem and blossom ends of the gooseberries and put them into a pot with the wine, elderflower heads, and sugar. Simmer until the gooseberries are soft.

Add the butter and nutmeg and then pass the mixture through a food mill, or blend in a food processor and sieve.

Elderflower and gooseberry ice cream

This recipe is for one of the best early summer ice creams. You can cook more of the fruit puree than you need and freeze it in ¼-pound and ⅓-pound blocks for making more ice cream throughout the year.

Serves 6
For the puree:
2 to 3 elderflower heads
⅓ cup gooseberries
¼ cup sugar

2 large eggs, separated
¼ cup superfine sugar
¾ cup heavy cream

To make the puree, put the elderflowers and gooseberries in a pan with just enough water to stop them catching on the bottom of the saucepan—you want a good concentrated flavor. Cook very gently until the fruit is reduced to a mush.

Push this mixture through a fine sieve or food mill and let it cool. Add the sugar. You can use more, but ¼ cup gives a lovely sharp taste.

To make the ice cream, whip the egg yolks with the sugar until they are pale yellow and foamy. Whip the cream and then in a separate bowl beat the egg whites to form stiff peaks. Mix together the gooseberry puree and the whipped egg yolk with the sugar, then add the cream, and finally fold in the beaten egg whites.

Spoon the mixture into individual pots or glasses and freeze.

There is no need to beat or churn this ice cream. The egg white keeps it from forming too many ice crystals and it will be a perfect consistency to eat after being removed from the freezer and spending 20 minutes in the fridge to soften.

Strawberries

Please don't ever buy out-of-season strawberries again. They are tasteless and likely to have been doused in chemicals and produced in a city of plastic row covers by cheaply paid, exploited labor. They're all looks and no substance. Everything that the strawberry should give you—sweet-scented, enveloping lusciousness—is missing from these fakes. What you want is the real thing, and the best way to get that is to go to a local pick-your-own berry farm, where you can see for yourself how the strawberries are being produced, or, even better, grow your own. There is something magically gratifying about picking them from outside your door.

They're at their best when eaten straight from the plant, still warm from the sunshine, which helps release their subtler flavors. Sprinkle vanilla sugar over them and leave them to bleed their juices for an hour or two before eating them with cream.

If you have too many to cope with, make ice cream. My children love nothing better than this—just a pint of strawberries, the juice of one orange and one lemon, one cup heavy cream, and three-quarters cup superfine sugar. For grown-ups, I like the surprising addition of black pepper (see page 147) or alternatively a dash of balsamic vinegar, which cuts through the sweetness.

If you want to grow your own, which are the strawberry varieties with supreme flavor? It depends on where you live but my early summer strawberry is 'Royal Sovereign', which gives giant-sized fruit, packed with taste. You can't go wrong with 'Cambridge Favourite', which has medium-sized fruit, good taste, and disease resistance. Also try 'Honoeye' and 'Florence'. 'Honoeye' is early and has excellent flavor, but is not very vigorous, so you only want to keep plants for a couple of years. 'Florence' is also delicious, with dark-red berries, but in contrast it is both late and vigorous, needing no drip-feeding to keep it cropping well, so it's ideal for the organic grower.

I am also fanatical about the perpetual 'Mara des Bois'. If you visit almost any French market during July or August, there will be whole stalls devoted to this deep-red fruit alone. It has a fantastic woodland flavor and is easy to grow, with good resistance to disease—including the dreaded powdery mildew. It's ideal for the domestic garden as it fruits lightly over two or three months.

Alpine strawberries are delicious. I grow 'Mignonette', which lines the paths down my south-facing vegetable garden. We start picking in April, and go on right until the frosts in November.

Strawberry and black pepper ice cream

This is wonderful with fresh strawberries and gooey meringues (see page 148). Leave the pepper out if you're making this for children.

Serves 6 to 8
   1 quart strawberries
   Juice of 1 orange
   1 cup heavy cream
   ¾ cup superfine sugar
   Black pepper

Hull the strawberries and puree them with the fruit juice in a food processor. Add the cream and sugar until well mixed. Season with pepper to taste—remember, the flavor is milder when frozen than at room temperature—and blitz a few more times to mix the pepper in.

Put the mixture in an ice cream maker and freeze/churn for 20 minutes. Serve immediately or pack in plastic containers for the freezer.

If you don't have an ice cream maker, place the mixture in a shallow container and freeze until half frozen. Put the mixture back into the food processor and blitz again until smooth before putting it back in the freezer to freeze completely.

Take the ice cream out of the freezer and put in the fridge for half an hour before serving.

Strawberry sauce for ice cream

This makes an excellent sauce for vanilla or strawberry ice cream.

Serves 4 to 6
   1 quart strawberries
   1½ cups blueberries
   1 tablespoon lime juice
   ⅓ cup honey
   3 tablespoons dark rum
   5 tablespoons unsalted butter
   2 tablespoons soft brown sugar

Hull the strawberries and cut into quarters. Combine the two fruits and pour over the lime juice.

Heat the honey, rum, butter, and sugar in a small saucepan over low heat until the butter is melted. Allow the mixture to cool.

Toss the berries in the sauce and pour over ice cream.

Marinated strawberries

This is the simplest way of serving strawberries—just one up from eating them straight from the basket. Do this when you want strawberries on top of ice cream or meringue, when you want to hull them a few hours before you eat. Adding the lemon and orange juice preserves them for several hours.

Serves 6
4 quarts strawberries
Juice of 1 orange
Juice of 1 lemon
Superfine or vanilla sugar

Hull the strawberries and slice them in half. Drizzle with the orange and lemon juice, and enough sugar to taste. Chill for an hour or until you are ready for them, stirring from time to time.

Strawberries with meringues

These slightly gooey-centered meringues, served with strawberries, remain one of the best ever desserts. My daughter Rosie has her birthday in the summer and we almost always have this then. Strawberries are, of course, also delicious with pavlova (see page 353).

Yield: 12 to 14 large meringues
Sunflower oil
4 egg whites, room temperature
½ cup granulated sugar
½ cup superfine sugar
2 to 3 quarts hulled strawberries
Heavy cream or ice cream

Preheat the oven to 225°F.

Cover a baking pan with a layer of parchment paper and rub a little sunflower oil over the surface or, if you have one, use a silicone mat.

Whisk the egg whites until very stiff and dry. Add the granulated sugar, one tablespoon at a time. Keep whisking and continue until the egg white regains its stiffness. Then carefully fold in the superfine sugar with a large metal spoon.

Put tablespoonfuls of this mixture on the prepared paper or mat and cook for 2 hours so that the meringues dry out. Leave in the oven to cool before taking them off the paper or mat.

Serve with strawberries and cream or ice cream.

Strawberries Romanoff

A more sophisticated version of a fruit sundae. Children may prefer sweet wine instead of Cointreau.

Serves 4 to 6
  1½ quarts strawberries
  ⅓ cup superfine sugar, or to taste
  ¾ cup heavy cream
  3 tablespoons Cointreau
  1 cup soft homemade vanilla ice cream (see page 201, Quick lavender ice cream, but leave out the lavender)

Hull the strawberries, halving the large ones, and sprinkle with the sugar. Chill well and, just before serving, transfer the strawberries to a glass serving dish (or individual glasses).

Beat the cream with the Cointreau and then beat the ice cream and fold the two together. Spoon the mixture over the strawberries.

Fresh strawberry and shortbread tart

I love this orange-flavored shortbread base from Scottish cookbook author Claire MacDonald with almost any fruit. You can also use cinnamon instead of orange—particularly good topped with raspberries.

Serves 6 to 8
For the crust:
  ¾ cup (1½ sticks) unsalted butter, softened and cut into little chunks
  ¾ cup all-purpose flour
  3 tablespoons semolina
  3 tablespoons superfine sugar
  Grated zest of 2 oranges

For the topping:
  1 cup heavy cream
  1 tablespoon superfine sugar
  Juice of ½ lemon
  2 quarts strawberries, hulled
  Confectioners' sugar or superfine sugar

Preheat the oven to 325°F. Grease an 8-inch tart pan.

Combine the crust ingredients in a food processor and blend for a minute, or mix together in a bowl, rubbing the butter into the dry ingredients. Press the shortbread mixture into the pan to cover the base. Prick with a fork and bake in the preheated oven for 40 to 45 minutes. Cover with foil if it begins to brown too soon. It should be a light biscuit color.

Let it cool for 10 minutes, then remove from the pan and leave on a wire rack to cool further.

Meanwhile, whip the cream, adding the sugar and lemon juice to taste.

Pile this on to the cooled shortbread base and add as many strawberries as you can.

Sprinkle confectioners' sugar or more superfine sugar over the top.

Strawberries with rosé wine

You'll find this dessert all over southern France, where it's eaten with a bottle of ice-cold rosé wine.

Serves 4
  2 quarts strawberries, hulled
  ½ cup superfine sugar
  ½ cup rosé wine

Put the strawberries (halving the large ones) into a large serving bowl. Sprinkle with the sugar and drizzle over the wine. Stir them from time to time.

Prepare this about an hour before you want to eat.

Champagne cocktail with alpine strawberries

Alpine strawberries are delicious but tiny. This is a luxurious summer drink that will make a little go a long way, as you don't need a lot of fruit.

Yield: 8 glasses
- **8 lumps of sugar**
- **8 dashes of Angostura Bitters**
- **About ½ cup alpine strawberries, mashed**
- **1 bottle chilled champagne or sparkling wine**

Put one sugar lump flavored with a dash of Angostura Bitters in each glass.

Divide the mashed strawberries among the glasses and fill up with champagne or sparkling wine.

French strawberry jam

An excellent jam that is not too sweet and not too set, perfect with scones and cream.

Yield: about 5 jars
- **2 quarts strawberries (if you are not adding wild strawberries, add another pint)**
- **1 cup wild or alpine strawberries (optional)**
- **5 cups sugar**
- **Juice of 1 lemon**

Hull the strawberries and cut them in half or quarters, if very large. (Leave the wild strawberries whole, if using, and put them to one side.)

Put the halved strawberries into a large heavy-bottomed pot with the sugar and lemon juice. Warm the pot over very low heat, stirring until the sugar has completely dissolved, and then raise the heat and bring to a boil, stirring continuously. Allow the fruit to boil for 5 minutes, add the wild strawberries, if using, and boil for a further 2 minutes.

Remove from the heat, skim off the scum with a large metal spoon, and allow the jam to stand for at least 20 minutes before putting into warm sterilized jars. Cover with wax discs and seal.

This keeps well but is better kept in the fridge after opening.

Alpine strawberry gratin

A gratin usually implies cooking, but not here. This needs to sit in the fridge for a while but only takes 10 minutes to make, and everyone always loves it.

Serves 6
- **1 cup heavy cream**
- **1 cup plain yogurt**
- **1 cup alpine strawberries**
- **Grated zest of 1 lemon**
- **Superfine sugar, to taste**
- **Lemon juice, to taste**
- **½ cup Demerara or light brown sugar**

Whip the cream to form soft peaks and fold in the yogurt, a few of the alpine strawberries, and the lemon zest with enough superfine sugar and lemon juice to taste.

Fill the bottom of 6 ramekins—or a large dish if you prefer—with the remaining strawberries and cover with the cream mixture. Over this carefully spread the Demerara or brown sugar, smoothing it with the back of a spoon. Put into the fridge for at least 2 hours to form a crust. Add lots of extra strawberries on the plate around each ramekin.

July | August

Apricots, peaches, and nectarines

There are few things I love more for breakfast than a slice of fluffy white bread with sweet unsalted butter and golden-yellow apricot jam.

Apricots don't grow and ripen reliably in the open in colder parts of the United States, as they need plenty of warmth and shelter. There they are most successful with the trees fanned out against a south-facing wall or, better still, grown in a greenhouse. Although they are self-fertilizing, the blossom comes in early spring, before many bees are around, so to ensure a good crop they may need hand-pollination. Few of us bother with this, so if you're like me you'll almost certainly end up buying apricots from warmer climates.

I love the taste of apricots, but picked before they're fully ripe, they vary hugely in flavor and texture, and are almost always best cooked. Use the less interesting and slightly underripe ones for poaching. Keep the best for tarts and, of course, making jam.

It's a crime to cook ripe peaches or nectarines. They are best eaten just as they are. As children, if we were very lucky, we'd be given a prized white peach from a ramshackle Victorian greenhouse where we went on holiday on the west coast of Scotland. Peaches and nectarines grew surprisingly well there. I still remember those wonderfully juicy fruits as some of the best things I've ever eaten.

If you buy furry-skinned peaches and want to peel them, drop them into boiling water for thirty seconds. Lift them out with a slotted spoon, and plunge them straight into very cold water to stop them cooking. The skins then slip off easily. To remove the pit , slice them in half around the stone and carefully twist until they separate. Lever the pit out with a pointed knife.

The most luxurious way of using peaches is to make them into Bellinis, with a puree of skinned white peaches and a good Prosecco, one to five being the correct ratio. Just pour the peach puree into a champagne glass and top up with Prosecco, champagne, or sparkling wine. If you like your Bellini sweeter, whisk a little sugar syrup into the peach puree. If you want to give it more of a kick, add a splash of peach brandy instead.

French apricot jam

Apricot jam is one of the best. The French are excellent at making jam that is not too set and not too sweet.

Yield: about 3 to 4 jars
  2¼ pounds fresh apricots
  5½ cups sugar
  1 vanilla bean
  Juice of 1 lemon

Halve and pit the fruit, reserving a handful of the pits.

Put the fruit with the sugar into a preserving pot. Score the vanilla bean down its length and cut into three. Add to the fruit and sugar with the lemon juice, stir together, and leave to steep for several hours.

If you have the patience, crack the pits with a nutcracker, or wrap them in a kitchen towel, whack them with a hammer, and remove the kernels. Blanch them in boiling water for 1 minute, plunge into cold water, and remove the skins. Split the kernels in two and add to the fruit. They add a lovely extra taste.

When the sugar and apricots have softened, put over low heat and stir until the sugar has completely dissolved. Turn up the heat and boil for 20 to 25 minutes, until the mixture is thick.

Allow to stand for 20 minutes and bottle in warm sterilized jars, ensuring that the vanilla and kernels are divided between the bottles. Cover and seal while still hot. Once open, store in the fridge.

Apricot tart

Almond-flavored amaretti cookies sprinkled on the base of this tart absorb the juice from the apricots, giving another layer of texture and taste. The tart is delicious served warm with cream, and fantastic with a chunk of Stilton or any blue cheese.

Serves 6
  1½ pounds apricots
  ⅓ cup soft brown sugar
  6 to 8 amaretti cookies
  2 whole eggs
  ½ cup sugar
  ¾ cup heavy cream
  1 teaspoon vanilla extract
  **Cream, a chunk of Stilton, or
    any blue cheese, to serve**

For the crust:
  **6 tablespoons cold unsalted
    butter**
  1¼ cups all-purpose flour
  1 teaspoon superfine sugar
  1 egg, beaten
  A little ice-cold water

Preheat the oven to 400°F.

Halve the apricots and remove the pits. Unless they are very ripe, sprinkle them with a little light brown sugar and roast them in the oven for about 20 minutes.

To make the crust, using a food processor or by hand, rub the cold unsalted butter into the sifted flour until it resembles breadcrumbs and stir in the sugar. Add the egg mixed with a very little ice-cold water and bring the mixture together in a ball with your hand. Roll out and use to line a 10-inch tart pan, then put in the fridge to chill for 30 minutes or so.

Prick the bottom of the tart all over with a fork, cover with a round piece of parchment paper or foil, and weight it down with some baking beans or rice. Bake the crust blind in the preheated oven for about 15 minutes, until the crust is pale golden.

Take from the oven, but leave the oven on. Remove the beans or rice and the paper or foil, and let the crust cool.

Crush the cookies and spread over the crust. Put the apricots, cut-side up, on the crumbs in one tight layer. Whisk the eggs with the sugar until pale and thick. Add the cream and the vanilla extract. Pour this over the apricots and bake the tart for 15 minutes in the preheated oven. Lower the heat to 350°F and cook for a further 20 minutes, or until the custard is set and lightly colored.

Peaches with bourbon

This recipe, one step up from eating peaches just as they are, makes a wonderful summer dessert.

Serves 4
- **5 peaches, peeled and sliced**
- **6 tablespoons bourbon**
- **1 teaspoon almond extract**
- **3 tablespoons soft light brown sugar**
- **Whipped cream, to serve**

Put the peaches in a bowl with the bourbon, almond extract, and sugar, and stir them all together carefully, trying not to bruise the fruit. Cover and steep for a couple of hours. Serve with whipped cream.

Peach or nectarine zabaglione

Fluffy, light zabaglione is delicious with peaches and nectarines, or a mixture of the two.

Serves 4
- **4 egg yolks**
- **¼ cup superfine sugar**
- **1 tablespoon Marsala or dessert wine**
- **6 peaches or nectarines, skinned and sliced**

Lightly whisk the egg yolks and sugar together, and add the wine. Put the mixture into a metal bowl and sit it in a wide shallow saucepan half filled with simmering water. Whisk constantly until the mixture has swollen into a soft foam that nearly holds its shape.

Arrange the peaches or nectarines in individual gratin dishes or one large shallow dish, and pour over the zabaglione.

Peach melba

A simple combination of vanilla ice cream, fresh peaches, and raspberry coulis. It's not sophisticated, but it is delicious. You will probably make more of the coulis than you need, but it will keep in the fridge for a day or two and can be used on ice cream. Some toasted almonds or praline (see page 357) make a tasty addition to this pudding.

For a recipe for vanilla ice cream, see Quick lavender ice cream on page 201, but leave out the lavender.

For each glass:
- **2 scoops of vanilla ice cream**
- **1 white peach, peeled and sliced**
- **A few raspberries**

For the raspberry coulis:
- **1 pint raspberries**
- **2 to 3 tablespoons confectioners' sugar or superfine sugar to taste**

To make the coulis, put the raspberries and sugar into a food processor. Puree and then push the puree through a coarse sieve or food mill.

In each fluted glass, pile in a couple of scoops of vanilla ice cream. Scatter over the peach slices, pour over some raspberry coulis and finally add a few fresh raspberries.

Beets

You either love beets—they're one of my favorite vegetables—or you loathe them and, like my father, won't let one anywhere near your plate. I think he'd been forced to eat too many at school. It's true you don't want the purple juice bleeding all over other things, but as long as you keep it segregated, there's nothing prettier than a few chunks of beets. If the purple really puts you off, go for white or the lovely orange 'Burpees Golden', or choose those with pink and white stripes ('Chioggia').

As far as purple varieties go, my favorite is 'Pronto'. It is excellent whether eaten small or large, is slow to bolt (run up to flower before the root swells) and seldom forms that horrid black woolly heart.

Beets have a very dense texture, so the roots take much longer to cook than one expects. A fair-sized beet needs well over half an hour before it's properly soft. Boil the roots, leaving half to three-quarters of an inch of their tops, as well as roots and skins on, and then peel them once they've cooled. You can also bake or roast them. Wrap them in foil and bake for about an hour, or intersperse them with a couple of whole heads of garlic for a delicious smoky mild garlic taste. My favorite way of cooking beets is to lay them on top of a base of rock salt, mixed with different herbs and spices, and then roast them (see page 162).

Beets are emerging as another superfood, with the maximum health benefits gained from eating them raw. Grate them for salads (see page 163) or steam them to retain much of their rich vitamin and mineral content. You can cut them in half or quarter them to reduce the cooking time.

When beets are tiny, the leafy tops are also good. Try them as a sweet-tasting addition to a mixed leaf salad. A good tip the famous gardener Christopher Lloyd gave me when I first started growing vegetables is to leave a few of your beet roots in the ground through the winter. In the early spring, they start to sprout tasty tender leaves with a vivid purple midrib, which look beautiful. You can treat these as cut-and-come-again leaves to add to your early spring salads.

If you grow your own—or buy fresh beets—the roots will come with fully grown tops. Try cooking these in a little water and apple juice. This draws out the flavor and sweetness of the leaves, and they are delicious.

Roasted beets with lentils and goat cheese

The mixture of the texture of the lentils with the creamy sharpness of the cheese and the sweetness of the beets is wonderful. Eat this for lunch with a green salad or have it as a first course for supper.

Serves 6 as a starter

Coarse sea salt
1 tablespoon cardamom pods, lightly crushed
1 tablespoon caraway seeds
1 tablespoon cumin seeds
3 star anise
1 tablespoon juniper berries (optional)
8 small to medium-sized beets
3 tablespoons olive oil
1 cup lentils, preferably French (Puy) lentils
About ½ cup white wine
2 small garlic cloves, thinly sliced
10 cherry tomatoes, halved (optional)
Small bunch of flat-leaf parsley, finely chopped
Small bunch of mint, finely chopped
15 to 20 mint leaves, whole
Salt and pepper
8 ounces goat cheese, soft farmers' cheese, or cream cheese

For the dressing:

Juice and grated zest of 1 lemon
3 tablespoons olive oil

Preheat the oven to 350°F. Scatter the salt and spices over the base of a baking dish and lay the beets whole on top, then drizzle over a tablespoon of the olive oil.

Cook in the preheated oven for just under an hour, until the beets are completely soft to the tip of a sharp knife. Take them out of the oven and let them cool enough for you to peel. Peel and cut into small chunks. Cover to keep warm.

While the beets are roasting and cooling, cook the lentils in equal parts white wine and water, with the garlic and the remaining olive oil. Cover the lentils with about an inch of liquid in a pan and then add more if they need it. Once the lentils are soft but not mushy—this usually takes about 20 minutes—take them off the heat and drain off any excess liquid. Allow to cool for 5 minutes, add the tomatoes (if using), parsley, and mint, and season.

Lay out some lentils on each plate. Add a few whole mint leaves, then crumble the goat cheese (or spoon the farmers' or cream cheese) on top. Finish with the warm, fragrant beet cubes.

Make the dressing by whisking the ingredients together, drizzle it over the salad, and eat while still warm.

Pantzarosalata

This is a dish that I've had with my friend Kate Hubbard. It's a delicious puree with a very strong flavor, using walnuts and beets, best served as a dip with pita bread or with boiled potatoes and a green salad.

Serves 6

1 large beet (about ⅓ pound)
4 tablespoons chopped walnuts
A few slices stale white bread, crumbled
1 garlic clove
6 tablespoons olive oil
2 tablespoons red wine vinegar
½ teaspoon salt

Cook the beet in boiling water for 30 to 40 minutes, depending on size. Once cooked and cool enough to handle, peel it and chop it coarsely.

Blend this and the other ingredients together until smooth.

Grated beet salad with toasted mustard seeds and orange

This lovely nutty-flavored salad is a fantastic-looking dish with any beet, and sensational with the stripy variety, 'Chioggia'. Once cooked the colors of this beet merge into a pretty overall pink, but raw the stripes remain.

Serves 4 to 6

3 tablespoons mustard seeds
4 to 5 medium-sized beets (ideally an unusual-colored variety such as Chioggia)
1 tablespoon hazelnut oil
Grated zest and juice of 1 orange
Salt and pepper

Toast the mustard seeds in a dry frying pan for 2 to 3 minutes, stirring all the time.

Peel the raw beets, grate them, and put them into a large shallow bowl. Pour over the hazelnut oil and toss together with the orange zest and juice, toasted mustard seeds, salt, and pepper.

Nadah Saleh's Lebanese beet salad

Nadah Saleh—the great Lebanese cook—came to our cookery school last year and demonstrated lots of vegetable-based eastern Mediterranean dishes suited to the summer and autumn. This was my favorite. It's delicious eaten as one of many meze, and lovely with grilled meat and kebabs.

Serves 4

4 medium-sized beets
1 garlic clove
1 teaspoon salt
2 tablespoons tahini
2 cups plain yogurt
Handful of fresh mint leaves, coarsely chopped

Cut the beets into quarters and steam for 30 to 40 minutes, until tender. When cool enough to handle, peel them.

In a bowl, pound the garlic with the salt and stir in the tahini and yogurt, mixing thoroughly.

Cut the beets into chunks and put in a shallow dish. Spread the yogurt mixture over the top of the beets and scatter with lots of mint.

Beet relish

This relish is delicious with smoked fish, ham, and cold turkey.

Yield: 1 large jar
- ½ pound beets
- 1 teaspoon cumin seeds
- Olive oil
- 1 tablespoon grated fresh horseradish
- About ¼ inch of fresh ginger, peeled and grated
- ⅓ cup red wine
- ⅓ cup red wine vinegar
- Grated zest and juice of 1 orange
- 1 tablespoon soft light brown sugar
- Salt

Peel and grate the raw beets. In a dry frying pan, toast the cumin seeds and set aside.

Over low heat, add a splash of oil to the pan, then the grated beets, horseradish, and ginger, and stir together.

Add the toasted cumin seeds and the remaining ingredients, with salt to taste, and cook for 2 to 3 minutes. Lift out the beets with a draining spoon and put into a clean warm jar.

The relish will last a good 2 to 3 weeks in the fridge.

Roasted beet soup

There are many beet soup recipes, but this is my favorite. The secret here is to roast the beets first in the oven.

Serves 4 to 6
- 1 pound beets
- 2 to 3 large Swiss chard or beet leaves
- 6 cups homemade chicken stock
- 1 tablespoon olive oil
- 4 shallots or 1 onion, finely chopped
- 2 carrots, chopped
- 2 celery sticks, chopped
- 2 garlic cloves, crushed
- Salt and pepper
- ¾ cup plain yogurt or sour cream, as a garnish
- Chopped tarragon, as a garnish

Preheat the oven to 350°F. Tear the leaves off the beets, but do not cut off the roots. Scrub the beets clean and roast in the oven for an hour or so. The beets are cooked when the skin looks wrinkled and can be easily pushed off.

If using chard, separate the green part of the chard from the stalk. Chop up the stalk and boil in half the stock for 5 minutes. Then add the shredded leaves and cook for a further 10 minutes. If using beet leaves, just cook the shredded leaves in half the stock for 5 to 7 minutes.

In a frying pan, gently fry in the olive oil the shallots, chopped carrots, chopped celery, and crushed garlic, being careful not to burn them. Add all of these to the saucepan with the stock and chard or beet leaves, cover with the rest of the stock, and simmer for 8 minutes.

Rub the skin off the beets and chop them up. Put the beets in a food processor or blender together with a small amount of the stock mixture. As you blend, gradually add the rest of the stock mixture. You can do this in two batches, if necessary.

Put the soup through a sieve or food mill to remove any tough fibers.

Add a little water if the soup is too thick. Check the seasoning and serve either hot or chilled, with a swirl of yogurt or sour cream and a garnish of chopped tarragon.

Beets and mini onions in béchamel

This is fantastic comfort food, sweet and creamy, and wonderful with any roasted meat and roasted potatoes, especially roasted lamb.

Serves 4
- **4 medium-sized beets**
- **4 to 6 small onions or shallots**
- **1 tablespoon olive oil**

For the béchamel sauce:
- **1 to 1½ cups milk**
- **1 bay leaf**
- **2 tablespoons butter**
- **1 tablespoon all-purpose flour**
- **Salt and pepper**

Boil the beets for 40 minutes with their skins left on, until you can slide a fine-tipped knife straight into the flesh to the center. Leave them to cool for 10 minutes, then remove the skin with your fingers—it comes off easily. Depending on size, halve or even quarter the beets.

At the same time, peel the onions or shallots. These are best left whole, so go for small. Blanch them for 5 minutes in boiling water, then sauté them gently in a tablespoon of olive oil for another 5 minutes, until they are slightly colored and soft.

To make the béchamel sauce, bring the milk to a boil with the bay leaf and, in a separate pan, melt the butter. Stir the flour into the butter, allow it to cook for a couple of minutes, and then gradually add the hot milk, stirring continuously. Season with plenty of salt and pepper.

Pour the sauce over the onions and beets, and leave the flavors to steep for 10 minutes before serving.

Risotto of beets, dill, and fennel

Make this when you feel like something with full-on color and flavor. Serve it on a large white plate and eat it with a bright green romaine lettuce salad on the side.

Serves 6 as a main course, 8 as a starter
- **1 pound beets, washed but not peeled**
- **3 tablespoons olive oil**
- **1 onion, finely chopped**
- **½ pound fennel, finely chopped**
- **2 garlic cloves, finely chopped**
- **2 cups risotto rice**
- **7 cups vegetable stock, heated**
- **Small bunch of dill, chopped**
- **3 ounces goat cheese**
- **Salt and pepper**

Preheat the oven to 400°F. Wrap the beets in foil and bake for an hour. Leave them to cool. Peel them and then dice them into ½- to ¾-inch pieces.

Put the oil in a pan and sweat the onion, fennel, and garlic very gently until softened. Add the rice and coat it well in the oil. Then add the hot stock gradually, a ladleful at a time, stirring all the time, as the liquid is absorbed. Cook it until the rice is al dente. This usually takes 15 to 20 minutes.

Add the beets and cook for a further 5 minutes, then add the dill and the cheese.

Allow to stand, covered, for 5 minutes. Then season with salt and pepper to taste.

Stir-fried beet tops with chili and ginger

I first saw this Indian way of cooking beet greens in Madhur Jaffrey's book *World Vegetarian*, and I now cook them this way when I want a change from chard or spinach.

Serves 4
- **1 pound beet greens**
- **3 tablespoons vegetable oil**
- **1 fresh green chili, cut into long thin slivers**
- **1-inch piece of fresh ginger, peeled and cut into long thin slivers**
- **½ teaspoon salt**

Strip the beet greens from the stalks and cut them into fine ribbons.

Put the oil in a large pan and warm over high heat. When the oil is hot, put in the chili and ginger. Stir them around for a minute and then add the greens.

Cover the pan, turn the heat to low, and cook until the leaves have wilted. Add the salt and stir, then add 4 tablespoons of water and bring to a simmer.

Cover again and cook on low heat, stirring occasionally, until the greens are tender.

Blackcurrants, white currants, and redcurrants

Currants are an expensive rarity in the grocery store. To find them in abundance, you need to visit a pick-your-own farm or grow your own. Apart from a cherry in full fruit, there's nothing more perfect in a kitchen garden than a white or redcurrant bush covered in chains of glassy berries. Every branch looks as though it was made in a Venetian glass factory, with each bead shining as if it were lit from inside.

The more sultry blackcurrants can look wonderful too. The best method of pruning a blackcurrant is to cut out complete branches— a third of the oldest ones—while they are still dripping with fruit in July and bring them into the house to harvest. Put them in a vase to admire for a couple of days and then strip them. An early pruning allows the new wood to mature before winter and, if the pruning is done in time, to produce fruit the following year.

With redcurrants and white currants, you see their fruit most clearly when they're trained against a wall. As with most plants, they prefer an open sunny site with plenty of organic matter in the soil, but will still produce good yields in a less-than-perfect situation. Trained flat as espaliers, they are ideal for a smaller garden, as they take up a quarter of the space of a bush.

With currants, as with all the fruit in my garden, I aim to prolong the producing time for as long as possible, so I select varieties that fruit in succession. For reds, 'Junifer' starts me off, followed by the classic 'Laxton's No 1', which produces huge strings of brilliant red berries from midsummer, with 'Red Start' to end the season. This has excellent disease resistance and its late flowering helps to avoid frost damage, so it's ideal if you garden in a frost pocket or on a cold site in the north. For their translucent beauty and added sweetness, it's also worth having a white currant bush or two. I've put in 'White Versailles', an early-season heavy producer with large sweet, juicy berries and good disease resistance.

Blackcurrants are tougher and more tolerant, and they love a rich, heavy clay soil like mine, with plenty of organic material added. I grow 'Ben Hope', a midseason, exceptionally heavy fruiter, with tasty medium-sized berries.

A couple of other currant tips: always pick them when it's hot and dry—wet currants will quickly go moldy—and use a fork to remove the berries from the stalks. It's much quicker and easier than doing it by hand.

Blackcurrant and almond cake

This makes a good dessert, served warm with cream, crème fraîche, or Greek yogurt. You can make it in advance and reheat it gently, covered with a piece of foil.

Serves 6 to 8
   1 cup (2 sticks) butter, plus a little more for the tart pan
   1 cup superfine sugar
   3 eggs
   1½ cups ground almonds
   1 teaspoon vanilla extract
   1 cup blackcurrants, ends removed
   Confectioners' sugar

Preheat the oven to 350°F. Butter a 10-inch loose-bottomed tart pan and line the base with a circle of parchment paper.

Cream the butter and sugar in a mixer or with a hand beater until the mixture is pale. Add the eggs one at a time, beating well, and, after each addition, fold in some of the ground almonds and a few drops of vanilla extract.

Put the mixture into the tart pan and scatter over the blackcurrants. Their flavor is intense, so don't be tempted to use more fruit.

Cook for 30 minutes, until golden and just firm, and before serving, sprinkle over some confectioners' sugar.

Blackcurrant cupcakes

Use blackcurrants, instead of blueberries, to flavor these cupcakes. Their intense flavor is perfectly offset by the sweet softness of the cake.

Yield: 12 cupcakes
   ½ cup blackcurrants, ends removed, and a few more for decoration, plus 2 tablespoons blackcurrant juice
   1 tablespoon light brown sugar
   7 tablespoons butter
   ½ cup superfine sugar
   2 eggs
   ⅔ cup plus 2 tablespoons self-rising flour
   1 teaspoon baking powder
   1½ cups confectioners' sugar
   A little lemon juice

Preheat the oven to 400°F.

Pick over the blackcurrants, then rinse them and toss them in the brown sugar.

Cream the butter and sugar until pale and fluffy, and beat in the eggs. Sift the flour with the baking powder and add gradually to the sugar, butter, and eggs. Fold the blackcurrants into the mixture.

Spoon a bit of the mixture into the tins (remember that they will rise and you will need room for the icing once they are cooked).

Bake them for 15 to 20 minutes and then allow them to cool on a wire tray.

Mix the confectioners' sugar with a little lemon juice and the blackcurrant juice to create a pink icing. Ice the cupcakes and finally drop one blackcurrant on top of each.

Philippa's blackcurrant leaf sorbet

This is an approximation of a recipe that my husband, Adam, remembers his mother making. It's delicious—fresh and delicate.

Serves 4 to 6
   3 handfuls of blackcurrant leaves (young ones have more flavor)
   Grated zest of 2 lemons and juice of 3 lemons
   ¾ cup sugar
   1 egg white, lightly whisked with a fork

Bruise the blackcurrant leaves with a rolling pin to help release their flavor.

Make the sorbet base by putting the lemon zest, sugar, and 2½ cups water into a pan and gently stirring over low heat until the sugar is dissolved.

Bring to a boil and add the blackcurrant leaves. Take the pan off the heat. Let it cool and add the lemon juice, then leave the whole thing to infuse for a couple of hours until the flavor is strong enough.

Strain and put the liquid in an ice cream maker and churn. After 10 minutes, add the egg white, mixing it in well. Continue to churn for a further 10 minutes, or until frozen.

You can do this without an ice cream maker (see page 69), adding the egg white just before you pour the liquid into the a plastic container.

Take the sorbet out of the freezer and put in the fridge for half an hour before serving.

Cassis

Cassis, blackcurrant brandy, is traditional for making kir with white wine. If stored somewhere cool and dark, this will last for at least a year.

Yield: about 6 cups
1 pound blackcurrants, crushed
1 pound sugar
2½ cups brandy
A few tips of new blackcurrant leaves

Strip the berries from the stalks and crush them (no need to remove the ends). Put them and the other ingredients into a large screw-top jar. Leave on a sunny windowsill. Stir the mixture and turn the jars twice a week.

Leave for one month, strain, and then bottle the liqueur.

Blackcurrant jam

This wonderful jam, with a powerful taste, is good on fluffy white bread.

Yield: 5 to 6 jars
2½ pounds sugar
2 pounds blackcurrants
Juice of 1 lemon (optional, as the fruit is high in pectin, but good for flavor)

Warm the sugar in a bowl in a very low oven for about half an hour.

Strip the berries from the stalks—no need to remove the ends—and put them into a heavy-bottomed pan with 2½ cups water. Bring to a boil and simmer gently until the fruit is tender.

Add the warmed sugar and lemon juice (if using), and stir until the sugar is completely dissolved. Bring to a boil again and boil rapidly for about 20 minutes.

Remove from the heat whenever you test for gelling. Have a cold saucer ready and test by putting a teaspoonful of jam on the saucer and leaving it to cool in the fridge. If the jam wrinkles when you push it with your finger, that means it's ready.

Spoon off any scum from around the edge of the pan and allow the jam to stand for 15 minutes before stirring once and pouring it into warm sterilized jars.

Cover with wax discs and seal while hot. It will store unopened for about a year. Once opened, keep it in the fridge.

Redcurrant jelly

The classic jelly to eat with lamb, this is also invaluable for desserts (see right) and glazes.

Yield: 10 to 12 jars
5½ pounds redcurrants
Sugar (for exact quantity, see below)

Put the redcurrants, stalks and all, into a preserving pot with 7 cups of water and bring to a boil. Simmer gently until the currants are soft.

Put the pulp into a jelly bag and leave it to drip to extract the juice.

Put the juice into a clean preserving pot and for every 2½ cups juice add 1¼ pounds sugar. Stir over low heat to dissolve the sugar and bring to a boil.

Boil rapidly until it reaches the gelling point (see left) and then pour into warm sterilized jars. Cover with wax discs and seal. The jelly will store unopened for about a year. Once opened, keep it in the fridge.

Russian redcurrant and raspberry pudding

This is an adaptation of Margaret Costa's recipe for raspberries in her *Four Seasons Cookery Book.* The addition of redcurrants gives an excellent sourness to this summer classic.

Serves 4
½ pound redcurrants
½ pound raspberries
4 tablespoons superfine sugar, plus more as a garnish
1 cup sour cream
2 eggs
1 tablespoon all-purpose flour

Preheat the oven to 300°F.

Put the redcurrants and raspberries into a shallow oval gratin dish, scatter over 3 tablespoons of sugar, and place in the middle of the preheated oven, until the fruit is hot throughout.

Beat the sour cream with the eggs, flour, and remaining tablespoon of sugar.

Pour the mixture over the redcurrants and raspberries and put the dish back in the oven at the same temperature but nearer the top.

Cook for about 45 minutes, until the topping turns a pale golden brown and becomes firm.

Sprinkle with a little more sugar before serving. This is best served hot or warm.

Emma's redcurrant steamed pudding

A lovely old-fashioned pudding cooked for me by my friend, potter Emma Bridgewater.

Serves 4 to 6
½ cup (1 stick) unsalted butter, plus more for the bowl
½ cup superfine sugar, plus extra for the redcurrants
2 eggs
1 teaspoon vanilla extract
1¼ cups self-rising flour
½ tablespoon baking powder
½ pound redcurrants, stripped and rolled in a tablespoonful of sugar, plus more to garnish
1 small jar redcurrant jelly
Cream, as a garnish

Cream the butter and sugar together and then beat in the eggs, followed by the vanilla extract.

Sift the flour and baking powder together into another bowl, and lightly fold into the creamed mixture. Gently mix the redcurrants in.

Grease a small heatproof ceramic bowl with a little butter and spoon the mixture into it. Cover with 2 layers of parchment paper and then with a layer of foil, pleated to allow for expansion, and tied loosely with string. Stand the bowl in a large pan one-third filled with simmering water, cover, and boil for 3 hours, replenishing the water level with boiling water when necessary.

Heat the redcurrant jelly in a small pan. Turn out the pudding and surround it with more fresh redcurrants. Pour the redcurrant jelly over the pudding and serve with cream.

Frosted redcurrants with Chantilly cream

Make your redcurrants sparkle, and then dip them into this delicious flavored cream. This dish is good with Almond meringues (see right). Note that the recipe includes uncooked egg whites.

Serves 4 to 6
- **2 egg whites**
- **1 pound redcurrants, in clusters on their stalks**
- **Superfine sugar, for coating the currants**

For the Chantilly cream:
- **1 cup heavy cream**
- **1 level tablespoon vanilla sugar, superfine, or confectioners' sugar**
- **½ teaspoon vanilla extract**
- **1 egg white**

Lightly beat the egg whites and use them to coat the redcurrants, using a pastry brush. Dip the clusters into a bowl of superfine sugar to frost them and allow to dry on a rack or on paper towels.

To make the Chantilly cream, whip the cream with the sugar and vanilla until it reaches the soft-peak stage.

Whip the egg white until it just holds its shape and fold carefully into the cream. Do this just before you serve the redcurrants, as it won't hold its shape for long.

Arrange 5 or 6 redcurrant chains and a dollop of cream on each plate.

Almond meringues

These are the most wonderful nutty meringues, and they taste fantastic with Frosted redcurrants (see left).

Yield: about 20 small meringues
- **Peanut oil, for the baking sheet**
- **4 egg whites**
- **½ cup granulated sugar**
- **½ cup superfine sugar**
- **Pinch of salt**
- **Grated zest of 1 lemon**
- **⅓ cup almonds, blanched, chopped, and toasted until golden**
- **1 cup heavy cream**

Preheat the oven to 225°F. Rub a trace of oil over a sheet of parchment paper and use to line a baking sheet. Alternatively, use a silicone sheet.

Whisk the egg whites until stiff and dry. Continue whisking while you add the granulated sugar, one tablespoonful at a time, until the egg whites regain their former stiffness. Lightly fold in the superfine sugar, salt, lemon zest, and almonds with a metal spoon, being careful not to knock out the air. Put spoonfuls of the mixture onto the baking sheet and cook in the oven for a couple of hours until crisp. Turn off the oven and, with the door open, leave the meringues until completely cold.

Whip the cream. Sandwich the meringues together with whipped cream, lightly sweetened to taste.

Cherries

There can be few things more beautiful to me than a fifty-foot cherry tree, with a forty-foot canopy in full blossom, surrounded by clouds of cow parsley. Fifty years ago, that would have been a common sight in much of my area. There were extensive cherry orchards in Kent, Herefordshire, Hertfordshire, Suffolk, Devon, and Buckinghamshire. Even five years ago, there were spring auctions in the village halls around Faversham and Sittingbourne in Kent, with orchard owners selling off the right to pick their fruit.

In the last twenty years, though, swathes of large-scale cherry orchards have been grubbed out. They couldn't compete against cheaper fruit imported by supermarkets. Huge trees are also difficult to pick and almost impossible to net against birds. What commercial cherry trees there are now are almost always grafted onto dwarf rootstock. These can be easily grown under nets, or even under plastic, to protect them from the rain. Gone is that majestic vision of cherry trees as far as the eye can see.

To add to their problems, cherries have a short fruiting season and do not store for long. They first appear when imported cherries flood the market. These are good, but on the whole not as plump and juicy as the slower-to-develop local fruit.

The best thing to do with a sweet dessert cherry is just to eat it as it is, grazing from a brimming bowl in the middle of the table. Sweet cherries make a good sauce for ice cream and are lovely in a fresh fruit salad.

Sour cherries, the 'Morello' and 'Montmorency' varieties, are ideal for bottling and pickling, and they make delicious jam. The good thing about a self-fertilizing sour cherry is that the birds tend to leave the fruit on the branch for you to pick. It has beautiful single blossoms and is one of the few fruiting plants that will thrive grown against a north wall.

When you next visit a kitchen supply store, look for a cherry pitter. Hard to find here, this is a brilliantly simple tool for effortlessly pitting cherries or olives.

Cherry clafoutis

A classic no-crust tart, which keeps the flavor of the fresh cherries, this must be served warm. It is a brilliant and easy recipe for other fruit too—I also love it with plums.

Serves 6
Butter, to grease the dish or pan
⅓ cup all-purpose flour, plus more to dust the dish or pan
3 eggs
½ cup sugar
1 tablespoon vanilla extract
¼ teaspoon salt
1 cup milk
1 pound sweet cherries, pitted or not as you wish
Confectioners' sugar
Crème fraîche, as a garnish

Preheat the oven to 375°F.

Butter and flour a 9-inch ovenproof dish or cast-iron skillet.

Whisk the eggs in a large mixing bowl, add the sugar, vanilla, and salt, and then sift in the flour. When the mixture is quite smooth, mix in the milk. This can be done in advance and rested for 2 to 3 hours, but is not essential.

Pour about ½ inch of batter into the ovenproof dish or skillet, cover with the cherries, and then pour over the remaining batter.

Bake in the middle of the preheated oven for about 40 minutes, until it is puffed and golden brown.

Remove the clafoutis from the oven and allow it to cool a little. If you've used a skillet, turn it out onto a plate. Sprinkle the clafoutis with confectioners' sugar. Serve it warm with crème fraîche.

Cherry compote for ice cream

This is the simplest way of eating sweet cherries, almost as they are off the tree. Serve on top of vanilla ice cream.

Serves 6 to 8
7 tablespoons unsalted butter
1 bay leaf
½ cup soft light brown sugar
2 tablespoons lemon juice
⅔ cup orange juice
Pinch of salt
1 pound fresh sweet cherries, pitted

Melt the butter in a pan and cook until it is beginning to brown. Add the bay leaf. Reduce the heat, add the sugar, and make sure it has dissolved completely before adding the lemon and orange juices and the salt. Whisk while cooking, until the sauce has reduced by half.

Add the cherries and leave on the heat until the cherries are warmed through.

Sour cherry jam

Cherry jam can be very sweet and, certainly in France, it is often mixed with redcurrants to make the jam less sweet. Pulped and strained redcurrant juice (2 cups) can be added to the quantities below before boiling. Crack some of the cherry pits to reveal the kernels and add these—they give it a really lovely flavor.

Do this with a nutcracker or wrap them in a kitchen towel and whack them with a hammer.

Yield: about 6 jars
About 3 pounds sugar
6 pounds Morello or Montmorency cherries, weighed before pitting
Juice of 3 lemons

Warm the sugar in a bowl in a very low oven for about half an hour. Pit the cherries and tie the stones in a cheesecloth bag. Put the cherries into a pan with the lemon juice and the cheesecloth bag, and cook very gently until the juices begin to run and the fruit softens. Remove the bag. Stir in the warm sugar and make sure it is completely dissolved before raising the heat and boiling until the gelling point is reached (see page 170).

Remove from the heat. Skim the scum from the surface and allow the jam to stand for at least 20 minutes. Stir once before pouring into warm sterilized jars. Cover with wax discs and seal. It will keep unopened for up to a year, but refrigerate after opening.

Caroline's cherry tart

A good friend of mine, Caroline Owen-Lloyd, has a huge cherry tree and, in occasional bumper years, the birds fail to strip it bare. Then she uses the sweet black cherries to make lots of these tarts.

Serves 6 to 8
For the orange pastry crust:
6 tablespoons butter, plus more for the tart pan
1¼ cups all-purpose flour, plus lots more for dusting the pastry
¼ cup confectioners' sugar
Grated zest and juice of 1 orange

For the frangipane:
½ cup (1 stick) butter
¾ cup superfine sugar
2 eggs
3 tablespoons all-purpose flour
1 cup ground almonds

About 1 pound cherries, pitted and halved
Crème fraîche or cream, as a garnish

Preheat the oven to 350°F.

To make the pastry crust, mix all the ingredients together in a mixer or by hand. The mixture will look quite wet and sticky, but don't worry. Mold it into a ball and put it in the fridge for 30 minutes.

Butter an 8-inch tart pan and roll out the chilled pastry, using enough flour on your rolling surface so that it doesn't stick. The secret is to roll the pastry very, very thin. This recipe makes slightly too much pastry, which saves the usual anxiety of not quite having enough to line the base. Use any leftovers to make jam tarts.

Pierce the bottom of the tart with a fork, cover with parchment paper and rice or baking beans, and bake blind for 10 minutes. Take from the oven, leaving the oven on, remove the rice or beans and paper, and allow it to cool slightly.

To make the frangipane, cream the butter and sugar, and add the eggs one by one, then the flour and almonds. Put the frangipane mixture into the crust and then fill to the brim with the cherries.

Cook for 20 to 30 minutes in the oven, until the frangipane has turned slightly golden.

Allow to cool on a wire rack and then ease out of the pan.

Serve warm or cold with crème fraîche or cream.

Zucchini

So many people say they're bored with zucchini. They get oppressed by the huge quantities that even a couple of plants produce, and complain there aren't enough things you can do with them. I love them and think they're one of the most versatile vegetables you can grow or buy.

I grow the pale-green-skinned 'White Defender', dark green 'Defender', and bright yellow 'Taxi', all varieties bred for good flavor and disease resistance. They last for ages in the vegetable rack, not losing much in terms of flavor or texture. With three different colors, they also look good together.

Particularly when they grow large, it's worth removing the excess water from zucchini. Slice or grate them, sprinkle with salt, and then let them sit in a colander for half an hour before squeezing them out with your hands or by putting them in a kitchen towel and twisting either end. You'll get loads of liquid out of them.

I try not to let my zucchini get too large, but inevitably a few get away. I love the generous fatness of those that get to the size of winter squash, particularly the brilliant yellow ones, and so I often pick them to make an arrangement in the middle of the table. It's harvest festival time.

That uses up a few, but it's also worth having some recipes up your sleeve for eating larger squash through the summer and into the autumn. Stuffed squash can be watery and insipid, but it can be delicious too—and there are many more ways to use them.

Then there are glamorous zucchini blossoms. These aren't easy to buy, although you may find them at a good farmers' market, but if you grow your own zucchini, you'll have plenty opening in your garden every day. It's tempting to pick squash and pumpkin flowers too, but these tend to have a bitter flavor and are not as nice. If you've got only a few plants, harvest the male flowers only, but if you have a glut, then use the female flowers as well. These have a small zucchini forming behind the flower. As you pick, lay them in a single layer in the bottom of a basket and use them as soon as possible. Zucchini flowers are delicious stuffed (see page 189) or simply dipped in batter, fried, and then served with lemon juice and Parmesan.

Zucchini risotto

This risotto looks good with different colors of zucchini and plenty of zucchini flowers. It has a delicious, creamy and gentle taste.

Serves 6 to 8

About 6 cups good vegetable or chicken stock
2 shallots, finely chopped
1 garlic clove, chopped
2 tablespoons olive oil
6 small to medium-sized zucchini
A few strands of good-quality saffron
A few sprigs of tarragon
2½ cups Arborio rice
½ cup white wine
Salt and pepper
2 tablespoons unsalted butter
5 ounces Parmesan cheese, plus more as a garnish
Zucchini flowers (if you can find them)

Put the stock on to heat.

Gently sweat the shallots and garlic in the olive oil.

Slice the zucchini and add to the pan with the saffron and most of the tarragon, coarsely chopped.

Add the rice, making sure that it is well coated with the oil before you add any liquid.

Pour in the glass of wine and allow it to bubble up and evaporate before you season with salt and pepper and begin to add the stock, a ladleful at a time, while stirring continuously. The rice must absorb each addition of liquid before you add the next.

Keep adding more stock and stirring it in until the rice is al dente, which may take up to 20 minutes.

When the rice is ready, stir in the butter and Parmesan, and adjust the seasoning, adding a little more wine if necessary. Tear the zucchini flowers into strands and scatter most of them over the rice, mixing them lightly through. Allow to stand for 5 minutes or so.

Garnish with the remaining tarragon leaves and more zucchini flower strands, and serve with plenty of extra Parmesan.

Zucchini and dill farfalle

When we're not eating zucchini risotto, we're often enjoying zucchini in a pasta sauce. You can make this with tarragon or sweet cicely, but I like it best with lots of fresh dill.

Serves 4

6 small to medium-sized zucchini, thinly sliced
Salt and pepper
1 onion, finely chopped
2 garlic cloves, chopped
2 tablespoons butter
2 tablespoons olive oil
½ cup sour cream or crème fraîche
Small bunch of dill, finely chopped
12 ounces farfalle
Plenty of grated Parmesan cheese

Put the zucchini in a colander, sprinkle with a little salt, and let them drain. Dry on paper towels.

Sweat the onion and garlic in the butter and oil over low heat for about 10 minutes.

When the onion is soft, add the zucchini and cook them gently together for 5 minutes without allowing them to color. Add the sour cream or crème fraîche, and season to taste.

Let this bubble up, then add the chopped dill, and immediately turn off the heat.

Meanwhile, cook the farfalle in a large pot of salted boiling water until al dente.

Drain the pasta and combine with the zucchini sauce. Add more salt and pepper to taste, and plenty of Parmesan.

Zucchini soufflé

Delicate and subtle, this is an adapted version of Elizabeth David's recipe. It's also nice cooked in individual ramekins, in which case reduce the cooking time to 20 minutes.

Serves 3 to 4
2 tablespoons butter, plus more for the dish
1 pound zucchini
Salt and pepper
1 ounce Parmesan cheese or 2 ounces Gruyère cheese
2 eggs, separated, plus 1 extra egg white

For the béchamel sauce:
About ½ cup warmed milk
1 to 2 tablespoons butter
1 tablespoon all-purpose flour

Preheat the oven to 350°F and butter a medium soufflé dish.

Grate the zucchini, salt, and leave in a colander for 10 minutes or so. Squeeze out any juices and dry on paper towels.

While the zucchini are draining, make the béchamel sauce. Bring the milk to a boil and, in a separate pan, melt the butter. Stir the flour into the butter, allow it to cook for a couple of minutes, and then gradually add the hot milk, stirring continuously. Season with plenty of salt and pepper.

Sweat the zucchini gently in the butter until soft, then mix with the béchamel sauce. Add the cheese, remove from the heat, and allow to cool slightly. Add the egg yolks and plenty of pepper, stirring all the time.

Whisk the egg whites to stiff peaks and fold them in. The secret with any soufflé is to have the basic mixture roughly the same consistency as the beaten egg whites.

Spoon into the prepared soufflé dish and cook in the oven for 30 to 40 minutes, until risen and slightly firm on top but still wobbly in the middle.

Zucchini soufflé tart

This is a wonderful light fluffy tart of my assistant Tam's, which she has made for years using every vegetable imaginable. Her very favorite version is with zucchini.

It sounds like a bit of trouble, but I promise you it's worth it, and it's as good cold as it is hot. Serve it with a tomato salad.

Serves 6
For the crust:
1¼ cups all-purpose flour
Pinch of salt
5 tablespoons unsalted butter
A little paprika
1 tablespoon grated Parmesan cheese
1 egg yolk
A little iced water

For the filling:
2 onions, sliced
1 garlic clove, finely chopped
¼ cup (½ stick) butter or 2 tablespoons olive oil, plus more butter for cooking the onions, garlic, and zucchini
1 pound zucchini, sliced at an angle
2 tablespoons all-purpose flour
¾ cup hot milk
6 ounces Cheddar cheese
Dijon mustard, to taste
Grated zest of ½ lemon and 2 teaspoons lemon juice
Small bunch of tarragon or sweet cicely
Salt and pepper
3 eggs, separated
½ cup plain yogurt

Make the crust by combining the flour, salt, and butter, and pulsing in a processor or rubbing the flour and salt into the butter by hand, until it resembles breadcrumbs. Add the paprika and grated Parmesan, and mix well. Beat the egg yolk with a little iced water, and then add this to the flour mixture. Use just enough to make a soft, smooth dough that will hold together in a ball.

Roll out the pastry on a floured surface and use to line a 10-inch tart pan. Put it in the fridge for 30 minutes to rest.

Preheat the oven to 400°F. Prick the bottom of the crust all over with a fork, cover with a round of parchment paper or foil, and weight it down with some baking beans or rice. Bake the crust blind in the preheated oven for about 15 minutes. Take from the oven, but leave the oven on at 350°F. Remove the beans or rice and the paper or foil and let the crust cool.

To make the filling, sweat the onions and garlic in a little butter or oil for 3 to 4 minutes. Then add the zucchini, and cook together for a minute or two until they're soft.

In a saucepan, melt the butter or oil and stir in the flour. Cook for a minute and gradually add the milk, whisking continuously until smooth. Add the grated cheese, mustard, lemon zest and juice, herbs, salt, and pepper. Fold in the squash mixture and put to one side to cool slightly.

Mix the egg yolks with the yogurt and add to the cooled mixture.

In a clean bowl, whisk the egg whites until stiff and fold them carefully into the mixture, using a metal spoon. Pour into the crust.

Cook in the oven for about 25 minutes, or until set and golden.

Zucchini and lemon salad

Zucchini are tasty eaten raw, fresh, and simple. This salad looks lovely with different-colored zucchini, golden yellow and deep and pale green. It is good just as it is, or with a handful of toasted pine nuts or quartered almonds scattered over the top. It's ideal with a rich creamy pasta sauce or risotto.

Serves 6 to 8

3 to 4 zucchini
Grated zest of 1 lemon and juice of ½ lemon
Grated zest of 1 lime and juice of ½ lime
2 tablespoons olive oil
2 tablespoons chopped summer savory or tarragon
1 teaspoon honey
Salt and pepper

Cut the zucchini very thinly lengthwise with a potato peeler and put the slices in a shallow dish. Grate over the zest of the lemon and lime.

Make a dressing with the olive oil and lime and lemon juices, together with the herbs, honey, and salt and pepper.

Pour the dressing over the zucchini and toss gently.

Greek zucchini pie

This is delicious warm and almost as good cold. In Greece, it's made on the weekend and then eaten cold for breakfast or lunch for the rest of the week. It's good with a tomato and onion salad.

Serves 10 to 12

2 pounds zucchini
Salt
1 large onion, chopped
4 scallions, chopped
⅔ cup olive oil
1 (16-ounce) package phyllo pastry
10 ounces feta cheese
3 eggs
½ cup heavy cream
Small bunch of dill
Small bunch of parsley
Pepper
2 or 3 stems of mint, leaves
   stripped
Milk, for glazing the crust
Sesame seeds, as a garnish

Grate the zucchini and salt them, allowing them to drain for 30 minutes. Squeeze out the excess juice.

Sweat both types of onions in a little of the olive oil until they're soft and then add the zucchini. Sweat them together gently for 15 minutes until the excess liquid evaporates.

Meanwhile, preheat the oven to 400°F. Separate out 6 phyllo sheets and brush them with oil on both sides. If the pastry seems to be a bit dry, lay it between two damp clean kitchen towels.

Place 3 of the sheets in the base of a 10 by 15-inch baking pan, one oiled sheet layered on top of the next.

Pour in the squash mixture and crumble the feta over it. Beat the eggs and cream together and drizzle them on top. Add the herbs, pepper, and salt, and fork the cheese and egg mixture lightly into the zucchini.

Fold in the phyllo sheets, enclosing the zucchini mix and brush with oil. Then place another phyllo sheet on top and brush with oil, and repeat with 2 more sheets. Brush lightly with oil and snip most of the excess pastry around the edges, leaving just enough to tuck in all the way around the pan. Glaze the pie with a little milk and scatter sesame seeds over the top. Prick the pastry all over with a fork.

Put the pie in the preheated oven and cook it for about an hour. You can shake it in the pan to see if there's much movement. Remove from the oven when the pie is set and the pastry is golden. Put a kitchen towel over the top and leave it to cool for half an hour before you eat.

Crisp zucchini wedges with anchovy mayonnaise

I first had this dish at the restaurant De Kas in Amsterdam, and I've been making it every summer since. The triple layer of coating—flour, egg, breadcrumbs—gives these the most delicious crunch. If you're not one for anchovies, try the wedges dipped into Green mayonnaise (see page 83).

You'll probably have some of the mayonnaise left over, but it keeps well in the fridge.

Serves 4
For the anchovy mayonnaise:
1 whole egg, plus 1 extra egg yolk
1 garlic clove
6 canned anchovy fillets, drained
½ teaspoon English or other spicy mustard powder
Salt and pepper
1 cup sunflower oil (or one part olive oil to two parts sunflower oil)
2 tablespoons lemon juice

4 canned anchovy fillets, drained
1½ cups breadcrumbs
Grated zest of 1 lemon
1 tablespoon grated Parmesan cheese
1 egg, beaten
A little seasoned all-purpose flour (salt, pepper, and some English or other spicy mustard powder)
1 pound zucchini, cut into wedges about 2½ to 3 inches long
Peanut or sunflower oil, for frying

First, make the anchovy mayonnaise. Put the whole egg and the egg yolk in a food processor or bowl and mix them with the garlic, anchovy fillets, mustard, salt, and pepper.

When the mixture is quite smooth, carefully add the oil in a stream while blending continuously, until the oil emulsifies and makes a thick and smooth mayonnaise. Finally, stir in the lemon juice to taste.

Combine the anchovy fillets with the bread. Add the lemon zest and Parmesan to the breadcrumbs.

You need 3 shallow bowls, one containing the seasoned flour, a second with the beaten egg, and the third the breadcrumb mixture. Dip the zucchini wedges first into the flour, then the egg, and finally the breadcrumbs. Then shallow-fry them in the oil, with 5 or 6 only in the oil at one time, until they're golden but still with a good bite.

These can easily be made in advance and heated briefly in a hot oven to crisp them up.

Serve as soon as they are all cooked, with the mayonnaise.

Matthew's stuffed zucchini flowers

My friend Matthew Rice grows lots of zucchini plants, as much for the blossoms as for the fruit. This dish is rich, filling, and delicious.

Serves 8
For the tempura batter:
  1½ cups all-purpose flour
  Plenty of salt and pepper
  2 eggs
  1½ cups cold beer

  16 zucchini flowers
  ½ pound (8 ounces) peas (frozen is fine)
  8 ounces cream cheese
  Salt and pepper
  Small bunch of parsley, coarsely chopped
  1 tablespoon olive oil, plus more for frying

First, make the tempura batter. Sift the flour into a bowl with the salt and pepper and make a well in the center. Add the eggs and, with a whisk, mix in the cold beer to make a batter the thickness of heavy cream that is not too smooth. Keep this in the fridge until you need it.

Shake the zucchini flowers to dislodge possible insects and remove the stigma from the center. Cook the peas in salted boiling water for 3 minutes. In a mixing bowl, combine the peas, cream cheese, salt, pepper, parsley, and a little olive oil.

With your fingers, gently part the flower petals, leaving one finger inside to keep it open. Take a teaspoon of the mixture and carefully stuff the flower. The stickiness of the mixture will mean that you can seal the pointed end easily with a little twist.

Heat about 4 inches of olive oil (the oil is an important component of the taste) in a deep pan, making sure the oil doesn't come more than one-third of the way up the sides of the pan, until it reaches about 325°F. If you don't have an oil thermometer, it's easy to test the temperature. Drop a cube of bread into the oil. It should turn golden brown in less than a minute. Dip each stuffed flower in the tempura batter, then fry them in the hot oil.

Turn them after 30 seconds and again after 2 minutes. When they're golden, remove them from the oil and drain them on paper towels.

These are at their best eaten hot, sprinkled with sea salt and black pepper.

Tam's stuffed zucchini flowers

This makes a lighter stuffing. Sometimes I do some flowers stuffed with Matthew's mix and some with Tam's. One of each per person makes a good first course.

Serves 8
For the tempura batter:
  1½ cups all-purpose flour
  Plenty of salt and pepper
  2 eggs
  1½ cups cold beer

  1 tablespoon olive oil
  ½ teaspoon chopped fresh red chili
  A sprig of marjoram or thyme, stripped and chopped
  12 olives, pitted and chopped
  ¾ cup cooked couscous
  4 ounces fresh goat cheese
  ½ cup cooked baby fava beans or peas
  Salt and pepper
  16 zucchini flowers
  Olive oil, for frying

First, make the tempura batter. Sift the flour into a bowl with the salt and pepper and make a well in the center. Add the eggs and, with a whisk, mix in the cold beer to make a batter the thickness of heavy cream that is not too smooth. Keep this in the fridge until you need it.

Pour a little olive oil into a saucepan and, over low heat, add the chili, chopped herbs, and olives. Cook for 2 minutes or so.

Remove from the heat and combine with the cooked couscous. Crumble in the fresh goat cheese and the fava beans or peas, and season well.

Stuff the flowers with this mixture, then dip them into the batter and fry in olive oil until golden. Drain on paper towels.

These are at their best eaten hot, sprinkled with salt.

Zucchini chutney

Sometimes you feel as if you're sinking under a garden full of zucchini. You can leave them to grow into larger squash, but this stops the plants producing so much small fruit. This chutney is a good way of using them up. The recipe was given to me by the chef Paul Burton, taught to him by his grandmother.

Yield: 3 to 4 jars
> **Pickling spices (coriander seeds, yellow mustard seeds, dried chilis, allspice, ginger, black peppercorns, and a couple of bay leaves)**
> **1½ pounds zucchini**
> **1 cup raisins**
> **1 cup dried apricots**
> **1 small green apple**
> **1¼ cups sugar**
> **¾ tablespoon salt**
> **2 cups white wine vinegar**

Tie the spices in a cheesecloth bag. Cut the zucchini into cubes. In a large preserving pot, combine with all the other ingredients and tie the cheesecloth bag onto the handle so that it dangles into the mixture. Leave it for 24 hours.

Stir over low heat to dissolve the sugar gently.

Cover and simmer for at least an hour, pressing the bag of spices from time to time, until the pieces of zucchini are translucent and the liquid is golden and syrupy.

Pour into warm sterilized jars and cover or use the technique described on page 304.

Zucchini and coconut soup

You can make this fantastic soup with zucchini, and it's a delicious way of using those older ones that are bigger and fatter, but only if they are deseeded and salted. My godmother, Marni Hodgkin, cuts this recipe right down to softened onion, squash, some good stock, and a can of coconut milk. Try this if you want something really simple.

Serves 4 to 6
> **2 pounds zucchini**
> **Salt**
> **1 large onion, chopped**
> **1 tablespoon olive oil**
> **1 teaspoon grated fresh ginger**
> **2 garlic cloves, crushed**
> **2 tablespoons chopped basil, plus more as a garnish**
> **2 tablespoons chopped mint, plus more as a garnish**
> **4 cups chicken or vegetable stock**
> **1 cup coconut milk**

Peel and deseed the large zucchini if using and cut it, or cut the smaller zucchini, if using instead, into ¾-inch chunks. Put them into a colander, sprinkle with salt, and let them drain for 30 minutes to get rid of the excess water. Pat them dry.

Sweat the onion gently in the oil. Add the grated ginger and garlic, plus the zucchini chunks. Add the basil and mint with half the stock and cook for 10 minutes.

Blend in a food processor and then put the liquid back in the pan with the rest of the stock and the coconut milk. Simmer for about 5 minutes.

Throw in another tablespoon of mint and basil leaves as you eat.

Zucchini and ginger jam

This is an Edwardian recipe. The lemon jelly and pineapple may sound like bizarre additions, but this makes a heavenly syrupy jam out of older zucchini.

Yield: 4 to 5 jars
   2 pounds large zucchini
   1 (3-inch) piece of fresh ginger
   5 cups sugar
   Juice and grated zest of 2 to 3
      unwaxed lemons
   1 packet lemon gelatin
   1 (8-ounce) can pineapple, thinly
      cut, drained

Peel the squash, remove the seeds, and cut the flesh into cubes. This is long cooked, so there's no need to salt and bleed.

Bruise the piece of ginger and tie it in a cheesecloth bag.

In a large bowl, layer the squash with the sugar, lemon juice, and zest, and put the bag of ginger in so that it hangs over the side of the bowl. Leave the whole mixture steeping for 24 hours.

Place it all in a preserving pot with the ginger again tied to the handle and stir to dissolve the sugar gently over low heat. Add the lemon gelatin and pineapple, cover, and simmer gently (unlike the rolling boil usually used for jam or jelly). Press the bag of ginger from time to time.

Simmer until the pieces of squash are translucent and the liquid is golden and syrupy. Pour into warmed sterilized jars, cover, and seal. You can use this right away, but it will store, unopened, for years.

Roasted zucchini, eggplant, and onion with balsamic sauce

When you feel like something virtuous and simple, this is a good supper, eaten with a dollop of Cucumber raita (see page 196) or minty yogurt. Alternatively, serve it as a side vegetable with almost any meat or fish.

Serves 6 to 8
   1 medium- to large-sized zucchini
   Salt and pepper
   A little olive oil
   2 red onions, quartered
   2 eggplants, cubed
   ⅓ cup apple juice
   ⅓ cup balsamic vinegar
   2 tablespoons sunflower oil
   Small bunch of herbs, such as
      summer savory, tarragon, and
      parsley, chopped

Peel the squash, deseed it, and cut it into chunks about ¼ inch thick. Put in a colander and sprinkle well with salt, then leave to drain. If you have a younger squash less than 10 inches long, you shouldn't need to peel it.

Lay the chunks out in a single layer on a baking pan in a low (300°F) oven for about an hour. This will dry them out further. Then pour over a little olive oil and increase the heat to 425°F for another 15 minutes. This will brown the chunks around the edges.

Meanwhile, put the onions and eggplants on another baking pan. Pour over a little bit of olive oil and roast in a medium (350°F) oven for 45 minutes.

In a pan, mix the apple juice with the balsamic vinegar and reduce it by three-quarters over low heat. Add the sunflower oil.

Mix the roasted vegetables together and dress them with this mixture. Scatter the herbs over the top.

Cucumbers

It's the fresh, cool crunchiness of a cucumber's flesh that makes it so delicious. Unlike tomatoes, cucumbers—and almost everything made with them—are best served as cold as possible. They are also usually best peeled. Particularly when home-grown, towards the end of the season the skins can be tough. And for many recipes, it is worth salting them once they are sliced. You'll be amazed by the amount of liquid that they produce.

If you're growing your own cucumbers, choose a modern hybrid such as 'Burpless Tasty Green'. With modern varieties you have none of the bother of removing male flowers to prevent bitterness: this problem has been bred out of almost all cucumbers now. I've grown 'Burpless Tasty Green' for years. It's incredibly reliable and heavy cropping, grown both inside in a greenhouse and out, producing medium-sized, smooth-skinned cucumbers with sweet tender flesh.

Sometimes I also grow a mini cucumber variety such as 'Zeina', which produces large amounts of cucumbers the size of a large cigar. These are so prolific that it's difficult to eat enough, but keep picking: don't leave them to yellow on the plant or they'll stop producing. Make soup and pickles if you have a glut of them (see pages 195 and 197). Mini cucumbers are fantastic eaten freshly picked and cut lengthwise to dip into hummus (see page 85) or creamy herby goat cheese. I also like the old-fashioned round, so-called melon cucumbers such as 'Crystal Apples', which are sweet and very juicy.

The gherkin or cornichon, a mini cucumber pickled for eating through the winter with a plate of antipasti, is much more popular almost everywhere in Europe. A sweet dill pickle—not too acrid and vinegary—made from gherkins is delicious and, for the first time this year, I made lots. They are wonderful with salami and cold meat, and I love them sliced over the top of Lamb burgers with thyme and rosemary (see page 49).

Mint and cucumber soup

This is an easy soup to make; refreshing and light, it is ideal for lunch on a hot day or as an almost instant first course for a summer dinner. It's also a useful way of using cucumbers when there's a surplus. You can make a big batch and freeze it, but if you do, leave the garlic out, to be added when you eat.

Serves 6
- **1 head garlic**
- **2 large cucumbers**
- **1 bunch of mint**
- **1¼ cups olive oil**
- **2½ cups milk, plain yogurt, or fromage frais**
- **Salt and pepper**

Roast the garlic (see page 253) to give the soup a delicious smoky background taste. Peel the cucumbers, slice them in half lengthwise, and scoop out the seeds with a teaspoon.

Strip the mint leaves off their stems and coarsely chop them.

Blend the garlic, cucumbers, and mint in a food processor, then add the olive oil in a stream, with the machine still running. Stir in the milk, yogurt, or fromage frais and add plenty of salt and pepper.

Like all cucumber soups, this should be served really cold, with perhaps a flower-studded ice cube floating in the top of each bowl.

Cucumber and garlic soup with chives

Made with a stock base and plenty of yogurt, this soup is a meal in itself if eaten with bread. It has a lovely sharp taste from the chives, fresh garlic, and lemon juice.

Serves 4 to 6
- **1 large cucumber**
- **1½ cups Greek yogurt**
- **1 cup crème fraîche**
- **¾ cup cold vegetable or chicken stock**
- **1 to 2 garlic cloves, mashed to a very fine paste using a mortar and pestle**
- **2 tablespoons chopped chives, plus more as a garnish**
- **Salt and pepper**
- **Juice of 1 lemon**
- **Purple chive flowers, as a garnish (optional)**

Grate the cucumber. If the outer peel is tough, remove it; but if the cucumber is young and fresh it grates easily.

Mix together the yogurt, crème fraîche, and stock, and then add the cucumber, garlic, and chives. Give the mixture a quick blitz in a food processor to combine.

Season the soup with salt and pepper and a little lemon juice, then chill it for at least 1 hour.

Ladle the soup into bowls and finish with chopped chives and, if you like, dismembered purple chive flowers.

Marinated cucumber and dill salad

This is a recipe from my friend Lucinda Fraser, and it's fantastic for making in large quantities when you have lots of people to lunch. It's at its most delicious eaten fresh, but it's fine made the day before.

Serves 4 to 6
- **1 large cucumber**
- **6 tablespoons rice wine vinegar**
- **½ cup superfine sugar**
- **1 small bunch of dill**
- **Salt and pepper**

Peel the cucumber and slice it as thinly as possible. (If you have one, use a mandoline or the slicing disc on a food processor.) Remove the seeds only if there are lots of large ones, but you must remove the skin.

Heat the vinegar in a small pan over low heat and stir in the sugar until it has dissolved. Allow to cool.

Finely chop the dill. Layer a quarter of the cucumber in a small dish with high sides and season. Sprinkle a quarter of the dill over the cucumber. Repeat the layers.

Pour over the vinegar, season, cover, and leave for at least an hour.

Drain the liquid (of which there will be lots) before you eat.

Cucumber raita

This is a very basic dish, but I make it all the time. It's a good meze to eat alongside falafel, olives, baby fava beans, and bacon, or to have on its own with flat, pita-style bread (see page 46). Without the turmeric, it's Greek tzatziki. Greek cooks up the garlic to two cloves and add a tablespoon of olive oil.

Serves 4 to 6
    ½ cucumber
    ¼ teaspoon salt
    ¾ cup whole-milk yogurt
    Small bunch of mint
    1 garlic clove, finely chopped
    Small pinch of turmeric or paprika

Grate the cucumber—you don't need to skin it—and put it in a sieve over a bowl. Sprinkle it with the salt and leave it to drain for half an hour. Pat the cucumber dry with paper towels. Mix with the yogurt, mint, garlic, and just enough water to give you the consistency you want, usually in the region of ½ cup.

    Add a pinch of turmeric for extra flavor and pale yellow coloring or sprinkle paprika over the top.

Fresh horseradish and cucumber sauce

Horseradish is delicious mixed with all sorts of things. It's excellent with beets (see page 164) and with sour cream and new potatoes. I love it with cucumber, to eat with almost any fish, and it's famously good with smoked fish, but also superb with fresh salmon and sea bass.

Serves 8
    2 inches fresh horseradish root
    1 cucumber
    Salt and pepper
    4 tablespoons white wine vinegar
    ½ teaspoon superfine sugar
    1 cup heavy cream, whisked to hold its shape, or crème fraîche
    1 cup light cream

Wash the horseradish and peel it, then grate it either by hand or with the grating disc in a food processor.

    Peel the cucumber, slice it in half lengthwise, and scrape out the seeds. Grate or chop the flesh, sprinkle with salt, and leave in a colander for about 20 minutes.

    Put the grated horseradish into a bowl with the vinegar, sugar, and pepper. Stir in the heavy cream, followed by the light cream.

    Dry the grated cucumber with paper towels. Fold it into the cream and season.

Surinam pickled cucumber

This recipe is a wonderful way of storing cucumber for several weeks and it tastes delicious with ham and cold meat.

Yield: about 1 pint
1½ cucumbers
1 tablespoon salt
½ cup cider vinegar
1 onion, thinly sliced in rings or half rings
2½ tablespoons sugar
3 star anise
1 tablespoon pickling spice
1 red chili, pricked or chopped into large bits

Peel the cucumber, cut in half lengthwise, and deseed, then cut up into large strips. Put in a colander, sprinkle with most of the salt, and leave to drain for at least half an hour.

Slowly heat 1 cup water with the vinegar, onion, sugar, spices, chili, and a pinch of salt until boiling. Warm the sterilized jars.

Fill the jars with the cucumber chunks and pour over the boiling liquid.

Seal the jars and keep them somewhere cold and dark, but eat within a few weeks. Keep in the fridge once open.

Sweet cucumber pickle

This recipe is excellent for the long-term storing of cucumbers. It's sweet and tangy, with a good crunch, and is delicious eaten with potato salad, cold meat and pâtés, and in Cheddar cheese sandwiches. I am addicted to this and make loads of it. It stores for up to a year.

Yield: 5 small jars
3 large cucumbers
2 onions
¼ cup salt
2½ cups white wine vinegar or distilled white vinegar
2½ cups sugar
1 tablespoon mustard seeds
1 teaspoon celery seeds
5 cloves
½ teaspoon turmeric

Peel the cucumbers and cut lengthwise into thin sticks about 2 inches long and about ¼ inch deep and ½ inch wide.

Thinly slice the onions into half moons. Put the cucumbers and onions into a large mixing bowl and sprinkle with salt. Cover this with a weighted plate and leave for 2 to 3 hours.

Rinse the cucumbers and onions in cold water, and then let stand to drain. While they are draining, put all the remaining ingredients into a saucepan and stir over low heat until the sugar has dissolved. Add the cucumbers and onions, bring to a boil, and simmer for 1 minute.

Remove from the heat and lift the cucumbers and onions out of the liquid. Put into warm sterilized jars.

Return the liquid to the heat and boil rapidly for at least 10 minutes to reduce it. Pour the liquid over the cucumbers in the jars and cover. Keep in the fridge once open.

Dill-pickled cornichons

These mini cucumbers should be pickled and then eaten with grilled burgers or salami and cold ham.

Yield: 4 to 5 jars
2 pounds tiny gherkin cucumbers, about 2 inches long
3 tablespoons coarse sea salt
4 garlic cloves, peeled
3 to 4 sprigs of thyme
3 to 4 sprigs of tarragon
1 tablespoon black peppercorns
2 bay leaves, cut into strips
2 dried chilis, crumbled
White wine vinegar or cider vinegar, to cover

If they're small, leave the cornichons whole; if they're large, slice them. Wash and rub them gently to remove the spiny bits. Put them into a colander.

Mix them with the salt and allow them to stand and drain for 24 hours.

Either rinse and dry or rub with a cloth, and put into sterilized jars along with the garlic, herbs, peppercorns, strips of bay, and dried chili pepper.

Fill to the top with the vinegar and cover tightly, ideally with a plastic lid. These are best stored in a cool and dark place, and will be ready after one month. After opening, store them in the fridge.

Edible flowers

I love edible flowers. They may be perceived as a bit fussy, but so what? I like bright color in my food.

If you're patient, and I'm not, you can crystallize edible flowers and add them to cakes, but more realistic for most of us is to use them as they are, studding ice cubes, or scattered in salads. Pointy, star-shaped rubber ice cube trays look the best, with blue and white borage flowers or delicate pansies frozen in the cubes. These look pretty in any summer drinks or floating in a cold soup.

English marigolds (calendulas) look lovely in a salad, as do dandelions and chicory, with their distinct tart taste. As soon as the summer gets hot, lots of your herbs will start to flower. Arugula is usually the first and once the flowers begin to form, the leaves turn inedibly hot. Don't chuck your plants until you've stripped all the flowers for adding to a bowl of salad. These taste similar to the leaves, but milder. Do the same with parsley, cilantro, fennel, and dill—all tasty and colorful. You can also scatter the flowers of borage, chives, and any dianthus, rose, or pansy, but with the larger flowers, pull the petals off the bitter flower base first—don't add the whole thing.

Nasturtiums in salads have become so popular they're almost a cliché, but there are other ways of using these tasty, peppery flowers, and their buds and leaves. Add them to mashed potato or, even better, use them instead of black pepper in fish cakes (see page 202).

My favorite variety of nasturtium is 'Tip Top Mahogany', with deep crimson flowers, contrasting with the acid-green leaves. There's also a new variety, 'Black Velvet', with even richer, darker, nearly black flowers. Use these dipped in batter and fried for a Summer garden tempura (see page 207).

We think of lavender as a beautiful and fragrant ornamental plant, but it's also a lovely, unusual taste in desserts, cookies, cakes, and ice cream. Put a sprig into the custard when you're making crème brûlée (see page 202) and quiz everyone as to what they think the flavoring is. Rather than vanilla sugar, make lavender sugar for introducing this flavor to your food through the winter.

Stuffed lamb with lavender

The flavor of lavender is wonderful with meat, particularly lamb. To make the most of the fragrant taste, puncture the skin of the lamb with a sharp knife, push some lavender flowers into the meat, and also add plenty to the stuffing.

Serves 6 to 8
For the stuffing:
- ⅔ cup medium couscous
- 1 cup good lamb or vegetable stock, boiling
- 2 shallots, chopped
- ¼ cup raisins, soaked for a few minutes in warm water
- ¼ cup toasted pine nuts
- 5 to 6 lavender flowers, finely chopped
- Flat-leaf parsley, chopped
- Grated zest of 1 lemon
- Salt and pepper

- 1 boned leg of lamb
- Olive oil
- Bunch of lavender
- 2 garlic cloves, sliced
- Good bunch of hay* (optional)
- 1 cup white wine
- Salt and pepper

Preheat the oven to 400°F.

To make the stuffing, put the couscous into a mixing bowl and pour over the boiling stock, whisking with a fork to break up any lumps. Cover with a kitchen towel and put to one side for about 15 minutes, stirring occasionally.

Sweat the shallots until soft and translucent. Once the couscous is ready, add the shallots and the remaining ingredients, mix well, and season with salt and freshly ground pepper.

Stuff the cavity of the boned leg with the couscous mixture and tie it into a good shape.

Smear the surface of the lamb with olive oil, season really well, and then make a dozen or so cuts in the skin of the lamb with a sharp knife. Push into each incision a short lavender head and a sliver of garlic.

Wash the hay, if using, under cold running water. Make a nest of it in a casserole dish and put in the lamb.

Pour over the wine, cover, and roast the lamb for 20 to 25 minutes per pound plus 25 minutes. Remove the cover for the last 15 minutes till browned.

Lift the lamb out of the casserole, cover with foil and then a kitchen towel, and allow to rest while you strain the juices into a small saucepan and boil to reduce a little.

Check the seasoning and serve with the lamb and some Redcurrant jelly (see page 171), Mint and apple jelly (see page 231), or Rowan jelly (see page 324).

*Bagged timothy hay is sold as rabbit feed at pet stores.

Quick lavender ice cream

A delicately flavored lavender vanilla ice cream.

Serves 4 to 6
- 1½ cups milk
- ¼ cup honey (lavender honey, if possible)
- 4 to 6 stalks and heads of fresh lavender, plus a few more to serve
- 1 vanilla pod, split
- Pinch of salt
- ½ cup condensed milk
- 1¼ cups heavy cream
- Strips of lemon zest, as a garnish

Heat the milk with the honey, lavender, and vanilla pod until just below the boiling point and stir gently. Allow to cool completely, then pour through a sieve to remove the lavender and vanilla, and put in the fridge for half an hour or so.

Add the salt, condensed milk, and heavy cream to the chilled mixture and freeze/churn in an ice cream maker for about 20 minutes. Put into a plastic container and freeze for at least 4 hours. To serve, remove from the freezer and put in the fridge for about 15 to 20 minutes to soften slightly.

Decorate with fresh lavender and strips of lemon zest.

Lavender crème brûlée

Crème brûlée is ubiquitous, as it's so easy to prepare in advance, but the subtle addition of lavender gives it a whole new lease on life.

Serves 6
6 egg yolks
1 level tablespoon superfine sugar
2 teaspoons vanilla extract
3 cups heavy cream
4 lavender flowers
2 tablespoons Demerara or soft brown sugar

Beat the egg yolks with the sugar and vanilla extract.

In a heavy saucepan, heat the cream with the lavender flowers and bring to a simmer. Remove the pan from the heat and allow the flavors to infuse for 10 minutes or so. Strain through a fine sieve.

Put the cream into a bowl and stand this in a shallow saucepan of simmering water. Add the egg mixture and keep stirring. Gently cook the cream until just thickened enough to coat the back of a wooden spoon.

Remove from the heat and pour into an ovenproof dish or individual ramekins and chill in the fridge for at least 4 hours.

When well chilled, carefully sprinkle the sugar onto the cold cream and either use a blowtorch to caramelize or put under a preheated grill (about 3 to 4 inches below the heat and it must be really red-hot before you start), watching carefully, until the sugar has turned to a golden caramel.

Smoked fish and nasturtium cakes

This looks and tastes marvelous. Serve it with Really rich tomato sauce (see page 277) and a green salad.

Serves 4
1 pound smoked fish (I use haddock)
About 2 cups milk
A few black peppercorns
1 bay leaf
Some parsley stalks
1 onion, finely chopped
1 garlic clove, finely chopped
A little olive oil
4 medium-sized potatoes
1 to 2 tablespoons butter
1 egg yolk plus 1 other whole egg, beaten
3 ounces Parmesan cheese, grated
Salt and pepper
15 nasturtium flowers, torn or roughly chopped
Seasoned all-purpose flour
Breadcrumbs

Put the fish in a shallow heatproof dish and cover with milk. Add the peppercorns, bay leaf, and parsley, and poach until just cooked.

Lift the fish out of the liquor, reserving this for later, and carefully flake with a fork, keeping the flakes as generous as possible.

Fry the onion and garlic in a little oil until translucent.

Boil the potatoes until tender, drain, and add the butter and some of the reserved milk in which the fish was cooked. Mash, but keep the mixture quite stiff.

Add the cooked onion and garlic and the egg yolk to the potato, together with some of the Parmesan, and season well with salt and pepper.

Very carefully fold in the flaked fish and some of the torn nasturtium petals, without mixing it up too much, and then shape the mixture into small round cakes.

Preheat the oven to 375°F.

Have three plates ready— one with seasoned flour, a second with beaten egg, and a third with breadcrumbs mixed with Parmesan and nasturtium petals. Make sure that the fish cakes are lightly covered first with seasoned flour, then egg, and lastly the breadcrumb mixture.

Put into the fridge for a couple of hours and then either shallow-fry or bake in a 375°F oven until golden.

Green beans

A curious and inexplicable chic hangs about French green beans or haricots verts. If brussels sprouts remind you of a slightly ramshackle and tweedy farmer, haricots verts look as if they are dressed for the races—slim, elegant, and a cool pretty green.

I think that's why these green beans are almost always best on their own, but whether eaten in splendid isolation or mixed with other things, they need to be fresh. You can tell that by smelling and breaking them. They have a characteristic very clean smell and, just picked, will snap in half sharply. Many are imported from far away and perhaps doused in many chemicals as they grow.

If possible, grow your own, sowing an equal quantity of a yellow variety such as 'Roquencourt', a purple such as 'Purple Teepee', and regular green beans. I like 'Masterpiece' as a dwarf and 'Blue Lake Climbing' as a climber. All of these are slow to get stringy, have a great taste, and the three colors look fantastic together on a plate.

When you want to eat them, trim the ends and cook them in lots of already boiling water with no lid on the pan. With the lid on, the trapped steam and acidity from the cooking beans will turn the green ones olive. You want to dilute this effect as much as you can and allow the steam to evaporate. When they are just tender, plunge them into cold water and they'll stay bright green and firm. The yellows keep their color on cooking, but the purples will do so only if quickly fried or steamed with the lid off.

If you go away for a week or two and come back to big stringy bean pods, don't chuck them. Shell them and boil the beans inside in plenty of water with three bay leaves. Eat them, just soft, doused in really good olive oil. Alternatively, use them like borlotti or cranberry shell beans (see page 302).

Italian romano beans come after French beans in the garden. There is no such thing as too small a romano bean. The smaller and more tender, the nicer they are. Left to grow more than about 8 inches long, they'll get that horrid toenail-like membrane just inside their outer skin, so pick them as often as you dare. The more you pick, the more pods will form.

There are lots of ways of preparing romano beans, but I use a sharp knife to remove the sides and then cut them across into half-inch strips. Romano beans have wonderful-tasting flowers, similar in flavor to the bean. If you grow your own romano beans, don't grow a great long line of one variety: go for a pink and a white, as well as the more usual scarlet-flowered varieties.

Summer garden tempura

If you boil purple green beans, they turn a dark greyish green. By dipping them raw and whole into tempura batter and then shallow-frying them, they stay looking fantastic and taste even better.

Mix them with mini peppers, zucchini flowers, eggplants, and carrots for a wonderful plate of garden vegetable tempura. Dip them into Chili dipping sauce (see page 318) and soy sauce.

Serves 10 to 12
For the tempura batter:
  1½ cups all-purpose flour
  Plenty of salt and pepper
  2 eggs, beaten
  1½ cups iced sparkling water or
    cold beer

  3 cups sunflower or peanut oil
  2 handfuls of beans, ends left on
  2 red or green bell peppers, cut
    into strips or, if small, deseeded
    but kept whole
  3 to 4 mild peppers, such as
    Hungarian wax, with stems
  1 eggplant, cut into discs
  4 zucchini, cut in half or whole if
    small
  3 zucchini flowers
  2 globe artichoke hearts, cooked
    (see page 116)
  Selection of green herbs: leaves
    and flowers of parsley, chervil,
    basil, and single sage leaves
  8 nasturtium flowers
  A few root vegetables (beets,
    mini carrots, sweet potatoes),
    cooked briefly and sliced into
    bite-sized sections
  Sea salt and black pepper

First, make the tempura batter. Sift the flour into a bowl with the salt and pepper and make a well in the center. Add the eggs and, with a whisk, mix in the cold water or beer to make a batter the thickness of heavy cream but not too smooth. Keep this in the fridge until you need it.

Pour the oil into a deep pot so that it reaches about one-third of the way up the side. Heat the oil until it reaches about 325°F. If you don't have an oil thermometer, it's easy to test the temperature. Drop a cube of bread into the oil. It should turn golden brown in less than a minute.

Dip the vegetables, herbs, and flowers into the batter, a few at a time, and then into the hot oil until pale gold and crisp. Drain them on paper towels.

These are at their best eaten hot, sprinkled with sea salt and ground black pepper.

Spaghetti with beans and tomatoes

The team from the River Café in London demonstrated this at our cookery school five years ago, and I've made it many times during the summer ever since. It's an incredibly fresh-tasting and yet comforting pasta dish, perfect when the garden is full of beans and tomatoes.

Serves 6
  2 pounds tomatoes, ideally plum
    or small beefsteak
  ½ pound French beans, ends
    removed
  Salt
  ½ cup heavy cream
  1 garlic clove, whole and peeled
  Handful of basil leaves
  1 pound spaghetti
  2 ounces grated Parmesan
    cheese, as a garnish

Skin the tomatoes, deseed with a teaspoon, and chop them coarsely. Cook the beans in plenty of salted boiling water for 3 minutes until they are just tender. Cool them quickly in a bowl of cold water and drain.

Bring the cream to a boil and add the garlic. Take the pan off the heat and leave the cream to steep for 5 minutes before removing the garlic.

Then add the beans, tomatoes, and torn-up basil, and toss just for a minute to warm the vegetables through.

Cook the pasta in salted boiling water until al dente, drain, and mix with the tomatoes and beans. Serve with freshly grated Parmesan.

Trofie with potatoes, beans, and pesto

Trofie, a hard durum wheat pasta with a spiral shape, makes a delicious dish with Marcella's homemade pesto (see page 225), potatoes, and beans. Gemelli makes an acceptable subsitute.

Serves 4
1 pound trofie or gemelli
Salt and pepper
4 small new potatoes
½ pound green beans
2 tablespoons pesto (preferably homemade)
Plenty of grated Parmesan cheese

Cook the pasta in plenty of rapidly boiling salted water for 18 to 20 minutes, until just al dente.

Cook the potatoes, peel them, and cut them into ¼-inch slices or chunks. Cut or break the beans into short lengths and cook for 2 minutes, until tender.

Drain the pasta, leaving 3 tablespoons of the cooking water in the bottom of the pan, and add a generous amount of pesto to the water, stirring it in to make a thin sauce.

Add the drained pasta, beans, and potatoes and mix together gently to combine.

Serve with plenty of grated Parmesan and black pepper.

Green beans in truffle oil with steak and hollandaise

This hardly needs a recipe, but is one of my favorite summer garden meals— a rare steak and a big mound of beans tossed in truffle-flavored olive oil and topped with almonds. You also want a good dollop of tarragon hollandaise. Pick a good handful of beans for each person, harvesting them when the beans are still small and tender.

Serves 4
Tarragon hollandaise (see page 233)
¼ cup almonds, slivered
4 steak fillets, each about 5 to 7 ounces, at room temperature
1 pound green beans
1 tablespoon white truffle oil
1 tablespoon extra virgin olive oil
Sea salt

Make the tarragon hollandaise and store it in a Thermos to keep it warm. Roast the almonds in a hot oven until golden.

Preheat a hot cast-iron skillet, lightly oil the steaks, and cook on the hot pan for 3 minutes on each side. Let them rest for 5 minutes, wrapped in foil.

Cook the beans in plenty of salted boiling water for 3 minutes, tasting them at this point. They should be cooked but squeaky. Drain and drizzle the truffle oil and olive oil over them while they're still warm, and toss to coat. Add the almonds and sprinkle sea salt over the top.

Your meat should then be perfect—still warm and rested for just the right amount of time. Serve with the tarragon hollandaise.

Niçoise salad

An excellent salad which features crunchy, just-cooked beans, waxy new potatoes, salty anchovies, quails' eggs—if possible rather than chickens' eggs—and also if possible, fresh tuna. It feels right on a hot summer day.

Serves 4
- **½ pound (2 slices) sashimi-quality fresh tuna (or 2 six-ounce cans tuna)**
- **Olive oil**
- **12 quail eggs or 3 hen eggs**
- **1 pound green beans**
- **Salt**
- **1 pound new potatoes, cut into chunks**
- **10 roasted cherry tomatoes (see page 278)**
- **2 red chilis, cut into thin strips (optional)**
- **10 radishes, halved**
- **12 good black olives (always avoid pitted ones)**
- **12 canned anchovies, drained**
- **20 capers, rinsed**
- **Basil or chervil leaves**

For the dressing:
- **3 tablespoons olive oil**
- **2 garlic cloves, chopped**
- **1 teaspoon Dijon mustard**
- **1 tablespoon red wine vinegar**
- **Salt and pepper**

If you're using fresh tuna, preheat a hot pan. Brush the tuna with olive oil on both sides and sear for 1½ minutes on each side. Allow to rest for 5 minutes and then slice it at an angle into ¼-inch slices.

Boil the eggs for 4 minutes and leave them under cold running water to cool sufficiently for you to peel them.

Boil the whole beans in salted water for 3 minutes before plunging them in cold water.

Cook the potatoes for about 15 minutes, until they're tender, and let them cool a bit.

Make the dressing by combining all the ingredients and some seasoning.

On a large flat plate, make a bed with the beans. Dress and toss them. Then add the cherry tomatoes, chilis (if you want them), radishes, potatoes, olives, and anchovies. Add the shelled quail eggs or quartered hen eggs, throw the capers over the top, and lay the tuna on top of that.

Drizzle with the rest of the dressing and scatter over some basil or chervil leaves.

Lemon bean salad

This makes a wonderful bean salad that is particularly good with chicken.

Serves 4
For the lemon dressing:
- **Juice of 2 lemons and grated zest of 1 lemon**
- **1 tablespoon mascarpone cheese**
- **1¼ teaspoons Tabasco sauce**
- **1 garlic clove, chopped**
- **5 tablespoons olive oil**
- **1 teaspoon ground coriander seeds**
- **1 teaspoon English or spicy mustard powder**
- **2 teaspoons sugar**
- **Salt and pepper**

- **1 pound green beans (thicker ones if possible)**

First, make the dressing: whisk together all the ingredients and add salt and pepper to taste.

Cook the beans in salted boiling for water 3 to 4 minutes, until just tender. Drain and plunge them into cold water.

Mix the beans with the dressing. Serve cold or at room temperature.

Romano bean flower salad

Scatter romano bean flowers over any leaf salad or make this bean tabbouleh, where the flowers take center stage.

Serves 4 to 6

2 good handfuls of small tender Italian romano beans
Salt and pepper
½ cup bulgur wheat
1 cup vegetable stock (enough to cover the bulgur)
½ pound tomatoes, cut into small chunks
Juice of 1 lemon
2 tablespoons olive oil
3 scallions, thinly sliced
Very large bunch of flat-leaf parsley, finely chopped, tops of stems included
Large bunch of mint, finely chopped
¼ teaspoon ground cinnamon
½ teaspoon ground allspice
40 or so Italian romano bean flowers

String your beans and slice into thin strips at an angle. Like French beans, the best way to cook them is for 3 minutes in plenty of salted boiling water with the lid left off, until just tender. Then plunge them into a bowl of cold water and drain.

Prepare the bulgur by boiling the vegetable stock and covering the bulgur with it. If you don't have any homemade, use diluted organic bouillon or even water. Leave the wheat to stand for 15 minutes in a covered bowl, occasionally fluffing it up with a fork. Drain it and press with a spoon to get rid of any excess stock, then let it cool.

Add the beans, tomatoes, lemon juice, olive oil, scallions, and herbs. Finally add the spices and let the salad sit for half an hour for the flavors to combine. Add the flowers just before you eat.

Romano beans with cream and savory

This is a delicious soft, creamy dish that is good with roasted chicken. It also makes a tasty quick pasta sauce.

Serves 4

1 pound Italian romano beans
Salt and pepper
½ cup heavy cream
1 garlic clove, peeled
1 tablespoon chopped summer savory (or thyme), plus more as a garnish
Grated Parmesan cheese, as a garnish

String and slice the beans and cook them uncovered in rapidly boiling salted water for 3 minutes, until they are just tender. Plunge into cold water and drain.

Put the cream, garlic clove, and savory (or thyme) in a saucepan. Add salt and pepper. Bring to a boil and simmer gently for 2 minutes. Remove from the heat and leave for 10 minutes for the flavors to merge. Take out the garlic.

Add the beans, put back on the heat, and stir to heat them through.

Garnish with more savory (or thyme) and plenty of Parmesan.

Gooseberries

Gooseberries certainly don't look promising. Green, red, pink, purple, black, or yellow, hairy gooseberries are just not very alluring. But appearances can be deceptive—a gooseberry is a glorious fruit. I visited the Royal Horticultural Society fruit garden at Wisley this summer and was shown around by the maître d'. We looked at figs, grapes, kiwis, melons, as well as the more usual strawberries, raspberries, apples, pears, and currants, and at the end of the day, I asked him which was the one fruit that he'd take to a desert island. It was the gooseberry—good cooked unripe, excellent for freezing, lovely in jam and his number-one top flavor when eaten fully ripe from the bush in midsummer.

Gooseberries start fruiting early and you can usually begin to pick them in late May. At this stage, they won't be ripe and will need cooking, but especially combined with elderflowers, they are delicious in tarts, fools, and ice creams (see page 143), or as a sauce for grilled fish. Harvesting some will help thin the crop, so that the remaining fruit can grow and ripen. Dessert gooseberries will be ready in July and August, and can be picked and eaten straight from the bush. 'Leveller' is a good variety and was one of the great gardener-cook Christopher Lloyd's favorites, as it has thin skins.

Gooseberries are easy to grow, lower maintenance than most other fruit bushes, and tolerant of almost all types of soil and situation. They flower early (particularly in the case of 'Leveller'), so frost can be a problem, and they have quite brittle branches, so should be protected from strong wind. You will also need to net them when the fruit is ripening or the birds will strip the whole lot.

The simplest way of cooking gooseberries is to roast them in the oven sprinkled with soft brown sugar and a little bit of butter. This is delicious with yogurt or cream.

To freeze, just pack them into plastic containers and freeze them as they come off the bush. Remove both ends after freezing. It's much quicker when they're still rock-hard.

Gooseberry tart

A tart of sharp, delicious, just-cooked gooseberries in a very light crust.

Serves 6
For the crust:
1¼ cups all-purpose flour
¼ cup superfine sugar
5 tablespoons very cold unsalted butter
1 egg yolk
A little ice-cold water

1 pound gooseberries
3 eggs
½ cup superfine sugar
1¼ cups heavy cream, plus more as a garnish
1 teaspoon vanilla extract
Confectioners' sugar, for dusting

Preheat the oven to 350°F.

Make the crust by briefly processing the flour and sugar together. Chop the cold butter into chunks and add. Pulse carefully until the mixture resembles breadcrumbs, and put into a mixing bowl. Mix the egg yolk with a little ice-cold water, add to the bowl, and mix with your hands until the pastry comes together in a soft ball. Roll out onto a floured surface and use to line a 10-inch tart pan. Chill for half an hour in the fridge.

Remove both ends of the gooseberries. In a bowl, mix the eggs, sugar, cream, and vanilla extract.

Remove the crust from the fridge and pierce the bottom with a fork. Cover with parchment paper and baking beans or rice and bake blind for about 10 to 15 minutes, until golden. Take from the oven, leaving it on, remove the beans or rice and paper, and allow it to cool slightly.

Fill with the gooseberries and pour over the egg mixture. Bake in the oven for about 35 minutes, until just firm in the center. Dust with confectioners' sugar and serve warm with heavy cream.

Gooseberry fool

The tartness of gooseberries is wonderful with the sweetness of elderflower and plenty of whipped cream. Serve this pudding with shortbread or Hazelnut biscotti (see page 357). Another classic gooseberry fool is made with equal parts whipped cream and egg custard (see the recipe for homemade custard on page 256). Try that too.

Serves 4
1 pound gooseberries (no need to remove the ends)
¾ cup sugar
3 elderflower heads or 2 tablespoons elderflower cordial
1 cup heavy cream

Rinse the gooseberries and put them in a saucepan with the sugar and the elderflower heads or cordial. Bring to a boil and simmer gently until the berries are soft.

Remove from the heat, allow to cool, and then remove the elderflower heads, if using. Whip the cream to the soft-peak stage.

If you like a rougher texture, just crush the fruit; for a smoother texture, put the berries through a food mill or push them through a sieve into a large bowl. Fold in as much of the whipped cream as you like, depending on how strong a taste of gooseberry you prefer.

Chill in the fridge.

Gooseberry and thyme jelly

This is the jelly to eat with duck or goose, and it's lovely with lamb.

Yield: 8 jars
  4 pounds gooseberries
  Large handful of thyme sprigs
  Sugar (for exact quantity, see below)

Put the gooseberries into a large heavy-bottomed pot and cover with 4 cups of water.

Make a bunch of thyme and suspend in the liquid by tying it to the handle.

Bring to a boil and cook until the gooseberries are very tender.

Strain the gooseberries through a cheesecloth or jelly bag overnight. Don't be tempted to squeeze the bag or the jelly will be cloudy.

Measure the amount that has dripped from the bag. Warm the sugar in its packets or a bowl in a very low oven for about half an hour. For every 2½ cups of juice, add 2½ cups sugar. Allow the sugar to dissolve completely while you stir over low heat. Then bring to a boil and boil rapidly until the gelling point is reached (see page 170).

Leave to cool a little, then pour into warm sterilized jars. After 20 minutes, add a sprig of extra thyme to each jar. Cover with a wax disc and seal. It will keep unopened for up to a year, but refrigerate after opening.

Jane's gooseberry and elderflower sorbet

There is a gooseberry and elderflower ice cream on page 143. Here is a lighter but equally delicious sorbet recipe of my sister's.

Serves 6 to 8
  2 pounds gooseberries
  4 to 5 elderflower heads
  1 to 1¼ cups superfine sugar
  Grated zest and juice of 3 to 4 lemons

Stew the gooseberries and elderflower heads in a small amount of water until soft and pulpy. Take out the elderflower heads and put them aside. Then rub the rest of the mixture through a sieve or food mill.

Dissolve the superfine sugar in 2½ cups water and then boil hard for 7 minutes to get a light syrup. Remove from the heat and add the elderflowers, plus the lemon zest and juice.

Leave the flowers in the syrup until cold, then strain and add the juice to the gooseberry mixture.

If you have an ice cream maker, freeze/churn the mixture for 20 minutes; if you don't, put it into a plastic container and freeze, breaking up the ice particles a couple of times with a fork every 2 hours.

Take the sorbet out of the freezer and put in the fridge for half an hour before serving.

Baked cream with gooseberries

A delicate recipe that was given to me by a great friend, Pip Morrison.

Serves 4
For the gooseberries:
¾ to 1 pound gooseberries
2 or 3 elderflower heads
¼ cup superfine sugar

⅓ cup milk
2 elderflower heads
1 teaspoon vanilla extract
1¾ cups heavy cream
5 egg yolks
⅓ cup superfine sugar
4 tablespoons sparkling wine or
   1½ tablespoons brandy

Remove the ends of the gooseberries and put them in a saucepan. Add the elderflowers and just enough water to stop the gooseberries catching on the bottom of the pan. Cook gently until the fruit is tender and then either sieve or put through a food mill to make a puree or leave the fruit whole. Stir in the sugar. Leave to cool.

For the baked cream, preheat the oven to 300°F. Put the milk into a pan with the elderflower heads and bring to a boil. Remove from the heat, stir in the vanilla and the cream, and put to one side for the elderflowers to steep, ideally overnight.

Remove the elderflower heads, whisk the egg yolks with the sugar, and add to the mixture. Whisk for a couple of minutes, and then stir in the sparkling wine or brandy.

Divide the mixture between 4 ramekins and sit them in a baking tin half full of water. Bake in the preheated oven for 30 to 40 minutes until set. Allow to cool and then cover and refrigerate.

To serve, run a knife around the edge of the molds and turn them out into the middle of each plate. Surround them with the gooseberries.

High-summer herbs

I pick and use herbs every day. They can transform a mediocre dish into something marvelous. In the summer, it's the turn of sun-loving annuals—basil, lemongrass, oregano, and dill—which join the late-cropping perennials, such as mint, fennel, and tarragon, as well as the shrubby lemon verbena.

Basil is almost everyone's favorite herb, and it's easy to grow with a couple of tips up your sleeve. If you can grow basil, you'll be fine with lemongrass and oregano, as similar rules apply. If growing these herbs outside—and that's a good place to do it, with less of a risk of whitefly than in a hot contained environment—don't plant them out until you are happy to have supper in the garden. If it's warm enough for you, it's warm enough for them. If you try to put your plants out too early in summer, or leave them out too late, the foliage and stems turn black and stop growing. In the early autumn, dig up your plants with a good-sized root ball and pot them up for picking inside. Dill is a little hardier and will survive for longer in the garden, but bringing the sun-lovers under cover will keep them going for a few more weeks.

If you want to keep your plants growing fast, keep them well watered, dousing them in the morning, not in the evening. With basil in particular, if the leaves are damp, slugs and snails have a feast after dark, so plants are best left dry overnight. This will also help discourage mold.

There are many varieties of basil to choose from, but the most intense aromatic variety is 'Sweet Genovese'. I'm also addicted to 'Mrs. Burns' Lemon Basil'. It makes delicious herb tea, from a handful of leaves soaked in boiling water for 5 minutes. Basil is also easy to grow from cuttings. Any time during the summer, cut your plant back and wait for it to resprout to 1 to 1½ inches. Then take your cuttings, strip their lower leaves, and put the remaining stalk with leaf tips into water. In a short time roots will appear.

With oregano, it's the annual variety you want, not the perennial form, which looks good, but has less flavor. For mint, I grow 'Bowles' mint, also called apple mint, with furry leaves, and spearmint for cooking and salads, as well as Moroccan peppermint for tea. These perennial herbs need to be cut back often to keep them coming. They also benefit from a potash-rich feed a couple of times during the summer and cutting to within 2 to 3 inches of the ground in June. They will quickly resprout, and then provide you with plenty of fresh leaves to pick right through the summer into the autumn.

Basil ice cream

I first had this at the wonderful Amsterdam restaurant, De Kas. There they use sweet Genovese basil, but I also love making this with Mrs. Burns' Lemon Basil.

Yield: about 4 quarts
2 large bunches of fresh basil
5 cups superfine sugar
2½ cups mascarpone cheese
2½ quarts (or 85 ounces) plain yogurt

Pick the leaves from the basil stems and blend them with the sugar in a food processor. Combine with the other ingredients and pour the mixture into an ice cream maker. Freeze/churn for about 20 minutes and either serve immediately or pack into plastic containers for the freezer.

Allow the ice cream 15 minutes in the fridge before serving. This has a wonderful flavor if it is eaten as fresh as possible. Don't store it for too long in the freezer.

Basil custards

Another creamy basil dish, from *The Cook's Garden* by Lynda Brown, this is perfect for lunch or as a first course for dinner. I add pesto and a little Parmesan. The custards are best served warm, turned out onto plates, with the fresh tomato sauce and some toast or bread.

Serves 4
A small handful of basil leaves, stripped from their stalks
2 large eggs
¾ cup whole milk
4 level tablespoons plain yogurt
1 large teaspoon pesto (see page 225)
2 ounces grated Parmesan cheese
Salt and pepper

For the sauce:
½ pound ripe tomatoes, skinned and deseeded (see page 266)
1 to 2 tablespoons butter
1 garlic clove, peeled

Preheat the oven to 325°F and butter 4 ramekins.

Coarsely chop the basil and then put it with the eggs, milk, yogurt, pesto, Parmesan, and seasoning into a blender or food processor. Process until smooth.

Divide among the ramekins. Put them in a shallow pan and add hot water to come halfway up the side of the dishes. Bake for about 20 minutes, until the center feels just firm to the touch.

Meanwhile, prepare the tomatoes and cook them gently in the butter with the garlic for 5 to 7 minutes. Remove the garlic and blend.

Let the custards cool a little, run a knife around the edge, and invert onto warm plates, giving them a gentle shake downwards.

Spoon the tomato sauce around the custards and serve.

Gravlax

You can always buy gravlax, but as long as you think about it well ahead, it's easy to make and a fraction of the price of ready prepared. Serve it scattered with coarsely chopped dill, dill and mustard sauce, and Buckwheat pancakes (see right). Gravlax is excellent with Cranberry vodka (see page 418).

Serves 6 to 8
For the marinade:
1 heaped tablespoon sea salt
1 heaped tablespoon superfine
   sugar
1 teaspoon black or white
   peppercorns, coarsely crushed
1 tablespoon Calvados or brandy
Plenty of chopped dill

2 pounds tailpiece of salmon in
   two pieces, scaled, boned, and
   filleted, but with the skin on
Large bunch of dill

For the dill and mustard sauce:
1 egg yolk
2 tablespoons Dijon mustard
½ teaspoon sugar
1 tablespoon white wine or
   white wine vinegar
6 tablespoons vegetable oil
Salt and pepper
Small bunch of chopped dill

Prepare the marinade by mixing all the ingredients together in a small bowl. Line a shallow dish with plastic wrap and put a quarter of the marinade into the bottom of the dish. Lay the first piece of salmon, skin side down, on the marinade. Scatter half the dill over it.

Cover the salmon with half the remaining marinade, rub the marinade into the flesh, and then lay the second piece of salmon on it, with the skin side uppermost.

Cover with the remaining dill and marinade, rubbing the marinade well into the skin. Cover with plastic wrap and cover with a board weighed down with a heavy weight.

Chill for at least 12 hours, but 24 is even better.

Meanwhile, make the dill and mustard sauce. Beat the egg yolk with the mustard and sugar, and stir in the wine or vinegar. Slowly beat in the oil until the sauce emulsifies (see page 233). Add salt, pepper, and the chopped dill. Chill.

Drain the salmon from the marinade and slice it thinly with a very sharp knife. Serve with the sauce and buckwheat pancakes.

Buckwheat pancakes

I love making real blinis with whisked egg white, but these pancakes are quicker and easier to make. If you want, you can make a huge batch and freeze them. These taste delicious with Gravlax (see left).

Yield: about 16 to 20 pancakes
2 eggs
1 cup milk
3 tablespoons butter, melted
   and cooled
⅔ cup buckwheat flour
2½ teaspoons baking powder
½ teaspoon salt

Mix the eggs, milk, and melted butter in a bowl and whisk until smooth. Sift the flour, baking powder, and salt into another bowl. Make a well in the middle and gradually add the egg mixture and beat together until smooth. Leave for at least 2 hours, or overnight if possible.

Heat a nonstick frying pan and put in a tiny bit of oil or butter to coat. Use a large tablespoon as a measure and ladle 4 individual dollops of batter into the pan. Leave the pancakes to cook for a minute or two, until you see them begin to bubble on top and set. Then flip them over and cook for a slightly shorter time on the other side.

Keep warm in a napkin or kitchen towel while you make the rest.

Basil oil

I enjoy making a few bottles of basil oil at this time of year to give as presents at Christmas, and for adding flavor to winter salads. There are many different recipes for basil oil, but I like this one from Jane Dunn, who runs the lovely hotel near us, Stone House in Rushlake Green. Very good expensive olive oil is often recommended, but it seems wasted to me when what you're after is the flavor of the basil. This oil is a beautiful emerald green.

Yield: about 2 cups
Large handful of basil leaves
Iced water
1 cup sunflower oil
1 cup mild olive oil

Blanch the basil leaves briefly and put them into iced water.

Dry the leaves, using a paper towel. Put both the oils in a food processor, add the basil leaves, and process for about 3 minutes.

Transfer to a jug and leave in the fridge for a week.

Strain through a cheesecloth and then pour into a sterilized bottle and seal. This keeps for a couple of months. Once open, store in the fridge.

Ricotta al forno

This is my favorite recipe from the famous River Café in London. When I was a waitress there twenty years ago, I made this all the time and I still love it. It's rich and yet fresh—wonderful with bread and a crunchy green salad. Sometimes I make it with olives, sometimes without.

Serves 6
1 to 2 tablespoons butter
5 ounces Parmesan cheese, grated, plus more for the tart pan
2 handfuls of fresh basil
Handful of mint
Handful of flat-leaf parsley
1 pound fresh ricotta cheese
½ cup heavy cream
2 eggs
Salt and pepper
12 black olives, pitted and chopped

Preheat the oven to 375°F.

Grease an 11-inch springform pan using a little soft butter and then coat the buttered surface with a little grated Parmesan cheese. Shake off any excess cheese.

Put the herbs into a food processor with half the ricotta and half the cream. Blend until bright green. Add the rest of the ricotta and cream, and, while blending, add the eggs one by one. Season with salt and pepper and finally fold in the 5 ounces grated Parmesan.

Spoon the mixture into the prepared tin and spread the olives over the top.

Bake in the preheated oven for 20 minutes. It should rise and have a brown crust but the center should be soft. Serve immediately.

Marcella's homemade pesto

I use pesto in many recipes and hugely prefer the fresher taste of homemade to the bottled variety. Mix pesto with extra cheese to stuff baked potatoes (see page 339), have a dollop of it with grilled fish, and put a teaspoon on big tomatoes when you bake them in the oven. This version is based on author Marcella Hazan's recipe, although she adds 3 tablespoons of softened butter and I never do.

Serves 6

¼ pound fresh sweet basil
½ cup extra virgin olive oil
¼ cup pine nuts
2 garlic cloves, finely chopped
Salt
2 ounces Parmesan cheese, grated
2 tablespoons grated pecorino cheese

Put the basil, olive oil, pine nuts, chopped garlic cloves, and salt to taste into a food processor and blend, stopping from time to time to scrape the ingredients down towards the bottom of the bowl with a rubber spatula.

When evenly blended, pour into a mixing bowl and beat in the two grated cheeses by hand. Add a little more olive oil if necessary.

If you want to store the pesto, put it into a jar, smooth off the top with the back of a teaspoon, and cover completely with a thin layer of olive oil. Keep it in the fridge and it will last for several months.

After using some from the jar, make sure that there is still sufficient olive oil to cover the top completely. This will keep it fresh and prevent it from losing its color.

Before spooning the pesto over pasta, add a tablespoon or two of the pasta water.

Verveine sorbet

This is a delicious, sparkly-fresh sorbet, ideal for supper after a hot day. To give it a real punch, you need to use a lot of lemon verbena.

Serves 4

1 cup superfine sugar
About 80 lemon verbena leaves
1 cup dry white wine
Juice of 2 lemons

Make a syrup by dissolving the sugar in 2 cups water and then boiling hard for 7 minutes.

Wash and dry the lemon verbena leaves. Put them in a saucepan with the syrup and 1 cup water, and bring gently to a boil.

As soon as the mixture reaches the boiling point, draw the saucepan off the heat, pour the mixture into a bowl, and add the wine and lemon juice.

Cover and, when cool, put it in the fridge to steep overnight.

The next day, strain the liquid, put into an ice cream maker, and freeze/churn for 20 minutes, or until it is the right consistency to scrape into containers for the freezer. If you don't have an ice cream maker, put it into a plastic container and freeze, breaking up the ice particles a couple of times with a fork at 2-hour intervals.

This sorbet needs at least 3 hours in the freezer before you use it.

Take the sorbet out of the freezer and put in the fridge for half an hour before serving.

Whole fish stuffed with fennel

This is one of my favorite dinners: whole fish—sea bream, sea bass, or salmon—absolutely fresh, with the cavity crammed full of fennel leaves, barbecued over fennel stalks, and served with a salsa verde. It's also lovely with Lemongrass rice (see right).

Serves 6 to 8
- **4- to 4½-pound whole fish (see above)**
- **1 lemon, thinly sliced**
- **Large bunch of fennel**

For the salsa verde:
- **⅔ cup olive oil**
- **Juice and grated zest of 1 lemon**
- **About 5 stems and leaves of fennel**
- **2 tablespoons capers (ideally dry-salted), rinsed**
- **About 8 stems of flat-leaf parsley**
- **About 6 chives**
- **About 2 stems of summer savory**
- **About 3 stems of cilantro**

Light the barbecue or heat a grill pan until it's providing a constant low to medium heat.

Stuff the cavity of the fish with the lemon slices and as much fennel as you can fit into it.

Arrange a base of thick fennel stems (with a girth the size of the base of an average thumb—they then shouldn't ignite) and lay the fish on top of that.

Barbecue or grill it until the flesh is cooked to taste.

To make the salsa verde, put all the ingredients in a food processor and blitz for 5 seconds.

Lemongrass rice

The perfect accompaniment to barbecued or grilled fish or chicken. Just add a green salad.

Serves 6 to 8
- **1 onion, chopped**
- **2 garlic cloves, chopped**
- **2 small red chilis, chopped**
- **2½ cups basmati rice**
- **Salt and pepper**
- **2 lemongrass sticks, cut lengthwise and bruised**
- **Juice of 1 lime**

Blend the onion, garlic, and chilis to a paste.

Rinse the rice thoroughly under cold running water and place in a pan with a tight-fitting lid. Add enough water to cover it by 1 inch and some salt. Add the lemongrass and bring to a boil. Cover, reduce the heat, and simmer gently until all the water has been absorbed.

Fluff up the rice with a fork and stir in the chili paste. Cook over very low heat for a further 4 to 5 minutes.

Before serving, adjust the seasoning and lastly squeeze over the lime juice.

Lemongrass cordial

Lemongrass makes the most wonderful tea with a few leaves steeped in boiling water for 5 minutes. It also makes a delicious, thirst-quenching summer drink.

You can make it from the base of the lemongrass stems for sale in any supermarket, but if you grow your own lemongrass (which is easy to do from seed—see page 218), use the green, grassy part as well. You can marinate any fresh fruit in it; it's particularly delicious with melon (see page 234).

Yield: One 750ml bottle
   3 lemongrass sticks
   2-inch piece of fresh ginger
   2½ cups sugar
   Juice of 3 large lemons (to taste)

Chop the tips off the lemongrass and bruise the base with a heavy knife or mallet before slicing thinly. Peel the ginger and slice it. Put these into a saucepan over low heat with the sugar and 2½ cups water. Stir until the sugar has completely dissolved before raising the heat and then allow to simmer for 5 to 6 minutes.

Remove from the heat, add the lemon juice, and, when quite cold, strain into a screw-top bottle. Keep it in the fridge until needed, for up to about a month.

Serve as a cordial, with thin slices of lemon or lime, and filling the glasses with water—flat or fizzy— or tonic water.

Halloumi, mint, cilantro, and dill pitas

Ideal for a quick lunch or supper (or even better for a picnic around the fire), these are delicious pockets of herbs and salty toasted halloumi cheese. A great friend and cook, Ivan Samarine, made this for me, having had something like it in an Uzbek café in Moscow.

Serves 6
   8 ounces halloumi cheese
   6 pita breads
   Good bunch of dill
   Good bunch of mint
   Good bunch of cilantro
   2 tablespoons good fruity olive oil

Cut the halloumi into slices about ½ inch thick and grill or fry the slices until warm and beginning to melt.

At the same time, warm the pitas on the grill or covered in foil in the oven and then cut them open lengthwise. Strip the herb leaves and chop finely.

Stuff each pita with 3 to 4 slices of halloumi and a good fistful of the mixed herbs, then drizzle with a little olive oil.

Mint potato cakes

We ate these fantastic potato cakes sitting in a café in the Amari valley in Crete. They were served with a sharp ewes' milk yogurt dressing flavored with fresh mint leaves.

Yield: 8 potato cakes
   **1 pound potatoes (floury kinds
      are best)**
   1 onion
   2 tablespoons butter
   2 eggs
   Small handful of mint, chopped
   4 ounces feta cheese, crumbled
   2 tablespoons all-purpose flour
   Salt and pepper
   3 tablespoons olive oil

For the mint yogurt dressing:
   Small handful of chopped mint
   1 cup tangy yogurt
   Juice of 1 lemon
   **1 tablespoon fruity extra virgin
      olive oil**

Peel and grate the potatoes.
   Slice the onion very thinly and sweat it in a little butter to soften. Lightly beat the eggs and mix with the mint, feta, and flour, then add the potatoes and onion. Season and mix well.
   Flour your hands and make flat patties out of good dollops (about 2 tablespoons each) of the mixture. Fry these gently in olive oil on both sides for 5 to 7 minutes, until golden brown.
   To make the dressing, crush the mint, using a mortar and pestle. Add the yogurt and thin with the lemon juice and olive oil to the consistency of heavy cream.

Mint-and-gingerade

Another simple and delicious drink, based on a recipe from Bill Granger's book *Sydney Food*. This is good hot, but even better cold with lots of ice on a hot day.

Serves 4
   1 quart boiling water
   **Good handful of mint leaves,
      chopped, plus more as a
      garnish**
   Grated zest of 2 lemons
   **2 tablespoons peeled and grated
      fresh ginger**
   3 tablespoons sugar

Pour the boiling water over the mint, lemon zest, and ginger in a heatproof jug. Add the sugar and stir until it has completely dissolved.
   Allow the mixture to cool, sieve, and then pour it into glasses full of ice and a few fresh mint leaves.

Mint julep

This classic summer drink is good for a party or sipped on a porch.

Yield: 1 glass
   12 mint leaves
   Crushed ice
   **1 tablespoon sugar syrup (see
      page 225)**
   3 tablespoons bourbon
   **Thinly pared lemon rind (use a
      potato peeler)**

Put the mint leaves into the bottom of a tumbler and bruise with a spoon.
   Fill the glass with crushed ice and add the sugar syrup, bourbon, and lemon rind. Stir thoroughly. Decorate with mint leaves.

Mint and apple compote

Strongly flavored, sharp, and delicious, this compote is delicious served with cold meat. It's also lovely with Moussaka (see page 301) and simple shepherd's pie.

Yield: 3 jars
- **2 pounds apples**
- **2 lemons, plus juice of ½ lemon, for the water**
- **A good handful of peppermint leaves, chopped**
- **4½ cups superfine sugar**

Peel and slice the apples, and then put them in a bowl of water acidulated with lemon juice.

Drain the apple slices and put them in a large pan with the zest and juice of 1 lemon, the mint leaves, and 1 tablespoon of sugar. Bring this slowly to a boil, stirring from time to time, until the apples are soft. Skim the top as any scum forms.

Push the mixture through a coarse sieve or food mill to give you a green puree. Add the rest of the sugar and juice of the other lemon.

Cook the puree, stirring, until it has the consistency of marmalade.

Pour into warm sterilized jars and seal. This will keep for up to a year, but refrigerate after opening.

Mint and apple jelly

Apple forms the base of many a good herb jelly. This classic mint jelly is a lovely color and particularly delicious with lamb.

Yield: 4 to 5 jars
- **4½ pounds cooking apples**
- **¾ cup white wine vinegar**
- **Bunch of mint, plus some more finely chopped mint**
- **Sugar (for exact quantity, see below)**

Roughly chop the apples and put into a bowl of water acidulated with a dash of the vinegar. Keep the cores and seeds.

When all the apples are chopped, drain them and put into a large preserving pot.

Cover the apples with water, tie up the cores and seeds in a cheesecloth bag, and then hang the bag in the liquid from the handle.

Add the bunch of mint to the apple mixture and bring to a boil. Add the vinegar and cook until the apples are very soft.

Pour into a jelly bag and leave to drip overnight. Don't squeeze the jelly bag as this spoils the clarity of the jelly.

Measure the amount of juice and for each 2½ cups of juice add 2½ cups of sugar.

Put the juice in the pan and stir over low heat until the sugar is completely dissolved. Then boil rapidly until the mixture reaches the gelling point. Keep a saucer in the fridge and to check for gelling, put a teaspoonful of the jelly on the cold saucer. When it cools it should wrinkle when you push it with your finger. Pull the pot off the heat while you test.

Skim the surface with a spoon in order to get rid of any scum and then add the finely chopped mint. Let the jelly stand for 20 minutes to cool. Stir it once more, pour into warm sterilized jars, and seal.

Leave for a week or two before using to give the mint flavor time to infuse. It will keep unopened for up to a year, but refrigerate after opening.

Tarragon vinegar

There's nothing better than tarragon vinegar, with that characteristic smoky flavor, for winter salad dressings. It makes the best ever hollandaise sauce (see right).

You need:

As much tarragon as you can pick (see below)

As much good white wine vinegar as you can get your hands on

Making this is as simple as it gets. Before the plants begin to die back in late summer, pick lots of tarragon. Blanch the tarragon instantly by plunging the stems into a pot of boiling water to kill any possible bugs. Then submerge the tarragon in the vinegar and leave it to steep for a month before straining. This keeps for years.

Tarragon hollandaise

Make a bowl of hollandaise sauce using tarragon vinegar and stir in some chopped tarragon. Dip in your new baby carrots, new potatoes, beets, and sugar snap peas. There are speedier ways of making this sauce, but in my experience they are more likely to go wrong. This works.

Serves 6

3 tablespoons tarragon vinegar (see left) or white wine vinegar
6 black peppercorns
1 bay leaf
2 egg yolks
5 tablespoons unsalted butter, cut into small chunks
Salt and black pepper
Bunch of tarragon, chopped

Boil the vinegar and 1 tablespoon of water with the peppercorns and the bay leaf until reduced to about 1 tablespoon. Allow to cool.

Fill a wide shallow pot halfway with water and bring to a simmer. Put the yolks in a heatproof bowl, sit this in the pan of water, and whisk well. Add the butter bit by bit, whisking all the time. As the mixture warms, it will gradually become thick and shiny.

Remove from the heat and stir in the cooled reduced vinegar, together with salt and pepper to taste, and the chopped tarragon. If the sauce ever looks as if it is splitting, remove it from the heat immediately and beat in a tablespoon of cold water or an ice cube.

This sauce is best served tepid but can be reheated in a bowl standing in a pan of simmering water, or it can be put into a Thermos until needed.

I prefer the taste of the reduced vinegar, but if you like you can skip this bit and just add lemon juice to taste once the sauce is ready.

Chicken in tarragon cream

This is a classic chicken dish, but remains one of the very best ways of using tarragon.

Serves 4

Olive oil
¼ cup (½ stick) butter
1 free-range chicken, cut into 8 pieces
1 shallot, finely chopped
¾ cup dry white wine or vermouth
1 cup crème fraîche
Bunch of tarragon, chopped
Salt and pepper

Heat the oil and butter in a large sauté pan and brown the chicken pieces all over. Cover the pan and cook over low heat—in the oven or on the stovetop— for 25 to 30 minutes, until the chicken is cooked through but still tender and moist.

Remove the chicken pieces from the pan, add the shallot, and cook gently for 5 minutes until softened.

Add the wine and cook for a further few minutes, scraping up the juices from the pan.

Return the chicken to the pan. Add the crème fraîche and the chopped tarragon. Season and cook for 2 minutes, until the cream is bubbling and thickened.

Melons

How do you tell when a melon is ripe? It's all in the smell. If you pick it up to smell the base of the fruit and get a waft of sweet honey, it means it's perfect. This is a particularly reliable guide for 'Ogen' or 'Charentais' melons, which are often the best and most worth seeking out. If the flesh gives a little when pressing the end, that's also a good sign. Melons will ripen a bit off the plant, but the nearer they are to perfection when picked and brought out of the sun, the better the flavor.

If melons are truly ripe and fragrant, they are lovely eaten as a first course or as dessert. Have them just as they are, the flesh scooped out with a spoon, or cut them into segments to eat with slices of prosciutto. Eat them as they do in France, with salt and pepper or with slices of ginger in a fresh fruit salad. Crunchy cubes of watermelon are excellent in salads with nutty pumpkin seeds, or try filling 'Ogen' melons with a mixture of alpine strawberries and redcurrants, sprinkled with superfine sugar and ginger syrup or liqueur. I love chunks marinated for an hour or two in two-thirds of a cup Lemongrass cordial (see page 228). If the melon is good, you can't go wrong and if the melon is disappointing, this will transform it.

Try and keep melons at room temperature, not in the fridge; but if you do need to store them in the fridge, wrap them well, or everything else will catch their flavor. Bring them out of the fridge at least half an hour before you eat.

Melon, pear, and arugula salad

Melon is fantastic in salad, the sweetness particularly good with the peppery taste of arugula. This is good as a light first course and it's lovely with salami, bresaola, and prosciutto.

Serves 6
- **1 ripe melon (any variety, or a mixture of watermelon and sweet melon)**
- **3 ripe but still firm pears**
- **4 ounces pecorino cheese**
- **2 tablespoons olive oil**
- **Juice of 3 limes and grated zest of 1 lime**
- **Salt and pepper**
- **½ teaspoon superfine sugar**
- **Large bunch of arugula**
- **1 red onion, very thinly sliced**
- **⅔ cup roasted pumpkin seeds (see page 372)**

Peel the melon, remove the seeds, and cut it into chunks. Peel and quarter the pears and make shavings of the pecorino.

In a bowl, combine the olive oil, lime juice and zest, salt, and sugar to taste, and mix well together.

Put the arugula, melon, pears, and thinly sliced onion into a large shallow serving bowl. Pour over just enough of the dressing to coat the leaves and fruit, and scatter over the pumpkin seeds and pecorino.

Add freshly ground pepper.

Teresa's melon with blackberries

Teresa Wallace, my twin sister's mother-in-law, made up this simple recipe when she had a glut of blackberries in her garden in Edinburgh one summer, and she froze bagfuls of them. Throughout the year she used them in various combinations. This one was the most delicious.

Serves 3 to 4
- **1 ripe Ogen or Cantaloupe melon**
- **1 pint blackberries, fresh or frozen**
- **Sprinkle of sugar, depending on the sweetness of the melon**
- **3 tablespoons Cassis (see page 170)**
- **A few mint leaves, torn up**

Peel and deseed the melon, and cut it into chunks. Mix gently with the blackberries. Sprinkle over a little sugar and the Cassis. Add the mint and put into the fridge for a few hours to chill. It's lovely very cold, straight from the fridge.

Melon and ginger sorbet

This is light, refreshing, and very quick and easy to make.

Serves 4
- **1 pound ripe melon flesh**
- **½ cup stem ginger (or candied ginger in syrup) with 1 tablespoon of its syrup**
- **1 cup sugar**

In a food processor, puree the melon and chill well. Chop the ginger and add to the melon with the ginger's syrup and the sugar. Put into an ice cream machine and freeze/churn for about 20 minutes. Serve immediately or pack into a plastic container and freeze.

New summer carrots

Carrots can really be divided into two different vegetables. There are large cold weather maincrop carrots and there are small tender summer roots, and they suit different recipes. The large ones have less sweetness and taste, and benefit from strong-flavored dressings or long cooking. They're delicious grated in a salad with poppy seeds (see page 430), or slow-roasted to eat with Cucumber raita (see page 196) and any roasted meat.

In contrast, summer carrots are lovely just washed and eaten raw or cooked very simply. Eat them as you pull them up, or use them in a bowl of crudités with cucumber, fennel, and radishes. On a big plate, fill three or four bowls with a variety of dips, such as Masai mara (see page 369), Baba ghanouj (see page 299), aioli (see page 137), and Hummus with cilantro (see page 85), and surround them with raw vegetables cut to finger size. If the carrots are very small, leave them as they are, or cut them in half, with an inch or so of the leaves left on.

Young carrots are also delicious steamed. Don't bother to peel them. Cook them for six to seven minutes so that they're still firm but not too crunchy, and eat them with butter and coarsely chopped lovage or fennel, or steam them for a couple of minutes and then stir-fry them as the Chinese do with lots of other vegetables. With this double-cooking technique, they keep their brilliant color and a bit of crunch.

I grow three varieties of summer carrots. 'Early Nantes', for my first batch in June, is followed by 'Sytan', which can be harvested throughout the summer. You can leave some of these in for harvesting later in the year.

Right through from late spring until the end of summer, I also try to have a row of the spherical 'Parabell' going. These are at their best slightly bigger than a walnut and are ideal blanched and then dipped in tempura batter (see page 207). This is also an excellent variety for those of us who garden on heavy soil. Most carrots prefer a light, sandy ground; not these—they grow happily almost anywhere.

Sally Clarke's carrots and peas

A recipe that is at its best with freshly shelled peas and young carrots.

Serves 4 to 6
- **¼ cup (½ stick) unsalted butter, cut into small pieces**
- **1¼ pounds young carrots, scrubbed and thinly sliced at an angle**
- **Salt and pepper**
- **1½ cups small shelled peas**
- **2 tablespoons chopped tarragon leaves**

Choose a nonstick pan, only a little larger than is necessary to hold all the ingredients quite snugly.

Put the butter in with the carrots and a little salt and pepper, and add about ⅔ cup water. Then add the peas and the tarragon. Cover with a circle of parchment paper and a lid and cook over medium to high heat until all but a drop of water has evaporated and the vegetables are tender.

Stir the vegetables with the syrupy juices. Garnish with more tarragon and serve immediately.

Riverford new summer carrots and turnips

Jane Baxter, cook at the Riverford Field Kitchen in Devon, created this recipe. She cooks the local primary school lunch and the children love these.

Serves 10 to 12
For the carrots:
- **2 pounds carrots with their tops, trimmed and cut lengthwise**
- **¼ cup (½ stick) butter**
- **1 teaspoon honey**
- **1 tablespoon balsamic vinegar**
- **1 tablespoon chopped parsley**

For the turnips:
- **1¼ pounds turnips, halved**
- **1 tablespoon balsamic vinegar**
- **1 tablespoon chopped parsley**
- **¼ cup (½ stick) butter**
- **1 tablespoon honey**

To cook the carrots, put them in a pan with the butter, honey, and 3 tablespoons of water and cook them over high heat until the mixture is simmering away.

Turn down the heat, cover, and simmer for about 10 minutes, frequently checking and stirring the carrots to make sure they don't stick and burn.

When they're almost cooked, uncover and increase the heat slightly, then add the balsamic vinegar. Stir to combine, turn off the heat, and add the chopped parsley.

Cook the turnips separately in the same way until just tender. Don't cook the vegetables together as they cook at different rates. When the carrots and turnips are both cooked, mix them together and serve.

Grilled new carrots

This is a lovely way to cook many different summer vegetables—new carrots, baby fennel, zucchini, and green beans. Cook them all together or on their own. Grilled carrots are very good with chicken and lamb.

Serves 4

1 pound small new carrots
Grated zest and juice of 1 lemon
⅔ cup olive oil
2 garlic cloves, chopped
Salt and pepper
Handful of flat-leaf parsley, chopped

Scrub the carrots and trim the leaves to about ½ an inch. If you can only find larger carrots, halve them lengthwise and blanch them for a couple of minutes before you put them into the marinade.

Put the lemon zest and juice, oil, garlic, salt and pepper into a bowl, and turn the carrots in this to coat them well. Leave while you preheat the barbecue or grill pan.

Grill the vegetables (reserving the dressing), turning them every few minutes, until they're just tender to the point of a sharp knife.

Transfer to a plate, pour over a little more of the dressing, and add the parsley. These are lovely warm or cold.

New carrots and potatoes roasted with garlic and thyme

New summer roots are infused with the flavor of shallots, garlic, caraway seed, lemon, and thyme in this wonderful mixed vegetable dish. If you're vegetarian, eat this with Cucumber raita (see page 196) and a green salad. It's also the perfect all-in-one vegetable dish to eat with strong-flavored fish or meat.

Serves 8 to 10

2 pounds new carrots
¾ pound shallots
1¼ pounds new potatoes
2 tablespoons olive oil
Bunch of thyme, plus some to serve
Grated zest of 1 lemon
1 teaspoon caraway seeds
1 head garlic
Salt and pepper

Preheat the oven to 350°F.

If they are small, leave the carrots whole, or halve them lengthwise if larger. Trim the carrot stalks to about ½ inch. Peel the shallots and scrub or peel the potatoes, but leave them whole.

Heat the olive oil in an ovenproof dish and toss together all the ingredients, except the garlic, to coat with the oil.

Break up the head of garlic without peeling the cloves and add to the dish.

Put into the preheated oven for at least 45 minutes, stirring from time to time, until the vegetables soften and begin to caramelize.

Season with salt and pepper, and throw over some more fresh thyme before serving.

Onions, shallots, and garlic

I rarely cook a meal without reaching for one or other of these bulbs. They are some of the most versatile vegetables in terms of flavor, changing from sharp and punchy when eaten raw to incredibly sweet, syrupy, and mellow if cooked for ages. There is a range of tastes, too, from the sweeter, mild red onion to the strong, large white.

The thing that can be painful with onions is the slicing. First, cut off the bottom—not the more logical top—and peel the onion, leaving the bit where the bulb joins the stem. Held intact, the onion's quicker to chop and the main gland, which releases the stuff that makes your eyes water, is at the top of the bulb not the bottom. It's there to protect the plant from being eaten by grazing animals.

Then cut down towards the top in slices as narrow as you can, before turning the onion around and slicing again at right angles to the first series of cuts, still down towards the tip. Now turn the whole thing on its side, holding the bulb so that it doesn't fall apart, and slice across in a plane at right angles to the first and second cuts.

The more you chop garlic, the stronger its taste. Chopping releases the enzymes responsible for its flavor, so if you want a mild taste, leave the garlic whole and in its skin, and remove it all together before you eat. If you want power, chop it finely and use lots. For garlic, my friend Katie Boxer has a brilliant technique. Peel a clove and—similar to the onion-chopping technique above—cut several times down vertically to the base of the clove, but leaving it intact. Then swivel it around a little and do the same thing, still vertically. Finally, put it on its side and chop the flesh from nose to root. It should by now be almost a pulp.

Full-sized onions are widely available and cheap, so if you don't have much room in your garden, don't grow them.

Shallots can be expensive, look fantastic in the spring garden, and are easy, so I like to grow them. And I grow scallions, interspersing 'White Lisbon' and a red-bulbed variety, 'North Holland Redmate', among my carrots to protect against pests. 'Redmate' is an excellent strong tasty variety, which will fill out to a good full-sized onion if you fail to eat your whole row at the scallion stage.

Clove and onion pasta

The secret to cooking onions so that they're sweet and delicious is long, slow, gentle frying, so that they almost melt without turning brown. With this pasta sauce, you gradually add red wine, glass by glass, waiting between each addition to let the liquid reduce right down.

Serves 6
- **1½ pounds white onions, thinly sliced**
- **2 garlic cloves, finely chopped**
- **10 cloves**
- **3 tablespoons olive oil**
- **¾ cup red wine**
- **20 ounces spaghetti**
- **Salt and pepper**
- **Small bunch of flat-leaf parsley**
- **¼ cup (½ stick) unsalted butter**
- **5 ounces grated Parmesan cheese**

Put the onions, garlic, and cloves in the olive oil in a heavy-bottomed pan over very low heat.

To cook onions safely without browning, cover the onions with a circle of parchment paper cut to fit inside your pan. This will keep the moisture in and allow the onions to cook until they are translucent and soft. This takes about 20 minutes on low heat.

Once the onions are cooked, start to add the red wine, bit by bit, allowing the onions to cook more briskly until any excess liquid has evaporated. Remove the cloves.

Meanwhile, cook your spaghetti in salted boiling water until al dente and drain.

Add the parsley and a chunk of unsalted butter to the sauce.

Serve with the spaghetti, plenty of grated Parmesan, and some freshly ground black pepper.

French onion soup

This is a classic, and a symbol of celebration in France, often cooked for a wedding or housewarming party.

Serves 4
- **10 tablespoons butter**
- **1¼ pounds onions, very thinly sliced, plus 2 extra onions, thinly sliced**
- **3 large garlic cloves, peeled**
- **1 tablespoon sugar**
- **5 cups good stock (any type except fish stock will do)**
- **¾ cup white wine**
- **Salt and pepper**
- **4 slices from a baguette, each about ½ inch thick**
- **Gruyère or Cheddar cheese, as a garnish**

Melt three-quarters of the butter in a heavy-bottomed pan and add the very thinly sliced onions. Cover with parchment paper and a lid, and sweat over low heat for about 10 minutes, until the onions have softened.

Remove the lid and add 2 of the garlic cloves, chopped, and the sugar. Stirring from time to time, allow the onions to become a good brown without letting them burn, which will take 10 to 15 minutes (the flavor of the soup depends on the onions' color, so don't hurry this stage). Stir in the stock and wine, and season carefully. Simmer for 30 minutes.

Meanwhile, fry the 2 extra onions in the remaining butter until dark brown and slightly crisp. Put to one side. Toast the bread and rub one side with the remaining garlic clove.

Taste the soup and adjust the seasoning. Fill some warmed earthenware bowls with the soup and float a piece of toast on the top. Grate the cheese over the toast and put the bowls under the broiler until the cheese is starting to melt. Scatter the crisp onions over the cheese and serve immediately.

Pissaladière

The sharp saltiness of this classic onion tart from the south of France is the perfect thing on a hot day, eaten with a crunchy green salad. It takes more time to make than the average onion tart, but its intense flavor—with anchovies, onions, Dijon mustard, olives, and tomatoes—makes it well worth the effort.

Serves 6
For the crust:
1¼ cups all-purpose flour
Salt
½ teaspoon ground cinnamon
6 tablespoons unsalted butter
1 egg, beaten
A little iced water, if necessary

For the filling:
2 pounds onions
3 garlic cloves
6 tablespoons olive oil
1 pound skinned chopped tomatoes (see page 266) or canned tomatoes
1 tablespoon tomato paste
1 teaspoon sugar
2 sprigs each of thyme and oregano
Dijon mustard
10 canned anchovy fillets, drained
A few black olives

Make the crust by sifting the flour, salt to taste, and cinnamon together. Then rub the butter into it until it resembles breadcrumbs. This can be done by hand or by pulsing in a food processor, but make sure that the butter is cold and cut into chunks before you add it to the flour. Then add the beaten egg and just enough iced water to make a dry dough, which you can form easily into a ball.

Roll out the pastry, put into a 9- or 10-inch ungreased tart pan, and chill in the fridge for half an hour.

Preheat the oven to 350°F. Prick the bottom of the crust all over with a fork, cover with a round of parchment paper or foil, and weight it down with some baking beans or rice. Bake the crust blind in the preheated oven for about 15 minutes, until it's cooked but not browned. Take from the oven, but leave the oven on at the same setting. Remove the beans or rice and the paper or foil and let the tart base cool.

To make the filling, slice the onions and chop the garlic. Sweat these in 6 tablespoons of oil slowly over low heat, without allowing them to brown, for about 20 minutes, until translucent and soft (see page 245).

Meanwhile, in a separate pan, cook the tomatoes, tomato paste, sugar, and herbs for about 20 minutes, until well reduced. Stir into the cooked onions and season.

Spread a thin layer of Dijon mustard over the base of the cooked crust and fill with the onion and tomato mixture. Arrange the anchovy fillets in a lattice pattern over the filled tart and then place a pitted black olive in every square.

Bake in the center of the preheated oven for about 20 minutes, brushing the top with olive oil halfway through the cooking time.

Serve warm or cold.

Onion tart from Beamish and McGlue

This is the most delicious tart from my cousin's shop in south London. It has more onions than usual—and lots and lots of nutmeg.

Serves 6 to 8
For the crust:
   1⅓ cups all-purpose flour
   Pinch of salt
   4 tablepoons shortening
   ¼ cup (½ stick) butter
   1 tablespoon grated Parmesan cheese
   1 egg yolk
   3 tablespoons cold water

For the filling:
   1 pound (usually 3 large) onions
   1 to 2 tablespoons butter
   1 tablespoon all-purpose flour

For the custard:
   1 egg plus 2 extra egg yolks
   ⅔ cup cream
   ⅔ cup milk
   Salt and pepper
   Plenty of freshly grated nutmeg
   4 ounces grated Cheddar cheese

Make the crust by combining the flour, salt, shortening, and butter, and pulsing in a processor or rubbing the flour and salt into the shortening and butter by hand until it resembles breadcrumbs. Add the grated Parmesan and mix well. Beat the egg yolk with a little cold water, and then add this to the flour mixture. Use just enough to make a soft, smooth dough that will hold together in a ball.

   Roll out the pastry on a floured surface and use to line a 9-inch tart pan. Put it in the fridge for 30 minutes to rest.

   Preheat the oven to 400ºF. Prick the bottom of the crust all over with a fork, cover with a round of parchment paper or foil, and weight it down with some baking beans or rice. Bake the crust blind in the preheated oven for about 15 minutes. Take from the oven. Remove the beans or rice and the paper or foil and let the crust cool. Turn off the oven.

   To make the filling, slice the onions thinly (a food processor is good for this, using the fine blade). Melt the butter, add the onions, and give them a good stir. Cook them gently on the lowest possible heat for as long as it takes for them to soften and caramelize a little, stirring occasionally. This can take upwards of an hour. If you want to speed things up, turn the heat up and stir them more frequently to stop them catching on the bottom. When they are soft and slightly caramelized, turn off the heat and stir in a level tablespoonful of flour.

   Towards the end of this process, preheat the oven again to 375ºF.

   Make the custard by beating or processing all the ingredients together, but leaving out a couple of tablespoons of the grated cheese. Then stir in the cooked onions with a fork and spread the mixture over the tart shell.

   Scatter the reserved cheese over the top to make it lovely and brown. Bake in the preheated oven for about 30 minutes.

Shallot tatin

You can make this fantastic tart with onions, too, but the sweetness of the shallots is what makes this recipe particularly delicious.

Serves 6
   1 pound shallots
   6 ounces any leftover soft cheese, such as Brie or Camembert
   3 tablespoons unsalted butter
   2 tablespoons olive oil
   1 tablespoon soft brown sugar
   Salt and pepper
   1 pound puff pastry

Preheat the oven to 400ºF.

   Peel the shallots, leaving them whole, and cut the cheese into fairly thick slices. Bring a pan of water to a boil, add the shallots, and cook them for 5 to 7 minutes if they are small and 10 if they are larger. Drain and put to one side.

   Heat the butter and oil in an ovenproof pan. When the butter has melted, sprinkle in the sugar and allow it to dissolve gently before adding the shallots. Season well and allow the shallots to cook until a rich golden caramel.

   Remove from the heat and roll out the pastry to a circle a bit bigger than the pan.

   Spread the slices of cheese over the shallots and lay the pastry over the top, pressing it down slightly all around the edge.

   Bake the tart in the preheated oven for about 25 minutes, or until risen and golden.

   Allow to cool a little and then put a large serving plate over the pan and invert it quickly so that the shallots are now on the top, with the pastry underneath.

   Serve the tart warm with a crisp green salad.

Shallot dressing

With its perfect sharp creaminess, this is the best possible dressing for a straight tomato salad.

Serves 4

1 shallot, finely chopped
2 tablespoons red wine vinegar
4 tablespoons olive oil
4 tablespoons crème fraîche
Salt and pepper

Combine all the ingredients together with a fork and toss with a salad.

Onions baked whole in parchment paper parcels

You have to wrestle a bit with the skins of the onions as you eat them, but the flavor of the onion within is wonderful. These are lovely eaten with roast beef, venison, or sausages and mashed potatoes.

Serves 6

6 medium-sized onions
A little olive oil
2 to 3 canned anchovies, drained and chopped
¼ cup (½ stick) butter
6 tablespoons balsamic or cider vinegar
Salt and pepper

Preheat the oven to 350°F.

Cut the base of the onions so that they stand upright and take the tops off with a sharp knife, but leave the skins on.

Oil 6 squares of parchment paper and lay each on a square of foil. Sit each onion on one of these.

Rub the onions with oil, snip 1 or 2 anchovies over each onion, dot with butter, and then pour over the vinegar and season with salt and pepper. Wrap up and squeeze the foil parcels to make bag shapes and put them into a shallow ovenproof dish. Cook in the preheated oven for 50 minutes.

Undo the parcels, transfer to a serving dish, and spoon the liquid over the onions.

Ingrid Marsh's spring onion and cilantro vichyssoise

A sharp, fragrant chilled vichyssoise that knocks the socks off the usual mix of leeks and potatoes.

Serves 4

1 pound potatoes
4 scallions, chopped (the tender green parts as well as the whites)
½ teaspoon freshly ground coriander seeds
¼ teaspoon Chinese five-spice powder
Salt and pepper
4 cups good chicken stock, heated
A small handful of fresh green cilantro leaves and stems
1 cup heavy or light cream
Squeeze of lemon juice

Peel the potatoes and grate them coarsely. Put them in a heavy-bottomed pan with the chopped scallions.

Add the coriander, Chinese five-spice powder, a good pinch of salt, and then a really good grinding of black pepper.

Pour on the heated stock and bring to a boil over low heat, stirring to prevent the potato starch from sticking to the base of the pan. Add the finely chopped cilantro stalks but not the leaves.

Cover the pan halfway with a lid and cook gently for about 10 minutes, until everything is tender. Let it cool for a few minutes.

Whiz to a perfectly smooth puree in a blender and stir the cream gradually into the puree. Allow to cool for at least 5 minutes, then chop the cilantro leaves finely and stir them in. Cover and chill for several hours or overnight.

Check the seasoning before serving. A little more salt or five-spice powder or a squeeze of lemon may be a good idea. This soup will keep for 2 to 3 days in the fridge.

Red onion marmalade

Sweet red onion marmalade is the perfect thing to eat for lunch with bread and cheese. A good dollop also transforms Potato salad with capers and anchovies (see page 124), and it's delicious with sausages and mashed potatoes.

Yield: 3 to 4 jars
- **2 garlic cloves**
- **Sea salt and black pepper**
- **4 tablespoons olive oil**
- **1 pound red onions, sliced**
- **4 tablespoons red wine**
- **4 tablespoons balsamic vinegar**
- **1 tablespoon soft brown sugar**
- **Few sprigs of thyme**

Crush the garlic with some sea salt and heat the olive oil in a heavy-bottomed saucepan. Add the onions and garlic, and sweat gently, without allowing them to brown, for 20 minutes. To cook onions safely without browning, cover the onions with a circle of parchment paper cut to fit inside your pan. This will keep the moisture in and allow the onions to cook until they are translucent and soft.

Add the red wine, balsamic vinegar, and brown sugar, and simmer gently until most of the liquid has evaporated, which will take about 15 to 20 minutes.

Add the thyme, season with salt and pepper, and cook for a further 5 minutes. Put into warm sterilized jars and cover while still hot.

This keeps well in the fridge for up to a month.

Sweet onion compote

Another version of onion marmalade, with more complex tastes and textures from the added fruit.

Yield: 3 to 4 jars
- **½ cup mixed dried fruit, such as raisins, apricots, and prunes**
- **1 cup orange juice**
- **1 pound white onions**
- **1 tablespoon olive oil or 1 tablespoon butter**
- **1 tablespoon brown sugar**
- **½ pound apples, peeled, cored, and sliced**
- **4 tablespoons balsamic vinegar**
- **Salt and black pepper**

Chop the mixed fruit and marinate in the orange juice for an hour or so.

Slice the onions and sweat in the olive oil or butter with the sugar over low heat until they become translucent and golden brown (see left).

Add the apples, mixed fruit, and vinegar, and cook for about 25 minutes, until most of the liquid has gone.

Season, put into warmed sterilized jars, and cover while still hot.

This keeps well in the fridge for up to a month.

White beans with garlic and thyme

This is the most delicious dish—all creamy and garlicky—to eat with roasted lamb. Add a good spoonful of Redcurrant or Rowan jelly (see pages 171 and 324) and some Slow-roasted winter roots (see page 424) and you've got one of my favorite meals. Dried beans, soaked overnight, give a better, less slushy texture than canned, but if you're cooking at the last minute, they are also fine.

Serves 6

- **1 pound white cannellini or green flageolet beans, soaked overnight, or 2 (15-ounce) cans**
- **4 garlic cloves, thinly sliced**
- **6 small onions or shallots, thinly sliced**
- **3 tomatoes, halved**
- **2 cups beef or lamb stock**
- **4 sprigs of thyme**
- **Salt and pepper**

Preheat the oven to 350°F. Put the beans, garlic, onions, tomatoes, stock, and thyme in an ovenproof pot. Bring to a boil, then cover and transfer to the oven and cook for an hour (if using canned beans cook for only 30 minutes).

Add salt and pepper and cook for another 20 minutes (or 10 minutes for canned beans).

Pizza bianca

The nicest kind of garlic bread is not that oily and soggy French loaf but the type of garlic bread you get in Italy. There you have a slightly fluffier than usual pizza base, with a little garlic butter spread over the top. That's how I make mine, sometimes adding herbs, sometimes not. This is fantastic with any soup, or for eating with salad, such as Niçoise salad (see page 210), for lunch.

Yield: 8 garlic breads
For the topping:
- **½ cup (1 stick) butter**
- **Bunch of thyme, marjoram, savory, or rosemary, finely chopped, plus some as a garnish**
- **2 garlic cloves, finely chopped**
- **Salt and pepper**
- **Sea salt, to serve**

For the bread:
- **4½ cups bread flour**
- **1 teaspoon salt**
- **1 packet active dry yeast**
- **About 1 cup lukewarm water**
- **2 tablespoons extra virgin olive oil**
- **½ teaspoon sugar**

Soften the butter by leaving it out of the fridge for half an hour, and then cut it into cubes and mash it up with a fork or in a food processor with the herbs and finely chopped garlic cloves. Season with salt and black pepper.

To make the bread, put the flour and salt into a large bowl. Dissolve the yeast in the warm water with the oil and sugar. Mix and leave for a couple of minutes, and you will see bubbles start to form.

Mix the yeast mixture with the flour. Knead the dough for 3 to 4 minutes and then leave it to rest underneath a damp kitchen towel for a couple of hours. It should at least double in size.

Preheat the oven to 400°F. Break off about a 1-inch-diameter ball of dough and, on a lightly floured surface, roll it out as thinly as you can. Repeat to make 7 more.

Bake in the oven, in batches, for about 10 minutes, until the tops turn golden brown.

While still hot, cut slashes at an angle across the top of the breads and brush over the garlic and herb butter.

Scatter with sea salt and some more fresh herbs.

Roasted garlic

Roasted garlic is a crucial ingredient
in many sauces and soups, giving a
gentle, rich taste, rather than the sharp
hit of raw garlic. By roasting it you
remove sulphur compounds, making it
milder and sweeter, and reducing the
after-eating smell. It transforms Tomato
soup and sauce (see pages 268 and
277). You'll really miss it if you don't add
it to Chilled pea soup (see page 133).
You can roast several heads of garlic at
once and store them in a jar of olive oil.
You can then also use the flavored oil
for salad dressings and sauces.

You need:
   1 whole head garlic
   Sprig of rosemary and/or thyme
   1 tablespoon olive oil
   Salt and pepper

Preheat the oven to 350°F.
      Put the garlic in a roasting dish,
sitting it on top of the thyme and/or
rosemary sprigs. Add a tablespoon
of oil and 2 tablespoons of water, and
sprinkle with salt and pepper.
      Put it in the preheated oven and
cook for 45 minutes.

Microwave roasted garlic

If you're in a hurry for your roasted
garlic, this technique is nifty.

You need:
   1 whole head garlic
   **4 tablespoons vegetable stock or
   water**
   Sprig of rosemary and/or thyme
   1 tablespoon olive oil

Put the head of garlic in a ceramic or
glass bowl and add the stock, herbs,
and olive oil. Cook in the microwave on
full power for 4 minutes and leave to
stand for 5 minutes before using it.

Plums and greengages

I love a plum eaten cold in the early morning straight from the branch, when the flesh is soft but not mushy. The thing about a plum is that it's much friendlier than an apple. Everything about it says, "Eat me," whereas an apple says, "I'm perfectly happy to sit here for a few days." It's no coincidence that the English have traditionally described something at its very best as a "real plum."

Plums thrive in mild and moist seasons, and a plum tree is one of the easiest, lowest-maintenance fruit trees you can grow. A typical plum tree will produce top-quality fruit for twenty years.

For me, the plum season runs from mid-July until September. Supermarkets often stock only one or two types, primarily the trusty 'Victoria'; to experience plums at their best, grow your own, or go to a good pick-your-own orchard.

The number one rule is to buy locally whenever you can and avoid the horrid large imported black plums with no flavor whatsoever. The first to crop for me is the delicious, early 'Opal'. This is harvested from mid-July until the middle of August. It has reddish purple skin, contrasting beautifully with its yellow flesh, and medium-sized, plump fruit. The flesh parts easily from the pit, which makes it brilliant for spectacular-looking plum tarts.

Next comes 'Czar'. This is described as a cooking plum, but when I went to Brogdale in Kent, which holds the National Fruit Collection, for a tasting, I loved the strong acidic flavor of 'Czar'. It's lovely raw or cooked. Another more recently bred, midseason plum is 'Avalon'. It has huge, exceptionally juicy and delicious fruit.

Then comes 'Victoria', our most commonly grown and popular plum. It's a midseason plum, peaking in mid-August, and is delicious eaten raw or cooked, but contrary to popular opinion, it is not the best for flavor or disease resistance, having problems with both canker and silver leaf. Most orchards finish fruiting with the late 'Marjorie's Seedling', picked from the end of September to mid-October. It's another you can eat raw or cooked, with very sweet yellow flesh and deep-purple, blushed-blue skin. It's a vigorous grower, with late blossoms that miss the frosts; so, in colder northern areas, this is the one for you.

My husband, Adam, is also passionate about greengages, which are smaller and sweeter than dessert plums, but also lower yielding and more temperamental, so increasingly rare. They make wonderful sorbet (see page 259) and delicious tarts and jams.

Roasted plums with homemade custard

Homemade custard tastes delicious with this pudding. Try it flavored with a few scented geranium leaves steeped in the milk. It's also excellent with the addition of a bay leaf or two.

Serves 4
For the roasted plums:
   2 pounds plums
   Grated zest and juice of 1 to 2
      oranges (for ½ cup of juice)
   Grated zest of 1 lemon
   2 bay leaves
   1 cinnamon stick, broken into two
   A few juniper berries (optional)
   ⅓ to ½ cup dark brown sugar

For the custard:
   6 egg yolks
   ½ cup superfine sugar
   2 cups milk

Cut the fruit in half, removing the pits, or leave whole. Preheat the oven to 350°F.

Put the plums into an ovenproof baking dish and add the orange zest, bay leaves, cinnamon, juniper berries, if using, and sugar, and pour over the orange juice enough to cover the bottom of the dish.

Bake in the preheated oven for 15 to 20 minutes, until the plums are tender. Allow to cool and then cover and chill until you need them. If you want a thicker syrup, transfer the plums to a serving dish and then boil up the juice in a small pan until thick and glossy.

To make the custard, mix the egg yolks and sugar together in a large bowl. Bring the milk to a boil and pour over the eggs and sugar. Combine thoroughly and return to the pan.

Over low heat, cook the mixture very gently, stirring constantly, until it thickens enough to coat the back of a spoon.

Remove from the heat and strain through a fine sieve.

Roasted plums with bread and butter pudding

The combination of a good slice of bread and butter pudding with the syrupy sauce and soft flesh of a few plums is one of the best ever late-summer desserts. One of the keys to a really good bread and butter pudding is good white bread—never use sliced—or you can use brioche or panettone.

Serves 10 to 12
   5 tablespoons unsalted butter
   8 slices good white bread,
      brioche, or panettone
   Golden raisins, soaked in a little
      whisky, dessert wine, or water
      (optional)
   1 vanilla pod
   2 cups heavy cream
   2 cups milk
   1 cup superfine sugar
   6 eggs
   4½ pounds plums, roasted (see
      left for ingredients and method)

Preheat the oven to 350°F. Butter an ovenproof dish.

Butter the slices of bread and arrange them in the dish with the soaked raisins, if using, scattered over them.

Split the vanilla pod and put into a saucepan with the cream and milk. Bring to a boil and put to one side.

Cream the sugar with the eggs until pale and thick, and add the hot cream (removing the vanilla pod) and beat together.

Strain the mixture over the bread and leave it to soak for half an hour or so, or until you are ready.

Place the ovenproof dish in a roasting tin, and fill a pan with boiling water to come halfway up the dish. Cook in the preheated oven for 45 minutes. When set and golden, remove from the oven and allow to stand. Serve warm with the roasted plums.

Best ever plum crumble

This recipe is really good for plums, damsons, greengages, and rhubarb—and, of course, wonderful with blackberry and apple. The nice thing about a crumble is the sharpness of the fruit with the sweetness of the topping, so don't oversweeten the fruit. If you are using sweet ripe plums or greengages, there is no need to add any sugar.

Serves 8
  4 pounds plums
  Grated zest and juice of 1 lemon
  ¼ to ½ cup sugar, depending on the sweetness of the fruit
  Greek yogurt or cream, as a garnish

For the crumble topping:
  1 cup all-purpose flour
  ¾ cup roughly chopped hazelnuts, toasted
  2 tablespoons oatmeal
  ½ teaspoon ground cinnamon
  ⅔ cup soft brown sugar
  ½ cup (1 stick) cold unsalted butter

Cut the fruit in half and remove the pits, and put into a shallow ovenproof dish. Grate over the lemon zest and pour over the juice. Add ¼ to ½ cup sugar only if the fruit is very tart. Preheat the oven to 325°F.

To make the crumble topping: put the flour, hazelnuts, oats, cinnamon, sugar, and cold unsalted butter, cut into chunks, into a food processor and pulse until the mixture resembles large breadcrumbs. This can be kept in the fridge until you want it, or put straight over the prepared fruit. Bake in the preheated oven for 30 minutes, until the topping is pale gold.

Crumble is much better served warm rather than hot, with cream or Greek yogurt.

Darina Allen's Tuscan plum tart

We tried many plum tarts and upside-down cakes, and this one of Darina Allen's from her Ballymaloe Cookery School was exceptional. She cooked it for us when she came to our school. Serve it with crème fraîche or softly whipped cream.

Serves 10 to 12
  2½ cups sugar
  2 pounds plums
  1 tablespoon butter, softened
  1½ cups self-rising flour
  3 eggs
  Vanilla ice cream, crème fraîche, or softly whipped cream, as a garnish

Use a 10-inch oven-safe sauté pan or a cast-iron skillet. Preheat the oven to 325°F.

Put 1¼ cups of the sugar and ⅔ cup water into the pan and stir over medium heat until the sugar dissolves, then cook without stirring until the sugar caramelizes to a rich golden brown.

Meanwhile, cut the plums in half and remove the pits. Then arrange, cut side down, in a single layer over the caramel in the pan.

Put the butter, remaining sugar, and flour into the bowl of a food processor and whiz for a second or two. Add the eggs and stop whizzing as soon as the mixture comes together. Spoon over the plums and spread gently in as even a layer as possible.

Bake in the preheated oven for about 1 hour. The center should be firm to the touch and the edges slightly shrunk from the sides of the pan.

Allow to rest in the pan for 4 to 5 minutes before flipping over.

Serve with vanilla ice cream, crème fraîche, or lightly whipped cream.

Plum sauce

This intense plum sauce can be used to brush on lamb, beef, pork, or fish before barbecuing or grilling. Use it too to enrich the juices of pork, duck, and goose, adding a lovely sweet-and-sour taste. Thinned a little with a light oil, it is also wonderful as a dipping sauce.

Yield: 2 cups
  1 pound ripe plums
  2 to 3 garlic cloves
  2 dried chilis or 1 fresh red chili
  3 heaping tablespoons soft brown sugar
  1 tablespoon grated ginger
  4 tablespoons soy sauce
  Salt

Cut the plums in half and remove their pits.

Chop the garlic and the chili; or, if you are using dried chilis, crush using a mortar and pestle.

Put all the ingredients into a heavy-bottomed saucepan and simmer for at least half an hour until rich and thick and most of the liquid has evaporated.

Pour into warm sterilized jars, seal, and cover. This keeps very well in the fridge for 3 to 4 weeks and freezes for up to a year.

Savory plum jam

I prefer plum jam that is not too set or too sweet, so that I can use it in a sandwich with Cheddar cheese or as a compote with yogurt, crème fraîche, or ice cream. If you prefer a traditional set, very sweet jam, use equal parts of sugar to fruit.

Yield: 3 to 4 jars
1¼ pounds plums (pitted weight)
5 cups sugar
1¼ cups warm water
1 tablespoon finely chopped candied ginger

Depending on the size of the fruit, halve or quarter your plums and remove the pits.

Put all the ingredients into a thick-bottomed preserving pot. Stir it all together and then allow to stand for an hour.

Warm the mixture slowly to dissolve the sugar completely, stirring regularly for the first 10 minutes.

Turn up the heat to bring the fruit to a rolling boil. Keep stirring if it's catching on the bottom and cook for about another 15 minutes, until the gelling point is reached (see page 170).

Pour into clean sterilized jars, cover, and seal. This jam stores for at least a year. Once opened, it should be kept in a fridge.

Greengage sorbet

An utterly delicious sorbet which is easy to make and tastes intensely of greengage plums.

Serves 6
⅔ cup sugar
Juice of 1 lemon
1½ pounds greengage plums

Bring ⅔ cup water and the sugar to a boil, and cook for 3 minutes. Allow to cool and add the lemon juice.

Preheat the oven to 350°F.

Either cut the greengages in half and remove the pits, or just leave them, pits, skins, and all, put them in an ovenproof dish, and cover with foil. They need no extra liquid.

Bake in the preheated oven until they are really soft and, if you have left the pits in, just pick them out with a knife and fork. Put everything into a food processor and process until you have a thick, smooth puree.

Add the cooled sugar syrup, process to combine, and put into a bowl. Cool and cover until you are ready to make the sorbet.

If you have an ice cream machine, empty the contents of the bowl into the machine and freeze/churn for about 15 to 20 minutes, until the mixture is thick but still easy to transfer into plastic containers for the freezer.

If you don't have a machine, pour the mixture into a plastic container, making sure that you have a depth of about 1½ to 2 inches at least. Cover and freeze. After an hour or so, beat or process the mixture and put back into the freezer. Repeat a couple more times over the next 4 hours and then cover and freeze until you want it. Allow the sorbet to thaw for about 20 minutes in the fridge before eating.

Raspberries, tayberries, and loganberries

When picking raspberries, there's that great moment when you lift a branch and find a perfect colony, missed by the person before, stiff with ripe fruit that drops easily into the palm of your hand. I love going with the children to a pick-your–own berry farm and gathering bowl after bowl of them. But rather than a pick-your-own, why not grow your own? You need space to grow raspberries, but not much time. They're one of the best low-maintenance, generally healthy fruit crops there are. The star performer among all current raspberry varieties for us is 'Glen Ample', which fruits throughout July. Its fruit is vast—almost twice the size of a normal raspberry—so you can pick a meal of these in half the time. But it also has great flavor—slightly tart and strong.

If you love raspberries, you may want to add an autumn-fruiting variety to extend the season. I've put in 'Autumn Bliss'. Despite new varieties arriving on the scene, this is still the autumn mainstay. Here it fruits—admittedly at quite a low level—from early August to mid- to late September, even sometimes into October, and the good thing about autumn raspberries is that you don't have to net. With so many berries and fruit around, the birds aren't usually interested.

To freeze raspberries, lay them out individually in one layer on a tray and put them in the freezer for a couple of hours. You can then bag them up and they will stay as single fruit, rather than disintegrate into a mush (as strawberries do).

Raspberries are wonderful, but I also want to grow loganberries. These have large, juicy fruit, plump and soft, about twice the size of a standard raspberry, with a tart flavor that reminds me of kiwi fruit. They are excellent cooked or raw, and have very good disease resistance, making them perfect for gardens. Plants will carry on fruiting for twenty-five years or more.

Tayberries and loganberries are close relations, both the result of a cross between a blackberry and a raspberry. Tayberries also have good flavor and disease resistance, but without quite the intensity of flavor of the loganberry. They do, however, produce massive yields, twice the weight of fruit per plant. There is now also a thornless variety available, which makes picking and pruning much easier.

Both of these fruits make superb jam and you can freeze them by the bagful to use in the winter. I make syrupy purees to go with vanilla ice cream and use them instead of blackberries mixed with tart apples in fruit crumbles and tarts. There is one big disadvantage to the tayberry: each berry has a large central core which usually remains attached to the calyx as you pick. The berries need to be picked through to remove this before eating or jamming, and that's a pain!

Meringue roulade with raspberries

Caroline Davenport-Thomas, who has cooked for our garden openings, makes this delicious dessert, ideal for feeding lots of people.

Serves 8
Sunflower oil, for the pan
6 egg whites
1½ cups superfine sugar
3 tablespoons sliced almonds
1½ cups heavy cream
2 cups fresh raspberries

Preheat the oven to 400°F.

Line a Swiss roll baking pan (or any shallow baking pan) with parchment paper and brush with a trace of sunflower oil.

Whisk the egg whites in a clean, dry bowl until very stiff. Gradually add the sugar, one tablespoon at a time, whisking between each spoonful. Once all the sugar has been added, continue whisking until the mixture is very thick and glossy.

Spread this meringue mixture into the prepared pan and scatter with sliced almonds. Place the tin fairly near the top of the preheated oven and bake for 8 minutes. Then lower the oven temperature to 325°F and bake until golden brown. Don't cook the meringue too long, or else it will be difficult to roll up.

Remove it from the oven and turn it, almond side down, onto a sheet of wax paper. Peel off the paper from the base of the cooked meringue and allow to cool for 10 to 15 minutes.

Whisk the cream until it stands in stiff peaks and gently mix in half the raspberries. Spread the cream and raspberries evenly over the meringue. Letting the wax paper help you, roll the long side fairly tightly until it is all rolled up like a roulade. Wrap in parchment paper and chill before serving. Scatter the rest of the raspberries over the top to serve.

Juicy summer pudding

As with bread and butter pudding, the best summer pudding is made with panettone or brioche, not cheap sliced white bread. It must also be juicy, with no white showing anywhere. You can use any combination of summer fruit, even gooseberries, but don't use too many blackcurrants, as they will dominate the flavor.

Serves 8 to 10
6 to 8 slices brioche or good (not ready-sliced) white bread
2 pounds mixed soft fruit, such as raspberries, redcurrants, and loganberries
½ to 1 cup superfine sugar, depending on taste
Cream, as a garnish

Rinse (but don't dry) a 4-cup (32-ounce) nonreactive bowl or soufflé dish with cold water. This makes it easier to turn out and helps spread the juice evenly. Cover the base and sides of the dish with the sliced brioche or bread, reserving some to cover the top.

Remove the stem ends of the fruit, and put in a pan over low heat. Sprinkle the sugar over the fruit and simmer for just 2 to 3 minutes, until the juice begins to run and the fruit is softened. Remove it from the heat and spoon the fruit mixture into the lined bowl.

Put in three-quarters of the juice and cover the top with a lid of brioche or bread. Put the remaining juice to one side.

Put a plate that fits the inside of the bowl on top. Place a weight on this and leave in the fridge overnight.

Remove the weight and plate and invert onto a flat dish. Pour the saved juice over the top of the pudding and serve with a bowl of cream.

Raspberry and redcurrant jam

This is the most fantastic color and hardly cooked, so the fruit stays almost whole. The redcurrants counter the sweetness of the raspberries, making the best ever raspberry jam.

Yield: 5 jars
- **1 pound sugar**
- **2 cups raspberries**
- **¾ cup redcurrants, stems and ends removed**

Warm the sugar in a bowl in a very low oven for half an hour.

Gently crush the fruit and warm it in a saucepan over low heat. Bring just to a boil and add the warmed sugar. Stir over low heat until dissolved and then boil fast for 3 to 4 minutes.

To test for the gelling point, put a saucer in the fridge to cool. Put a spoonful of the boiling jam on the saucer. Return the saucer to the fridge and, when it is cold, the jam should wrinkle when you push the surface with your finger.

Pour into warm sterilized jars. Cover with a wax disc and seal. Once open, store in the fridge.

Spectacular rice pudding with raspberry and redcurrant jam

Rice pudding is one of the best British desserts, particularly topped with Raspberry and redcurrant jam (see left). You need to prepare it a couple of hours before you want to eat, but it only takes 5 minutes to combine the ingredients.

Serves 4
- **2 tablespoons unsalted butter**
- **1 vanilla pod**
- **2½ cups whole milk**
- **2 tablespoons short-grain rice**
- **Freshly grated nutmeg**
- **2 tablespoons superfine sugar**
- **Heavy cream**
- **Raspberry and redcurrant jam, as a garnish**

Preheat the oven to 300°F. Butter an ovenproof dish.

Split the vanilla pod, put it in a saucepan with the milk, and bring this to a boil.

Rinse the rice and put it in the dish with some butter, grated nutmeg, and the sugar.

Remove the vanilla pod from the hot milk, pour the milk over the rice, and stir.

Put the ovenproof dish into the preheated oven and take out to stir two or three times over the next hour. After about an hour, stir in a good dollop of heavy cream and leave in the oven until the rice is quite cooked, but before all the liquid has been absorbed; this will take about 20 minutes. Keep checking, as you don't want it to be dry.

Serve with the Raspberry and redcurrant jam.

Tiramisu with red berries

Molly, my ten-year-old daughter, makes this dessert. It's also my husband Adam's favorite, and my middle stepson William chose it for his eighteenth birthday party, so it's popular here! Strictly speaking, a true tiramisu has alcohol in it and no fruit, but I leave out the alcohol—so that younger children can eat it—and add plenty of raspberries or, even better, tart loganberries to cut through the gooey creaminess.

Serves 12
- **½ cup superfine sugar**
- **4 eggs, separated**
- **1½ cups mascarpone cheese**
- **1 pound raspberries, loganberries, or tayberries**
- **14 ounces ladyfingers**
- **About 2 cups strong coffee, cold**
- **Cocoa powder**

Cream together the sugar and egg yolks. Add the mascarpone, and then beat the egg whites until stiff and fold into the mixture.

Put a layer of fruit in the bottom of a shallow dish and then prepare the ladyfingers. Douse these in the strong coffee by dipping rather than soaking them and arrange them in a layer over the top of the fruit.

Cover this with about half an inch of the mascarpone, making sure you cover the ladyfingers completely. Repeat these layers until you reach the top. With a sieve, dust the top with cocoa powder.

Put the tiramisu in the fridge for 3 to 4 hours for the tastes to amalgamate.

Tomatoes

Good tomatoes are the defining taste of summer, when their round, juicy softness comes into its own. The more of that just-picked, slightly acrid —almost poisonous—smell that they have the better. They are, after all, related to deadly nightshade.

When you're shopping, pick them up and sniff them. If they have a strong smell, they're likely to taste good. Tomatoes sold on the vine look lovely, but they're more expensive than those off the stem and they don't have better flavor. I picked a truss of 'Sungold' and left them on the stem and another that I stored as separate fruit. I tasted them both after three days and there was no difference at all. The ones still attached had a stronger tomato scent, but that came from the stem, not the fruit. It's the variety, if anything, that makes the difference and it may be that growers take more trouble with varieties they choose for selling on the vine, because they can charge more.

For eating raw, choose sweet cherry tomatoes or big juicy varieties. For stuffing and cooking, the drier-textured, almost seedless plum tomatoes are best. They keep their shape and when long cooked reduce to a sweet and intense tomato sauce. Whenever you can, select a mix of varieties with different colors, shapes, and sizes— you'll usually find several different types at farmers' markets. If you grow your own, go for an interesting range.

My top cherry tomato is the yellowy-orange 'Sungold', a heavy-cropping, healthy variety with small, very sweet fruit. My favorite large beefsteak is 'Costoluto Fiorentino', as well as the stalwart Russian variety 'Black Krim'. These are both full of flavor, and more prolific and easier to grow than the foodie favorite 'Brandywine'. Here, unless it's a very hot summer, 'Brandywine' tends to get end rot in the base of the fruit before it's ripe. I also like two heavy-producing plum tomatoes: 'Harlequin', with small to medium-sized fruit that need to be cooked, and the larger 'San Marzano'.

Don't store tomatoes in the fridge; it changes their texture and diminishes their taste. Keep them in a bowl somewhere warm. Skin tomatoes by pricking each one lightly with a sharp knife, then dropping them in a bowl of boiling water and leaving for 20 to 30 seconds. Scoop them out of the water with a perforated spoon and strip off the skin. If they're to be used raw, don't be tempted to leave them in the water too long or they'll start to cook. If the skins are difficult to remove, drop them back for another stint. On the whole, try not to deseed tomatoes. There's lots of flavor in the jelly around the seed, so process the whole fruit and then press through a food mill or sieve; this removes seeds but allows the jelly to get pushed through.

Baked tomatoes with cream

A friend of mine, Belinda Eade, first cooked this for me when we were at university. It's real comfort food—creamy and slightly sweet—and delicious eaten with new potatoes and a green salad, but I love it most with mashed potatoes or rice.

Serves 6
  2 tablespoons butter
  4½ pounds tomatoes
  3 tablespoons thyme leaves, chopped
  2 teaspoons sugar
  Salt and pepper
  2 garlic cloves, finely chopped
  ¾ cup heavy cream
  1 (2-ounce) can anchovies
  3 ounces Parmesan cheese, grated

Preheat the oven to 375°F. Lightly butter an ovenproof dish.

Skin and chop the large tomatoes, but leave the small ones whole and lay half of them out, tightly packed, in the buttered ovenproof dish. Scatter 1 tablespoon of thyme, 1 teaspoon of sugar, some salt, pepper, and half the garlic over the tomatoes. Add another layer of tomatoes and scatter the same amount of thyme, sugar, salt, pepper, and garlic over the top. Pour over the cream.

Add the remaining thyme, chopped anchovy fillets, and oil from their tin. Season with salt and pepper, and spread this mixture over the top. Finish by scattering little bits of the remaining butter and add the grated Parmesan. Bake in the preheated oven for 20 minutes, until the top is turning a nice brown.

Tomato soup

This recipe comes from my twin sister's mother-in-law, Teresa Wallace, via Mary Contini at Valvona and Crolla in Edinburgh, who in turn got it from La Potinière restaurant in Gullane, East Lothian. The soup is hugely tomatoey and fresh. It's ideal for making when you can buy huge quantities of rather battered, very ripe tomatoes cheaply. Make lots and freeze it. You can use port or Marsala (to add sweetness if the tomatoes are not tip-top quality) instead of sherry.

Serves 4 to 6
  ½ pound onions, chopped
  ¼ cup (½ stick) unsalted butter
  2 pounds tomatoes
  5 tablespoons dry sherry
  1 tablespoon sugar (optional, according to the quality of the tomatoes)
  3 tablespoons torn basil, plus some as a garnish
  Salt and pepper
  Vegetable stock (optional)
  A little cream, as a garnish

Sweat the onions very slowly in the butter. You don't want them to brown, but they should be cooked through. Add everything else except the cream and cook for about 10 minutes, until the tomatoes are softened. Whiz the soup in a blender and sieve, or push through a food mill. It will be fairly thick but can be thinned, if necessary, with some stock. Serve with a dribble of cream and more fresh basil.

Cleopatra's tomato soup

This is a South African recipe which makes a delicious rich tomato soup. It comes from Cleopatra's Mountain Farmhouse in the Drakensberg Mountains, the hotel belonging to Richard Poynton, a passionate cook. The ingredients list looks long, but it's very easy to make and it's as good cold as it is hot.

Serves 8

3¼ pounds ripe tomatoes
2 large onions, quartered
Generous drizzle of olive oil
Salt and pepper
3 garlic cloves, crushed
2 teaspoons grated ginger
½ small red chili, chopped, or 1 dried chili, crumbled
Bunch of cilantro, leaves and stems chopped, plus more to serve
1 (14-ounce) can tomato juice
2 (14-ounce) cans coconut milk
1 rounded tablespoon soft brown sugar
2 tablespoons Thai fish sauce
Bunch of fresh cilantro, to serve

Preheat the oven to 350°F and roast the tomatoes—you don't need to skin them—and onions with olive oil, salt, and black pepper for about 30 to 40 minutes, until slightly browned on the edges.

Meanwhile, heat a little olive oil in a saucepan and cook the garlic, ginger, chili, and cilantro (leaves and stems) for 3 to 4 minutes.

Add the tomato juice and coconut milk, and cook for a few minutes. Cover, remove from the heat, and allow the flavors to infuse.

Add the tomatoes, onions, sugar, fish sauce, and seasoning. Cover and simmer for 10 minutes.

Blend in a food processor and serve with plenty of fresh cilantro.

Gazpacho

This punchy garlicky soup, served very, very cold on a hot day, is absolutely delicious. The flavor improves if it is made the day before. You can use canned tomatoes, but the taste isn't the same as fresh.

Serves 6 to 8

3 to 4 thick slices good white bread, preferably a day old
2 garlic cloves
Generous drizzle of olive oil or equal parts olive oil and sunflower oil
1½ tablespoons red wine vinegar
1½ pounds tomatoes
2 sweet red peppers, bottled or fresh, grilled/roasted and skinned (see page 369)
1 large mild onion
1 cucumber
1¾ cups tomato juice
Salt and pepper
Iced water (optional)
A few fresh chives or a couple of ice cubes, as a garnish

Cut the crusts off the bread and discard. Tear the bread into small pieces in a large bowl. Crush the garlic and add it to the bread. Add just enough oil for the bread to absorb and then stir in the vinegar. Skin, deseed, and chop up the tomatoes.

Chop the roasted skinned peppers and roughly chop or grate the onion. Deseed and chop the cucumber. Add these to the bowl and mix well. Add the tomato juice and season with salt and pepper.

Blitz the whole thing with an immersion blender, or put the mixture into a food processor and process until it becomes quite smooth.

Check the seasoning and add iced water to get the consistency you want. Chill and serve very cold, with a few fresh chives or ice cubes.

Sungold tomato focaccia

This is a garden version of a focaccia recipe given to me by our local organic bakery—Judges in Hastings. It tastes deliciously of olive oil, which you slurp over and then press into the bread just before it goes into the oven. As Emmanuel Hadjiandreou from Judges says, this pressing action is like playing the piano, just using the tips of your fingers.

Serves 6 to 8

1 teaspoon active dry yeast
1¼ cups warm water
1 level teaspoon sea salt, and a little more for topping
2¾ cups bread flour
8 tablespoons olive oil
20 cherry tomatoes, such as Sungold, left whole
1 teaspoon rosemary leaves

In a large mixing bowl, dissolve the yeast in the warm water. Stir in the salt and all the flour to make a fairly sticky dough. If the dough is very soft it makes the yeast work more quickly and then you get the characteristic holes forming in the bread, so try not to add extra flour.

Cover it with plastic wrap and leave to rise for 30 to 45 minutes. When it has doubled its volume, add 2 tablespoons of the olive oil. Fold the dough in the bowl to integrate the oil and then cover again with plastic wrap and leave the dough to rise as before.

Repeat this whole process twice, each time adding another 2 tablespoons of the oil and folding.

When the dough has risen for the fourth time, place it on a small flat baking sheet (about 9 by 12 inches) lined with parchment paper or greased with olive oil. Push the dough out to the corners (it should be about ¾ inch thick) and then add another couple of tablespoons of olive oil and press it into the bread. You're aiming to make ¼-inch dents.

Cover the dough with a cloth and leave to rise again for another hour or so until it has doubled in volume and begun to bubble.

Preheat the oven to 400°F. Sprinkle the dough lightly with sea salt, scatter over the tomatoes and rosemary, and bake in the preheated oven. Place a heatproof bowl of water in the bottom of the oven. This creates steam, which gives a lighter, fluffier texture to the bread.

Bake until the focaccia has a nice golden color. Allow to cool for half an hour and then place on a wire rack to cool further.

Andalusian soup-salad

My mother found this recipe in a 1970s copy of *Vogue*. It's a kind of coarse gazpacho, with many of the same punchy raw ingredients. It is just as good the next day and even the day after that. If I'm making this for the children, I add less onion and leave out the chili. You can use tomato juice instead of tomatoes.

Serves 4 to 6

   2 pounds tomatoes (should give you about 4 cups tomato juice, but the quantity varies according to the ripeness and juiciness of the tomatoes), plus an extra 2 to 3 tomatoes
   4 eggs, hard-boiled
   1 teaspoon Dijon mustard
   4 tablespoons extra virgin olive oil
   2 tablespoons red wine vinegar
   2 garlic cloves, crushed
   1 slice good white bread that is a couple of days old, crusts removed, torn up
   ½ large cucumber, deseeded and chopped
   1 red pepper, roasted, peeled, deseeded, and chopped (see page 369) or 1 bottled pimento, drained and chopped
   4 scallions, thinly sliced
   1 mild chili, thinly sliced
   Salt and pepper

Start making this soup at least a couple of hours before you want to eat. Like gazpacho, it's best eaten really cold and so, once assembled, needs an hour or two in the fridge. Skin the 2 to 3 extra tomatoes (see page 266) and coarsely chop them.

Puree the rest of the tomatoes in a food processor and press through a sieve or food mill to get rid of the skin and seeds.

Shell the hard-boiled eggs and separate the whites from the yolks. In the bottom of a large bowl, mix the mustard, olive oil, vinegar, garlic, broken-up bread, and egg yolks to make a paste. Add all the chopped vegetables and then the tomato juice. Stir it all together.

Season with plenty of salt and pepper, and add the coarsely chopped egg whites before putting the soup in the fridge to chill.

Tabbouleh

I love tabbouleh made with only a little bulgur wheat, but lots of tomatoes, mint, and parsley. As in the fresh tabboulehs of Lebanese restaurants, the herbs and tomatoes should be flecked with bulgur, not the other way around. This is good with a plate of different meze—hummus (see pages 85 and 305), falafels, and Baba ghanouj (see page 299)—or serve it with roast or barbecued lamb.

Peeled chopped cucumber or chopped melon make delicious additions to this recipe. If you don't have homemade stock, use very weak organic bouillon or plain water.

Serves 4 to 6

   1 cup bulgur wheat
   1 cup boiling vegetable stock (enough to cover the bulgur)
   1 pound tomatoes, skinned (see page 266), deseeded, and cut into ¼-inch chunks
   Juice of 1 lemon
   2 tablespoons olive oil
   3 scallions, thinly sliced
   Large bunch of flat-leaf parsley, finely chopped, tops of stems included
   Bunch of mint, finely chopped
   ¼ teaspoon ground cinnamon
   ¼ teaspoon ground allspice
   Salt and pepper

Prepare the bulgur first by covering it with boiling vegetable stock. Leave the wheat to stand for 15 minutes in a covered bowl. Drain it, press with a spoon to get rid of any excess liquid, and let it cool.

Add the tomatoes, lemon juice, olive oil, scallions, and herbs. Finally add the spices and seasoning, then let it sit for half an hour to allow the flavors to meld before you eat.

Fattoush

This is a Lebanese dish similar to tabbouleh, but made with toasted flat bread, not bulgur wheat. This is a crunchier and more textured salad. You can make a robust and extra-delicious fattoush with olive and thyme tapenade (see page 49) spread over the flat bread before it goes into the salad. This is also good eaten with hummus (see pages 85 and 305) or Baba ghanouj (see page 299) and more hot pita bread.

Serves 4

2 to 3 pita breads
½ pound cucumbers
¾ pound tomatoes
2 handfuls of flat-leaf parsley, finely chopped
2 handfuls of mint, finely chopped
¼ pound radishes
3 scallions
2 tablespoons olive oil
Juice of 1 lemon
Salt and pepper

Toast the pita breads in a single layer in a hot oven for 10 minutes until they're crisp. You may need to cook them for 10 minutes and then split the two sides, break them into bits, and put them back into the oven for another couple of minutes to get them properly crunchy.

Peel the cucumber, halve, and deseed it, then cut it into ½-inch chunks. Skin the tomatoes (see page 266), then thinly slice the radishes and scallions.

Break up the toasted pita into small chunks and combine these with the vegetables, herbs, oil, lemon juice, and seasoning in a shallow bowl.

If you want to add tapenade, spread this onto the pita after you've toasted it, before breaking it up into chunks and adding to the salad.

Saganaki

This Cretan shepherd's dish of baked feta with tomatoes is simple and delicious, its salty flavor offset by the odd sweet burst of tomato. You can cook it in foil parcels on a griddle or in a fire, or bake it quickly in a shallow heatproof dish. A warm flat bread, straight from the oven, works well with this dish (see page 46).

Serves 6

3 (8-ounce) packs feta cheese, broken into rough ½-inch pieces
20 large or 30 small cherry tomatoes
20 capers
15 kalamata olives, halved and pitted
2 tablespoons olive oil
6 sprigs of thyme or marjoram

To make the saganaki as individual parcels for cooking on an open fire or grill, place about half a packet of feta on a square of foil. Add a few cherry tomatoes, a teaspoon of capers, and 3 olives, and drizzle with a little olive oil. If using larger tomatoes, cut them up into cherry tomato–sized cubes.

Put a sprig of the herbs on top and fold up the parcel loosely. Cook in the fire or on the grill for 10 to 15 minutes.

If you want a communal dish in the middle of the table, preheat the oven to 400°F, put the cheese into a shallow ovenproof dish with everything else, and bake it in the hot oven for about 15 minutes until the cheese is bubbling and browning on top. This must be eaten hot or warm.

Panzanella

When I worked as a waitress at London's River Cafe, this was one of the first recipes I learned. Using bread in a salad may seem odd, and you might think it would be heavy, but this is one of the best summer tomato salads.

Serves 4 as a main course,
8 as a starter

2 pounds ripe tomatoes
2 thick slices coarse white bread,
**   such as Pugliese or ciabatta**
2 garlic cloves, crushed
Salt and pepper
3 tablespoons extra virgin olive oil
2 tablespoons red wine vinegar
1 generous tablespoon capers,
**   roughly chopped**
1 (2-ounce) can anchovies, drained
**   and roughly chopped**
1 small red onion, very thinly sliced
12 black olives, pitted
Large bunch of basil (sweet and
**   purple if you can find it), roughly**
**   chopped**
Large bunch of flat-leaf parsley,
**   roughly chopped**
2 mild fresh red chilis, thinly sliced
**   (optional)**

Skin the tomatoes (see page 266). Put one large tomato aside and deseed and roughly chop the rest. Place the chopped tomatoes in a sieve over a bowl to catch any juices.

Tear the slices of bread into small chunks and put them in a large bowl. Season the collected tomato juice with garlic, salt, pepper, oil, and vinegar, and pour this over the bread. Add the tomatoes and then stir a little. If the bread still looks dry, add more oil.

Put a layer of the bread and tomato mix on a large plate and add some capers, anchovies, onions, olives, herbs, and, if you want them, chilis. Then add another layer of bread and tomatoes, then more capers, anchovies, olives, and so on.

Leave the panzanella for at least an hour to let the different tastes soak into the bread before you eat. Add a few more leaves of fresh basil and one freshly chopped tomato just before serving.

Raw tomato pasta

This is one of the simplest things you can do with tomatoes, but they need to be really tip-top. We eat this at least once a week in July and August, when the greenhouse is full of varieties like Black Krim and Costoluto Fiorentino. It's worth using a good oil: you'll really taste the fruity flavor.

Serves 4
  2 pounds tomatoes
  1 tablespoon coarse rock salt
  ½ cup extra virgin cold pressed olive oil
  2 garlic cloves, finely chopped
  Grated zest and juice of 1 lemon
  12 ounces pasta
  Small bunch of basil leaves, torn
  Grated Parmesan cheese, to serve

Peel (see page 266) and halve the tomatoes, then deseed with a teaspoon and chop them into chunks. Scatter the rock salt over them and leave them to drain in a colander for half an hour to get rid of some of their juice.

Move the tomatoes to a pan and mix them with the olive oil, garlic, lemon zest, and juice, and heat just to warm the sauce but not cook it.

Cook the pasta in salted boiling water until al dente, drain, and stir in the tomato mixture along with the torn basil leaves.

Serve with plenty of freshly grated Parmesan.

Really rich tomato sauce

This is an excellent tomato sauce, which forms the basis of many different dishes. Spread it on Pizza (see page 281), use it for Moussaka (see page 301), or serve it as it is with pasta.

Serves 8 to 10
  2 pounds tomatoes
  1 large onion
  2 garlic cloves
  2 tablespoons olive oil
  1 tablespoon tomato paste
  1 heaping tablespoon chopped fresh oregano
  1 large teaspoon sugar
  ¾ cup red wine
  Salt and pepper

Skin the tomatoes (see page 266) and chop them roughly. Chop the onion and the garlic. Heat the olive oil and sweat the onion over low heat until it begins to soften, but don't let it brown. If the onion begins to catch, place a lid on the pan. Add the chopped tomatoes, tomato paste, garlic, oregano, sugar, and wine, and simmer gently over low heat for at least for 40 minutes, until it has reduced and thickened.

Season well. This is excellent for freezing, but leave out the garlic (freezing garlic makes it taste moldy) and add it when you reheat.

Pasta with roasted tomatoes and garlic

This sauce can be eaten fresh, or frozen to use in the winter and spring, when tomatoes with any taste are hard to find. There's a lot of garlic in this dish, but it's not overwhelming. Once garlic is roasted, it becomes sweet and mild. Enrich the sauce at the end with a bit of butter to give a creamier taste. Eat with a mixed leaf and herb salad. Removing cherry tomato skins after you've roasted them is easier than the usual boiling water technique. Once they've cooled enough to handle, gently squeeze each fruit until it pops out of its skin.

Serves 4
- **1 pint cherry tomatoes**
- **3 tablespoons olive oil**
- **1 tablespoon balsamic vinegar**
- **2 level teaspoons sugar or honey (exclude with sweet cherry tomatoes)**
- **Salt and pepper**
- **12 to 14 ounces spaghetti**
- **3 or 4 cloves of Roasted garlic (see page 253)**
- **7 tablespoons butter**
- **1½ tablespoons fresh herbs, such as marjoram, oregano, basil, or thyme**
- **Grated Parmesan cheese, to serve**

Preheat the oven to 350°F.

Prick the cherry tomatoes several times with a sharp knife and lay them out in an ovenproof dish. Add the oil, vinegar, and sugar or honey. Season well with salt and pepper, and put the dish in the preheated oven for 20 minutes. Skin them when they come out of the oven.

Meanwhile, cook the pasta in salted boiling water until al dente.

Add the roasted garlic to the tomatoes by squeezing out the creamy flesh of each clove into the mixture. Put the dish back into the oven for another 5 minutes to allow the flavors to combine.

Remove the sauce from the oven and add the butter and the fresh herbs, with the leaves torn or chopped at the last minute.

Drain the pasta and serve lots of freshly grated Parmesan with the sauce. If you want to freeze the sauce, leave the garlic out (freezing garlic makes it taste moldy) and add it when you reheat.

Tomato bruschetta

A mix of yellow and red cherry tomatoes works well on bruschetta, as do juicy beefsteaks. Use white bread: a robust white Italian bread like Pugliese makes the best crostini.

Serves 4
- **2 pounds tomatoes**
- **Salt**
- **1 teaspoon white sugar**
- **2 tablespoons olive oil**
- **20 basil leaves, plus more as a garnish**
- **2 teaspoons red wine vinegar**
- **8 finger-thick slices white bread (see above), cut at an angle**
- **2 garlic cloves (optional)**
- **Extra virgin olive oil**
- **Black pepper**

If you're using cherry tomatoes, chop them in half, scatter with salt, and leave them to bleed for half an hour in a colander. You don't need to skin cherry tomatoes, but if you're using full-sized ones, skin them before chopping (see page 266).

In a bowl, mix the tomatoes with the sugar, oil, basil, and vinegar. If you're using very sweet cherry tomatoes such as Sungold, leave out the sugar and double the red wine vinegar to make them sharper. Try to keep the basil leaves whole. Once cut or torn, basil blackens quickly. If the leaves are too big and you need to halve them, just add at the last minute.

To make the crostini, preheat the oven to 350°F. Drizzle the olive oil over the bread. Toast the bread in the oven for 10 minutes, but don't let it become too hard. You can also cook it on a preheated medium-hot barbecue or grill pan until brown and crispy.

Lightly scrape one side with fresh garlic, if you are using it, and then add the tomatoes. Sprinkle with salt and black pepper, and garnish with extra basil.

Quick tomato tart

This tomato tart is special because you can throw it together very quickly and it needs few ingredients. You can use any old tomato, except for cherry varieties. I always make mine in a skillet with a metal or removable handle so that I can slot the whole thing into the oven for final cooking.

Serves 6 to 8

**10 medium-sized tomatoes
   (about 2 pounds)
2 red onions, thinly sliced
Drizzle of olive oil
2 garlic cloves, finely chopped
½ tablespoon coarsely chopped
   fresh thyme
1 teaspoon sugar
Salt and pepper
2 ounces anchovies, drained
20 capers
1 (1-pound) package puff pastry**

Preheat the oven to 400°F.

Skin the tomatoes (see page 266) and cut them in half horizontally.

Sauté the onions gently in a little olive oil with the garlic, thyme, sugar, salt, and pepper for about 10 minutes. If you are planning to freeze, leave out the garlic (freezing garlic makes it taste moldy).

Lay out the anchovies on top of the onion mix and sprinkle on the capers. Add the tomatoes, placing them cut side down and pushing them into the mix, and cook gently for a further 3 to 4 minutes.

Roll out the pastry to a thickness of about ¼ inch. If you're using store-bought pastry, it's often pre-rolled to about this size. Put the pastry over the pan, cutting away any excess, and push it down gently onto the tomatoes.

Put the pan into the preheated oven for 15 to 20 minutes, until the puff pastry has risen and is golden brown.

Remove it from the oven and allow the tart to rest and cool slightly. It tastes much better warm or cold rather than hot and it's easier to turn out when slightly cooler. Before you turn the tart, check there's not too much juice. Tip the pan on its side and drain any excess before turning.

Place a large flat plate—the ideal size is one that sits perfectly just inside the pan—over the top and flip the whole tart. Scatter a few extra sprigs of thyme over it.

Pizza

The secret of a good pizza is a crisp wafer-thin base. The keys to obtaining that are in the dough recipe and in rolling it very thinly. You'll need to use a good solid baking sheet on the bottom of a very hot oven.

If you don't have time to make Really rich tomato sauce (see page 277), use canned tomatoes cooked with a good 3 tablespoons of olive oil and 2 whole garlic cloves, which I later take out, and reduce.

We've done taste trials of different types of mozzarella and, once your pizza is cooked, you really can't tell the difference between the uninviting blocks and the more expensive buffalo spheres. Use the ordinary mozzarella for cooked toppings and save the delicious buffalo for eating fresh, sliced on top of the cooked pizza base with a handful of arugula and slices of juicy fresh tomato drizzled with olive oil.

Yield: 8 medium-sized pizzas
For the pizza dough:
   4½ cups bread flour, plus more for dusting
   1 teaspoon salt
   1½ teaspoons active dry yeast
   About 1¼ cups lukewarm water
   2 tablespoons extra virgin olive oil
   ½ teaspoon sugar
   Sunflower oil, for the baking sheet

For the pizza topping:
   Really rich tomato sauce (see page 277)
   1¼ pounds (20 ounces) mozzarella cheese, grated
   2 (2-ounce) cans anchovies, drained
   ¼ cup capers, rinsed
   ½ cup pine nuts
   12 slices prosciutto
   24 thin slices chorizo
   12 asparagus spears
   6 artichoke hearts

½ pound spinach
A few eggs

To make the dough, put the flour with the salt into a large bowl. Dissolve the yeast in a cup with the warm water, oil, and sugar, and leave to froth. It's worth doing this, rather than just adding the yeast straight into the flour, so that you know that the yeast is working. If it is active, you'll see bubbles starting to form within a couple of minutes.

Mix the yeast mixture with the flour. If your mix is too dry, add a little more water. A moist, sticky dough makes a light pizza base with a crisp crust, so don't be put off by the mess.

Once the dough is well mixed, there's no need to knead if you don't have time. Leave it to rest under a damp kitchen towel for a couple of hours. It should at least double in size, but even if it hasn't, it will still make fine dough. This is not a precise science.

To make your pizza dough, break off a ball 1 to 2 inches in diameter—depending on the size required—and roll it out as thinly as you can on a lightly floured surface, then transfer to a lightly oiled baking sheet.

To make the topping, you need to spread only a thin coating of tomato sauce—really ladling it on makes the crust soggy. Top the sauce with a light, even covering of grated cheese. Let people construct their own toppings. As well as cheese and tomato—the straight Margherita—I put out a couple of cans of anchovies, capers, pine nuts, a plate of prosciutto and thinly sliced chorizo, and maybe some asparagus spears or artichoke hearts. My husband, Adam, loves the classic Fiorentina with wilted spinach and an egg broken over the top.

The temperature of the oven should be at least 475°F—in which case 5 minutes is all a pizza will take.

De Kas tomato jam

This is my adaptation of a recipe from one of my favorite restaurants, De Kas in Amsterdam. A delicious sweet tomato pickle with a fragrant taste from the spices, it is fantastic on crostini and lovely with bread and cheese, sausages, pork, or thinly sliced cured and dried ham.

Yield: 1 quart
  **3½ pounds tomatoes (use lots of
    different varieties for a good
    structure and taste)**
  2 star anise
  3 cardamom pods
  1 teaspoon coriander seeds
  **1 teaspoon juniper berries
    (optional)**
  3 cloves
  1 teaspoon black peppercorns
  1 vanilla pod
  1 orange
  1 lemon
  Salt
  1½ cups sugar

Put a small saucer into the fridge to cool. Cut the tomatoes in half and scrape out the seeds. Roughly chop the halves into pieces and put into a large heavy-bottomed pan.

Cook the spices in a small frying pan over moderate heat until they begin to pop and smoke. Allow them to cool and then grind them quite finely using a mortar and pestle or in an electric grinder.

Split the vanilla pod and add the whole pod to the pan with the spices. Grate the zest from the orange and lemon, and squeeze the juice. Add these, together with salt to taste and the sugar, to the rest of the ingredients in the pan and heat slowly until the sugar has dissolved completely.

Simmer for at least 30 minutes to thicken and reduce, stirring regularly. Test for gelling by putting a teaspoonful on the chilled saucer—it should just hold its shape and be the consistency of soft jam.

Remove from the heat and put into warm sterilized jars. Cover with greaseproof discs and lids. Allow to mature for a few days before using it. This will keep well in the cool and dark for a couple of months, but refrigerate after opening.

Stuffed tomatoes
with roasted potatoes

Last spring I had a fantastic cooking lesson from two Greek women, Efi Polis and her sister Marina, in the town of Stavros on Ithaca. This is one of Efi's favorite vegetable-based recipes. The rice grains need to have a bit of a crunch and the tomatoes must be slightly charred for the texture to be as good as the taste.

It is delicious for lunch served with a lemony-dressed crunchy green salad or the typical Greek mix of one part coarsely grated carrot with two parts thinly sliced white cabbage, dressed with plenty of salt, lemon juice, and olive oil.

Serves 6

**10 large beefsteak tomatoes,
    or 12 large plum tomatoes
1 large onion, finely chopped
1 garlic clove, finely chopped
⅔ cup olive oil
3 serving spoons of white rice
3 serving spoons of brown rice
Generous bunch of herbs (a mix of
    one or all of fresh basil, oregano,
    dill, mint, and marjoram)
1 teaspoon sugar
Salt and pepper
1¼ pounds medium-sized to large
    waxy potatoes**

Preheat the oven to 350°F.

Cut the tops off the tomatoes, scoop the seeds and central flesh out with a teaspoon, and put them in a colander over a bowl.

Cook the onion and garlic in the oil until they're soft. Add the tomato seeds and flesh, but keep the juice that's dripped out into the bowl separate, then add the rices and most of the herbs, the sugar, and salt and pepper.

Stuff the tomatoes three-quarters full with the mix (as the rice cooks, it swells a bit). Arrange the tomatoes in a baking pan.

Parboil the potatoes for a few minutes in salted boiling water and then halve or quarter them lengthwise. Add these to the tray full of tomatoes, poking them into any gaps.

Add a couple of tablespoons of olive oil to the tomato juice and pour this over the top of everything in the tray. Sprinkle over more salt and the remaining herbs, and cook the potatoes and tomatoes together in the preheated oven, uncovered, for about an hour.

Sun-blushed tomatoes

This soft, succulent way of preserving tomatoes—admittedly for only a couple of weeks—is totally delicious. These tomatoes are expensive to buy but inexpensive to make. Made without vinegar, they're not long-term preserved, but taste all the sweeter for that. Eat them straight with a slice of bread, or as part of an antipasti with mint and crumbled feta cheese, or mix them with mozzarella and basil-flavored olive oil (see page 224).

Yield: about 2 pounds
- 6½ pounds small tomatoes or large cherry varieties about 1 inch in size
- 1 teaspoon salt
- Black pepper
- 1 tablespoon fresh or dried oregano
- 1 teaspoon muscovado or superfine sugar (optional)
- 1 to 2 garlic cloves, peeled but left whole (optional)
- Organic sunflower oil

Don't slice the tomatoes completely in half, but cut them almost through from the top to the stem end and open them out into a figure eight. Lay them out in a single layer on a wire rack in a baking tray.

Sprinkle the tomatoes with the salt, pepper, and oregano—and if you like things sweet, you can add one teaspoon of muscovado or superfine sugar. Put them in a tray in a very cool oven. About 6½ pounds on a rack tightly covers an oven tray for a standard-sized oven. The length of time they take will depend on their size and texture. Look at and taste them after 3 hours. Their flavor should have intensified hugely and their skin should be a bit wrinkly but not collapsed.

Put them in a sterilized jar, add the garlic, if using, and cover them with sunflower oil. One's instinct is to use olive oil, but lighter good organic sunflower oil allows the flavor of the tomatoes and herbs to come through fully. It's also less heavy and gloopy.

Properly covered in oil, these should last in the fridge for a couple of weeks. If you want to keep them longer, put them in the freezer.

Green tomato chutney

At the end of the season, bring the last tomatoes inside before they blacken during a cold night and ripen them in a paper bag or in a drawer with a banana. There will be some tomatoes that refuse to turn, so it's good to have a recipe like this up your sleeve for using them.

Yield: 5 to 6 jars
- 2½-inch piece of ginger
- 2 to 3 red chilis, halved
- 3 pounds green tomatoes
- 2 pounds apples
- 1 pound shallots, chopped
- 1 pound golden raisins
- 7 cups wine vinegar
- 2½ cups soft brown sugar
- Juice of 2 lemons
- 1 tablespoon mustard seeds
- ¼ cup salt

Bruise the ginger by whacking it with a rolling pin and then tie it in a cheesecloth bag with the halved chilis. Slice the tomatoes. Peel, core, and chop the apples. Put all these and the remaining ingredients into a large preserving pan.

Tie the cheesecloth bag to the handle and let it dangle into the pan to release the flavor of the ginger and the chilis while the mixture is cooking. Stir over low heat to dissolve the sugar and then simmer for 2 hours, uncovered, until the consistency is rich and thick.

Remove the cheesecloth bag and put the chutney into warm sterilized jars, cover, and seal. It's worth leaving the taste to mature for a couple of months before you eat this chutney.

Apples

When I think of paradise, it's an orchard full of apple trees in full pink-flushed flower, with a carpet of cow parsley and the occasional sheep grazing below. Among my fruit blossoms, apples come last, flowering in May, and they are arguably the most beautiful, with their simple single flowers and bright golden anthers.

We grow plenty of good apples, ranging from early dessert varieties, such as 'Discovery', to the late cooker 'Bramley'. I love 'Discovery', one of the first native apples ready for picking in early August. It's delicious, with small slightly sharp-flavored fruit and lovely crunchy flesh, creamy-white with a beautiful pink flush below the skin. It needs to be eaten within a few days.

'Egremont Russet' and 'Rosemary Russet' come next, both ready here in September. They will store until Christmas. They have that classic acidic, russet flavor and are an acquired taste, but are often the favorites of the apple connoisseur. Then there are the Cox varieties such as the traditional 'Cox's Orange Pippin'. These are all late dessert apples with an aromatic, almost pineapple flavor. If kept cool, they will last well into the new year.

My daughters love 'Estival', another mid- to late season apple. This has vast fruit, with a sweet flavor and excellent crunchy flesh. You'll only find these at a good pick-your-own fruit farm.

My outstanding cooking apple is 'Bramley's Seedling', with its characteristic large irregular, flat fruit. When you cook this variety, the released acids break down the flesh, giving the perfect fluffball texture and tangy taste. 'Bramley' is a late-flowering and -harvesting variety that stores brilliantly.

'Orleans Reinette' is another cooker, bred by the French to make tarte tatin. It keeps its structure perfectly when cooked and is the variety to use for perfect crescent-shaped slices.

In addition to the full-sized apples, there are many varieties of the smaller crabapples. The fruit of the crabapple ranges from jawbreaker to golf ball size, and all are superb for jelly. They have a high pectin level, so you won't need to add much sugar for setting, and many of them produce a beautiful warm coral-pink jelly.

It's important to store only perfect fruit. Put it on slatted wooden trays (the slats help with air circulation). Keep each variety separate, as storing times vary. They are best kept in cool, dry dark conditions, individually wrapped in newspaper. If you have a barn or tool shed, put them there, or line a drawer with newspaper in the coolest room in the house.

Baked apples

A British classic that should be eaten at least once during the apple season. Serve it with thick cream. The apples are also lovely filled with mincemeat.

Serves 4

5 or 6 tart apples
6 tablespoons butter, plus more for the dish
½ cup soft brown sugar
¾ cup golden raisins
Grated zest of 1 whole lemon and juice of ½ lemon
1 tablespoon brandy or Calvados (optional)
1 tablespoon slivered almonds or pine nuts, toasted

Preheat the oven to 350°F.

Core your apples and, with a sharp knife, score a line just through the apple skin around each apple two-thirds of the way up. This will stop them from exploding in the oven as they expand during cooking. Place in a buttered shallow open dish.

Mix together the butter, sugar, raisins, lemon zest, and juice. Stir in the brandy or Calvados, if you are including it. Fill the cavities of the apples with the mixture, piling it up on top on the apples.

Bake in the preheated oven for about half an hour. Spoon the remaining syrup over the apples and scatter with the toasted almonds or pine nuts.

Jane's apple hotpot

This, my sister's recipe, is a quick and easy way of using up extra apples and mincemeat. It is lovely for breakfast or supper, served with Greek yogurt or ice cream.

Serves 8

2 pounds mixed tart baking and sweeter eating apples
¾ cup orange juice
8 ounces mincemeat, preferably homemade
Butter, for the dish
¾ cup soft brown sugar (optional)
Grated zest of 1 lemon

Preheat the oven to 350°F.

Peel, core, and thinly slice the apples. Mix the orange juice into the mincemeat.

Butter a deep ovenproof dish and lay half the apples in the bottom. Sprinkle with half the brown sugar, if necessary, and some of the lemon zest. Cover this with half the mincemeat and on that layer the remaining apples, then sprinkle them with the rest of sugar, if you are using it, and the rest of the lemon zest. Top with the remaining mincemeat, cover with foil, and cook in the preheated oven for 30 minutes.

This will make a lot of juice, so leave it until it is lukewarm to serve, when the liquid will have been partially absorbed and thickened to a syrup.

Pheasant with Calvados, apple, and chestnut

Pheasant can be dull and dry, but with this recipe the flesh remains succulent and full of flavor.

Serves 6
  2 pheasants
  2 tablespoons seasoned all-purpose flour
  ¼ cup (½ stick) butter
  About 5 tablespoons Calvados
  4 to 6 apples (depending on size), plus a few slices for caramelizing
  4 onions, quartered
  ⅔ cup dry white wine
  2 teaspoons soft brown sugar
  Salt and pepper
  ½ pound chestnuts
  1 tablespoon superfine sugar
  2 tablespoons crème fraîche

Preheat the oven to 350°F.

This recipe works equally well either with each bird quartered or kept whole. Roll the pieces or the whole birds in a light coating of seasoned flour and brown them well in hot foaming butter. When they are golden, pour in the Calvados and carefully ignite. Wait until the flames subside and allow to bubble up for a few seconds. Stir well.

While the pheasant is browning, peel, core, and quarter the apples. Put both the onions and apples in an ovenproof dish. Lay the browned pheasant on top of them and pour over the pan juices and white wine. Sprinkle with the brown sugar and season well.

Cover and cook in the preheated oven for about an hour (50 minutes if the pheasant is quartered). Then add the chestnuts and cook for a further 10 to 15 minutes.

While the pheasant is cooking, make the caramelized apple slices. Sauté a few thin slices of apple in butter and sugar.

With a slotted spoon, lift out the pheasant, apples, onions, and chestnuts, and place on a serving dish. Cover and keep warm.

Scrape up the juices from the pan and simmer over medium heat until the liquid has reduced by one-third and thickened slightly.

Take off the heat and stir in the crème fraîche. Adjust the seasoning, pour a little of this sauce over the pheasant, and serve the rest separately.

Decorate with a few of the caramelized apple slices on each plate as you serve the pheasant.

Crabapple and herb jelly

A good jelly to make when there are plenty of crabapples around, though it also works well with tart apples. The apples provide the pectin, and you can use almost any herb. Thyme and mint are my favorites. It's good with meat and poultry, and whisked into sauces and gravies.

Yield: 5 to 6 jars
  3 pounds tart cooking apples or crabapples
  Small bunch of thyme or mint, plus 3 tablespoons chopped fresh thyme or mint
  ⅓ cup white wine vinegar
  Sugar (see below)

Peel the apples and chop them in half. Put them into a large heavy-bottomed pan with 4 cups water.

Tie the bunch of whichever herb you're using to the saucepan handle, letting it sit in the mixture of apples and water. Simmer until the fruit is really tender. Add the vinegar and cook for a few more minutes.

Put the fruit into a jelly bag (or cheesecloth) and allow it to drip into a nonreactive bowl overnight or for several hours. Don't be tempted to squeeze the bag or the jelly will be cloudy.

Warm the sugar in a bowl in a very low oven. When the fruit has stopped dripping, measure the juice in the bowl and pour it back into the pan. For every 2½ cups of liquid, add 2½ cups of warmed sugar.

Over low heat, dissolve the sugar, making sure it is completely melted before raising the heat and boiling rapidly to the gelling point (see page 170). Always take the saucepan off the heat while checking for setting.

Skim the scum off the surface. Once the jelly has rested for 10 to 15 minutes, stir in the freshly chopped herbs. Then pour into warm sterilized jars and cover.

Apple juice

Freshly pressed apple juice is really worth making. We have a juicer, which turns two apples into an extraordinarily good drink that bears little resemblance to the urine-like pasteurized filtered apple juice you find in the supermarket.

My favorite juice is apple with pineapple and lime—bright, sharp, and delicious. If you want a sweet juice, choose Discovery or James Grieve or for something more tart, use a Russet or a mix of two—a sweet and a sour, such as Cox and Bramley or Granny Smith. Try adding other things instead of the pineapple, such as watercress or arugula.

Yield: a jug for 4
2½ cups apple juice from tart apples
½ cup pineapple juice
Juice of 1 lemon or lime
Crushed ice

Mix all the ingredients in a jug. If you're not drinking it right away, a little lemon or lime juice will stop the apple from oxidizing and turning brown so quickly.

Toffee apples

Our Guy Fawkes Night or Bonfire Night in early November coincides with the apple season. We make plenty of these for it.

Serves 6
6 small dessert apples (small is best here)
You will need 6 (6-inch) pieces of wooden dowel (or use popsicle sticks if you have them)
1¼ cups soft brown sugar
1 tablespoon golden syrup or corn syrup
2 tablespoons butter
2 teaspoons lemon juice

Wash the apples in very hot water to remove any oils from the skin that would otherwise prevent the toffee sticking. Remove the stems and dry them well. Push a piece of dowel or a popsicle stick into the center of each apple.

Put all the other ingredients into a heavy-bottomed pan with 4 tablespoons water. Cook over gentle heat until the sugar has completely dissolved and then bring to a boil and boil rapidly for 5 to 10 minutes.

Line a baking tray with nonstick paper to stand the apples on once they've been dipped. Have a jug of cold water with you at this stage and, every minute or so, test the toffee by dribbling some into the water—gradually you will see it form thick threads that will become increasingly brittle. When you have a toffee that hardens instantly into a crisp thread, remove the pan from the heat and stir to cool a little—this helps prevent the toffee from overcooking and burning.

Dip the apples into the toffee one at a time—swirling as you go—until they are evenly coated. Lift them up and let the excess toffee drip back into the pan. Immediately dip the coated apples in a bowl of iced water so that the toffee sets quickly, and put them on the lined baking tray until they are needed. If the toffee hardens or thickens too much as you dip, put it back on the heat to allow it to soften.

Kentish apple cake

Living on the Kent/Sussex border and being surrounded by orchards, I'm obliged to have a quick and simple apple cake recipe up my sleeve. This is a lovely one, with plenty of cinnamon and raisins. It makes a good cake for tea or you can serve it warm as a dessert with lots of thick cream.

Serves 8 to 10
- ½ cup (1 stick) unsalted butter, plus a little extra for the pan
- 2½ cups self-rising flour, sifted
- 1 teaspoon ground cinnamon
- Pinch of salt
- ½ cup raisins or golden raisins, soaked for an hour or two in water or fruit juice
- ¾ cup superfine sugar
- ½ cup toasted hazelnuts, roughly chopped or halved (optional)
- 1 pound tart cooking apples
- Grated zest of 1 lemon
- 3 large eggs
- Plenty of light brown sugar, for dusting

Preheat the oven to 350°F. Grease or line an 8-inch springform cake pan.

Pulse the sifted flour, cinnamon, salt, and butter in a food processor until it looks like fine breadcrumbs. Put this mixture in a bowl and stir in the raisins, sugar, and toasted nuts, if using.

Peel, core, and chop the apples roughly, and add to the other ingredients with the lemon zest. Lightly beat the eggs and stir them in.

Spoon the mixture into the prepared cake pan and bake in the preheated oven for about 1 to 1¼ hours, or until firm to the touch. You may need to cover the cake lightly with foil to prevent it from becoming too brown on the top. While it's still hot, sift over plenty of brown sugar. Let it cool in the pan on a wire rack.

Uncooked autumn chutney

As this chutney is uncooked, it is very quick and easy to make. It's wonderful with cheese and ham, and try it under grated cheese on a piece of toast to make the best ever Welsh rarebit.

Yield: 7 to 8 jars
- 2 pounds apples, peeled and cored
- 1 pound onions, quartered
- 2½ cups pitted dates
- 2½ cups golden raisins
- 2½ cups soft brown sugar
- 1 teaspoon ground ginger
- 1 teaspoon salt
- Cayenne pepper, to taste
- 2 cups white wine vinegar

Chop the apples, onions, and dates or pulse them carefully in a food processor. Don't overdo it, as you don't want a puree. Put the mixture into a large nonreactive bowl and add the raisins, sugar, ginger, salt, cayenne, and white wine vinegar.

Leave for 36 hours, stirring occasionally, and then put into warm sterilized jars. It keeps for months, if not years.

Apple and plum chutney

Another chutney that is delicious in great dollops with bread and Cheddar cheese. Windfall apples are fine for it.

Yield: 7 to 8 jars
- 1 pound light brown sugar or raw cane sugar
- 2 pounds plums
- 2 pounds apples
- 2½ cups cider vinegar
- 1 pound onions, chopped
- 1 pound golden raisins
- 2 level teaspoons salt
- 1 teaspoon whole cloves
- 1 teaspoon whole allspice
- 1 teaspoon black peppercorns
- 1 medium-sized piece of ginger

Warm the sugar in an ovenproof bowl in a very low oven for about half an hour. Halve and pit the plums and peel, core, and chop the apples. Put the fruit into a large saucepan and add the cider vinegar, onions, raisins, salt, and spices. Bruise the ginger, tie it in a cheesecloth bag, and let it dangle from the handle into the mixture.

Bring the pan to a boil and simmer gently for about 30 minutes, until the fruit has softened.

Remove from the heat, discard the ginger, and stir in the warmed sugar. Stir over low heat until the sugar has completely dissolved, and then bring to a boil and simmer. Stir the mixture from time to time and make sure that it is not sticking to the bottom of the pan—use a heat diffuser if necessary. Cook until the mixture has reduced considerably to a thick mass, with only a little excess liquid in the pan. (The mixture will thicken even more as it cools.)

Once the chutney has reduced and thickened, stir well, pour into warm sterilized jars, and cover with a disc of parchment or wax paper. Seal and leave for 6 weeks before using. This keeps for ages.

Eggplants

Eggplants are one of the most beautiful fruits of the edible plant world, ranging from small, tomato-sized varieties such as 'Slim Jim' to the handsome glossy fat 'Violetta'. You may choose early-ripening varieties such as 'Moneymaker' or little ones, which, like cherry tomatoes, ripen more easily in a cooler climate. They will continue to fruit outside until the end of October, and keep even longer on the plant in a greenhouse.

Whether you're buying or growing eggplants, you can tell if they are ripe by looking under the calyx—the greeny-purple star where the fruit joins the stem. If the skin there is pure white, the fruit is ripe; if it is tinged green, wait a few days before you use the fruit. It will ripen on or off the plant. In a perfect state, the skin at the apex should be soft and have a slight give as you squeeze. Overripe fruit is easy to spot too: when you cut it open, the flesh is full of seeds.

Unripe or overripe, you can still eat eggplants, but they won't be as nice. They'll have a chewy texture, so will need a longer cooking time. They can also be bitter, so if you have to use them unripe or overripe, scatter some salt over the sliced flesh to draw out the juices for half an hour before you start to cook. You won't need to use this old-fashioned technique with perfectly ripe fruit. Modern hybrids—and almost all you come across to buy will be—have been bred specifically to get rid of the bitter juice.

There are many great recipes for eggplants, but sometimes simple is best. One of my favorite ways of eating them is in slices, dipped into Cucumber raita (see page 196). Slice the eggplant into discs about three-quarters of an inch thick. Fry these on both sides until they are golden and dry them on paper towels. Alternatively, slice the eggplant and cut shallow diagonal cuts into the flesh. Rub fennel seed, a little salt, and extra virgin olive oil into the cuts, and grill them for a few minutes on each side until they're slightly charred and tender. Eat them on their own or dipped into crème fraîche flavored with fresh dill or fennel leaf.

Spiced eggplant salad

This fragrant salad is lovely served warm as a first course, with Cucumber raita (see page 196) and flat or naan bread (see page 46 and right).

Serves 6 to 8

- 3 large to medium-sized eggplants (about 2 pounds)
- 3 tablespoons good extra virgin olive oil
- 1 large onion, finely chopped
- 2 teaspoons cumin seeds
- 2 teaspoons coriander seeds
- 1 teaspoon allspice berries
- 1 star anise
- 1 teaspoon ground cinnamon
- 1 teaspoon paprika
- 5 medium-sized tomatoes, skinned (see page 266), or 1 (14-ounce) can chopped tomatoes
- Generous handful of cilantro, coarsely chopped
- Generous handful of mint, coarsely chopped

Preheat the oven to 400°F. Dice the eggplants into ½-inch chunks. Drizzle 2 tablespoons of olive oil over the top and roast them in the preheated oven for about 30 minutes. The oil really adds to the flavor, so use a good one. Cook until the edges start to char.

Meanwhile, fry the onion gently in the rest of the oil until it's glassy and soft. In a separate pan, toast the cumin and coriander seeds, allspice, and star anise for a couple of minutes until they begin to smoke, and then grind them to a coarse powder in a spice grinder or using a mortar and pestle. Add the toasted spices to the onion, together with the cinnamon and paprika, and then add the cooked eggplants and tomatoes. Cook the mixture over gentle heat for 20 to 30 minutes.

Once the tomato juice has reduced so that there's little liquid left, take the pan off the heat and stir in the fresh herbs.

Baba ghanouj with naan bread

I have tried lots of baba ghanouj recipes and this is my favorite, from *The Moro Cookbook* by London chefs Samuel and Samantha Clark. It has a nutty, lemony taste and the texture is light and creamy.

Serves 6

- 3 large to medium-sized eggplants (about 2 pounds)
- 2 garlic cloves, crushed to a paste with 2 teaspoons salt
- Juice and grated zest of 1 lemon
- 3 tablespoons tahini
- 4 tablespoons olive oil
- Salt and pepper

For the naan bread:

- 2½ cups bread flour
- 1 teaspoon active dry yeast
- 2 teaspoons salt
- ½ teaspoon baking powder
- 4 tablespoons milk
- ¼ cup (½ stick) butter, plus a little extra for brushing
- 4 tablespoons plain yogurt
- ¼ teaspoon baking soda
- 1 egg
- Plenty of poppy seeds

Pierce the skins of the eggplants and grill or barbecue them whole, turning them until they are cooked and the skin is charred and crisp all over.

Or you can cook them in a 425°F oven for about 45 minutes.

Let the eggplants cool, then cut them in half lengthwise and scrape away the skin from the flesh. Put the flesh and juices in a food processor and whiz until nearly smooth. Add the garlic, lemon juice and zest, tahini, and olive oil. You may need to thin with a little water—you are aiming for a hummus-like consistency. Season.

To make the naan bread, put the flour, yeast, salt, and baking powder into a food processor. Warm the milk, butter, and yogurt, and add the baking soda and egg. Add this to the flour in the processor. (This saves a lot of time and washing up.)

Whiz to a bread dough consistency—you may need to add a little more milk. Let the dough rise in the container for about an hour, covered with a damp cloth in a warm room.

Whiz again to break it down, and shape it into 12 balls. Roll these into teardrop shapes and leave for 10 minutes (you can start cooking the first one by the time you've rolled the last one). Brush one side with melted butter and sprinkle with poppy seeds. It's nice to have different textures on each side, so don't be tempted to butter and poppy seed both sides.

Flip onto a large hot griddle or a cast-iron skillet.

You can do 4 at a time. They swell brilliantly. When they color, flip them over to cook on the other side

Eggplant and feta salad

Another, much sharper-tasting eggplant salad which you can eat warm or cold. The smoky flavors of roasted eggplant work well with the acidity of lemon and saltiness of feta.

The finishing touch to this salad is a good handful of any green herb, and coarsely chopped flat-leaf parsley is ideal.

Serves 8

3 large to medium-sized eggplants (about 2 pounds)
2 tablespoons olive oil
8 ounces feta cheese
2 tablespoons extra virgin olive oil
Juice and grated zest of 1 lemon
Salt and pepper
Handful of coarsely chopped parsley

Cut the eggplants into large chunks and roast them in oil as in the Spiced eggplant salad on page 299. Meanwhile, break up the feta into small lumps.

Take the eggplant out of the oven and, while it is still hot, stir in the extra virgin olive oil, lemon juice and zest, and feta. Season with salt and pepper to taste. Once it has cooled down a little, add plenty of parsley.

Caponata

This classic Italian dish is a good way of storing eggplant. The balsamic vinegar preserves it, so it can be kept in a jar in the fridge for at least 2 weeks. Serve this cold, as a starter. It is lovely with prosciutto and cold meats and cheeses. Salted instead of brined capers have the best flavor, so find these if you can. Drain and rinse them under cold running water and then dry on a paper towel.

Yield: about 3 cups

1 large or 2 small eggplants (about 1 pound)
2 to 3 tablespoons olive oil
1 large onion, sliced
2 garlic cloves, finely chopped
A few basil leaves
2 tablespoons capers
5 tomatoes, skinned (see page 266) and roughly chopped, or 1 (14-ounce) can chopped tomatoes
2 tablespoons balsamic vinegar
1 tablespoon brown sugar
1 teaspoon cocoa powder
Handful of black olives, pitted and quartered
Salt and pepper

Preheat the oven to 350°F. Peel and chop the eggplants. In a pan, heat the olive oil and sauté the eggplants until they begin to brown. Add the onion and garlic, and cook for a further 5 minutes.

Tear up the basil leaves and add these to the eggplants and onion, together with all the other ingredients, and cook gently over moderate heat or in the preheated oven for about 40 minutes. Check to make sure that the mixture is not catching on the bottom of the pan and add a little water if necessary.

When the caponata has finished cooking, the mixture should look dark and rich, with most of the excess liquid absorbed.

Baked eggplants with mozzarella

Eggplants and mozzarella—melanzane Parmigiana—is an Italian classic and the ultimate comfort food—ideal for a chilly autumn night, eaten with a spicy green salad. It's good then and there, and even better reheated. Don't compromise with anything but the best mozzarella. You can really taste the difference.

Serves 4

3 large to medium-sized eggplants (about 2 pounds)
Olive oil
Salt and pepper
½ cup freshly grated Parmesan cheese
2 cups Really rich tomato sauce (see page 277)
1½ pounds buffalo mozzarella
Handful of flat-leaf parsley
Handful of basil, torn up

Preheat the oven to 325°F.

Slice the eggplants lengthwise into slices about ½ inch thick. Brush the surface of each side with a little olive oil and sprinkle with salt. Bake or cook them in a grill pan until they are tender. (Make sure, if you are baking them, that they don't dry out or brown too much. You can cover them with foil.)

Oil an ovenproof dish and cover the bottom with a layer of eggplant. Season with black pepper and a scattering of Parmesan. Spread a layer of tomato sauce over the eggplant and top that with thick slices of mozzarella and a scattering of herbs. Add another layer of eggplant and continue as before. Make sure you finish with a layer of tomato and a generous amount of Parmesan.

Cook in the preheated oven for an hour, then allow to rest for at least 20 minutes. It will hold its heat well. As with so many recipes, this tastes far better warm rather than piping hot.

Moussaka

For years my assistant Tam Lawson has been trying to recreate the best moussaka ever, which she had in a backstreet restaurant in Heraklion years ago. This is pretty faithful to the original. The key ingredients are feta, yogurt, cinnamon, nutmeg, and allspice.

Unlike many adaptations of this dish, it does not contain Parmesan, Cheddar, or Gruyère.

Serves 4 to 6

3 large to medium-sized eggplants (about 2 pounds)
Olive oil
1 large onion, chopped
1 pound ground lamb or beef
½ teaspoon freshly ground allspice
½ teaspoon freshly ground cinnamon
Salt and pepper
2 cups Really rich tomato sauce (see page 277)
1 tablespoon chopped thyme

For the béchamel sauce:
2 cups milk
3 bay leaves
6 tablespoons butter
8 tablespoons all-purpose flour
1 heaping teaspoon nutmeg, freshly grated is best
1 level teaspoon cinnamon, freshly ground is best
6 ounces feta cheese, finely crumbled
1 cup Greek yogurt
2 egg yolks
Salt and pepper

Preheat a grill pan or the oven to 350°F.

Cut the eggplants lengthwise into slices about ½ inch thick and brush them on both sides with a little olive oil. Bake the eggplants in the preheated oven or cook them in a grill pan until they are soft but not charred.

If you were using the oven, keep it on or preheat as above if not. Over moderate heat, sweat the onion in a little olive oil and, when it has softened, add the meat, allspice, cinnamon, salt, and pepper. When the meat begins to brown, add the tomato sauce and the chopped thyme. Cover and simmer gently for half an hour, checking from time to time. If the mixture begins to stick, add a little water. When the meat is ready, there should be no extra liquid in the pan. Put the meat to one side.

For the béchamel sauce, bring the milk and bay leaves to a boil, then take off the heat to allow the bay to infuse the milk. Melt the butter in a saucepan, stir in the flour, freshly grated nutmeg, and cinnamon, and cook for 2 minutes. Using a balloon whisk, gradually add the strained hot milk and keep stirring until you have a perfectly smooth sauce. Cook gently for a couple of minutes and put to one side. When the sauce has cooled for a few minutes, add the feta, Greek yogurt, and egg yolks. Season with a little salt and plenty of black pepper. Whisk gently until the mixture is smooth.

Lightly oil an ovenproof dish and cover the bottom with a layer of the eggplant slices. Spread over a layer of the meat and tomato mixture, then another layer of eggplant, another layer of meat, and finally a thick layer of the béchamel sauce.

Bake for an hour in the pre-heated moderate oven, covering the moussaka with foil if it colors too much on the top. Allow to stand for at least 20 minutes before serving.

Again, this is much better eaten warm rather than hot.

Cranberry beans

The eau de nil and crimson-stippled cranberry (or borlotti) bean is a beautiful thing. Climbing up a tepee or sprawling over a frame, they look so handsome you'd want them in your garden even if they didn't taste so good, but they do. They have a creamy flavor and a meaty, hearty texture, which is just what you need as the weather gets colder at this time of year.

You can grow cranberry beans quite successfully, but they can be difficult to buy. If you can't get hold of them fresh, use dried. Canned don't have the flavor or the texture, but they'll do as a last resort.

The key to growing the perfect cranberry bean is climate. In Italy, it is said that their ideal conditions are high altitude, poor soil, heat in the day, and cool moisture at night. To grow them elsewhere, sow in late spring with your runner or Italian romano beans, although, unlike runners, you don't need to add lots of organic material to their planting soil.

In my garden, cranberry beans produce best in a sunny, sheltered spot out of the wind, and in soil which is not enriched. If overfed, they produce lots of lush green growth and fewer flowers and beans. For this reason, cranberry beans are ideal for growing in a large planter with a tepee of canes. Pick them as the bean pods turn from green to cream. This is when the beans inside are ripe. Or you can pick them earlier and dry them somewhere bright and warm inside. You can use them at this stage, or shell them and dry them out of their pods in the same place for another week or so, then store them in a jar for use in the winter.

Cranberry bean ratatouille

This is my absolute favorite recipe for cranberry beans. It's good as a starter, but can also be eaten as a main course, with a green salad and perhaps some roasted or grilled eggplant.

Serves 6 to 8 as a starter or a side dish
   1 large onion, finely chopped
   2 garlic cloves, finely chopped
   **Splash of olive oil, plus extra for
      drizzling**
   **15 medium-sized tomatoes,
      skins removed (see page 266)
      and roughly chopped, or
      3 (14-ounce) cans chopped
      tomatoes**
   **1 pound fresh cranberry beans (or,
      if using dried beans, use 1 to 1¼
      cups soaked overnight in cold
      water)**
   Salt and pepper
   **Really generous bunch of fresh
      cilantro, coarsely chopped**
   Fine slivers of Parmesan cheese

Cook the onion and garlic gently in the oil until they are soft. Add the tomatoes and the beans, and stew gently for about 45 minutes. Add a little water if they become too dry at any time.

   When the beans are tender but not mushy, remove them from the heat and leave for 15 minutes to cool. Season with salt and pepper.

   Just before you eat, add the cilantro, a drizzle of olive oil, and the slivers of Parmesan.

Sweet-and-sour cranberry beans

This is a classic northern Italian antipasto, eaten speared with a toothpick, or as a dollop on a plate with ham and salami. In this country you may not find enough fresh cranberry beans to want to preserve them, but you can make this with dried. It's a good starter.

Yield: 2 quarts
   **2½ pounds fresh cranberry beans
      (or, if using dried beans, use
      3 cups soaked overnight in
      cold water)**
   Salt
   2 white onions, sliced
   **2 red peppers, deseeded and cut
      into slim matchsticks**
   **3 small glasses of white wine
      vinegar**
   1 tablespoon sugar
   3 cups extra virgin olive oil

Boil the beans in salted water until they're tender but retaining their shape. This will take about half an hour. Drain and let them cool.

   Put them into a large pan with the onions, red peppers, vinegar, sugar, and oil. Bring them to a boil again and bottle them in warm sterilized jars, filled right to the top. Seal well.

   Turn the jars upside down immediately and wrap them in a wool blanket or thick cloth. Leave them wrapped up for a couple of days so that the liquor cools very slowly, preserving the cranberry beans. They will keep for at least a year.

Cranberry bean hummus

Cranberry beans also make a delicious lighter-than-chickpea hummus. If you don't have any cranberry beans, cannellini beans, soaked overnight, work well. Eat this hummus with black olives and Rosemary flat bread (see page 46).

Serves 6
- ½ pound fresh cranberry beans (or, if using dried beans, use ½ cup soaked overnight in cold water)
- 1 (2-ounce) can anchovies
- 1 garlic clove
- Juice and grated zest of lemon, to taste
- 2 tablespoons yogurt
- 2 tablespoons extra virgin olive oil
- Salt and pepper
- Handful of chopped cilantro

Cook the beans for half an hour or until tender in plenty of salted water. Strain, reserving the cooking liquid, allow to cool, and then puree them with the drained anchovies, garlic, lemon juice and zest to taste, yogurt, a little of the cooking liquid, and olive oil. Season well and add the chopped cilantro.

Cannellini, cranberry, or white butter bean soup

This soup is filling, so serve it in small bowls, with a dollop of Greek yogurt or a splash of a good fruity extra virgin olive oil over the top. There's no need for bread.

Serves 8
- 3 garlic cloves, finely chopped
- 1 teaspoon ground cumin seeds
- 2 small Preserved lemons (see page 35), pith removed (or you can use strips of lemon rind)
- ½ hot chili (left in one piece so that you can remove it)
- Olive oil
- 2 pounds fresh or canned cannellini, cranberry, or white butter beans (or, if using dried beans, use 2 cups soaked overnight in cold water)
- 4 cups chicken stock
- Juice of ½ lemon
- Good handful of cilantro leaves, coarsely chopped
- Salt and pepper

Sweat the garlic, cumin, lemons or lemon rind, and chili in a splash of olive oil for a couple of minutes. Then add the beans and stock, and cook them for about 40 minutes, until the beans are soft. Remove the chili.

Puree the mixture with an immersion blender or in a food processor. You may want to dilute the soup with stock or water and a little lemon juice to taste.

Stir in the cilantro, season with salt and pepper, and serve.

Cranberry beans with sage

I first had this simple dish in the Madonna restaurant in Venice to accompany slow-roasted belly of pork. The River Cafe in London serves a similar cranberry bean recipe as a first course with lots of arugula.

Fresh beans make this extra delicious as they have a softer, creamier texture than dried.

Serves 6 as a starter, 8 as a side dish
1 pound fresh cranberry beans (or, if using dried beans, use 1 cup soaked overnight in cold water)
1 garlic clove, peeled
3 or 4 sage leaves, chopped, plus plenty extra for garnishing
3 tablespoons extra virgin olive oil, plus a little extra for drizzling
3 ounces pancetta, chopped
Dash of red wine vinegar
2 tablespoons Dijon mustard
Salt and pepper
3 handfuls of arugula or young spinach leaves (optional)

Put the beans, garlic, and chopped sage into a pan, bring them to a boil, and simmer for 30 to 40 minutes, until the beans are soft. Drain them and, while still warm, add 1 tablespoon of oil and put aside.

Meanwhile, fry the pancetta in a very little olive oil until crisp and add to the beans. Mix together the vinegar, mustard, salt, and pepper, and slowly add the rest of the olive oil to give a very creamy dressing. Pour this over the still-warm beans, retaining a third of it if you are using the salad leaves. Garnish with plenty of chopped sage leaves over the top.

If using the salad leaves, dress the leaves, divide among the plates, and spoon the beans over the leaves. Drizzle with a little extra virgin olive oil.

Cranberry bean brandade

Marseilles is the home of this dish, which is served as an accompaniment to lamb. There, they eat it topped with croutons fried in olive oil. It is rich, robust, and delicious, and also lovely spread on crostini.

Serves 4
½ pound fresh cranberry beans (or, if using dried beans, use ⅓ cup soaked overnight in cold water)
1 onion, halved
1 carrot
2 bay leaves
6 cloves
½ head garlic
5 anchovies
½ cup milk
2 to 3 tablespoons extra virgin olive oil
1 to 2 tablespoons lemon juice
Sea salt and pepper

Cook the beans in a saucepan filled with lots of water, along with the onion halves, carrot, bay leaves, and cloves for 30 to 40 minutes, until tender.

Roast the garlic in the oven until soft (see page 253).

Rinse the anchovies if they are salted and chop finely.

Bring the milk to a boil in a small saucepan.

Drain the beans and remove the vegetables, bay leaves, and cloves. Squeeze out the soft, sweet roasted garlic from its skins and puree with the beans. Return the mixture to low heat and stir constantly while gradually adding the oil.

Stir in the boiled milk, anchovies, and lemon juice to taste and season with a little sea salt and plenty of ground black pepper. Keep warm and serve as soon as possible.

Fennel

It's the gentle aniseed-y flavor as well as the texture of bulb fennel—or so-called Florence fennel—that makes it such a great vegetable. The texture can change from a delicious water-filled crunch when raw to soft squidgy caramel when cooked. Very fresh fennel makes a good addition to a green salad and very thinly sliced, it is delicious on its own. I also love the everyday French way of preparing fennel—blanching thick slices of it for a couple of minutes in salted water and then cooling it quickly in cold water before dressing with a little warm olive oil, black pepper, and topping with halved black olives. Try grilling slices too, and then dress them with lemon juice, olive oil, and a thinly sliced chili. This is lovely hot or cold the next day.

If you're going to cook whole bulbs, they benefit from a long, slow roast. This softens any fibers—even of the outer layers—and brings out the sweet syrupy flavor. Always keep them covered in the oven, so that they steam and roast at the same time and don't start to char. They're perfect eaten with chicken, and they also taste fantastic with fish.

Growing bulb fennel is worthwhile if you avoid sowing from mid-May to late July. Sown early in the year under cover, or outside in August or early September, it will bulb up well before it tries to flower. The most reliable variety of all I've tried is the late season 'Romanesco'. It's slow to bolt or flower and forms huge bulbs. If you get a few bulbs that flower, use the beautiful acid green umbels in salad, or dip them in tempura batter (see page 207) and panfry them. They are delicious.

Braised fennel

Slow-cooking bulb fennel makes it one of the best vegetables to eat with any meat or poultry.

Serves 4
   2 pounds fennel bulbs
   1 whole head garlic
   4 tablespoons olive oil
   Salt and pepper
   5 tablespoons white wine (or ½ cup if not using Pernod)
   5 tablespoons Pernod (optional)

Trim the fennel bulbs, removing any damaged outer leaves and the stalks. Keep some of the feathery tops to one side. Split the bulbs in half. Separate the garlic cloves but leave the skins on.

In a heavy-bottomed pan, heat the olive oil and add the fennel bulbs, cut side down. Put in all the garlic cloves and season with salt. Cover and cook the fennel very gently, until the undersides are golden. Turn and allow the other sides to color—this takes about half an hour. (This can also be done in the oven, preheated to 325°F.) Squeeze the garlic flesh out of the skins and mix it in.

Add half the white wine and the Pernod, if using, turn the fennel once more, cover, and continue to cook very gently for about an hour. Add a little more wine or Pernod from time to time if necessary. Pernod, with its higher sugar and alcohol content, gives a creamier flavor.

When the fennel is tender and a rich gold, season and serve with some of the reserved, chopped fennel leaves on the top.

Bulb fennel and grape salad

One of the best salads for eating at this time of year—refreshing with a hint of aniseed.

Serves 2 to 3
   2 medium-sized fennel bulbs, plus 1 tablespoon finely chopped fennel tops and a little extra to garnish
   Extra virgin olive oil
   Black pepper
   Grated zest of ½ lemon
   1 teaspoon toasted crushed fennel seeds
   1 to 2 tablespoons crème fraîche or fromage frais
   Small bunch of seedless green grapes

Take off any tough or discolored outer layers from the fennel. Slice the bulb as thinly as you possibly can—a mandoline is the best tool for this—and combine with the ferny tops. Arrange in a deep bowl with a little extra virgin olive oil, black pepper, lemon zest, and fennel seeds. Fold in the crème fraîche.

Halve the grapes and add them to the ingredients in the bowl. Stir to combine and decorate with more chopped fennel tops.

Sage, Florence fennel, and Pernod pasta

The wonderful smoky taste of sage and aniseed infuses this pasta sauce.

Serves 4

6 shallots, peeled and roughly sliced
3 medium-sized fennel bulbs, outer leaves removed and roughly chopped
20 sage leaves, coarsely chopped
5 tablespoons Pernod
4 tablespoons butter
3 tablespoons olive oil
Salt and pepper
¼ cup pine nuts
6 ounces pasta (tagliatelle is ideal)
Freshly grated Parmesan cheese, as a garnish

Preheat the oven to 300°F.

Put the shallots, fennel, sage leaves, Pernod, butter, and olive oil in a covered ovenproof dish with some seasoning. Braise gently in the preheated oven for an hour, until the bulbs are soft. Check every so often to make sure that they are not sticking and, if the liquid has been absorbed, add more Pernod or water.

Chop or pulse once in a food processor to combine the ingredients, but do not reduce to a puree.

Towards the end of the braising time, toast the pine nuts for 3 to 4 minutes and cook your pasta in salted boiling water until al dente.

Drain the cooked pasta, leaving in about 3 tablespoons of water, and fold in the sauce.

Garnish with plenty of Parmesan and more salt and pepper to taste.

Fennel and prawn risotto

For this, it's worth finding fresh prawns or shrimp, not frozen shelled ones. The quickest and best fish stock is made from the cooking liquid, reduced after you have removed the cooked prawns.

Serves 4

2 teaspoons salt
1 pound uncooked tiger prawns or jumbo shrimp, shells on
3 tablespoons butter
1 tablespoon extra virgin olive oil
1 large onion, thinly sliced
1 large or 2 medium-sized fennel bulb(s), cut into ½-inch slices
1 cup Arborio rice
⅔ cup white wine
Grated zest and juice of 1 lemon
Black pepper
Chopped parsley
A few fennel tops, as a garnish

In a saucepan, bring 1 quart of salted water to a boil. Throw in the prawns or shrimp and, when the water comes back to a boil, remove from the heat. Allow to stand for a couple of minutes.

Remove the prawns or shrimp with a draining spoon, leaving the liquid in the saucepan, and plunge them into cold water. When the prawns or shrimp are cool enough to handle, peel them, put them to one side, and put the shells back into the saucepan. Boil up the shells in the water to make the stock.

While the shells are boiling, melt half the butter in a large saucepan and add a generous splash of olive oil. Sweat the onion and fennel together in the saucepan and then cover with a circle of parchment paper so that they don't color.

After a few minutes, add the Arborio rice and stir to make sure the rice is well coated before adding the white wine. Allow this to bubble up and wait until the wine has evaporated before adding the hot stock gradually in strained ladlefuls. Before each addition keep stirring until the stock has been absorbed. (You will need to add about three-quarters of the stock.)

It will take about 15 to 20 minutes for the rice to become al dente and, when it reaches this stage, add the lemon zest, lemon juice to taste, and the cooked prawns. Stir over the heat for a few seconds to warm the prawns.

Season with black pepper and take the pan off the heat. Stir in the parsley and the remaining butter.

Cover and leave for a few minutes. Check the seasoning and serve with some of the chopped feathery fennel tops.

Celery

Celery is good raw when it's crunchy and fresh, ideal for eating with strong cheese or in a tall Bloody Mary. It's also delicious cooked, a fundamental flavor for a good stock, and excellent sliced and slowly braised. A lot of commercially mass-produced celery is now grown hydroponically and, in my experience, has almost no taste, and has among the highest pesticide residues you'll find in any vegetable.

I grow 'Mammoth Pink', which needs blanching (a gardening technique of excluding the sunlight) to make the stems paler, more tender, and less bitter. You can blanch with mounded earth, newspaper, or cardboard, but earth seems to work the best. Dig a celery trench—a beautiful thing—adding as much compost as you would for hungry runner beans. As soon as the last frosts are over, plant your young celery seedlings in the bottom of the trench in a double row (eight inches between each) and cover with soil. When the tops of the plants rise above soil level, bank up the soil around them and continue to do so as often as you can. To grow well, celery benefits from a steady water supply and a rich soil.

Whether you're eating celery raw or cooked, choose a good head and remove the damaged outside branches. With a potato peeler, strip away the fibrous strings of the outer layer. This will stop you from wasting the outer stalks, which are usually the tastiest. Remove the top branches at the joints and rinse the celery under cold running water. Another good thing about celery is that the leaves are useful, too. They are an excellent addition to soups and stews, and the young leaves in the heart are lovely in salad.

Braised celery

The intensified flavor of the braised celery stems is delicious and, like fennel, perfect with the gentle flavors of chicken and fish. Another version of braised celery is to finish it off with cream. After braising, warm ½ cup of crème fraîche. Add 1 tablespoon Madeira and pour over the celery. Season and serve with plenty of chopped parsley.

Serves 6
- **3 heads celery**
- **Salt and pepper**
- **3 tablespoons butter**
- **3 shallots, thinly sliced**
- **2 cups good vegetable or chicken stock**
- **Juice of 1 lemon**
- **1 tablespoon sugar**
- **Bunch of parsley, finely chopped**

Tie some string around the top of the celery branches to hold the hearts together as they cook. Bring a large saucepan of salted water to a boil and add the celery. Simmer gently for 10 minutes and then cool the celery quickly by plunging it into cold water. Dry on a kitchen towel. Remove the strings from the celery stalks and then trim the ends.

Melt the butter in a pan. Add the celery, shallots, stock, lemon juice, sugar, and a little salt. Simmer for about 30 minutes over low heat without covering, making sure that the water doesn't boil away.

When the celery is tender, lift out onto a serving plate and add some freshly ground pepper and plenty of parsley. If there is more than a little liquid in the pan, boil to reduce it and pour over the celery.

Braised beans and celery

I had a wonderful lunch this summer in a simple restaurant outside Asolo in the Veneto. We had roast rabbit with chard, mashed potatoes, and these very delicious cranberry beans. The beans—boiled in vegetable stock—were braised quickly with finely cut celery. The crunch of the celery made a perfect contrast to the softness of the beans.

Serves 4 to 6
- **1 cup dried cranberry beans (or any other dried beans)**
- **4 cups vegetable or chicken stock**
- **2 tablespoons butter**
- **Olive oil**
- **½ onion, finely chopped**
- **½ pound celery, finely chopped**
- **1 garlic clove, finely chopped**
- **Large glass of white wine**
- **1 teaspoon sugar**
- **Several sprigs of thyme**
- **Salt and pepper**

Soak the beans for about 6 hours and then drain and cook in the stock for about half an hour, until tender but still holding their shape.

Heat the butter with a little olive oil in a pan and sweat the onion, celery, and garlic, covering them with a circle of parchment paper and a lid to prevent them from coloring. Cook for about 10 minutes, until they become just translucent and the celery is still a little crisp.

Add the wine, sugar, and thyme, and cover and simmer gently for another 5 minutes. Add the cooked beans. Warm them through and season.

Celery and cucumber salad in mustard dressing

The tastes and textures of cucumber and celery make a very good salad with a punchy mustard dressing.

This is good with any cold meat—especially beef, chicken, turkey, or ham—and is an excellent salad for casual Christmas gatherings.

Serves 6

1 cucumber
Salt and pepper
1 head celery
1 tablespoon Dijon mustard
1 teaspoon Colman's English or other smooth, spicy mustard
1 tablespoon red wine vinegar
Juice of 1 lemon
4 tablespoons sunflower oil
Bunch of parsley or winter savory, finely chopped

Peel and deseed the cucumber (cut in half and use a teaspoon). Slice the halves into ½-inch-thick half-moons, put in a colander, and sprinkle with salt. Leave to drain for half an hour.

Meanwhile, prepare the celery as described on page 312, and then slice it into similar-sized chunks.

Put the mustards in a bowl. Add the vinegar and lemon juice, and then slowly add the oil to make a thick mustard dressing.

Pour the dressing over the celery and cucumber, and mix in plenty of salt and pepper and finely chopped parsley or winter savory, if available.

Bottled celery

The Italians have a glorious tradition of spreading out various bowls of different antipasti to dip into before lunch or supper. Eat this celery antipasto with salami, prosciutto, salted almonds, sweet roasted peppers, grilled eggplant slices, and olives. The lovely thing about bottled celery is not just its flavor, but also its texture—crunchy but not raw.

Yield: about 6 jars

2 heads celery, stringy outer stems removed
Plenty of salt
1 large white onion, chopped
Olive oil
½ cup white wine vinegar
Freshly ground white pepper

Slice the celery into 1-inch chunks and put in a colander. Cover in a dusting of salt and leave to drain for about an hour. Then rinse off the salt and pat the chunks dry.

Sweat the chopped onion gently in plenty of olive oil for 10 minutes without browning and then add the celery, vinegar, freshly ground white pepper, and a little salt, cooking it enough to soften the celery slightly but keeping its crunch.

Fill about 6 warm sterilized jars right to the top, filling with oil so that the celery is completely covered.

Seal the jars and turn them upside down right away. Wrap in wool blankets or thick cloth, and leave them wrapped up for a couple of days, so that the liquid cools very slowly. The celery will last for at least a year.

Chili peppers

Once you've had one or two sessions of tasting and eating chili peppers, you'll find that they are addictive. They contain an oil, capsaicin, that sends a burning sensation from the nerve endings in the mouth to the brain. The body defends itself against this "pain" by secreting endorphins, natural painkillers, which cause a physical rush in the same way as the opium-derived drug morphine. As a result, you feel good and the high keeps you coming back for more.

The highest concentration of capsaicin is in the seeds and the lighter-colored ribs attaching them to the fruit walls. If you've got mild chilis such as 'Hungarian Hot Wax' in their unripe green stage and want to maximize their heat, chop them whole, leaving the seeds in. If you've got a hot variety, such as the pretty tangerine-colored 'Habanero', you may want to cut the chilis open and discard the seeds.

A chili's heat is measured on the Scoville Scale, named after the chemist Wilbur Scoville. A number was assigned to each chili, based on how much it needed to be diluted before you could taste no heat. The Scoville grade of 'Hungarian Hot Wax' is 5,000 to 10,000, a similar range to that of the popular 'Jalapeño' (2,500 to 8,000). 'Scotch Bonnet' is considerably hotter (100,000 to 325,000). The heat varies according to how and where it's grown. Grown outside in the garden, chilis can be noticeably hotter.

When you're preparing chili peppers, wear rubber gloves and don't touch your eyes until you've taken the gloves off. Capsaicin is not water soluble, so you can't just wash it off and, if you burn your mouth eating chilis, drinking water won't help. Dairy products are very effective in cooling you off. They contain the protein casein, which breaks the bond between the pain receptors and the capsaicin.

You can buy your chilis, but some of the most interesting varieties are not widely available. Get these from specialist mail order suppliers, or grow your own. 'Hungarian Hot Wax' produces heavily over a long season, and is excellent if you like a mild to medium chili. 'Jalapeño' is of similar heat, with chunky, fleshy fruits and fantastic productivity. If you like them hot, there's 'Habanero', but this needs more attention and higher growing temperatures than others, or 'Twilight', a beautiful chili with multicolored cream, green, red, and purple fruit. It makes an ideal house plant.

With all the following recipes, the amount and variety of chili pepper you use will depend on the heat of that particular crop and your tolerance of it. The quantities given are just a guide—make sure you taste as you go.

Pickled chilis

Long thin chilis like the Hungarian Hot Wax are best for this, with a strength that is slightly surprising but doesn't burn. If you like things a bit hotter, jalapeño is also good. These pickled chilis are lovely with a glass of wine before supper. They are also excellent with a grilled burger and fries, and are one of my favorite things for lunch with bread and Cheddar cheese.

Yield: 1 small jar
- **6 mild to medium-hot chilis**
- **1 teaspoon sugar**
- **1 teaspoon mustard seeds**
- **½ teaspoon salt**
- **5 tablespoons white wine vinegar**

You can leave the chilis whole and pickle them, but they're easier to eat, and more versatile, when sliced into quite thick rings. If you want to maximize the heat, leave the seeds in; if you want them mild, remove them.

Meanwhile, bring the pickling mix of sugar, mustard seeds, salt, vinegar, and 1 tablespoon of water to a boil.

Stuff the chili rings tightly into a warm, sterilized jar and pour on the hot pickling mix. Seal and cover.

These are best left for a few weeks to mature. The longer you leave them, the hotter they get. They'll keep for a year.

Chili dipping sauce

A wonderfully simple dip that is delicious for any tempura (see page 207). Have a bowl of this and one of good soy sauce so you can alternate from sweet to salty. This one has some punch, but it's not too fiery. Many commercial varieties have too much sugar and contain unnecessary preservatives, so it's worth making your own.

Yield: 2 jars
- **2 cups sugar**
- **2 chopped red jalapeño or Cherry Bomb chilis, seeds left in**
- **1 cup cider vinegar**
- **1 cup orange juice**

Warm the sugar in a bowl in a very low oven for about half an hour.

Put all the ingredients, including the warmed sugar and chilis, into a saucepan over low heat to dissolve the sugar. Simmer for about 15 minutes—until it's syrupy—and then pour into sterilized bottles or jars and seal. The vinegar in the sauce acts as a preservative and so, kept cool, this lasts for months.

Chili jam

This is fantastically versatile stuff. Try it spread on corn on the cob instead of butter, or on top of cream cheese on a crostini. I use it instead of mint jelly with lamb or red meat and it's famously good with fish cakes or calamari rings. I have taken to having it on toast on top of cream cheese for a late breakfast!

Yield: about 6 jars
- **1 pound very ripe tomatoes**
- **4 garlic cloves, peeled**
- **4 large red chilis (seeds left in if you want your jam hot)**
- **2½- to 3-inch piece of ginger, peeled and sliced**
- **1½ cups golden superfine sugar**
- **2 tablespoons Thai fish sauce**
- **½ cup red wine vinegar**

Blitz half the tomatoes with all the garlic, chilis, and ginger in a food processor. Pour into a heavy-bottomed saucepan. Add the sugar, fish sauce, and vinegar, and bring to a boil, stirring slowly. Reduce to a simmer.

Dice the remaining tomatoes finely and add them to the pan. Simmer for 30 to 40 minutes, stirring from time to time. The mixture will turn slightly darker and sticky.

Store in warm dry sterilized jars and seal while the mixture is still warm. The longer you keep this jam, the hotter it gets. It keeps for about 3 months in the fridge.

Plum, apple, and chili jelly

There are many chili jellies, but I particularly like the color and flavor of this one, which has the taste of plum and apple, and the heat of the chilis. It tastes excellent with any meat or cheese.

Yield: about 2 quarts
- **2 pounds tart apples or crabapples**
- **2 pounds plums (any variety), pitted**
- **¾ cup cider vinegar**
- **Sugar (for exact quantity, see below)**
- **3 jalapeño or medium-hot chilis, sliced into rings (deseed them if you don't want it hot)**

Roughly chop the unpeeled apples and put them into a large preserving pot with the plums and 7 cups water. Bring to a boil, cover, and simmer for 1 hour. Add the cider vinegar and boil for 5 minutes.

Strain overnight through a jelly bag or cheesecloth. Don't be tempted to squeeze the bag as this will make the jelly cloudy.

Warm the sugar in a bowl in a very low oven for about half an hour. Measure the juice and for every 2½ cups of juice use 2½ cups of warmed sugar. Pour the juice into the preserving pot and add the sugar. Dissolve the sugar completely, while stirring over gentle heat, and add the chilis.

When the sugar has dissolved, raise the heat and boil vigorously until the gelling point is reached (see page 170). Leave the jelly to stand for at least 20 minutes and stir once more to ensure the chilis are distributed evenly through the jelly.

Pour into warm sterilized jars and seal. Keeps for up to a year.

Barbecued stuffed chilis

The two best varieties for barbecuing are the mild Hungarian Hot Wax and the medium-hot Cherry Bomb. They have a decent-sized cavity for you to stuff and don't collapse when cooked. It's good to have a variety of heat and flavor, so also think of using the mini red pepper Jingle Bells.

These are delicious served with barbecued meat, or as part of a mix of starters with Grilled corn (see page 384).

Yield: 20 chilis or mini peppers
- **8 ounces cream cheese or goat cheese**
- **¼ cup pine nuts, dry roasted for 3 to 4 minutes**
- **4 basil leaves, chopped**
- **Juice of ½ lemon**
- **Salt and pepper**

For the long, horn-shaped chilis, slice them in two lengthwise and scrape out the seeds. For the round ones, slice off the top, trying to keep as much of the globe as you can, and scrape out the seeds.

Mix your stuffing ingredients together and scoop them into the chilis with a teaspoon.

Put them in a hot grill pan or barbecue and cook them, skin side down, for 5 minutes. They may pop and jump slightly on the heat, so you need to watch them. Cook them until the undersides just begin to char.

Chili chocolate

You may think this recipe, given to me by the South Devon Chili Farm, sounds revolting, but it's extraordinary and delicious. It will make all the difference if you make it with top-grade chocolate, and it is the perfect thing for eating after dinner. It also makes a lovely Christmas present.

The amount of chili will vary, depending on which variety you use and the amount of heat you want, so the quantities given here are only a rough guideline.

Yield: about 1 cup
- **2 red chilis, fresh or dried**
- **4 ounces really good dark chocolate**

If you're using fresh chilis, remove the seeds and chop very finely.

If you're using dried ones, grind them to a powder using a mortar and pestle.

Melt the chocolate in a bain-marie and add the chili bit by bit—and keep tasting.

Cool quickly by sitting the bowl in iced water and, before the chocolate sets, pour onto baking parchment. Leave to cool for 10 minutes, and score into squares with a knife. Once it's cooled completely, cut it up and bag it. Store it somewhere cool.

Damson plums, sloes, rowans, blackberries, mulberries, and elderberries

Every one of these fruits—some of which you're unlikely to find in a supermarket—is worth seeking out. They make some of the most delicious desserts, as well as jams and jellies that you can eat through the year. Some of these, like sloes and rowans, will be difficult to find in the United States. I may have to make an early autumn visit to a good pick-your-own farm or, in the case of rowans, elderberries, blackberries, and sloes, search them out in the countryside or woods. Sloes are the fruit of the European blackthorn tree, a relative of cherries and plums, and the rowan is a European tree related to the American mountain ash.

Blackberries and elderberries are great baked or stewed with apples and they, as well as rowan berries and sloes, make fantastic jelly. These last two are excellent for serving with game, particularly venison. Damson plums make one of the best ice creams (see page 322), and a damson plum compote made with lots of spices (see page 322) is superb to eat with cheese. Mulberries used to flavor vinegar (see page 324) make a wonderful aromatic sauce to drizzle over almost any fresh fruit. Mulberries are often the connoisseur's favorite fruit, rich and full of flavor, with the right balance of sugar and acidity, at their best when very black. I've never seen them for sale, so to eat this delicacy you've got to know someone with a tree in their garden, plant your own, or you may be lucky enough to find them at your local farmers' market.

Mulberries are the bloodiest and juiciest of all fruits, which is why they feature in a Greek myth. The handsome youth Pyramus, thinking that his lover Thisbe was dead, lay under a white mulberry tree and plunged his sword into his heart. His blood spurted all over the tree and sank into its roots, so that the tree became the black mulberry. If you want a fruiting mulberry, it's the black, not the white one—grown to feed silkworms—that you want.

Damson plum compote

There are various preserves that you can make with damson plums—damson cheese, damson chutney, and jelly—but this is my favorite. Tart from the fruit and spicy from the cinnamon, star anise, and cloves, this compote is wonderful with cheese and with meat.

Yield: about 6 jars
- **2 pounds damson plums**
- **1½ cups malt vinegar**
- **2 cinnamon sticks**
- **12 cloves**
- **4 star anise**
- **4 cups sugar**

Pick over the damson plums and remove the stems. Put the vinegar, spices, and sugar into a saucepan and over gentle heat stir gently to dissolve. Add the damson plums and simmer until the fruit is softened but still whole. Carefully lift out the fruit and put into a bowl.

Boil the poaching liquid for 10 minutes and pour over the fruit. Leave overnight or for a few hours. Strain and boil the liquid once more for a further 10 minutes and then add the damson plums and simmer for 1 minute.

Remove the cinnamon sticks. Divide the fruit among warm sterilized jars and fill with the liquid. Put a disc of wax paper into each jar and seal. It keeps for 3 months. Once open, store in the fridge.

Damson plum chutney

My sister Anna makes and sells lots of jams, jellies, and chutneys. This is her favorite and most popular recipe. She recommends it to be used like quince jelly in Spain, with cheese, and with cold leftovers of ham, beef, or game.

Yield: 10 to12 jars
- **4 cups soft dark brown sugar**
- **½ pound apples**
- **1 pound damson plums**
- **3½ cups vinegar (cider or wine vinegar, or a mixture of dark brown malt and one of these)**
- **2½ cups raisins**
- **2 onions**
- **1 tablespoon sea salt**
- **2 garlic cloves, crushed**
- **A few chilis, fresh or dried**
- **1 teaspoon ground allspice**
- **1 teaspoon ground ginger**

Warm the sugar in a bowl in a very low oven for about half an hour.

Peel, core, and chop the apples. Add to the damson plums in a large pan with the vinegar and all the remaining ingredients, except the sugar, and simmer until soft. (Stir the pan regularly to prevent the chutney from sticking.) Remove from the heat. After this you can don your rubber gloves and pick out the pits if you want to.

Add the warmed sugar, put back on the heat, and stir constantly over low heat, until the sugar has completely dissolved. Simmer until the volume is sufficiently reduced to a thick mass. This may take some time and it will be necessary to stir it regularly to keep it from sticking. (Use a heat diffuser if necessary.) The mixture will thicken even more when it is cold, but there should not be much excess liquid at the end of the cooking time. Spoon into warm sterilized jars, seal, and store for a month before use. This chutney keeps really well for up to 2 years.

Damson ice cream

A delicious ice cream that is tart and packed with flavor.

Yield: about 3 pints
- **1 pound damson plums**
- **1½ cups heavy cream**
- **5 egg yolks**
- **1½ cups sugar**
- **1½ cups plain yogurt**

Put the whole damson plums into a medium-sized saucepan with 5 tablespoons water and poach over gentle heat until the fruit is soft. Rub through a sieve to extract the pits and chill the puree in the fridge.

Bring the cream to the boiling point and pull off the heat while you whisk the egg yolks and sugar together in a heatproof bowl until pale in color. Pour the scalded cream over the egg mixture and stir to combine.

At this point you can return the mixture to the rinsed saucepan and very carefully thicken the custard over gentle heat (preferably with a heat diffuser under the pan). Do not allow it to simmer. Alternatively, sit the saucepan in a wide shallow pan containing 2 inches of simmering water.

For either of these methods, stir the mixture until it thickens enough to coat the back of a wooden spoon. If you are worried that the mixture has overheated, plunge the base of the bowl or saucepan into very cold water and keep stirring until it loses some of its heat. Strain the custard into a bowl, cover with a sheet of wax paper, and chill in the fridge.

Combine the custard with the yogurt and fruit puree and freeze/churn for 20 minutes in an ice-cream machine, or put into a plastic container in the freezer and, after an hour or two, whisk with a hand mixer and return to the freezer, repeating this twice at intervals of about 1½ to 2 hours.

Remove from the freezer to the fridge about 20 minutes before serving.

Damson plum
and almond pudding

This is a really old-fashioned pudding, with very sharp damson plums contrasting with the sweet almond top.

Serves 8

- **6 tablespoons cold unsalted butter, plus a little extra for the dish**
- **2 pounds damson plums**
- **½ cup superfine sugar**
- **⅔ cup brown sugar, plus an extra spoonful for sprinkling**
- **¾ cup all-purpose flour**
- **¾ cup ground almonds**
- **3 level teaspoons baking powder**
- **Salt**
- **¾ cup buttermilk (or ¾ cup whole milk with 1 teaspoon lemon juice and a pinch of salt)**
- **2 drops natural almond extract**
- **2 tablespoons sliced almonds**

Preheat the oven to 400°F. Lightly butter a 2-quart ovenproof dish.

Pile the washed damson plums (unpitted) into the buttered dish and sprinkle over the superfine and brown sugars.

Combine the flour, ground almonds, baking powder, and a pinch of salt, and blend for a few seconds by hand in a bowl or in a food processor. Chop the butter into chunks and add to the flour mixture, pulsing until it looks like breadcrumbs. Add the milk and almond extract and mix again.

Spoon the mixture in mounds on top of the damson plums. Stick the sliced almonds into the mounds and sprinkle with a little extra brown sugar.

Cook in the preheated oven for 25 minutes, until risen and golden. Keep an eye on the almonds as they tend to brown quickly.

Sloe or damson plum
vodka or gin

This makes good Christmas presents and is perfect for drinking after dinner over Christmas. If you use damson plums, when you strain them from the vodka, eat them with ice cream or yogurt.

Yield: about a 750ml bottle

- **1 pound sloes or damson plums**
- **3 cups vodka or gin**
- **1¾ cups superfine sugar**

Make sure that the sloes or damson plums are really dry and remove any stems. Prick the fruit with a fork and put them into a large sterilized preserving jar with the vodka or gin and sugar. If you're doing a large batch and can't face pricking every one, shove the sloes or damson plums in the freezer overnight. This will have the effect of breaking the skins but doesn't affect the flavor.

If you prefer things less sweet, add less sugar (1¼ cups). You can then add a little more once you have tasted it, when rebottling.

Close the jar tightly and put in a dark place for 3 months, turning it as often as you remember—ideally, every few days—until the sugar has completely dissolved.

After 3 months, strain off the sloes or damson plums, pour the alcohol through a funnel into a dry warm sterilized bottle, and seal.

Sloe and apple jelly

A lovely jelly with a tart taste and beautiful color. It tends to be a bit sticky, so put it in the jars when it is a little runnier than most jellies. It will firm up anyway after a few months.

Yield: 2 jars
- **Sugar (for exact quantity, see below)**
- **3 pounds apples, chopped but not peeled or cored**
- **3 pounds sloes**

Warm the sugar in a bowl in a very low oven for about half an hour.

Cook the apples and sloes separately, adding just enough water to cover the fruit. Simmer gently until tender. Strain the juices separately.

Measure the juice, take equal parts of sloe and apple, and combine in a preserving pot.

Add 2½ cups warmed sugar for each 2½ cups of juice, stir until dissolved, and then boil rapidly until the gelling point is reached (see page 170). Pour into warm sterilized jars, cover, and seal. You can eat this right away or store for up to a year.

Rowan jelly

This is a recipe from my brother-in-law, Norrie MacLaren, who has made this jelly every year for twenty years. It's smoky and tart, perfect with venison or any game.

Yield: about 8 jars
- **4½ pounds rowan berries**
- **Sugar (for exact quantity, see below)**
- **Juice of ½ lemon and peeled rind of 1 lemon**
- **2 cloves**
- **Chili and mint, to taste (optional—use both or neither)**

Pick the berries from the stalks and wash out any insects. Put the rowans in a pan and just cover with cold water. Simmer them until they're pulpy. This takes about an hour.

Strain through a jelly bag, ideally overnight.

Warm the sugar in a bowl in a very low oven for about half an hour. Measure the juice and add 2½ cups warmed sugar to 2½ cups of liquid and the lemon juice. Add the lemon rind and cloves, tied in a cheesecloth bag so that you can fish them out later.

Heat until the sugar has dissolved and then boil briskly to the gelling point (see page 170). This usually takes about 20 minutes, but test every 10 minutes until you get a set on a saucer in the fridge.

Let the mixture cool for half an hour before stirring in the chopped herbs, if using. Pour into warm sterilized jars and seal. You can eat this right away, but it will keep unopened for up to a year.

Sweet black mulberry vinegar

Try splashing this over fresh fruit, particularly blueberries, melon, and pineapple. It's a wonderful way of storing away the extraordinary flavor of mulberries for a rainy day. I have bought this in the past from Stratta (see page 35), but when I can get my hands on mulberries, I make my own.

Try it also as part of a salad dressing or as a marinade for red meats and game. The exact amounts depend on how many mulberries you can lay your hands on.

You need:
- **Black mulberries**
- **White wine vinegar**
- **Superfine sugar (for exact quantity, see below)**

Cover the mulberries in vinegar—with liquid about one and a half times the volume of the fruit. Cover and leave somewhere cool and dark for 2 weeks.

Strain, measure the liquid, and add 3 cups sugar for each quart liquid. Dissolve the sugar in the juice and slowly bring to a boil, simmering very gently, for 15 minutes.

Decant into warm sterilized bottles and seal immediately. You can use this immediately, but unopened it will keep for up to 2 years and more.

Bramble jelly

This jelly is lovely on toast for breakfast and good with lamb.

Yield: about 5 jars

2 pounds blackberries
Sugar (for exact quantity, see below)
Juice of 1 large lemon

Put the blackberries and ½ cup water into a pan and simmer until they are soft. Allow the juice to drip through a jelly bag overnight (don't be tempted to squeeze the bag).

Warm the sugar in a bowl in a very low oven for about half an hour. Measure the juice and add 2½ cups warmed sugar for every 2½ cups of juice.

Put the juice into a large preserving pot with the lemon juice and warmed sugar, and stir over gentle heat until the sugar has completely dissolved. The pectin in the lemon is critical to get the jelly to set.

Bring to a rolling boil until the gelling point (see page 170) is reached. Pour into clean warm jars, cover, and seal. Keeps for up to a year.

Baked blackberries and mascarpone

Rose Gray, co-owner of the River Café in London, demonstrated this recipe at our cookery school recently, and I've made it several times since.

Blackberries are excellent when quickly cooked. A bit of heat releases their strange, sweet mellow flavor and yet—unlike raspberries—the fruit does not collapse.

Serves 6

2 pounds blackberries
2 vanilla pods
2 cups mascarpone cheese
3 egg yolks
2 tablespoons confectioners' sugar

Preheat the oven to 400°F. Wash the blackberries and pick them over. Scrape the seeds from the vanilla pods.

Mix the mascarpone, egg yolks, vanilla seeds, and confectioners' sugar together.

Put the blackberries in a small baking dish. Spoon the mascarpone over and bake in the preheated oven for about 5 minutes, until the mascarpone begins to brown.

Cranachan

This is a child-friendly version of a Scottish classic of whiskey, cream, raspberries, and oatmeal. In this one, I add dessert wine instead of whiskey, and I make a sweet granola with toasted oats. This is excellent with blackberries, or you can use raspberries.

Serves 6
For the granola:

2 tablespoons sunflower oil, plus more for the baking pan
2 tablespoons honey
¾ cup light brown sugar
Pinch of ground cinnamon
Pinch of freshly grated nutmeg
½ cup steel-cut oatmeal
½ cup rolled oatmeal
½ cup sesame seeds
About 1½ cups mixture of chopped nuts (pecans, hazelnuts, and almonds)

1¼ cups heavy cream
1¼ cups plain yogurt
Grated zest of 1 lemon and a little lemon juice, to taste
Superfine sugar, to taste
Beaumes-de-Venise, or any sweet white dessert wine, to taste
1 pound blackberries or raspberries

First, make the granola. Preheat the oven to 350°F. Warm the oil, honey, sugar, and spices together in a small saucepan. Mix together the remaining ingredients and put on a lightly oiled baking pan or cookie sheet. Pour over the warmed honey mixture and toss really well together, making sure everything is coated. Roast in the preheated oven for about 15 to 20 minutes, checking the mixture often to see that it is not burning. Remove from the oven and leave to stand. The mixture will crisp up.

When it's cool, break it up into small pieces and store in a screw-top jar. This is delicious for breakfast, sprinkled on porridge, or with yogurt or added to cereal. It keeps for a month in a screw-top jar.

Then whip your cream to the soft-peak stage and fold in the yogurt. Add the lemon zest, lemon juice, sugar, and dessert wine to taste.

Layer the cream with the fruit and scatter the granola over the top.

Figs and grapes

I think of figs and grapes under the same umbrella, both ready at this time of year and at their best eaten plain and simple, just as they come off the vine or tree. When they're perfect, they're perfect—you need do nothing to them.

Having said that, it's still worth having a few ideas up your sleeve for when you've got an enviable glut, when they're abundant and cheap in a market, or when the fruit is slightly over- or underripe. You can then use them to make some delicious things.

Grapes make wonderful jelly and, mixed with oranges, they make a good dessert (see page 330). The fresh leaves from a vine are also delicious stuffed. As far as grape varieties go, 'Phoenix' and 'Orion' (both white grape varieties) grow and fruit well outside for me. They have been specially selected for their suitability to cold climates, have good mildew resistance, and are sweet enough to eat just as they are. The delicious fat, sweet 'Muscat' fruits best here in a greenhouse.

If you have room, plant a fig and, if you want it to fruit, restrict its roots in a container. Left to get on with it, figs grow huge and barely fruit. Pruned and their roots restricted, they make a good small tree and produce well. To get the maximum fruit, protect the fruit buds from frost. Site a fig tree against a south-facing wall or, if you have anywhere frost-free under cover, grow it in a large pot and bring it in for the winter.

White gazpacho with grapes

This is delicious, but very rich, so don't be tempted to serve large portions of this autumn gazpacho.

Serves 6 as a starter
- ¾ cups blanched almonds, plus some toasted as a garnish
- 2 garlic cloves, peeled
- 4 slices stale white bread, crusts removed
- Salt
- 4 tablespoons sunflower oil
- 2 tablespoons extra virgin olive oil
- 3 tablespoons sherry vinegar
- 3 cups iced water
- 8 ounces seedless white grapes, halved

Blend the almonds, garlic, bread, and salt in a food processor until you have a smooth mixture. Gradually add the oils, vinegar, and half the iced water.

Pour into a bowl and, with a balloon whisk, mix in enough of the remaining iced water to give you the exact consistency you want—something rather like a granular heavy cream. Adjust the seasoning, stir in the grapes, and chill.

Serve very cold, with toasted almonds scattered over the top of each bowl.

Black and white grape salad

This is originally from Marcella Hazan's *The Classic Italian Cookbook* and it is not only beautiful but light, refreshing, and utterly delicious. It is perfect on its own after a large meal.

Serves 6 to 8
- 1 pound black or red grapes, seedless if possible
- 1 pound seedless green grapes
- Grated zest of 1 lemon
- ⅓ cup superfine sugar
- 3 oranges

Detach the grapes from their stems and cut the black grapes around the middle. If they have seeds, make sure you slice not right through them but just until you can feel the seeds; then twist the two halves, and you will easily be able to remove the seeds. If the green grapes are small, leave them whole; if not, slice them in half lengthwise.

Put the grapes into a bowl and add the lemon zest and the sugar. Squeeze the juice from the oranges. There should be just enough to cover the grapes—add a little more if not.

Mix thoroughly, cover, and chill for at least 2 hours before serving.

Grapes with caramel

Another quick, easy, and delicious dessert with grapes.

Serves 6
- 6 cups sugar
- 3 pounds grapes, ideally mixed green, red, and muscat
- ½ cup green ginger wine or other sweet wine
- 1½ cups crème fraîche
- Grated zest and juice of ½ lemon
- 1½ cups Greek yogurt or mild plain yogurt
- Superfine sugar, to taste

Put the sugar into a heavy-bottomed saucepan with 1½ cups water and stir over gentle heat so that the sugar dissolves completely. Place a silicone mat or a layer of parchment paper on a baking tray. Boil the syrup until it becomes a rich caramel color and then carefully pour into the lined tray and allow to cool.

Halve the grapes, or at least do half of them, and put them into a large glass dish. Spoon over the wine. Mix the crème fraîche, lemon zest, and yogurt together, and add a little superfine sugar and lemon juice to taste. Pile on to the grapes, cover the dish, and chill.

Just before serving, break up the caramel into shards and pile on to the cream.

Grape jelly

This is lovely on bread or toast and wonderful whisked into a sauce with meat or game.

You need:
Sugar (for exact quantity, see below)
Juicy grapes
Juice of ½ lemon

Take the grapes off their stalks and put them into a preserving pot. Put enough cold water into the pan just to cover them and bring them to a boil. Simmer the grapes over moderate heat until they are tender. Pour through a jelly bag and allow to drip overnight into a nonreactive bowl. Don't be tempted to squeeze the bag.

Warm the sugar in a bowl in a very low oven for about half an hour. Measure and then warm the grape juice in the preserving pot, and add 2½ cups warmed sugar for every 2½ cups of juice and the lemon juice. Dissolve gently over low heat and, when the sugar is completely dissolved, raise the heat and bring to a rolling boil. Boil until it reaches the gelling point (see page 170).

Take off the heat, skim the surface to remove any scum, and pour into warm sterilized jars and seal.

Jude's stuffed grapevine leaves

I love dolmades—hot as well as cold. This is a vegetarian recipe of Jude Maynard, who cooked in our school for several years. Serve with yogurt.

Serves 4 to 6
½ pound young grapevine leaves, or preserved bottled leaves
2 large onions, chopped
⅔ cup olive oil
2 tablespoons pine nuts
½ teaspoon tomato paste
2 tablespoons dried currants
1 cup Arborio rice
1 teaspoon ground allspice
Handful of dill, chopped
Handful of mint, chopped
Salt and pepper
1 (14-ounce) can chopped tomatoes
1 teaspoon sugar
Juice of 1 lemon
3 cups vegetable stock

If you are using fresh grapevine leaves, remove the tough part of the stem and blanch for about 3 or 4 minutes in salted boiling water. Drain and refresh in cold water. If you are using bottled or canned grapevine leaves, soak them in hot water for about 20 minutes, rinse, and drain.

Fry the onions in 3 tablespoons of olive oil until they are soft. Add the pine nuts and stir until they are golden. Add the tomato paste and stir in the currants, rice, allspice, and herbs—but do not cook. Season to taste.

Place a small mound of the filling on the grapevine leaf and roll up tightly, folding in the sides as you go, to make a secure parcel. Pour the canned tomatoes into a heavy pan and pack the rolled leaves on top. Mix the remaining oil, the sugar, and the lemon juice together and pour over the grapevine leaves. Cover these with the stock and then a plate to weight them down, and simmer gently for an hour, adding a small amount of water if necessary.

Roasted stuffed figs with Gorgonzola and walnuts

This is good eaten as a first course or for lunch, served with slices of Parma ham and a pile of watercress and arugula leaves.

Serves 4 as a starter
8 ripe figs
5 ounces Gorgonzola cheese
1 cup chopped walnuts, toasted
Black pepper
2 teaspoons honey
2 teaspoons balsamic vinegar
2 tablespoons extra virgin olive oil

Preheat the oven to 350°F. Place the figs in an ovenproof dish. Mix together the Gorgonzola and the toasted chopped walnuts, and season with black pepper. Cut a cross shape in the top of each fig, but leave ½ inch at the bottom intact.

Squeeze the centers to open the figs out a little and then pile in the cheese and walnut mixture. Warm the honey, balsamic vinegar, and a little extra virgin olive oil and then pour over the figs.

Bake in the preheated oven for about 8 minutes and serve.

Fresh fig tart

This is a really wonderful tart, with that characteristic taste of figs only just cooked. It looks good too.

Serves 6
- 1⅓ **cups all-purpose flour**
- **Pinch of salt**
- **6 tablespoons unsalted butter**
- **4 eggs**
- **1 tablespoon superfine sugar**
- **1 cup heavy cream or crème fraîche**
- **1 tablespoon green ginger wine or other sweet wine**
- ⅓ **cup sliced almonds, toasted**
- **9 fresh figs**

Sift the flour and salt together and rub in the butter, or pulse in a processor, until the mixture resembles breadcrumbs. Mix 1 egg with a little very cold water and add just enough of this to be able to pull the pastry together into a ball. Roll the pastry out and use to line an 8-inch tart pan. Chill for 30 minutes.

Preheat the oven to 350°F. Prick the bottom of the crust with a fork, cover with a round of parchment paper or foil, and weight this down with some baking beans or rice. Bake the crust blind for about 20 to 25 minutes. Take it out of the oven, but leave the oven on, and let it cool, then remove the beans or rice and the paper.

Mix together the superfine sugar, cream, remaining beaten eggs, and wine. Scatter the toasted almonds over the crust. Quarter the figs, arrange them on the almonds, and pour over the cream mixture.

Put into the preheated oven and cook until the custard has set and is just beginning to brown on the top. This should take about 15 minutes. Serve the tart warm.

Quail with figs

A simple dish full of the sweet flavor of figs. I think that one quail per person is plenty, but just double the quantities if you want two each.

Serves 4
- **4 quails**
- **Salt and pepper**
- ¼ **cup (½ stick) butter**
- **4 slices bacon or pancetta**
- **2 tablespoons extra virgin olive oil**
- **3 shallots, finely chopped**
- ¾ **cup dry white wine**
- **16 figs**

Preheat the oven to 350°F.

Season the quail with salt and pepper. Put a generous bit of butter inside the cavity and wrap each bird with the bacon or pancetta. Secure with a toothpick. Heat the olive oil and sweat the shallots until softened but not browned and put them in a casserole dish. Brown the quail and add them to the shallots. Pour over the white wine, cover, and then either simmer or cook in the preheated oven for 30 minutes.

Remove the quail from the casserole dish and keep warm. Quarter the figs without cutting through the base and then put them into the casserole dish with the juices. Cook for 10 minutes.

Remove the bacon or pancetta from the quail and serve them surrounded by the figs. Pour over the juices and, with scissors, snip the bacon or pancetta over the top.

Fig confit

The most delicious fig preserve I've tasted. Unlike some versions, where the fruit has been stewed for too long, this does not feel like a waste of precious figs. It is fresh and chunky, delicious served chilled with game or cheese, as well as lovely on toast.

Yield: 1 jar
- ¾ **cup Marsala wine**
- ½ **cup sugar**
- ¾ **pound figs**
- **Sprig of rosemary**
- **2 small bay leaves**
- **Piece of thinly pared lemon rind and juice of ½ lemon**

Put the Marsala into a saucepan with ⅓ cup water and the sugar. The Marsala will preserve the figs. Over gentle heat, stir to dissolve the sugar completely. Trim the stems from the figs, quarter them lengthwise, and add them to the pan with the rosemary, bay, and lemon rind. Simmer until the figs are tender but not too soft.

Remove them with a slotted spoon and put them into a warm sterilized jar, leaving enough space for the liquid.

Remove the rosemary, bay and lemon rind. Add the lemon juice and bring the syrup to a fast boil to reduce for 5 minutes. Pour the hot syrup over the figs in the jar and cover. You can and should use this right away since it will only last a couple of weeks. To store it, keep in the fridge.

Maincrop/floury potatoes

Maincrop potatoes—the ones that are stored through the winter—could not be more different from newly lifted, waxy new potatoes. Many maincrops, the fluffy ones with a high starch and low water content, make good baked and mashed potatoes, as well as crunchy roast potatoes, chips, and rösti. I have a huge range of floury varieties, from the white-skinned, long-storing 'Maris Piper' to the pinky-red-skinned 'Red Duke of York'. There are also waxy types such as 'Pink Fir Apple' and 'Ratte' that perform a different culinary role. With a high water, low dry-weight content, these don't collapse when boiled and so make the best salad potato (see pages 122–127).

Here is how you make delicious roasted potatoes: Preheat the oven to 400°F and put in a baking sheet, with a thin layer of oil covering the bottom of the tray. Meanwhile, parboil your potatoes for five minutes in salted water. Drain them, dry them off over low heat, and bash them around a bit to break up the outside flesh, or use a fork. Season with salt and put them into the hot oil. You can scatter thyme, rosemary, or sage over them, ensuring that the herbs as well as the potatoes are well coated with oil. After thirty minutes, you could scatter finely chopped garlic over them, then put them back in the oven to finish cooking. After forty-five minutes, they should be perfect.

You'll need to bear the following in mind if you want to make the best french fries. After cutting the potatoes, they need to be soaked in water for a good hour before frying (dry them thoroughly beforehand). Use peanut oil and fill the oil to only one-third of the depth of the fryer. Have the oil very hot (take care) and fry them in small batches. Lastly, the secret is to cook them twice. Fry them in hot oil for five minutes until cooked but not brown; drain them on paper towels, let them rest, and then reheat the oil to 325°F, giving them a refrying to make them perfectly crisp.

Finally, don't forget sweet potatoes. I love the color of the pink-fleshed ones and seek these out in preference to the white (though the taste is the same).

Rösti potatoes

Rösti potatoes might be fattening, but no more so than french fries, and they have infinitely more flavor.

Yield: 6 large rösti
  3 or 4 potatoes
  2 tablespoons chopped onion
  Handful of chopped flat-leaf parsley
  1 tablespoon all-purpose flour
  Salt and pepper
  2 tablespoons vegetable oil
  ¼ cup (½ stick) butter

Preheat the oven to 350°F.

Grate the potatoes on a coarse grating disc and twist them in a kitchen towel to squeeze out the moisture. Once the potatoes are fairly dry, put them into a bowl with the onion, parsley, and flour, and season them well with salt and pepper.

Heat the oil and butter in a heavy-bottomed pan and spread the potato mixture over the pan. Push it down hard with the back of a spoon. Cook until the bottom is brown and crisp—it will then hold together better—and turn to cook the underside until golden brown.

Allow to cool and cut into either wedges or rounds. Reheat them in the preheated oven for a few minutes to make them really crunchy.

Nutmeg mashed potatoes

I first had this with my brother-in-law, Andrew Wallace, and now almost always add nutmeg to my mash. If you want to try something different, add 3 bay leaves to the potato cooking water and another couple of bay leaves when you heat the milk.

Many chefs are keen on using baked potatoes, scooped out, for mash, claiming this method gives better flavor and creamier texture. I've done a taste and texture comparison between the baking and boiling techniques, and I don't think it makes any difference.

Serves 4
  6 large potatoes
  Salt and pepper
  ½ cup (1 stick) butter
  ⅔ cup milk (or cream)
  Freshly grated nutmeg, to taste

Cut the potatoes in half (not into small chunks, as this makes them watery) and boil in salted water for about 15 minutes until they're soft but not overcooked.

Drain and mash thoroughly with butter, salt, pepper, and some milk or cream with grated nutmeg.

You can keep this warm in the oven, covered in little knobs of butter and some foil, for up to an hour, or dot with butter and brown the top.

Rosemary saddleback potatoes

These are delicious and quicker to cook than roast potatoes, and you really get the taste of rosemary. While they are raw the potatoes are sliced, but not quite to the bottom, so that they fan out slightly when they're cooked. The flavors of the herbs and oil—it's worth using extra virgin olive oil—soak right into the potatoes. If you can find them, blue potatoes make the showiest-looking saddlebacks. Pesto is a good alternative to rosemary, and try them with garlic and anchovies pounded in a mortar with black pepper.

Serves 8
  1½ pounds potatoes
  6 tablespoons extra virgin olive oil
  Leaves from 5 sprigs of rosemary
  Salt and pepper

Preheat the oven to 375°F. Peel the potatoes, or keep the skins on if you prefer. Cut them in slices just under ½ inch thick, stopping just before the bottom of the potato.

Put them on an oiled baking sheet and scatter over the rosemary, pushing the herbs right down into the slices. Douse with olive oil and season with salt and pepper.

Put them in the oven and roast for about 1 hour, until they're golden brown.

Stuffed baked potatoes with pesto

My children love these. In the autumn, I make them with basil pesto (see page 225), while in the spring I make them with Wild garlic pesto (see page 95).

Serves 4

4 baking potatoes
½ cup crème fraîche
¾ cup grated cheese (Wensleydale or another crumbly hard cheese; Parmesan is also good, but use half the amount)
⅔ cup pesto (homemade or bought)
2 garlic cloves, peeled and crushed
Salt and pepper

Preheat the oven to 350°F.

Wash the potatoes and score around the full diameter of the potato with a sharp knife, only just piercing the skin. This makes it easier to cut them precisely, so that you get two perfect halves.

Bake the potatoes for about an hour, until they're cooked all the way through. Remove them from the oven, keeping it on, and cut them in half. Carefully scoop out the potato from the skins and put it into a bowl.

Add all the other ingredients to the potato flesh and mix thoroughly with a fork. Spoon the mixture back into the potato skins, piling them up above the edges so that they look generously filled. You may need to sacrifice a couple of skins to get enough filling to do this. Return them to the oven for about 15 minutes, until the tops become golden.

Stuffed baked potatoes can be made in advance and kept in the fridge for up to two days to cook when needed. They are also suitable for freezing at the just-stuffed stage.

Warm potato and lentil salad

This is lovely for lunch with a mixed leaf salad or as a side dish to accompany meat or fish. If you want something more substantial, add chunks of soft cheese—either goat or sheep.

Serves 8 as a starter or a side dish
  2½ cups lentils (preferably French Puy lentils)
  2 tablespoons extra virgin olive oil, plus more for drizzling
  2 garlic cloves, peeled but not chopped
  ½ onion, chopped
  Some parsley stalks and handful of coarsely chopped parsley
  1 bay leaf
  Plenty of salt and pepper
  1 pound potatoes
  Plenty of mint leaves
  Grated zest and juice of 2 lemons

Cook the lentils in enough water to cover together with the olive oil, garlic, onion, parsley stalks, bay leaf, and salt. For a richer taste, use half water, half white wine. Simmer gently for about 15 minutes, until the lentils are soft but not collapsing. Drain.

Boil the potatoes in salted water with most of the mint. When they are cooked and after they have cooled slightly, peel and cut them into chunks.

Add the potatoes to the lentils with more olive oil, the lemon zest and juice, and plenty of chopped parsley and mint.

Season well and eat while the salad is still warm.

Bubble and squeak cakes

This is a great way of eating leftover mashed potatoes and vegetables, but the best bubble and squeak is made from floury potatoes that are broken up, not mashed. These cakes are good with bacon and baked beans for brunch, or with grilled salmon and chili jelly or chili jam for lunch or dinner. Bacon fat, if you have some, is excellent for frying the onions and then the potato cakes.

Yield: 16 cakes (enough for 8 people)
  1 onion, sliced
  1 leek, thinly sliced
  Olive oil (or butter or bacon fat), for frying
  3 pounds potatoes
  1 small savoy cabbage
  Small bunch of spinach (about ½ pound), stems removed
  Salt and pepper
  4 tablespoons flour, seasoned with salt and pepper

Gently fry the onion and leek in olive oil. Peel and cook the potatoes until they're soft. Drain them and put aside.

Meanwhile, cut up the cabbage into ribbons and boil it for 3 minutes in salted water. Cook the spinach for 5 minutes and coarsely chop. Add plenty of salt and pepper to the potato, and then mash roughly.

Combine everything well. Shape the mixture into palm-sized cakes, roll them in seasoned flour, and fry them gently in olive oil, until they are brown and crunchy on the outside but heated through to the middle.

You can keep the unfried mixture in the fridge for a couple of days.

Sweet potato gratin

Sweet potatoes have some of the densest flesh of any root vegetable and so take some cooking. Slice them thinly to get the best texture and taste. This is filling and good with a green salad on its own or as a side dish to eat with any red meat.

Serves 4
   2 sweet potatoes, peeled and
      thinly sliced
   2 tablespoons extra virgin olive oil
   2 red chilis, deseeded and finely
      chopped
   1½-inch piece of ginger, peeled
      and chopped
   2 garlic cloves, chopped
   Salt and pepper

Preheat the oven to 350°F.

   Oil an ovenproof dish and layer the sweet potatoes, with a scattering of chili, ginger, garlic, seasonings, and a little olive oil on every second or third layer. Cover with foil and bake in the preheated oven for 1 hour.

Grilled sweet potato with ginger, chili, and lime

I love the look and the taste of these grilled pink sweet potatoes.

Serves 8 to 10
   4 medium-sized sweet potatoes
   ¾ cup extra virgin olive oil

For the dressing:
   5 tablespoons lime juice
   3 tablespoons chopped fresh
      cilantro
   2 tablespoons honey
   4 teaspoons grated ginger
   1 red chili, deseeded and finely
      chopped
   2 garlic cloves, crushed
   Salt and pepper

Peel the sweet potatoes and cut into thin slices. Blanch the slices in boiling water for a couple of minutes. Drain them and allow to dry. Put the slices in a bowl and smother with the olive oil.

   Heat a grill pan and cook the potato slices for 3 to 4 minutes on each side. This is fine when you're cooking for a few, but for this sort of number, it takes quite a few batches. It's quicker, but produces less handsome striping, if you put the whole lot in a baking sheet and do it under the broiler.

   Make the dressing by mixing all the ingredients together and drizzle over the sweet potatoes while still warm. This is delicious hot or cold.

Roasted sweet potato and feta salad

An excellent salad that is ideal as a first course with crusty bread.

Serves 8
   8 good-quality tomatoes
   Salt and pepper
   Pinch of sugar
   3 tablespoons extra virgin olive oil,
      plus more for drizzling
   2 red onions
   4 sweet potatoes
   1 pound baby spinach
   1 tablespoon balsamic vinegar
   6 ounces feta cheese

Preheat the oven to 250°F. Halve the tomatoes, sprinkle with salt, pepper and a pinch of sugar, and drizzle with olive oil. Place on a baking sheet and put in the oven for 4 hours. Remove, and cover to keep warm.

   Increase the oven setting to 350°F. Peel and quarter the red onions. Put them on a baking sheet and roast for 45 minutes.

   Peel the sweet potatoes and chop them into ½-inch rounds, and add them to the roasting sheet with the onions after 15 minutes, giving them 30 minutes' cooking time. The onions should be well cooked and caramelized and the sweet potato starting to brown around the edges.

   Arrange the spinach in a shallow bowl or plate, and dress with the extra virgin olive oil and balsamic vinegar and some pepper. Scatter the still-warm roasted tomatoes, onions, and sweet potatoes over the dressed spinach (if the spinach wilts a bit, all the better), and throw the juices from the roasting pan over the vegetables.

   Dice the feta into small cubes and arrange over the top. Grind some pepper over the top and serve immediately.

Mushrooms

Strictly speaking, mushrooms aren't garden vegetables, but you couldn't have a garden cookbook without them. Many people are fearful about eating fungi, anxious that they'll pick the wrong one when foraging for them in the wild. We can abandon a lawn full of the most perfect mushrooms to the slugs just because we're not sure. We're unique in this and, unlike most Europeans, we miss out.

All you need is a good book that clearly tells you the ten or fifteen best wild mushrooms to search for, and which are the non-edible or poisonous ones that look similar. It will take you a couple of seasons to feel confident. I learned from Antonio Carluccio's mushroom book. He has the good, the less good, and the dangerous close together on the page, so it's difficult to make a mistake. Roger Phillips has also written a definitive guide.

My favorites are all quite common in the late summer and autumn around my home, Perch Hill. These are field mushrooms, parasols, shaggy ink caps (when they've just emerged from the ground), chanterelles (beware of the false ones: not deadly, but disappointing), porcinis, and hedgehog fungus. Chicken of the wood—the sulphur polyphose—is also good and so much like chicken that some will be completely fooled by its long-grained meaty texture. It requires longer cooking than the others I've mentioned, but is equally delicious.

With lots of these recipes, a mixed basket will give you a range of color and texture and make for a more interesting dish, so when you're out foraging, try to find a few of several different types. There is now a wide range of interesting mushrooms available in good grocery stores. I don't often buy tight button mushrooms, but the big flat ones have fantastic flavor and my local farm shop now almost always has tasty oyster mushrooms as well. Just a couple of thin slices of each with a splash of cream and a sprinkle of nutmeg transform a simple baked egg into a wonderful quick supper dish. And of course mushrooms—wild or bought—make a great omelette.

Jane's chanterelles

My twin sister, Jane, is a great fungi enthusiast and a fantastic cook. She lives in Scotland, where there are lots of chanterelles. If you're lucky enough to find them, this wine-rich sauce with garlic is the best way to eat them. It's good with rice—brown gives an extra crunch—or any pasta. This recipe also works well with a mix of mushrooms—porcini and hedgehogs, as well as chanterelles.

Serves 6

1 medium-sized onion (preferably red), finely chopped
1 tablespoon olive oil
3 ounces smoked bacon or pancetta, cut into strips
1 large garlic clove, finely chopped
1½ pounds chanterelles (and some porcini and hedgehog fungus, if possible)
1 glass of white wine
A little cream (optional)
Handful of chopped parsley
Salt and pepper
3 ounces Parmesan cheese, grated

Fry the onion in olive oil gently for 10 minutes, until just soft. Add the bacon or pancetta and cook for another 5 minutes, until browned. Add the garlic and cook for 1 minute. Add the mushrooms, breaking up the large ones so that they cook consistently.

Cook for about 5 minutes—after a couple of minutes they will exude water, which you want to evaporate (a wide pan helps with this). Before the mushrooms become mushy, add the white wine and cook until there is just a little sauce left. Add the cream (if using), parsley, salt, and pepper and heat for another couple of minutes. Add the Parmesan cheese.

Raw mushroom salad

A mix of wild mushrooms is the most interesting fungi to use for this salad, but they must be very young. If store-bought are used, pick only the young ones with the closed cups. These stay firm, not going soggy in the marinade. This is perfect for eating before a rich main course. It's good with homemade brown bread and butter.

If you cannot find hazelnut oil, you could use walnut oil and warm chopped walnuts.

Serves 4

½ pound very young wild or closed-cup store-bought mushrooms
Bunch of flat-leaf parsley
A little hazelnut oil
1 teaspoon freshly grated nutmeg
Squeeze of lemon juice
Salt and pepper
¼ cup hazelnuts, skinned
Warm brown bread or toast

Trim the mushroom stalks and slice them thinly.

Chop the parsley and add to the bowl with the mushrooms. Pour over just enough hazelnut oil to coat the mushrooms— don't drown them—and stir in the nutmeg and a little lemon juice. Stir to combine and season carefully with salt and pepper.

Leave this to one side to marinate for 20 minutes or so, stirring from time to time.

Just before serving, toast the hazelnuts, chop them into halves, and serve warm on top of the mushrooms with a little more hazelnut oil if you wish. Season.

Serve with warm brown bread or toast.

Mushroom soup

You can practically stand your spoon up in this soup, it is packed so full of mushrooms.

Serves 6

2½ cups good chicken stock
1 large onion, finely chopped
1 garlic clove, finely chopped
5 tablespoons butter
1 pound mushrooms (a mixture of mushrooms is delicious, including some button or closed-cup)
¼ cup all-purpose flour
Generous pinch of ground mace or freshly grated nutmeg
2½ cups milk
⅔ cup light cream
1 tablespoon lemon juice
Salt and pepper
Handful of parsley, finely chopped

Warm the stock and put to one side. Fry the onion and garlic in the butter to soften. Roughly chop half the mushrooms and add to the onion. Cook until the mushrooms are soft.

Stir in the flour and mace or nutmeg, and cook for a couple of minutes.

Using a large balloon whisk, gradually add the hot stock and bring to a boil. Cover and allow to simmer for 15 to 20 minutes. Puree the soup and return to a clean pot.

Season well. You can freeze the mixture at this point in batches.

Finely chop the rest of the mushrooms and add to the pan with the milk. Bring to a boil and simmer for a further 10 minutes. Take off the heat and add the cream, lemon juice, and seasoning to taste. Garnish with some parsley in each bowl.

The soup can be reheated gently, but do not bring to a boil once the cream and lemon juice have been added.

Porcini and prosciutto pasticcio

Another of my sister Jane's recipes. This is a dish that she made with author Hugh Fearnley-Whittingstall. She still remembers it as one of the best feasts she's ever had. They found so many porcinis in Morayshire in Scotland that they had to think of different ways to cook them.

Serves 8

- **1 pound porcinis or mix of wild and farm-grown mushrooms**
- **½ onion**
- **1 garlic clove**
- **6 tablespoons extra virgin olive oil, plus a little more to oil the dish**
- **8 ounces lasagne sheets, either homemade or the no-pre-cook store-bought variety**
- **Salt**
- **10 slices Parma ham (or prosciutto)**
- **A few bits of butter, to finish**

For the béchamel sauce:

- **4 cups milk**
- **6 tablespoons butter**
- **⅓ cup all-purpose flour**
- **1 egg yolk**
- **1 cup mascarpone cheese**
- **Freshly grated nutmeg, to taste, plus a bit extra to garnish**
- **Plenty of salt and pepper**
- **½ cup grated Parmesan cheese**

Preheat the oven to 350°F.

Slice the mushrooms and onion, and peel the garlic clove, crushing it with the side of a knife but ensuring you leave it whole.

Heat the olive oil in a deep saucepan and cook the onion and garlic on gentle heat until golden brown. Remove the garlic and add the mushrooms to the pan. Cook for 10 minutes, until the fungi are soft.

While the mushrooms are cooking, make the béchamel sauce. Bring the milk to a boil and, in a separate pan, melt the butter. Stir the flour into the butter, allow it to cook for a couple of minutes, and then gradually add the hot milk. Add the egg yolk, then the mascarpone and plenty of nutmeg, stirring continuously. Season with plenty of salt and pepper. Add almost all the grated cheese and stir until it melts.

If your pasta needs precooking, boil the sheets in plenty of salted water and allow them to dry flat on a clean cloth.

In an oiled ovenproof dish, build up thin layers of mushroom, ham, béchamel, and pasta, repeating in this order. Finish with the remaining béchamel, then the rest of the grated cheese, and dot the top with the butter and a bit of extra nutmeg. Cook in the preheated oven for 35 to 40 minutes.

Mushroom pasta

This is a more everyday way of eating mushrooms, and makes a good quick weekday supper.

Serves 4
For the sauce:
   1 large onion, finely chopped
   1 tablespoon olive oil
   3 tablespoons butter
   1 garlic clove, finely chopped
   6 large flat field or mixed
      mushrooms, sliced
   1 glass of white wine
   Juice and grated zest of 1 lemon
   Freshly grated nutmeg
   Salt and pepper
   1 cup crème fraîche
   2 tablespoons finely chopped
      parsley or 1 tablespoon finely
      chopped thyme
   Grated Parmesan cheese

   10 to 16 ounces pasta

To make the sauce, gently fry the onion in the olive oil and butter for 10 minutes and then add the garlic and mushrooms.

   Just stir enough to combine everything, as you don't want to knock the mushrooms about too much or they'll bleed lots of black juice. Add the white wine, lemon juice and zest, and then nutmeg, salt, and pepper to taste. Continue to cook for 10 minutes. Pour in the crème fraîche and three-quarters of the parsley, and just heat through without boiling.

   Meanwhile, boil the pasta in salted boiling water until just al dente. Drain the pasta. Mix with the sauce and garnish with the rest of the parsley and the Parmesan on top.

Mushrooms with polenta

Anything with a strong flavor and a gunky soft texture is good with polenta. I love polenta with Braised endive (see page 25) and it's wonderful with garlicky mushrooms. You can use a real mix of mushrooms for this—porcinis, field mushrooms, parasols, and very fresh shaggy ink caps.

Serves 8
   ⅔ cup quick-cooking polenta
   ¼ cup (½ stick) butter
   3 ounces grated Parmesan
      cheese, plus a bit extra as a
      garnish
   Plenty of salt and pepper
   Double quantity of Mushroom
      pasta sauce (see left)
   Extra virgin olive oil, for drizzling
   A bunch of parsley, coarsely
      chopped, as a garnish

To cook the polenta, bring 6 cups of salted water to a boil and then remove from the heat while you whisk in the polenta.

   Keep whisking until the mixture is quite smooth and then put the pan back on the heat. It will start to bubble furiously, but keep stirring and turn the heat down. Cook the polenta for a few minutes, until it becomes thick and creamy. Add the butter and Parmesan, and season well. This dish really does benefit from plenty of salt and pepper.

   To grill or fry the polenta, turn it out on a large shallow plate or dish (ideally, the depth of the polenta should be about 1 inch) and allow it to cool completely while you cook the mushrooms. When the polenta is cold, cut it into triangles or fish finger–sized slices ready for cooking.

   Make sure the grill pan is really hot and put the wedges of polenta on to grill them for about 5 minutes on either side. For a richer option, fry the slices in butter or olive oil.

   To serve, heat the mushroom sauce and put a slice of polenta and a good dollop of sauce on each plate. Drizzle with a little olive oil and garnish with the parsley and grated Parmesan.

Nuts

My husband's family has a brilliant tool for roasting chestnuts. It's a small iron pot, with a few holes punctured through the base and sides, and a well-fitting lid. You can fit fifteen or twenty chestnuts in one go—each one first pierced with the tip of a sharp knife—and then you poke the pot into the middle of the fire to roast. After five minutes, tipped out to cool, they're perfect.

That's one of the best ways to eat chestnuts—hot, smoky, soft, and sweet—but there are other delicious things to do. They are good in desserts (with meringue) and savory dishes—mixed with brussels sprouts (see page 391), added as invaluable texture in a terrine, or used as a rich center for stuffed meat (see page 350) or soup. Either buy your chestnuts vacuum-packed or cook and skin them yourself. This takes time and is a process, but it can be done. Make a decent-sized nick in the skin on the flat side of each chestnut and then put them in a pan of boiling water for ten to twelve minutes. Try one and see if it's soft after ten. If you overdo them, they fall apart. Drain them and let them cool a bit before you peel them. They are very rich and full of protein, so a few chestnuts go a long way.

This spring I spent a morning in a hazel orchard full of hundred-year-old trees. It was a beautiful place on a slope overlooking Plaxtol in Kent. At the top end of the field was a large wooden shed, standing a couple of feet up on stone stilts. The shed floor was lined with sheets of tin, which were bent to a third of the way up its walls. This was a hazel storehouse, armored against squirrels and mice. There aren't many of these buildings left and there aren't many nut orchards either. In 1900, there were seven thousand acres of hazelnut orchards in Britain; now there are only two hundred fifty. Like chestnuts, they're incredibly good for you and have a unique and wonderful taste. Eat them green—fresh, straight off the tree—with cheese, or use them dried in ice cream (see page 357), salads, biscuits (see page 357), and cakes.

Picking green walnuts, leaving one's hands black for days, is an activity that immediately makes me feel eight years old. That acrid yet oddly addictive smell is a powerful memory press. Dried walnuts are a big part of Christmas. Cut up and toasted, they make a good addition to salads (see page 26), while green, they are wonderful to eat with cheese. Instead of pecans, they also make an excellent toffee walnut tart (see page 355).

Chestnut-stuffed pork tenderloin

Stuffing things often feels a step too far, but once you've made this, you'll realize how quick and easy it is to do, and that the chestnut filling makes an ordinary bit of meat into something very delicious.

Serves 4

1 pork tenderloin (about 1 to 1¼ pounds)
1 onion, finely chopped
2 tablespoons olive oil
6 ounces pancetta or bacon
Several garlic cloves, finely chopped
½ pound spinach, chopped
Freshly grated nutmeg
Bunch of sage leaves, finely chopped
1 tablespoon breadcrumbs
Salt and pepper
15 prunes, pitted and roughly chopped
15 to 20 chestnuts
6 full slices prosciutto, for wrapping the tenderloin
8 to 10 baby onions or shallots
2 glasses of white wine
1 tablespoon redcurrant jelly
2 tablespoons crème fraîche

Preheat the oven to 350°F.

Make a cut along the length of the pork tenderloin, without cutting it in two, and open it out. Put the pork between 2 sheets of plastic wrap and beat it out until it is at least twice the size.

Chop the onion and sauté it in the olive oil with the pancetta or bacon and garlic for a few minutes, until the onion is softened. Add the spinach, nutmeg, sage, and enough breadcrumbs to absorb any liquid given off by the spinach. Season and take off the heat.

Stuff the length of the pork fillet with this mixture. Add the prunes and chestnuts, scattered through, and roll it up. Wrap the roll with the prosciutto and tie at intervals with string.

Brown this for a couple of minutes all over in the pan in which the stuffing was made and then put it in a shallow ovenproof dish with the baby onions or shallots—whole if small, cut in half if large—and cover with the white wine.

Roast in the preheated oven for 40 minutes, and then remove the meat from the roasting dish and keep it warm. Scrape up the juices from the dish, add the wine (or some stock), and allow to bubble up and reduce a little before adding a little redcurrant jelly and the crème fraîche. You can add more chestnuts at this stage. Pour this sauce over the meat.

Chestnut pavlova with caramelized apples

The nuttiness of this chestnut meringue with the tartness of the apples is wonderful. This is a fantastic party dessert for autumn.

Serves 8

For the meringue:
- ½ **cup granulated sugar**
- ½ **cup superfine sugar**
- 4 **egg whites**
- ½ **teaspoon cream of tartar**
- 1 **teaspoon vinegar**

For the filling and topping:
- ¾ **pound cooked chestnuts, fresh or canned**
- 1 **cup heavy cream**
- **Splash of brandy**
- **Superfine sugar, to taste**
- 2 to 3 **tart apples**
- 1 **tablespoon unsalted butter**
- **Confectioners' sugar**

Preheat the oven to 325°F.

To make the meringue, mix the two sugars together. Whisk the egg whites until they are really stiff and continue whisking while you add three-quarters of the sugar, one tablespoon at a time. Make sure that the mixture regains its former stiffness and finally, carefully fold in the remaining sugar with a metal spoon. Add the cream of tartar and vinegar. Sparsely oil 2 circles of parchment paper (or use silicone mats) and divide the mixture between the two, spreading it out as lightly as possible.

Cook in the preheated oven for about 45 minutes, until the meringue is crisp and has turned coffee colored. Turn off the heat and allow the meringue to cool completely in the oven before removing from the baking sheet.

To make the filling, first puree ½ pound of the chestnuts in a food processor. Then whip the cream with a bit of brandy and sugar to taste, and carefully fold into the chestnut puree just till combined.

Peel and core the apples, and cut into fairly thick slices. Toss these in melted butter and a little sugar over high heat until they begin to go brown, but remove them to a bowl before they become soft, and keep warm.

Add the remaining whole chestnuts to the pan in which you heated the apples and toss them until they are glazed with the sugar and butter mixture. Add to the apples.

Sandwich the 2 meringue layers together with the chestnut cream and a layer of caramelized apples and chestnuts, sift the confectioners' sugar over the top, and serve with the rest of the apples and chestnuts.

Pickled walnuts

These are good just as they are with smoked meats and cheese, and also lovely added to hot game or beef dishes. You really need freshly picked nuts for this treatment.

Yield: 1 quart
- 2 **pounds freshly picked green walnuts, shelled weight**
- **Salt**
- 1 **cinnamon stick**
- 4 **cups malt or wine vinegar**
- 1 **teaspoon freshly grated ginger**
- 1 **teaspoon ground allspice**
- 1 **teaspoon cloves**
- 12 **black peppercorns**
- 2½ **cups soft brown sugar**

Prick the walnuts with a sharp fork or needle. Put them into a nonreactive bowl, cover them with water, and add a handful of salt. Leave this for 5 or 6 days, stirring from time to time.

After this time, drain them, cover with fresh water, salt again, and leave for another few days.

Drain and lay the walnuts out in a dry place. They will turn black after 2 or 3 days.

Crumble the cinnamon, put it into a pan with the remaining ingredients, and put over gentle heat until the sugar has completely dissolved. Bring to a boil and simmer for 10 minutes. Add the blackened walnuts and simmer for a further 10 minutes. Lift out the walnuts with a slotted spoon and divide among 3 or 4 large jars, filling the jars about two-thirds full. Pour over the strained syrup and cover.

Leave the walnuts for at least 6 to 8 weeks before using them. They will last for ages.

Parmesan and walnut crisps

You can eat these as a snack before supper with a glass of wine, or they are lovely with a salad and make a wonderful autumn starter with Poached pears (see page 361).

Yield: 12 crisps

½ cup grated Parmesan cheese
2 tablespoons chopped walnuts
½ teaspoon crushed peppercorns (ideally, Szechuan peppercorns for their aromatic flavor)

Preheat the oven to 350°F.

Mix the grated Parmesan with the chopped walnuts and peppercorns and, using a tablespoon, put little circular heaps of the mixture on to either a silicone baking mat or a sheet of parchment paper on a baking sheet. Press the mixture down with the back of a wooden spoon or your fingers and bake in the preheated oven for a few minutes, until just beginning to color. Allow to cool a little before using a metal palette knife to transfer them to a wire rack. (As they cool, they will crisp up and are much less likely to break.)

Pappardelle with walnuts

This classic Italian dish is great as it is, and also good with the addition of whole walnuts and sliced meaty cremini mushrooms.

Serves 4

1 tablespoon unsalted butter
½ cup walnuts, plus a few more as a garnish
2 tablespoons extra virgin olive oil
2 shallots, finely chopped
1 garlic clove, chopped
3 tablespoons white wine
Generous grating of nutmeg
5 tablespoons heavy cream
Salt and pepper
14 ounces pappardelle
Grated Parmesan cheese (optional)

Put a tablespoon of butter into a pan and cook the walnuts for 3 to 4 minutes (or roast in a moderate oven). Be careful not to overcook them as they will turn bitter.

Put them to one side and add 1 tablespoon of oil and the shallots to the pan and gently sweat the shallots until they have softened but not browned. Add the garlic and cook for a couple of minutes.

Remove the shallots and garlic and put them into a food processor with the cooked walnuts. Add the remaining oil, the wine, and a generous grating of nutmeg. Then pulse only briefly to combine the ingredients. Do not puree. Add the cream and season.

Cook the pasta in plenty of salted rapidly boiling water until al dente. Drain all but 2 tablespoons of the cooking liquid and keep the pasta warm. Combine the cooking liquid with the walnut sauce and warm gently.

Toss a few more walnut halves in butter. Combine the sauce with the pasta, pile on to warm plates, and serve with the walnut halves and a bowl of freshly grated Parmesan if you wish— I don't think it is necessary!

Walnut tart

Rather like a toffee pecan tart, this recipe replaces pecans with my native walnuts. It is rich and delicious, a little going a long way. Serve it with crème fraîche or, even better, vanilla ice cream.

Serves 10 to 12
For the crust:
   2 cups all-purpose flour
   Salt
   Grated zest and juice of 1 orange
   1 stick plus 2 tablespoons
      unsalted butter

For the filling:
   8 eggs
   1¾ cups superfine sugar
   1 cup honey
   1 cup maple syrup
   1 teaspoon vanilla extract
   Salt
   1 pound walnuts, halved

To make the crust, sift the flour and a pinch of salt into a bowl, mix in the orange zest, and rub in the butter until the mix resembles breadcrumbs. This can be done by pulsing in a food processor. Add just enough orange juice to make the pastry hold together in a ball, roll out, and use to line an 11-inch loose-bottomed tart pan. Chill for half an hour in the fridge.

Preheat the oven to 400°F. Prick the bottom of the crust with a fork, cover with a round of parchment paper or foil, and weight this down with some baking beans or rice. Bake the crust blind for about 10 minutes, or until it is cooked but not colored. Take it out of the oven, but leave the oven on, and let it cool slightly, then remove the beans or rice and the paper.

To make the filling, beat the eggs together in a bowl, adding the sugar, honey, syrup, vanilla, and a pinch of salt. Place the halved walnuts over the base of the cooked crust and pour over the egg mixture. Cook the tart for 20 minutes, and then reduce the oven

setting to 350°F and cook for a further 30 minutes, until the filling has set. Cover the tart with foil if it begins to brown too much.

Allow to cool a little before removing from the pan. This is best eaten warm.

Hazelnut biscotti

A delicious crunchy hazelnut biscuit, traditionally served in Italy after dinner. The biscuit is baked hard so that it will hold its shape when dipped into a glass of vin santo. They are also lovely with poached fruit or ice cream.

Yield: about 24 biscotti
1¾ cups all-purpose flour
Salt
1 teaspoon cream of tartar
½ teaspoon baking soda
1 cup light brown sugar
2 eggs, beaten, and 1 extra egg white
¼ cup pine nuts
½ cup skinned hazelnuts (see right)
¼ cup raisins

Preheat the oven to 350°F and line a baking sheet with parchment paper.

Sift the flour with a pinch of salt, the cream of tartar, and the baking soda. Add the sugar and the beaten eggs and extra white, and mix well together. Fold in the nuts and fruit. As the mixture will be sticky, flour your hands and make it into 3 or 4 rolls about 6 inches long and 1½ inches in diameter. Space them out well on the parchment paper and bake for about 25 minutes in the preheated oven until firm. Remove from the oven, turning the oven setting down to 275°F, and allow the biscuits to cool for 10 to 15 minutes.

Cut the rolls at an angle into slices about ¾ inch thick and then put them back into the oven for another 10 minutes.

After that time, turn them over and cook them for another 10 minutes, or until they are golden.

These biscuits will become very crisp and will keep very well in an airtight container.

Hazelnut ice cream and praline

In our family we're obsessed with this creamy-textured nocciola ice cream.

Serves 6 to 8
1 pound hazelnuts
½ cup superfine sugar
3½ cups milk
8 egg yolks
1 cup soft brown sugar
½ teaspoon vanilla extract
1¾ cups heavy cream

Preheat the oven to 350°F and roast ¾ pound of the hazelnuts in it for 5 minutes until golden brown, but watch them, as they burn readily. While they are hot, skin them by rubbing them in a dry cloth. Process in a food processor until very fine.

To make the hazelnut praline, put the superfine sugar in a pan over low heat and let it dissolve very slowly. Add the remaining hazelnuts, some halved, and keep on the heat until the liquid is a rich brown. Pour the mixture onto an oiled marble slab or baking sheet and, when it is cool, break it into shards or crush it with a rolling pin.

To make the ice cream, bring the milk to a boil, remove from the heat, add the ground hazelnuts, and allow to cool completely. Line a sieve with cheesecloth, or use a very fine-meshed sieve, and push through as much of the mixture as you can.

Whisk the eggs and brown sugar together and add the vanilla extract and the hazelnut mixture. Put this over gentle heat or in a bowl over simmering water, and keep stirring until the mixture is thick enough to coat the back of a spoon. Do not allow it to boil. Strain into a bowl and, when it is cool, mix in the cream. Then put it into an ice cream machine to freeze/churn for 25 minutes.

Remove the ice cream from the freezer and put it in the fridge about 20 minutes before serving. Top with the praline.

Pears

One of the best things I've ever eaten is a 'Doyenne du Comice' pear with a slice of Gorgonzola, sitting in the Madonna restaurant next to the Rialto Bridge in Venice. Once peeled, the pear was pouring juice and the flesh so ripe it was collapsing. The sweetness of the pear was perfect in contrast to the creamy yet punchy taste of the cheese. It made me want to rush home and plant a tree.

'Conference' pears appear on my shelves first at the end of summer. It's one of the best for storing, and excellent for cooking, the best for poaching, as well as being good straight from the tree. I love its characteristic long, odd-shaped narrow fruits. They look unpromising, but they are, in fact, delicious and juicy once peeled. 'Williams' is around early too, with more elegant plump, oval smooth-skinned fruit. These are beauties, as lovely to look at as they are to eat. A plate of these yellow-skinned, streaked, and stippled red pears makes a wonderful still life. But 'Williams' pears don't store—you need to eat them good and quick before the flesh gets fuzzy. They are too often picked very unripe and then cold stored for ages. They then lose their scent and their true sweet flavor.

After 'Williams' and 'Conference' come 'Beurre Hardy' and 'Doyenne du Comice'. 'Beurre Hardy' is less widely available but is one of the finest dessert pears, with tender, juicy sweet flesh which, as the name suggests, has a buttery texture that melts in the mouth. The foodie's favorite, 'Comice', comes next, in September/October. Grab it whenever you see it—it's tops for flavor and texture, but doesn't travel well, so is often sold unripe.

One of the last to ripen is 'Concorde', which is not ready until mid-October. Its parents are 'Conference' and 'Comice', a fantastic pedigree. It's shaped like the nose of an airplane, and has melting, juicy flesh.

You'll get the best pears if you grow your own or find them at a greenmarket or pick-your-own fruit farm. Store them carefully, in a cool and dark place—checking on them almost every day to catch them when they're just right.

Darina Allen's pears poached in saffron syrup

A fragrant recipe from the chef of the famous Ballymaloe Cooking School in Ireland. These poached pears are fresher and lighter than the more wintry dish of pears poached in port (see right). They are good eaten with almost any ice cream.

Serves 4
- **1 cup sugar**
- **6 whole cardamom pods, lightly crushed**
- **¼ teaspoon good-quality saffron**
- **3 tablespoons freshly squeezed lemon juice**
- **4 firm pears**

Put the sugar, cardamom pods, saffron, and lemon juice in a wide shallow pan with ¾ cup water. Stir to dissolve the sugar and bring to a simmer.

Meanwhile, peel the pears, halve and core them, and immediately put them into the simmering syrup, cut side uppermost. Cover with parchment paper and the lid of the pan and cook gently for 20 to 30 minutes, spooning the syrup over the pears every now and then.

Carefully remove the pears and arrange in a single layer in a serving dish, cut side down. Pour the syrup over them and allow to cool.

Chill in the fridge and serve very cold. These keep for several weeks, covered, in the fridge.

Poached pears

These make an excellent easy dessert with Parmesan and walnut crisps (see page 354), which make a good savory contrast to the sweetness of the syrupy poached pears. These pears are also good with crème fraîche or vanilla ice cream.

Serves 6
- **6 firm pears**
- **2½ cups port (or wine, see below)**
- **¼ cup sugar**
- **1 star anise**
- **Peel of 1 lemon, cut into strips**
- **1 cinnamon stick**

Choose a saucepan that will hold the pears snugly. Peel the pears with a potato peeler, leaving the stems on the fruit, and cut a thin slice off the bottom so that the pears will stand upright.

Put the port into a saucepan with ¾ cup water, the sugar, star anise, lemon peel, and cinnamon, and stir to dissolve the sugar. You can substitute red wine for the port, but the flavor is less interesting. Poached in dessert wine, the pears are delicious, but you'll need less sugar.

Add the pears and simmer, covered, until the pears are tender but not soft.

Remove the pears to a bowl and return the liquid to the heat. Reduce by simmering, until the mixture is slightly thicker and the taste intense.

Pour the syrup over the pears and leave for several hours, turning the pears occasionally, until they have taken on the rich color of the syrup. Chill.

Pears, bananas, and grapes with fudge sauce

A wonderful standby for unexpected visitors, this is always loved by adults and children alike. Make some of the fudge sauce and have it at the ready in the fridge. It keeps well. Dried apricots are a lovely possible addition to this, and toasted sliced almonds are delicious scattered on the top. Serve with vanilla ice cream.

Serves 6
For the fudge sauce:
- **¼ cup (½ stick) butter**
- **⅔ cup soft light brown sugar**
- **⅔ cup light corn syrup**
- **½ cup heavy cream**
- **1 teaspoon vanilla extract**

For the fruit:
- **6 just-ripe pears, peeled and quartered**
- **3 bananas, sliced**
- **1 pound green or black grapes**

First, make the fudge sauce. Heat the butter, sugar, and syrup gently until the sugar has completely dissolved. Turn off the heat and allow the mixture to cool for a few minutes before adding the cream and vanilla extract. This sauce is delicious hot or cold.

Put the fruit into a dish and generously pour the sauce over it.

Toffee pear tart

This is my standard quick-to-rustle-up dessert, using pastry that is kept in the freezer.

Serves 6 to 8
   4 to 5 firm pears
   Juice and grated zest of 1 lemon
   ½ cup (1 stick) unsalted butter
   ½ cup superfine sugar
   1 (1-pound) pack puff pastry
   Cream or ice cream, to serve

Preheat the oven to 375°F. Peel, halve, and core the pears, and cover them with lemon juice to prevent them from turning brown.

   Melt the butter in a nonstick frying pan with a metal or removable handle and add the sugar. Cook the two together gently until the sugar has dissolved completely. Add the pear halves and lemon zest and continue to cook until the sugar mixture deepens to a dark brown, but take care not to burn the sugar at this stage. Take off the heat.

   Roll out the pastry to a circle a little bigger than the pan and press it down gently on the pears. Bake for 20 minutes in the preheated oven, or until the puff pastry has risen and is golden. If you don't have a frying pan with a metal handle, cook the pears in an ordinary frying pan. Let the butter and sugar mixture become well caramelized and tip into an ovenproof dish. Cover with the pastry and then bake in the oven.

   Allow the tart to cool slightly. Run a knife around the edge of the pan, and invert on to a plate. Serve warm with cream or ice cream. If you need to prepare this tart a few hours ahead, leave the cooked tart in the pan and warm through thoroughly before turning it out on a plate.

Pear and almond tart

Another classic pear tart, with a wonderfully sweet and nutty taste.

Serves 6 to 8
For the crust:
   1 ¾ cups all-purpose flour
   Pinch of salt
   1 tablespoon superfine sugar
   1 stick plus 2 tablespoons
      unsalted butter
   1 egg yolk mixed with a little very
      cold water

   4 to 5 ripe (but not soft) pears
   6 tablespoons unsalted butter
   3 tablespoons all-purpose flour
   ½ cup sugar
   3 eggs
   1 cup ground almonds
   1 teaspoon vanilla extract
   ¼ cup sliced almonds
   2 tablespoons apricot jam,
      warmed and sieved
   Confectioners' sugar, for dusting

To make the crust, sift the flour with the salt and sugar. Either by hand or with a food processor, work the butter into the flour until it resembles breadcrumbs. Add just enough of the egg and water mixture to hold the pastry together. Wrap in plastic and chill for 30 minutes.

   Preheat the oven to 375°F. Roll out the pastry and press into a 10-inch tart pan. Prick the bottom of the crust with a fork and bake blind by covering the crust with parchment paper weighted down with baking beans or rice and placing in the oven for 12 to 15 minutes. Remove the baking beans or rice and paper and allow to cool.

   To make the filling, peel and core the pears and then slice them up or leave them in halves. Beat the butter, flour, sugar, eggs, ground almonds, and vanilla extract together and pour over the crust. Arrange the pears on top, scatter with sliced almonds, and brush with the apricot jam.

Bake in the preheated oven for 15 to 20 minutes, until set and golden. Serve warm, dusted with confectioners' sugar.

Spiced preserved pears

These pears are delicious cold with Parma ham and are a good addition to a cheese board. Warmed slightly, they are wonderful with roast duck or goose. If you have a pear tree in your garden, this is one of the best ways of preserving the pears. They make a great Christmas present.

Yield: 1 quart

- 2½ cups light brown sugar
- 1 cup white wine vinegar
- 1 cup cider vinegar
- 3 cinnamon sticks
- ½ lemon, cut into slices
- ½ teaspoon whole cloves
- 1 teaspoon juniper berries (optional)
- 1 tablespoon mixed peppercorns
- 2 pounds firm pears (Conference are best, but any hard pear will do)

Warm the sugar in a bowl in a very low oven for about half an hour.

Put all the ingredients, except for the pears, into a saucepan over low heat and bring slowly to a boil, making sure the sugar dissolves.

Peel the pears, but leave the stems on them. Quarter and core them, trying to keep the stems, or leave them whole. Add the pears to the pan, bring up to a gentle simmer, and let the pears cook for about 20 minutes, until just tender but not too soft.

Using a slotted spoon, transfer the pears and slices of lemon to a warm sterilized preserving jar. Boil the syrup hard for about 5 minutes to reduce it, pour in enough to fill the jar to its neck, and completely cover the pears. Scoop out the spices from the pan and add them to the jar.

Cover, seal, and store for a month before using. The pears will keep for up to a year.

Pear, apple, and quince Charlotte

I like apple Charlotte, the crunchy buttery bread a good contrast to the soft sweet apple inside. It's even better when the apple is mixed with quince and pear, more interesting and less sweet.

If you want to prepare this in advance for a party, allow it to become completely cold, run a knife around the edge to loosen it, and invert on to a board. With a round cutter, cut rounds of the Charlotte and put on a lightly greased baking tray. Bake at 350°F just to heat through and to crisp up the top.

Serves 6 to 8

- 3 large apples
- 3 firm pears
- 2 quinces
- Juice of ½ lemon
- ⅓ cup sugar
- A loaf of good white bread, cut into slices (don't be tempted to use cheap white sliced bread)
- 1 cup (2 sticks) butter, melted
- Crème fraîche or Greek yogurt, as a garnish

Preheat the oven to 350°F.

Peel, core, and quarter the apples and pears, and cut the quinces into smaller slices, as they take longer to soften. Poach the fruit gently in ½ cup water and the lemon juice, adding a little more water if the fruit begins to stick. When the fruit is soft, add the sugar. Mash the fruit to break up any large pieces, but do not puree.

Choose an ovenproof dish about 8 by 11 inches. Cut the crusts off the bread and, with a pair of scissors, cut the slices into shapes that will completely cover the bottom and sides of the dish. Put some for the top to one side. Using a pastry brush, brush a layer of melted butter over the bottom and sides of the dish. Sprinkle with a little sugar and shake the dish to distribute it over the sides and base. Brush each side of all the pieces of bread with melted butter and lay them in and around the dish. Spoon over the fruit mixture and cover with the remaining bread, then brush the top generously with melted butter.

Bake in the oven for at least 40 minutes, until the top is golden brown.

Serve with crème fraîche or Greek yogurt.

Sweet peppers

Imported red and yellow bell peppers can be very bland. You're more likely to find them sweet and tasty if you eat them during their natural cropping season, from the middle of August right through the autumn.

Green bell peppers are quicker to produce and therefore cheaper, but they aren't nearly as sweet. This sharper taste suits some Oriental dishes and they're an essential ingredient in Jambalaya (see page 370). As a general rule, they taste better when fully matured to red or yellow. Look out for the less uniform, more unusually shaped reds. These may be rare in supermarkets, but they have the most flavor.

I grow only three sweet peppers that seem to be uncharacteristically prolific varieties. 'Unicorn' is a large red pepper, in the classic bell shape. This is ideal for filling with capers, anchovies, and cherry tomatoes (see page 370), and delicious with mozzarella. I also grow the medium-sized, highly productive 'Marconi Rosso', with a narrower, horn-like shape and an excellent sweet flavor. 'Jingle Bells' is another good one, with miniature fruit right through the summer and into the autumn, that gradually turn from green to red. This variety looks good long enough to make ideal house plants. The fruit is small, two inches or so—the perfect size for eating whole, stuffed, and barbecued alongside milder chili peppers (see page 319) or eaten as tempura (see page 207).

I rarely eat bell peppers raw. They have a reverberating taste, but cooked—roasted, grilled, or fried—they can be magnificent. Removing the skin makes them more digestible.

To peel, roast them in a 375°F oven for thirty to forty minutes until they begin to blacken and the flesh is soft to the point of a knife. Put them in a plastic bag, or in a bowl covered with plastic wrap, and leave them to steam for another fifteen minutes. They will taste deliciously sweet and warm—and the peel comes off easily in your fingers.

Roasted pepper soup

A lovely rich soup. Serve it warm with a dollop of Greek yogurt and some just-torn-up basil leaves; or, if it's a beautiful warm autumn day, serve it cold with a floating ice cube.

Serves 6 to 8
- **4 to 5 red bell peppers (about 1½ pounds)**
- **1½ pounds ripe tomatoes**
- **1 red onion**
- **3 garlic cloves**
- **½ red chili**
- **1 tablespoon balsamic vinegar**
- **3 tablespoons extra virgin olive oil**
- **Handful of basil leaves**
- **5 cups good chicken or vegetable stock**
- **Salt and pepper**
- **1 cup Greek yogurt, as a garnish**

Preheat the oven to 350°F.

Quarter the peppers and deseed them. Halve the tomatoes and roughly chop the onion, garlic, and chili. Put all the vegetables and basil on a baking pan, mix the vinegar and oil, and pour it over the vegetables, making sure everything is well coated.

Roast them in the preheated oven, turning them from time to time, for 45 minutes. Put everything through a food mill or sieve to get rid of the skins. If you pulse it in a food processor the flavor will be less mellow, as it will include that of the skins, but it will still be delicious.

Thin the soup with the stock to the consistency you want and season with salt and freshly ground pepper. Tip into a saucepan and warm for a couple of minutes, or put it in the fridge to cool. Before serving, add a dollop of Greek yogurt.

Pheasant soup

My friend Matthew Rice gave me this recipe for a light, elegant Oriental-tasting soup, with a subtle flavor of red peppers. Matthew is a keen shot and an inventive cook. Ideally, you want to start making this recipe the day before.

Serves 4
- **2 pheasants**
- **2 red bell peppers, deseeded**
- **1 onion, chopped**
- **3 (6-inch) lemongrass sticks, chopped**
- **2 garlic cloves, chopped**
- **2-inch piece of ginger, peeled and chopped**
- **1 teaspoon Chinese five-spice powder**
- **8 scallions**
- **2 tablespoons sherry**
- **Salt and pepper**
- **Small bunch of cilantro, roughly chopped**

Cut the breasts from the pheasants and put them to one side. Chop one of the red peppers and put with the rest of the pheasants, the onion, lemongrass, garlic, ginger, and the Chinese five-spice powder in 2 quarts of water in a pan.

Cook these together, simmering gently, for an hour. Strain and leave to cool overnight.

Skim any fat off the surface of the stock. Measure out 6 medium-sized ladlefuls of stock (i.e., 1½ per person) into a saucepan and bring it up to a rolling boil.

Cut the raw pheasant breasts into fine slivers. Slice the scallions and the other red pepper into equally fine strips. Put the vegetables and pheasant breast strips into the hot stock and cook them gently for 5 minutes. Add the sherry and season.

Add the chopped cilantro to each bowl.

Masai mara

This is from *The African Kitchen* by Josie Stow and Jan Baldwin and it is by far the most interesting and delicious way of using red peppers as a dip. It beats all the comparable Greek, Italian, and Spanish recipes. Have it as part of a selection of starters and dip into it with strips of Rosemary flat bread (see page 46).

Serves 8
- **4 large sweet red peppers**
- **1 cup extra virgin olive oil**
- **6 garlic cloves, thinly sliced**
- **¾ cup pecans or walnuts, toasted for a few minutes**
- **¾ cup white breadcrumbs**
- **Juice of 2 lemons**
- **2 teaspoons freshly ground cumin seeds**
- **2 teaspoons sugar**
- **1 teaspoon finely chopped red chili (or to taste)**
- **Salt and pepper**

Preheat the oven to 400°F.

Cut the peppers in half and remove the ribs and seeds. Coat them with a little of the oil and bake them in the preheated oven until they begin to blacken. Then flip them and do the same on the other side. Remove the skins that come off easily, but don't worry about getting every last bit.

Put the roasted peppers, garlic, pecans, breadcrumbs, lemon juice, cumin, sugar, chili, and some salt and pepper into a food processor and whiz until smooth. Pour in the rest of the oil and continue processing until the mixture is glossy. Season.

This is good warm or cold.

Roasted red peppers with mozzarella

A brilliant easy starter, this is ideal if you're cooking for lots of people and have little time. You can use goat cheese instead of mozzarella for a stronger taste. Anchovies packed in salt have the best flavor: rinse them carefully in cold water. If you use anchovies in oil, use the oil from the tins, plus a bit more. For lunch, serve two stuffed pepper halves, a few slices of mozzarella, a dollop of Caponata (see page 300) or Spiced eggplant salad (see page 299), some arugula, and plenty of bread for dipping.

Serves 6 as a starter

3 sweet red peppers
12 cherry tomatoes, cut in half
2 garlic cloves, chopped
12 anchovy fillets, salted or in oil, chopped (see above)
24 capers
3 to 4 sprigs of thyme
Salt and pepper
Extra virgin olive oil
2 slices mozzarella or 6 to 8 ounces goat cheese, sliced
Small bunch of basil leaves

Preheat the oven to 350°F. Cut through the peppers, including the stem, and remove the ribs and seeds. Put the halved peppers on a baking sheet and, starting with the tomatoes, add the different filling ingredients. Bright Sungold cherry tomatoes, cut in half, look best. Then add the garlic, anchovies, capers, thyme, a little salt and pepper, and a drizzle of olive oil.

Bake the peppers in the preheated oven for 30 minutes, until the edges are beginning to blacken. Take them out, put the slices of cheese over the top, and cook for a further 10 minutes.

Finally, before you eat, garnish with the freshly torn basil leaves. These peppers are best eaten just warm.

Jambalaya

This recipe involves more ingredients than many, but jambalaya is a great dish for a gathering. Make it when you have lots of people to feed. Prawns—still in their shells—added at the end are a good extra. Serve the jambalaya with a big mixed salad.

Serves 6 to 8

2 tablespoons olive oil
2 skinless, boneless chicken breasts, each cut into 3 pieces
¾ pound pork, shoulder or loin, cut into pieces
2 onions, roughly chopped
3 green bell peppers, sliced into strips
2 garlic cloves, finely chopped
1 tablespoon tomato paste
6 tomatoes, skinned (see page 266) and roughly chopped, or 1 (14-ounce) can chopped tomatoes
4 ounces chorizo, cut into chunks
½ teaspoon cayenne pepper
½ teaspoon ground cloves
½ teaspoon ground mace
1 or 2 red chilis, finely chopped
4 bay leaves
Salt and pepper
1 cup good-quality long-grain rice, rinsed
1½ cups good vegetable or chicken stock
Large glass of white wine
Good handful of flat-leaf parsley

Preheat the oven to 350°F.

Heat some olive oil in a sauté pan and brown the pieces of chicken and pork. Put them in an ovenproof dish. Then fry the onions and peppers until the onions are just beginning to soften. Add the garlic, tomato paste, tomatoes, chorizo, spices, chilis, bay leaves, salt, and pepper.

After a couple of minutes, mix in the uncooked rice. Stir to make sure the rice is well coated with oil. Transfer everything into the ovenproof dish with

the chicken and pork. Add the stock and wine and cover with a lid. Cook in the preheated oven for about an hour, stirring 2 or 3 times during the process. Remove from the oven and stir in plenty of parsley.

Peperonata

Peperonata is as simple and delicious as it comes: ribbons of pepper, preserved in oil and vinegar, to eat then and there or bottle and store for later. The vinegar preserves the peppers and the sugar softens the flavor. This takes a lot of peppers for just one jar, so this recipe is one for when they're cheap in a market or you have more than you can eat from the garden. Peperonata is lovely eaten with hot or cold meat and excellent with cheese.

Yield: 1 jar
   4 red sweet peppers
   2 yellow sweet peppers
   2 tablespoons superfine sugar
   ¾ cup white wine vinegar
   ¾ cup extra virgin olive oil

Roast the red and yellow peppers whole for half an hour in a 350°F oven. Put them in a plastic bag or covered bowl for 5 minutes and then skin, deseed, and cut into thin strips about 1 inch long. Put them in a pan. Add the sugar and vinegar and cook over medium heat for 5 more minutes.

Put the mixture into a warm sterilized preserving jar, filling it right to the very top, and cover the peppers with olive oil. Secure the lid, turn it upside down, and wrap it in a wool blanket or thick cloth. Leave it wrapped up for a couple of days so that the liquor cools very slowly. It will then be safely preserved. This is the traditional bottling technique used all over Italy and the peperonata should keep for up to a year. Once open, keep it in the fridge.

Red pepper frittata with prosciutto

The peppers are the dominant flavor in this Spanish omelette, which is delicious either warm or cold, when the flavors of the sweet peppers and herbs really come to the fore. This is ideal outdoor food; wrap it up and take it on a picnic. Serve with crusty bread and a green salad.

Serves 6 to 8
   3 medium-sized potatoes, chopped
   4 red peppers
   2 tablespoons olive oil
   1 tablespoon butter
   1 onion, sliced
   1 garlic clove, crushed and chopped
   6 eggs
   ¾ cup heavy cream
   Salt and pepper
   Freshly grated nutmeg
   2 ounces prosciutto, sliced into strips
   4 ounces goat cheese
   3 ounces Parmesan cheese, grated
   Bunch of chives, chopped

Preheat the oven to 400°F.
Rinse the potatoes under cold water and dry.

Roast the peppers whole until the skins are well charred—this will take about half an hour—and then put them into a plastic bag to sweat for a few minutes. Skin and cut the peppers into strips and lower the oven setting to 350°F.

Heat the olive oil and butter in an ovenproof pan (preferably with a removable handle or one which has a metal handle). When the oil and butter are foaming, add the chopped potatoes. After a few minutes, add the onion and garlic, and cook until the potatoes are tender. This will take about 15 minutes. Remove from the heat.

Whisk the eggs with the cream and season with plenty of salt, pepper, and nutmeg. Add the prosciutto, goat cheese, most of the Parmesan, the chopped chives, and the peppers, and pour over the onion and potatoes in the pan, stirring gently to combine. Put the pan back on the heat and cook for just a couple of minutes, until the bottom of the frittata is beginning to set. Put into the preheated oven and cook for 10 minutes, until just firm to the touch. Invert the frittata on to a large plate. I think the top looks nicer, so flip it back again. Allow it to rest. It has far less flavor when it's piping hot. Garnish with more Parmesan cut into wedges.

Pumpkins and winter squashes

Pumpkins and winter squashes are fantastically buttocky and bosomy, and generous of form. Their sheer pregnancy makes you want to gather them up like a flock of expectant mothers. Get out the biggest bowl you can find and put it on your kitchen table. Don't just buy or pick one squash or pumpkin: find lots in different shapes and sizes and pile them up in a great multicolored mass—amber-oranges, golds, and vermilion, as well as the subtler bottle-green, lichen grey-greens, clear cream, and faded apricot. They come small and large, ribbed and warty, knobbly, and perfectly smooth. Admire them, and cook and eat them from the bowl. Most will last for months.

Winter squash will give you a huge range of flavors and textures, from soft and sweet ('Butternut' or 'Crown Prince') to parsnip-like ('Sweet Dumpling') and chestnut-flavored ('Red Kuri' or onion squash). Some are tasteless and boring, such as the widely available 'Jack-O-Lantern', but you'll find delicious giant varieties ('Giant Pink Banana'), ideal for making a huge batch of soup, and small ones that can be eaten easily in one sitting ('Baby Blue', 'Red Kuri', or onion squash). You can use either pumpkins or squash, but on the whole squashes have better flavor and texture.

Save the seeds of the ones you like for growing next year and, whenever you scrape decent-sized seeds from your pumpkin or winter squash, keep a few and clean the stringy flesh from them. These are rich in good oils and make a delicious snack. For every pound of pumpkin seeds, you want two teaspoons of salt and five tablespoons of water. Roast the seeds for five minutes in a preheated 350°F oven until they are slightly brown. Dissolve the salt in the water and sprinkle over the hot seeds. Stir them around to make sure that they're evenly coated and return them to the oven for a couple more minutes.

Many winter squash or pumpkin varieties are hugely prolific growers and put out shoots in every direction. If you're growing your own, once one vine gets to about six feet, it's a good idea to pinch out the tip. This stops the vegetative growth and encourages the plant to flower and fruit. These growth tips are delicious. Boil them in salted water for about five minutes and dress them in olive oil or a little butter. They have an unusual taste, not unlike spinach but more fragrant.

Stuffed butternut squash

This is a simple butternut squash recipe that we often cook for lunch in the autumn, when there are lots of them about. You can use any squash, but with butternut, it's perfect.

Serves 2
- **1 medium-sized butternut squash**
- **Generous drizzle of olive oil**
- **Salt and pepper**
- **1 teaspoon freshly ground cumin seeds**
- **3 tablespoons crème fraîche**
- **3 tablespoons chopped sage (or chives)**
- **2 tablespoons grated Parmesan cheese**

Preheat the oven to 400°F. Cut the squash in half lengthwise. Drizzle the cut flesh with olive oil and sprinkle with salt, pepper, and cumin. Bake, cut side upwards and covered in foil, on a baking tray in the preheated oven for about 45 minutes. Prick it with a fork to check that the flesh is soft. If not, give it 10 minutes more.

Take the squash out of the oven, lower the oven setting to 350°F, and leave the squash until it is cool enough for you to handle.

Scoop out the seeds and stringy bits and discard, then scoop out most of the flesh with a tablespoon into a bowl and mix this with the crème fraîche and 2½ tablespoons of the sage (chives are good in the summer). It is best to do this with a fork, or give the mixture a quick zap in the processor to get rid of any lumps of squash. Check the seasoning. Spoon the squash back into the empty skins.

Scatter the Parmesan and remaining herbs over the top and then bake in the oven for 15 minutes, or until the top starts to look brown and crunchy.

Sage and winter squash soufflé

These twice-cooked soufflés are a lovely orangey color and—with the goat cheese and sage—have a fantastic flavor. They can be prepared ahead and will rise again when you bake them a second time, which makes them ideal for a party.

Serves 4
- **Several tablespoons of butter, plus more for the ramekins**
- **Oil, for the ramekins**
- **1 small butternut squash**
- **1 tablespoon soft light brown sugar**
- **1 cup milk**
- **1 bay leaf**
- **Pinch of mace**
- **1 tablespoon butter**
- **2 tablespoons self-rising flour**
- **1 teaspoon finely chopped red chili**
- **1 tablespoon finely chopped sage**
- **4 ounces aged goat cheese, grated**
- **2 large eggs, separated, and 1 extra egg white**
- **Salt and pepper**
- **Freshly grated Parmesan cheese, as a garnish**

Preheat the oven to 400°F. Butter or oil 4 ramekins.

Cut the squash into 2 halves, scrape out the seeds, add the butter and sugar to each half, and season well. Cover lightly with foil and bake in the preheated oven for about 40 minutes, until the squash is really tender. Spoon out the flesh and blend to a puree. Leave the oven on.

Bring the milk to a boil with the bay leaf and the mace, and leave to infuse for a few minutes off the heat. In another pan, melt the butter and stir in the flour. Allow to cook for a couple of minutes and then gradually add the hot milk, stirring continuously. Allow to simmer very gently for another minute or two. Transfer this mixture to a bowl and add the squash puree, chopped chili, sage, and goat cheese. Mix well. Add the egg yolks and mix thoroughly to combine. Check the seasoning.

In another bowl, whisk the 3 egg whites until stiff and dry, and fold very carefully into the squash mixture with a large metal spoon. You must retain the lightness of the egg white.

Spoon into the ramekins and place in a baking pan. Add about an inch or so of boiling water to the pan and bake the soufflés in the oven for about 15 minutes, until they are puffed up and just firm but not too brown. Remove from the oven and allow to cool.

They can now be left, covered, in the fridge until you need them.

Again, preheat the oven to 400°F. With a sharp knife, ease the cold soufflés out of the ramekins and put them on a lightly oiled baking sheet. Dust the tops with freshly grated Parmesan and rebake until they have risen and browned.

Winter squash and cumin soup with squash chips

One of the most flavorful autumn soups for pumpkin or squash. The flavor improves if you cook it some time before eating. It also freezes well.

Serves 6

- **3 teaspoons cumin seeds**
- **1 teaspoon coriander seeds**
- **1 teaspoon caraway seeds**
- **½ teaspoon cayenne pepper**
- **1 medium-sized Red Kuri or butternut squash (at least 2 pounds)**
- **Generous drizzle of olive oil**
- **3 medium-sized onions**
- **2 garlic cloves**
- **¼ cup (½ stick) butter**
- **3 cups vegetable or chicken stock**
- **Salt and pepper**
- **1 cup crème fraîche**
- **Peanut oil, for frying the chips**

Preheat the oven to 375°F.

Toast the seeds in a dry frying pan for a couple of minutes and grind to a powder with the cayenne.

Take a small slice off your squash and put aside for making chips. Then cut your squash in half, remove the seeds, drizzle with the olive oil, and bake in the preheated oven for 45 minutes to 1 hour, or until it is soft. Scrape the flesh from the skin and put to one side.

Finely chop the onions and garlic and sweat them gently in the butter for about 10 minutes, until they are soft but not browned. Add the spices, squash, and stock, and simmer gently for a few minutes.

Blend if you want a very smooth soup. Season well and whisk in the crème fraîche.

To make the chips, slice thin strips of squash from the reserved piece with a potato peeler and shallow-fry them in very hot peanut oil until they begin to brown. Drain on paper towels and serve them scattered over the top of the soup.

Winter squash and arugula salad with pears and rosemary

Without the arugula, this is a great side dish to eat with almost anything, and it's good on its own as a first-course warm salad, with arugula tossed in at the last minute.

Serves 6

- **1 medium-sized pumpkin or winter squash, such as Red Kuri or butternut (about 2 pounds)**
- **2 tablespoons olive oil**
- **Salt and pepper**
- **2 firm pears, cored and sliced lengthwise into quarters**
- **¼ cup (½ stick) butter**
- **1 teaspoon finely chopped rosemary**
- **4 handfuls of arugula**
- **Slivers of Parmesan cheese**

Preheat the oven to 350°F.

Peel the pumpkin or winter squash and cut it into large chunks. Drizzle with olive oil, salt, and pepper, and roast in the preheated oven for 35 minutes, until the outside of the chunks begin to brown.

Sauté the pears quickly in foaming butter with a teaspoon of finely chopped rosemary until the pears are slightly brown but still with a good bite.

Lay out a base of arugula on one large or several smaller plates. When the pumpkin or winter squash and pears are cool, garnish with slivers of Parmesan.

Pumpkin, sage, and pecorino ravioli

This sounds like quite a production to make, but it's so delicious that it's worth giving it a try. Sadly, the widely available fresh lasagne sheets are too thick to use, but if you have a good Italian deli near you, you can order the ready-made ravioli sheets from them, and then it's much easier.

Serves 6 to 8
For the pasta:
- **1 pound pasta flour**
- **2 good pinches of fine salt**
- **5 eggs**

For the filling:
- **1 pumpkin or winter squash (about 2 pounds)**
- **Olive oil**
- **Salt and pepper**
- **5 ounces pecorino or Parmesan cheese, plus extra as a garnish**
- **2 tablespoons finely chopped sage, plus 36 whole sage leaves, as a garnish**
- **6 tablespoons butter, melted**

To make the pasta, tip the flour and salt into a round pile in the middle of a table. Make a well in the center, break the eggs into that, and then mix. Work the dough, kneading it with your hands, until it becomes elastic and soft. Every now and then throw the ball down from a height. The force of this knocks the air out and helps the dough to soften.

Work it for about 10 minutes until it has a really smooth texture. Allow the dough to rest, covered with a damp kitchen towel, for half an hour or so. You will end up with a mound of smooth dough.

Cut the dough into 5 chunks. Flatten these with the palm of your hand and start to feed the first one into a pasta machine. To begin with the roller must be on the widest setting, then progress through the other settings. With every rolling, the dough becomes silkier. If it begins to get a bit sticky, dust it with a little flour. If the sheets break at any time, just roll them up into a ball and start again.

When you reach the top setting, lay the long, thin smooth sheets on clean kitchen towels dusted with flour. Space them well, so they can dry out for half an hour. You can freeze the pasta at this stage, rolled carefully in a towel or parchment paper to keep the sheets apart. You may have a little pasta left over from the sheets—freeze it, or put it through the cutting disc on the pasta machine to make fettuccine.

To make the filling, preheat the oven to 400°F, peel the pumpkin or squash and cut it into small chunks. Remove the seeds. Drizzle with olive oil and season well. Cover it with foil and roast in the oven for about 30 minutes, until tender. When cooled a little, mix it with the freshly grated pecorino and chopped sage. Check the seasoning. The pecorino is salty, but you'll want plenty of black pepper. Mash or pulse it in a food processor.

For 6, you will use 4 sheets of pasta. Put teaspoon mounds of the filling at intervals and brush with water between the mounds. Then cover with another sheet of dough, and press the top piece down gently to seal each mound of filling, starting at one end and working to the other, ensuring that all the air is released around the dollops of mix. Cut into squares or rounds with a pasta cutter or knife.

Poach the ravioli, a few at a time, in a wide shallow pan in plenty of salted gently boiling water for 8 to 10 minutes until al dente, then drain and dry on a clean towel.

Serve the pasta with melted butter and freshly ground pepper. Sprinkle generously with grated pecorino and scatter over the whole sage leaves quickly fried in a little bit of olive oil.

Pumpkin pie

The best pumpkin pie I—and, with a bit of luck, you—have ever tasted.

Serves 6
For the crust:
- **¼ cup (½ stick) butter**
- **¾ cup all-purpose flour**
- **1 egg yolk, beaten**
- **Confectioners' sugar**

For the filling:
- **1 pound pumpkin, peeled, and cut in chunks**
- **¾ cup soft brown sugar**
- **Pinch of salt**
- **½ teaspoon ground cinnamon**
- **½ teaspoon ground ginger**
- **½ teaspoon freshly grated nutmeg**
- **1 tablespoon honey**
- **Grated zest of 1 lemon and juice of ½ lemon**
- **Grated zest of 1 orange and juice of ½ orange**
- **3 eggs, beaten**

To make the crust, rub the butter into the flour until the mixture resembles breadcrumbs. Add the egg yolk and just enough very cold water to gather it into a ball. Roll out the crust and line an 8-inch loose-bottomed tart pan. Chill in the fridge for 30 minutes.

Preheat the oven to 350°F. Prick the bottom of the tart with a fork, cover with parchment paper, and weigh this down with some rice or beans. Bake the pastry blind for 20 to 25 minutes. Take it out of the oven, but leave the oven on, and let it cool slightly, then remove the rice or beans and paper.

To make the filling, having removed its seeds, steam the pumpkin until tender. Put the pumpkin and all the remaining ingredients, except the eggs, into a food processor and puree until smooth. Add the eggs and blend.

Pour into the crust and bake for 55 minutes, until a skewer comes out of the center clean. Allow to cool and dust with confectioners' sugar.

Quinces
and medlars

The quince is a handsome yellow-green fruit, like an irregular, furry-skinned pear with a fragrant, fruity-rose smell that reminds me of Turkish delight. If you can bear not to eat them all right away, put a bowl of quinces somewhere warm—near a fireplace or radiator—and they'll look good and scent the room for several weeks. They are currently fashionable with chefs, so let's hope they become more widely available, as they are a very delicious fruit.

Quinces are good eaten in savory dishes as well as desserts. They're invaluable added to almost any stew—just include a few peeled pieces as an odd but pleasant surprise. And there's the Spanish classic membrillo, or quince paste, eaten with manchego cheese (see page 380). I also love quinces as jelly: Make this just as you would Medlar jelly (see page 381). Spread it on toast, or mix up a couple of tablespoons with Greek yogurt or crème fraîche to eat with fresh fruit. It's lovely with pineapple and blueberries.

Medlars aren't as good to eat as quinces, but they make a lovely fragrant jelly. This is delicious eaten on toast for breakfast and is perfect with pork and gentle-tasting spring lamb. Medlars are odd-looking fruits, like a cross between a russet apple and a rose hip, traditionally eaten on the high tables of Cambridge and Oxford colleges, where they were said to be a great delicacy. You can only eat them uncooked once soft, almost decayed or "bletted", but I think that at this stage they're like a rotten pear and revolting!

Quinces and medlars both make good trees for a smaller garden, with large single pink (quince) or white (medlar) flowers in late spring. If you have room, plant your own. Medlars have wonderful autumn color and an interesting bark and shape that look good even in the winter. In late autumn they're covered in fruit.

Membrillo

A classic way to eat quince. It is easy to make and stores well. Eat it with cheese, on its own, or add a little to flavor casseroles and sauces.

Yield: 4 pints
Sugar (for exact quantity, see below)
4½ pounds quince (or quince and cooking apples if you are short of quince)
A little ground cinnamon

Warm the sugar in a bowl in a very low oven for about half an hour.

Roughly chop the unpeeled quinces and put into a pan with 1¼ cups water. Cover and stew gently until the fruit is soft. Sieve or food mill the fruit and measure the puree. For each 2½ cups of puree, add 1¾ cups of sugar. Gently heat in a deep saucepan until the sugar has completely dissolved. Raise the heat and bring to a boil, stirring continuously to prevent it from sticking. Stir in cinnamon. As it reduces, it will spit and splatter, so cover your hand with a cloth.

After about 45 minutes, the mixture will have turned a lovely reddish brown and will begin to come away from the side of the pan as you stir. Pour into baking pans lined with oiled parchment paper or an oiled mold. Leave, uncovered, at room temperature for 2 to 3 days before cutting into blocks or chunks.

Baked quinces in orange syrup

This takes a couple of hours to bake, but it is very easy to do and is delicious with yogurt or cream.

Serves 6
3 large quinces
1 large orange
1 ⅓ cups superfine sugar
5 tablespoons orange juice
½ teaspoon orange flower water

Preheat the oven to 375°F.

Wipe the quinces with a damp cloth and then prick them all over with a skewer. Wrap each one individually in foil and stand them close together, upright, in an ovenproof dish. Bake in the preheated oven for about an hour, until they are just tender.

Remove from the oven and allow to cool sufficiently for you to be able to handle them. Reduce the oven setting to 350°F.

Cut the quinces in half, core them, and put them, cut side down, in the same ovenproof dish.

With a vegetable peeler, pare the orange peel in thin strands. Put this in a small pan with the sugar, 1 cup water, the orange juice, and the orange flower water. Stir over the heat, without boiling, until the sugar dissolves. Bring to a boil and simmer for 5 minutes, not stirring.

Remove the orange peel and reserve, pour the syrup over the quinces, and bake, uncovered, in the preheated oven for about an hour, until the fruit is soft and everything is syrupy.

Garnish with a few strands of orange peel over the top.

Windfall apple and quince cake

This is a brilliant recipe given to me by authors Montagu and Sarah Don, and one of the richest and fruitiest of autumn cakes. It's wonderfully gooey with cream or ice cream.

Serves 6
1 quince
2 to 3 large apples
2 lemons
1½ cups brown sugar
1 stick plus 6 tablespoons unsalted butter
2 eggs
⅔ cup self-rising flour
¾ teaspoon baking powder
½ cup whole blanched almonds, ground to breadcrumb consistency
¼ cup sliced almonds

Preheat the oven to 350°F. Line a 10-inch round springform baking pan with parchment paper.

Peel, core, and roughly chop the quince and apples, and place them in an ovenproof dish. Grate the zest from one lemon and squeeze the juice, pouring it over the fruit with the zest. Sprinkle over ¼ cup of the sugar, cover with parchment paper, and bake for 20 minutes until the fruit is soft.

Cream 10 tablespoons of the butter and 1cup of the sugar in a mixer. Add the eggs one at a time, mixing each in. Fold in the flour, baking powder, and ground almonds. Add the cooked apples and quinces, and lightly mix it in. Spoon the batter into the prepared pan and bake for 30 minutes.

Grate the zest from the remaining lemon and squeeze the juice. Melt the remaining 4 tablespoons butter and ¼ cup sugar in a small saucepan, stir in the zest and juice, and mix in the sliced almonds. Take the cake out of the oven and spread this mixture on top. Bake for another 10 to 15 minutes, until golden brown. Cool it in the pan.

Greek pork with quince

The nutmeg, lemon, and quince give the pork in this recipe a fabulous flavor. It is good when you eat it hot and just as good cold, when the different flavors really emerge. This is a traditional Greek dish taken from *Real Greek Food* by Theodore Kyriakou and Charles Campion.

Shoulder of pork is the best cut to use, as it doesn't harden with long cooking and the fat in the joint keeps the texture good. The difficulty is that it makes a ragged joint, so it is tricky to roll yourself. Ask your butcher to roll it loosely for you, so that you can push in the lemon rind yourself later and then tie it up more firmly.

Serves 6
- **2 lemons**
- **1 (3-pound) boned shoulder of pork (rolled and tied by your butcher, see above)**
- **Salt and pepper**
- **6 tablespoons unsalted butter**
- **2 pounds quinces**
- **3 tablespoons olive oil**
- **½ teaspoon freshly grated nutmeg**
- **2 tablespoons honey**
- **1 tablespoon sugar**

Preheat the oven to 350°F. Pare the lemon peel in long strips from the 2 lemons and then squeeze the juice. Poke the lemon peel into the pork and season well.

Weigh the pork to calculate the cooking time. Allow 25 minutes per pound for the oven cooking, plus 30 minutes on top of the stove.

In a heavy-bottomed casserole dish, heat a little oil and brown the pork well to seal it, then add 1¼ cups water, the lemon juice, and the butter. Cover and simmer gently for 30 minutes.

Peel and quarter the quinces, and warm the olive oil in a frying pan. Cook the quinces gently in the oil for a few minutes. Put them into a bowl and mix thoroughly with the freshly grated nutmeg, honey, and sugar.

Spoon the quince mixture over the top of the pork and add a little more water if necessary. Cover and bake in the preheated oven according to the weight of the pork as above.

When the meat is ready, remove it with the quinces, cover, and allow it to rest while you prepare the sauce.

Boil the juices rapidly to reduce by at least a quarter, until slightly thickened and syrupy. Skim with a spoon if there is too much oil on the surface. Season and serve separately.

Medlar or quince jelly

Medlar jelly is sweet and mellow, with a fragrant taste, rather like quince, that is lovely with meat and game. Gather the fruit so that some of it is ripe and soft and some still hard; such a mixture is best for this recipe. The amounts all depend on how many medlars or quinces you can get.

You need:
- **Medlars or quinces**
- **Juice of 1 lemon (optional)**
- **Sugar (for exact quantity, see below)**

Put the medlars or quinces into a large pot and just cover with water. You can add the juice of a lemon if you want the flavor to be sharper, but it is not necessary from the gelling point of view. Boil gently until the fruit breaks. Do not be tempted to break up the fruit yourself.

When the fruit is soft, strain off the liquid through a jelly bag and allow it to drip overnight or for several hours.

Warm the sugar in a bowl in a very low oven for about half an hour. Without squeezing the jelly bag (as this will make the jelly cloudy), measure the amount of juice in the bowl and return the juice to the pan. For each 2½ cups of juice add 2½ cups of warmed sugar.

Over gentle heat, make sure that the sugar is completely dissolved before bringing it to a rolling boil. Continue to boil until the gelling point is reached (see page 170). Both medlars and quinces have a very high pectin content, so the jelly will set easily.

Remove from the heat and take off any scum with a spoon. Pour into warm sterilized jars and seal.

Corn

Corn keeps getting sweeter and sweeter, with new breeding programs forever aiming at a higher sugar content. Try to get the ears as fresh as you can and, if possible, grow your own. As soon as the ears are picked, the sugar starts turning to starch and noticeably loses some of its taste.

Don't put salt in the water when cooking them. It toughens the kernels—better to serve with coarse sea salt as you eat them. If you have very fresh corn, cook it briefly in strongly boiling water for three or four minutes. This heats the corn through and softens it, but you still get a good crunch. If you've bought the corn, it may need boiling for longer—about ten minutes. The flavor and texture are better if you leave the outer husks on while the corn cooks; let them act as insulation until you eat. Only remove them when they have cooled enough to handle. When you're ready to eat, smother the ears in butter, olive oil, or Chili jam (see page 318), and plenty of salt and pepper.

Try roasting corn on the cob too, in the oven with the husks on, or wrap the cobs in foil if you've bought them with no husks.

Corn is more fun eaten straight from the cob, but you can remove the kernels with a very sharp knife and toss them in butter or olive oil with plenty of black pepper and salt.

Grilled corn with thyme butter or chili jam

Grilled corn concentrates its sweetness. You get a delicious smoky, sweet taste. This is also good with garlic butter.

Serves 8
8 ears of corn
Thyme butter (see page 80) or
Chili jam (see page 318)

Cook the corn in boiling water for 10 minutes—or less if home-grown (see page 382)—with the husks on but silks removed before cooking. Plunge into cold water and then dry them as much as you can. Peeling back the husks, smear the herb butter or chili jam over the corn and then fold the casing back. Put on a slow-burning barbecue grill, turning occasionally. When the husks are charred, they're ready.

Smoked haddock and corn chowder

This is comforting, filling, and delicious. It is enough as a meal on its own.

Serves 4
1 bay leaf
A few peppercorns
A pinch of mace
2 cloves
3 cups milk
1 pound undyed lightly smoked haddock (or substitute smoked trout)
¼ cup (½ stick) butter
1 onion or leek, chopped
A spoonful of all-purpose flour
6 small new potatoes, cut into quarters
Kernels from 2 ears of corn, removed with a sharp knife
Good bunch of flat-leaf parsley, chopped
⅔ cup cream
Salt and pepper
Juice of ½ lemon

Put the bay leaf, peppercorns, mace, and cloves into a saucepan with the milk. Bring just to a boil, add the haddock (cut into 2 pieces, if it is too long), and simmer for a further 2 minutes. Take off the heat, cover, and allow to cool in the liquid.

Strain, reserving the liquid, and lift out the fish. Gently flake the haddock or trout, discarding the skin and bones, and cover until you're ready.

Put the butter into a saucepan and sweat the onion or leek until soft but not brown. Stir in the flour and cook for a couple of minutes. Gradually whisk in the reserved liquid until the mixture is quite smooth. Add the potatoes and cook gently until just tender, adding the corn for the last 3 or 4 minutes. (If the soup seems to be a little thick, you can add some water at this stage.)

Turn down the heat and add the chopped parsley, the flaked fish, and the cream, and make sure that everything is heated through without boiling. Remove from the heat and season with salt and pepper and a little lemon juice.

Smoked haddock and corn soufflé

The cheesy taste, fluffy soufflé top, and crunch of the corn make this one of our family favorites. It is from my aunt Fortune Stanley's cookbook *English Country House Cooking*. It goes down well with children, including those who do not normally like fish.

Serves 4 to 5

1 pound undyed smoked haddock
1 ⅔ cups milk
2 tablespoons butter
2 heaping tablespoons all-purpose flour
7 ounces sharp Cheddar or Gruyère cheese, grated
Kernels from 2 ears of corn, removed with a sharp knife
Salt and pepper
3 whole eggs and 1 extra egg white

Preheat the oven to 350°F. Poach the fish in the milk gently for 3 or 4 minutes. Strain and reserve the milk. Skin the haddock and separate it into pieces.

Melt the butter in a fairly large saucepan. Add the flour and cook gently for a minute. Using a balloon whisk, add the warm milk gradually while stirring. Carefully fold in the cheese, fish, and corn, then season.

Separate the eggs. Add the yolks to the slightly cooled soufflé base. Whisk the whites to stiff peaks and then fold them into the mixture as carefully as you can, to avoid losing the volume.

Butter a deep ovenproof (ideally soufflé) dish. Pour the mixture into the dish and bake in the preheated oven for 20 minutes. The outside and top will be well risen, browned, and slightly crunchy, and the middle a little gooey and soft.

Corn blinis

These blinis are lighter than fritters, with a better texture and more flavor. My children like making these with canned corn at any time, but they are more delicious when they're made from newly picked corn. Serve them with grilled salmon or tuna, some sour cream, and a dollop of Chili jam (see page 318). This is good with a peppery mixed leaf salad.

Serves 6

4 ounces ricotta cheese
2 eggs, beaten
Kernels from 2 ears of corn, removed with a sharp knife
⅓ cup self-rising flour, sifted
1 red chili, finely chopped (optional)
2 good handfuls of chopped cilantro
Salt and pepper
Butter or olive oil, for frying

Put the ricotta into a bowl with the eggs, corn, flour, chili (if using), cilantro, salt, and pepper. Mix well and leave to stand for 15 to 20 minutes.

Melt the butter or oil in a heavy-bottomed pan and, when it's hot, add spoonfuls of the mixture to the pan. Turn when the blinis are browned and cook the other sides.

Brussels sprouts

Brussels sprouts are not something I want to eat every day, but I love them once in a while. Well cooked, sprouts are not the grey-blue-green blobs I remember from school but a brilliant cheery green. I also grow a crimson variety, 'Red Rubine'. It is smaller than green varieties, with a mild flavor and a nutty taste.

Brussels sprouts, like many winter vegetables, occupy their ground from early summer until you harvest, and require lots of space, so unless you have a large vegetable patch, they're not a good choice. Keys to success include selecting a good variety (I grow 'Fortress' for green) and stabilizing each plant firmly with a stout stake from the moment you plant it out. Wind will rock the tall heavy stems and weaken the root, compromising overall growth.

Don't start to harvest until the cold weather sets in. They then become sweeter and have more taste. November and December are their best months. Pick from the bottom upwards, choosing the largest sprouts first.

To keep the clarity of either color, put your brussels sprouts in a pan with a couple of inches of salted water, bring to a boil, and don't cover them with a lid. They'll take about eight minutes, but you can poke them to see that they're cooked—they should be firm but not mushy or losing their outer leaves.

If you have brussels sprouts growing in the garden and have just picked them, all you need do is remove any damaged outer leaves. If they've been picked for a while, recut the base—they develop a nasty greyish heel—but you don't need to make that traditional cross cut. It's meant to help the center cook at the same pace as the outer leaves. I've experimented with cut and uncut sprouts and, as long as they are not huge, cutting doesn't make any difference.

Brussels sprouts are good with almost any meat and in order to get the colors on the plate to sing, have them with something bright orange—carrots, squash, or sweet potato—and crunchy roast potatoes. If I have crimson brussels sprouts such as 'Red Rubine', I tend to sauté them with a little chili pepper and toasted almonds (see page 391). They look as good as they taste. Once you've eaten all the sprouts, eat the sprouting tops too. These are rather like more tender spring greens and are best cooked in the same way (see page 62).

Sauté of red brussels sprouts with almonds

Sautéed with a dash of vinegar, these amazing crimson brussels sprouts keep their color.

Serves 6
- **1½ pounds small red brussels sprouts**
- **2 tablespoons unsalted butter**
- **1 tablespoon olive oil**
- **½ red chili or a few dried chili flakes, to taste**
- **1 tablespoon white wine vinegar**
- **⅓ cup whole almonds, cut in half lengthwise and toasted**
- **Salt and pepper**

Trim the brussels sprouts. Melt the butter with the olive oil in a sauté pan. Add the sprouts, sliced chili (or flakes), and vinegar, and cook over moderate heat.

Keep shaking the pan to keep the sprouts from cooking too much and losing their color. While they are still crunchy, take them off the heat and stir in the toasted almonds. Sprinkle generously with salt and freshly ground pepper.

Pureed brussels sprouts in nutmeg cream

I remember having this as a teenager when we went to lunch with friends of my parents and, having always hated brussels sprouts, I was converted. The sprouts are best lightly cooked and then pulsed quickly in a food processor, so that you're left with some texture. Stir in a few chestnuts for extra crunch and flavor. This is fantastic with Christmas turkey and any roast meat.

Serves 8
- **2 pounds brussels sprouts**
- **⅔ cup crème fraîche**
- **Freshly grated nutmeg, to taste**
- **½ pound (10 to 15) chestnuts, roasted or vacuum packed**

Halve the sprouts and cook them for 5 minutes so that they're still quite firm. Drain them, and coarsely mash in a food processor, adding the crème fraîche and nutmeg before you blitz.

Add the chestnuts, roughly chopped, to the sprout puree and heat in a heavy open pan for a couple of minutes.

Professor Van Mons's brussels sprouts

This is a recipe from *Jane Grigson's Vegetable Book,* which I first cooked twenty years ago and have done countless times since. It's straight up, old-fashioned, and delicious, best with chicken or game.

Serves 8
- **2 pounds brussels sprouts**
- **5 tablespoons butter**
- **3 tablespoons white wine vinegar**
- **Handful of chopped green herbs, such as parsley, fennel, thyme, chives, and tarragon**
- **Salt and pepper**

Steam or boil the brussels sprouts for about 8 minutes, drain, and keep them covered so that they stay warm.

Heat the butter in a frying pan until it turns nut brown (not dark brown or black). Quickly stir in the wine vinegar and let the mixture sizzle for a few seconds.

Mix in the herbs, pour the sauce over the sprouts, and season with salt and pepper.

Chard

Chard is a rarity in our grocery, so it's good to grow my own—and easy too. 'Fordhook Giant' is the one I grow. If you keep picking it, preventing it from running to flower and seed, one sowing should keep producing for four or five months.

Here, from a July or August sowing, I can grow and pick it right the way through the winter. The outer leaves may get a bit frost and wind frazzled, but they are usually protecting a blemish-free heart. Space your plants well, allowing at least one foot (and ideally one-and-a-half feet) between them.

In my cooking I use white-stemmed Swiss chard (or silverbeet) rather than the decorative varieties such as 'Rainbow', 'Bright Lights', or 'Ruby'. It's much more productive and the flavor is better, with a cleaner, less muddy taste.

The key to cooking chard is to realize you have two vegetables in one. The white stems take two to three minutes longer to cook than the green, so strip the leaf from the stem before you cook and use the two parts separately. The whites need about eight minutes; the green only five to six. Or cook together: Start off with just the whites, giving them a head start before adding the greens. The cut stems brown quickly left uncovered in the air, so, after slicing, drop them into a bowl of acidulated water.

In the summer, you can just slice off the whole plant with a sharp knife and within a couple of weeks it will be ready to be picked again. To get the best out of chard when it's truly cold, use a different picking technique. In the winter, I do what's called "picking around," harvesting only the outer leaves, leaving the heart to continue to grow. This gradually creates a trunk, with the leaves sprouting at the top, and makes the plant much hardier, lifted away from the cold wet soil.

Many of the recipes for chard are also good with spinach but, particularly in the winter, chard is more prolific and easier to grow. Chard has a stronger taste and a coarser texture. It takes more cooking and is not good raw, but it suits slow-cooked gratins, pasta, and pies (see Ithaca pie, page 74) and is delicious in a nutmeg béchamel with roasted meat.

Chard and feta parcels

These delicious cheesy parcels freeze well, so you can make them in large batches when you have lots of chard or spinach. Just heat them through, straight from the freezer.

Yield: 12 parcels

1 leek, finely chopped
1 tablespoon butter
½ pound chard (greens only), chopped
6 ounces feta cheese, half grated, half in small lumps
3 ounces Parmesan cheese, grated
1 egg, beaten
Salt and pepper
1 (1-pound) package phyllo pastry in sheets of about 14 by 18 inches
A little melted butter
A few sesame seeds

Fry the leek in the butter until soft. Wash and dry the chard so that there is very little water and sweat it with the leek for a few minutes. Take the pan off the heat and add the grated feta, Parmesan, egg, and seasoning, mixing all together.

Take one sheet of phyllo pastry and cut into 4-inch strips. Brush this strip on one side with melted butter. Put 1 tablespoon of the mixture in the top right-hand corner. Fold this over, making a triangle, and then keep folding the triangle down the length of the strip, ending up with a triangular parcel several layers thick. You can freeze at this stage.

Preheat the oven to 400°F. The parcels look good garnished with a dusting of sesame seeds. With a pastry brush, brush on a light coating of butter and dip into a plate of sesame seeds.

Bake the parcels in the hot oven for 10 to 15 minutes, until golden brown.

Chard and coconut soup

A wonderful sweet and earthy soup. It is best served warm, rather than piping hot.

Serves 6

½ pound chard
¼ pound Red Giant mustard, kale, or more chard
2 medium-sized onions, finely chopped
1 garlic clove, finely chopped
2 tablespoons olive oil
6 cups vegetable stock
1 (12-ounce) can coconut milk
Salt and pepper

Prepare the chard and/or Red Giant mustard or kale, stripping the green from the stem and shredding it into ribbons.

Sweat the onions and garlic gently in olive oil for about 10 minutes, until they're soft. Add the greens, stock, and coconut milk, and bring to a boil. Simmer for 10 minutes and then whiz everything up together with an immersion blender or food processor. Season to taste, and serve.

Horta

This is an adaptation of the wilted wild greens you'll find in almost every Greek household and restaurant, particularly in the spring. Among many different leaves, they use wild arugula, dandelion, wild beet greens, chicory, and herbs, such as savory, marjoram, and mint. This dish feels virtuous and yet delicious. Particularly in the early spring, it's what our bodies are craving—iron- and vitamin-rich leaves.

Serves 8 as a side dish

3 handfuls of chard stems and leaves
2 handfuls of spinach stems and leaves
1 handful of wild bitter leaves (as above, if you can find them)
2 garlic cloves, peeled
Bunch of parsley, winter savory, or mint (whichever green herb you can find), coarsely chopped
Grated zest and juice of 1 lemon
3 tablespoons olive oil
Salt and pepper

Boil the chard, spinach, and mixed leaves with the whole garlic cloves in salted water for about 7 to 8 minutes, until the leaves are tender but not mushy.

Drain the leaves in a sieve or colander and press them down gently with the back of the spoon to get rid of any excess water but without mashing them. Add the herbs.

In a bowl, whisk the lemon zest and juice into the olive oil.

Pour this over the leaves, adding salt and pepper as you eat.

Chard and nutmeg farfalle

This is an excellent quick family supper, popular with everyone. We eat it all the time in winter.

Serves 6
1 pound pasta, such as farfalle
1 pound chard
Salt and pepper
2 tablespoons butter
2 tablespoons extra virgin olive oil
¾ cup crème fraîche
Plenty of grated nutmeg
3 ounces Parmesan cheese,
   grated, plus more as a garnish

Cook the pasta in a large pot of salted boiling water.

Strip the green chard from the leaves. Put the stems aside into a bowl of acidulated water to cook another time. Coarsely chop the greens.

Put a sprinkling of salt in the bottom of a saucepan, together with a bit of butter or splash of olive oil, and add the chard. The water caught in the washed leaves is plenty to cook with.

Cook gently for 6 to 7 minutes, until the chard is tender, and then strain in a sieve or colander, squeezing out as much water as you can with the back of the spoon. When the pasta is al dente, drain well.

Add the crème fraîche, nutmeg, Parmesan, pepper, and if needed, a pinch more salt to the chard, and heat through for a minute or two. Then whiz the mixture up with an immersion blender or food processor and add it to your pasta.

Serve with more Parmesan.

Chard and risotto balls

It's good to make too much risotto so that you can fry up balls of it again the next day, as in this recipe. This is made more delicious by putting a lump of melting mozzarella in the middle and wrapping it in chard. There's no point giving quantities for this recipe. Just use up all you have left over.

You need:
Chard
Leftover risotto
Mozzarella cheese
Olive oil, for frying
Grated Parmesan cheese

Lay the largest leaves of chard you can find on a board. Cut out the thickest two-thirds of the midrib of each of the leaves.

Bring a pan of water to a boil and blanch the ribless chard for 2 minutes.

Lay the leaf out on the board and place on it a tablespoon-sized ball of risotto folded around a small lump of mozzarella. Wrap the leaf around the rice ball as though it is a present. It will hold in place.

When you want to eat them, fry the balls in hot olive oil carefully on both sides and garnish with grated Parmesan.

Chard gratin

A fantastic meal-in-one recipe, which is delicious just as it is, served with a few potatoes. It's also lovely with good olives cut in half and added to the chard. Or you can add mussels cooked in white wine—a Provençal version—which we had as the first course of our wedding dinner.

Serves 6 to 8
- **3 pounds Swiss chard**
- **Salt and pepper**
- **3 garlic cloves**
- **3 tablespoons olive oil**
- **10 anchovies in olive oil, drained (or rinsed if salted), finely chopped**
- **4 to 6 tablespoons butter**
- **A few stems of fresh marjoram (if available)**
- **Plenty of grated nutmeg**
- **¾ cup heavy cream**
- **Grated Parmesan cheese, as a garnish**

For the mussels (optional):
- **2 pounds mussels**
- **2 tablespoons butter, plus some for the dish**
- **1 tablespoon olive oil**
- **1 onion, finely chopped**
- **1 garlic clove, finely chopped**
- **1 cup white wine**

Preheat the oven to 350°F. Put a pan of salted water on to boil.

Strip the green leaves from the chard stalks and cut the stalks about ½ inch wide across. Wash both leaves and stalks in a colander. Cook the stalks in the boiling salted water. When they're just cooked (no longer resistant to the point of a knife), remove with a slotted spoon and drain on a kitchen towel.

Blanch the greens for about 2 to 3 minutes, remove, and drain any excess water, pushing with the back of a spoon in a colander or sieve, or twist in a kitchen towel. Then coarsely chop.

Chop the garlic finely and heat in a pan with the olive oil. When the garlic begins to color, add the finely chopped anchovies. Add the chard stalks and cook gently until the anchovies start to dissolve. Remove from the heat.

To cook the mussels, if you are using them, debeard and clean them, discarding any open ones that don't close when tapped. Melt the butter and 1 tablespoon of olive oil in a large pan. Add the finely chopped onion and garlic, and sweat until translucent.

Add the mussels with the wine and cook them for 3 minutes, until they open, but no more.

Drain the mussels and allow to cool enough for you to be able to handle them, then remove from the shells.

Roughly butter a baking dish and spoon in the chard stalks and anchovy to cover the base of the dish, then scatter over half the shelled mussels, if you are using them. Lay the green chard leaves lightly over the top. Scatter the marjoram if using, grated nutmeg, and remaining shelled mussels over them. Pour over the cream. Season with salt and pepper and grate some Parmesan over the top. Some of the chard will be uncovered and some submerged. Cook the gratin in the preheated oven for 25 to 30 minutes.

Chard stems in a mustardy dressing

Many chard recipes are quite substantial. You may want something plainer and lighter. This recipe—using the stems with a mustardy dressing— is ideal. The stalks are also good with lemon butter and toasted pine nuts.

Serves 4
- **1 pound chard stems**
- **Salt**
- **1 garlic clove, peeled**
- **Bunch of flat-leaf parsley, chopped**

For the dressing:
- **2 tablespoons Dijon mustard**
- **Juice and grated zest of 1 lemon**
- **4 tablespoons extra virgin olive oil**
- **Salt and pepper**

Cut the chard stems into long fingers and cook them in a pan of salted water, with the garlic clove, for 8 minutes.

Make the dressing by mixing the mustard, lemon juice and zest, then slowly adding the oil. Season. Drain the chard and, while still warm, pour over the dressing and scatter over plenty of parsley.

Kale

I'm obsessed with kale. When you buy it, all too often it's tough and leathery, and, once cooked, it makes you feel like a giraffe eating old leaves. The flavor may be good, but there's too much fiber in the way. The other extreme is the sopping-wet, overcooked kale that I ate through the winter at school. This mushy stuff, with a nasty bitter aftertaste, is not worth bothering with.

I promise that this isn't the full story. If you grow your own, or can find the right varieties to buy, there is another side to kale. As Harold McGee relates in his book *On Food and Cooking*, growing conditions affect the strength of flavor and the bitterness in the leaves. What happens is the opposite of what one might think. In the summer, high temperatures and lack of water give kale a very strong, sometimes bitter, taste, whereas the cold and damp and dim sunlight of autumn and winter make for a milder flavor and creamier texture. The flavor is said to improve after the first frost.

'Redbor' is the most impressive looking, with statuesque, deep-red, trunk-like stems covered in crimson crinkly leaves. This makes the best deep-fried "seaweed" (see page 403). It's easy and quick to shallow-fry and, once crisped up, it will stay so even when cold.

I love the soft-textured 'Red Russian' kale, another beautiful plant with a strong purple wash over greyish leaves. The purple deepens as the weather gets colder. Stir-fry it, or it is wonderful just as steamed leaves, washed and shaken by hand with the central stems removed. Throw it into a pan with only the water left in the creases, a chopped garlic clove, and a good splash of olive oil. Cook over high heat for two to three minutes, with the lid off, stirring it around as it cooks. I sometimes add a splash of soy sauce. 'Pentland Brig' and cavolo nero or Tuscan kale are also ornamental and tasty, with the leaves at their best quite young.

Kales will grow almost anywhere for me, in any month of the year. They are the easiest to grow and hardiest productive plants. They can be used as a cut-and-come-again crop, continuing to grow strongly here right through the depths of winter and providing countless meals.

With all varieties, before you cook remove the stems with all but the youngest leaves. These are tough and need a much longer cooking time.

Kale and chickpea curry

My sister Jane gave me this very good Oriental-tasting and healthy curry recipe. She discovered it while on a detox diet but now cooks it all the time. It's one of my children's favorite meals. The mushrooms and chickpeas make it taste meaty. Serve with basmati rice and Cucumber raita (see page 196).

Serves 8

1 large onion, finely chopped
3 garlic cloves, finely chopped
A little vegetable oil
1 heaping teaspoon medium curry powder
2 tablespoons grated ginger
2 green chilis, or 1 red, finely chopped
Salt and pepper
1 cup chickpeas, soaked overnight and cooked (see page 44), or 2 (15-ounce) cans
1 (12-ounce) can of coconut milk
½ pound button mushrooms, halved
Juice of 1 lime
2 (6-inch) lemongrass stalks
15 medium cavolo nero leaves
2 tablespoons soy sauce
2 tablespoons Thai fish sauce
Large bunch of cilantro

Fry the onion and garlic gently in the oil until soft. Add the curry powder, fresh ginger, chilis, salt, and pepper, and stir.

Next, add the cooked chickpeas, coconut milk, mushrooms, lime juice, and lemongrass, and simmer for 30 minutes.

Remove the stems from the kale and chop the leaves into strips. Steam them for 5 minutes and then add them to the chickpea mixture. Add the soy and fish sauces.

Garnish with coarsely chopped cilantro. This is best served warm, when all the flavors seem to sing out.

Quick-fried kale

A quick and delicious vegetable dish that can be easily rustled up.

Serves 4
4 ounces pancetta, cut in chunks
2 tablespoons butter
1 tablespoon olive oil
¾ pound kale, roughly chopped
1 tablespoon white sugar
Salt and pepper

Fry the garlic with the pancetta in the butter and olive oil until the pancetta is crisp.

Add the kale and scatter over the sugar and seasoning. Cook on low heat for 10 minutes.

Ribollita

Ribollita is an amazing meal in a soup. It is good hearty stuff and one of my favorite winter recipes. You can put almost any winter vegetable into it, but kale is an essential.

Serves 8 to 10
½ pound cranberry or other
beans, fresh or dried and
soaked
3 pounds kale
1 pound chard (or just more kale)
3 tablespoons olive oil
2 onions, chopped
2 garlic cloves, chopped
2 carrots, diced
Bunch of flat-leaf parsley,
chopped
1 head celery or 2 fennel bulbs
5 slices good white bread, crusts
removed and bread
torn up
Salt and pepper
Grated Parmesan cheese, to serve

Cook the beans until they're soft, which usually takes about 40 minutes, and leave them in their liquid. You can use canned, but the texture is better with fresh or presoaked dried beans.

Prepare the kale and chard, removing stalks and chopping the leaves.

Cover the base of a big saucepan with olive oil and sweat the onions, garlic, carrots, parsley, and celery or fennel gently for about 15 minutes, until they are all soft.

Add half the beans, together with the kale and chard, cover everything with 6 cups of water, and cook for half an hour.

Put the other half of the beans in a food processor and puree them with their cooking liquid. Add the puree and the bread to the soup, also adding a little water if the soup is too dry.

Drizzle on a little olive oil. Season and have plenty of Parmesan on the table for scattering over the top.

Kale seaweed

One of my favorite snacks for a winter party—a big plate of kale seaweed, with everyone dipping in. Because of the amount of oil in the cooking, a little goes a long way. Redbor is the best variety for seaweed, but any kale will do. You can scatter cashew nuts or toasted sliced almonds over the top. You want one kale leaf per person if you're making it for a party, or one and a half leaves per person for a first course.

Serves 8 to 10
**1 pound kale leaves, with midrib
    removed, torn or cut into strips
1 teaspoon soft brown sugar
2 good pinches of salt
¼ cup crushed cashew nuts
    or toasted sliced almonds
    (optional)**

Heat some oil to 325°F. Use a deep-fat fryer if you have one; if not, the oil should fill only a third of the pan, so use a wide heavy-bottomed pot rather than a frying pan. You can use an oil thermometer or the more basic technique of dropping a strand or two of kale into the oil. If it sizzles immediately but doesn't burn, the oil is at the right temperature.

Before you cook a batch, dry the kale thoroughly in a clean kitchen towel or salad spinner.

Carefully drop a handful of kale into the hot oil. Don't try to cook it all at once as the oil temperature will drop and it won't crisp up the kale.

Fry for about a minute until the color darkens. It will crisp up as it cools. Drain it on paper towels.

Scatter soft brown sugar and salt over the top, and add the crushed cashew nuts or flaked toasted almonds, if using.

Always serve this immediately; it's far nicer hot.

Kale bruschetta

This recipe is akin to a robust winter salsa verde, with plenty of olive oil and parsley. It's good spread on bruschetta as a first course and I also love it as a pasta sauce. Add plenty of Parmesan and more olive oil, and eat it with tagliatelle or spaghetti. The softer-textured kale varieties—cavolo nero or Red Russian—are best for this dish.

Serves 8
**½ pound kale
Salt and pepper
2 garlic cloves, peeled
Juice and grated zest of 1 lemon
3 tablespoons chopped capers
3 tablespoons chopped gherkins
    or cornichon pickles
3 tablespoons chopped shallots
3 tablespoons chopped black or
    green olives
3 tablespoons chopped flat-leaf
    parsley
1 cup mascarpone cheese
    (optional)**

For the bruschetta:
**Fresh good-quality white bread
1 garlic clove
Extra virgin olive oil**

Prepare the kale by removing the stalks.

Bring 2 quarts of salted water to a boil. Add the kale and whole garlic cloves. Cook for 3 to 4 minutes, until the kale is tender, and drain, squeezing out as much water as you can from the leaves with the back of a spoon in a colander or sieve, or twist in a kitchen towel.

Chop the kale and garlic (ideally by hand so that you have a coarsely textured mix).

Add the lemon juice and zest, capers, pickles, shallots, black or green olives, and flat-leaf parsley, and check the seasoning.

To make the bruschetta, cut the bread into finger-thick slices and drizzle over olive oil. Grill or toast the bread in the oven at about 350°F for 10 minutes. Keep an eye on it to make sure it doesn't become too hard.

Lightly scrape one side of the bread slices with fresh garlic and sprinkle with salt. Once they've cooled a bit, spread a little mascarpone (if using) on the bread and add the kale topping. Sprinkle with olive oil.

Leeks

I love leeks when they're finely chopped; left in large chunks or whole, they can be stringy and slimy. You so often see them left on the side of a plate. As well as improving the texture, slicing leeks thinly makes cleaning them much easier. If they're store-bought, they might not be as sandy, but if they're home-grown, your leeks may be particularly dirty. Cut across the flesh all the way down the shaft of each leek, dividing it into four sections attached at the bulb. Then soak the whole thing in a sink of cold water for half an hour. This will get out any soil and dirt between the layers. If the leeks already look quite clean, just slice them into thin discs, whoosh them around in a sink of water, and roughly dry them on a kitchen towel.

Leeks are good as a side vegetable, gently fried in a good amount of butter, lemon juice, lemon zest, and a few sage leaves. They are invaluable in soups and stews, and will transform a fish, chicken, or pheasant pie (see page 407).

Leeks are also easy and reliable to grow, and look great, giving a good vertical spire in the vegetable garden amidst all those fat, round-leaved cabbages and kales. I plant strips of a green leek such as 'Hannibal' (which has exceptionally long white stems) next to a panel of the silver, washed-purple French leek 'St Victor'. Out in the frosty garden, they look superb.

I grow leeks at almost any time of the year, but they have less of a problem with disfiguring rust when it's cold. The fungal spores are wiped out by frost, so as long as your crop is relatively clean in the autumn, it should remain so all the way through the winter.

I leave a few unharvested leeks lining my paths, or on the outside of your beds in an ornamental vegetable patch. Remaining there in the garden from the previous year, they will bud and flower in the late spring. They always look fantastic in full flower, and you can easily harvest your own seeds to sow the next winter crop right away.

Potato and leek soup

A standard quick-to-make soup, and one of my favorites in the winter. An added bonus is that the taste improves after a day or two in the fridge. Just before you eat, add the herbs and cream.

Unlike many recipes for this soup, this one uses loads of leeks and few potatoes, making the soup full of flavor and not too stodgy, with a lovely color.

Serves 8
- **1 onion, thinly sliced**
- **1 tablespoon olive oil**
- **1 tablespoon butter**
- **6 large leeks, cut into ½-inch slices**
- **3 medium-sized waxy potatoes**
- **1 quart vegetable or chicken stock**
- **2 cups milk**
- **Handful of fresh basil or chervil, chopped**
- **Freshly grated nutmeg, to taste**
- **5 to 6 tablespoons light cream or crème fraîche**
- **Salt and pepper**

In a large heavy-bottomed pan, sauté the onion in olive oil and butter until soft. Add the leeks and potatoes, and cook for 6 to 7 minutes. Add the stock, which should just cover the vegetables, and simmer until the vegetables are tender. If you cut the potatoes very thinly, 10 minutes is plenty of cooking time.

Puree in a blender and add enough milk for the consistency you want, then return to the pot and bring to a boil.

Remove from the heat, add the herbs, nutmeg, and cream, and warm through on low heat.

Season with plenty of salt and pepper.

Creamed leek and haddock

Seafood restaurateur Mitch Tonks is a really wonderful fishmonger and cook. One of his basic recommendations is to serve creamed leek with almost any fish, especially haddock or turbot, but also salmon, hake, brill, or scallops.

Serves 4
- **2 medium-sized leeks**
- **2 tablespoons butter**
- **1 tablespoon olive oil**
- **½ cup heavy cream**
- **Salt and pepper**
- **1 teaspoon English mustard or smooth spicy mustard**
- **Vegetable oil, for frying**
- **½ pound skinless fish fillets**
- **Bunch of chervil, coarsely chopped (or parsley if chervil not available)**

Preheat the oven to broil.

Chop the leeks as finely as you can and fry them gently in the butter and olive oil. Add the cream, salt, pepper, and mustard and continue to cook for a few more minutes.

Put some vegetable oil into a hot frying pan with an ovenproof handle. Season the fish fillets with a little salt and fry, flesh side down, for about 5 minutes, until golden. Put the pan in the oven for another 3 to 4 minutes.

Put a spoonful of leeks on each plate and place the fish on top. Add the chervil as you are about to serve.

Ray Smith's pheasant and leek pie

This is a recipe from the River Cottage restaurant in London. It is perfect for when you have lots of people around at a weekend. It's good warm or cold.

Serves 6

Breasts of 4 hen pheasants
2 cups ruby port
2 teaspoons crushed juniper
 berries
Ground black pepper
A little olive oil
½ cup (1 stick) butter
2 pounds leeks, white parts only,
 finely chopped
½ cup heavy cream
24 ounces puff pastry, ready made
 or homemade (see below)

For the puff pastry:

6½ cups all-purpose flour
2 pinches of salt
1½ cups (3 sticks) butter (cold and
 diced into small pieces)
Juice of ½ large lemon
Beaten egg, to brush

Marinate the pheasant breasts in a deep bowl with the port, juniper berries, and pepper overnight.

If you are making the pastry, sift the flour with the salt and work the butter into the flour, or pulse in a food processor until the mixture resembles breadcrumbs. Drizzle in the lemon juice and just enough cold water to bind, and bring together to form a ball of dough. Flour a surface and roll out to an oblong. Fold over into three, turn the pastry by 90 degrees, and repeat the whole process another couple of times. Cover with plastic wrap, chill, and rest for 30 minutes.

Take the pheasant breasts from the marinade and fry in a little oil over medium heat, until just colored on both sides but not cooked through, and put to one side.

Melt the butter in a pan, add the leeks, and cook gently, until they are tender. Stir in the cream, season, and leave to cool. Preheat the oven to 400°F.

Transfer the marinade to a pan and, over low heat, simmer to reduce it by half.

Roll out half the pastry and line a pie dish. Add a layer of the leek mixture and lay the pheasant, cut into thick slices, on the leek. Add the reduced marinade and put the remaining leek mixture on top.

Cover with the second half of the pastry, moisten the upper edge with water, and pinch together to seal. Brush with an egg wash and bake in the preheated oven for 30 minutes, until the pastry is crisp and golden.

This pie can be difficult to serve neatly. Allow it to cool and it will be easier to slice.

Leek and goat cheese tart

This stands out from the plethora of recipes for this tart. It's adapted from a recipe by Scottish cookbook writer Claire Macdonald with very short pastry and the addition of Dijon mustard.

Serves 6 to 8
For the crust:

1½ cups all-purpose flour
½ teaspoon salt
6 tablespoons butter

2 tablespoons Dijon mustard
2 large eggs plus 2 large
 egg yolks
1 cup light cream
Salt and pepper
4 leeks, thinly sliced
2 tablespoons olive oil
8 ounces soft goat cheese

First, make the crust. Sift the flour with the salt and work the butter into the flour, or pulse in a food processor, until the mixture resembles breadcrumbs. Add just enough cold water for it to bind together as a dough. Roll out and use to line a 9-inch tart pan. Put this in the fridge for at least an hour.

Preheat the oven to 350°F. Prick the base of the pastry with a fork and bake blind by covering the crust with greaseproof paper weighted down with baking beans or rice and placing in the oven for 20 to 25 minutes. Remove the baking beans or rice and paper and allow to cool. Leave the oven on at the same setting.

Allow the crust to cool a little, then spread Dijon mustard all over the base. Beat together the eggs, extra yolks, cream, and seasoning.

Fry the leeks in the oil gently until they're soft and put them in the crust. Crumble the goat cheese over the leeks and pour over the egg mixture.

Bake in the oven for 20 minutes, until the tart is set.

Boiled chicken with leeks and salsa verde

Buy a really good chicken—slow-reared, organic, free-range. Put it in a pot with a mound of leeks and carrots, some white wine, and herbs, and eat it with creamy mashed potatoes and a winter salsa verde. It makes one of the best Sunday lunches for this time of year. It's also lovely if you extract some stock halfway through and cook a simple risotto as a change from mashed potatoes.

Serves 6

1 medium-sized organic free-range chicken
1 cup dry white wine
Salt and pepper
A few parsley stalks
8 large carrots, peeled and chopped into thumb-length chunks
8 large leeks, chopped into thumb-length chunks

For the salsa verde:
Large bunch of flat-leaf parsley
Small bunch of winter savory or thyme
4 gherkins or cornichon pickles
30 capers
¾ cup olive oil
Juice of ½ lemon

Preheat the oven to 350°F.

Cover the chicken halfway with equal parts wine and water. Season, add a few parsley stalks and half the carrots and leeks, and bring to a boil. Cover and cook in the preheated oven (or leave gently simmering on the stovetop) for about an hour, depending on size. The good thing about cooking chicken in liquid is that it doesn't matter if it's slightly overcooked. It won't be dry, but it will start to fall apart if you really overdo it.

Take the bird out and put it on a warmed plate, then cover it with foil and a thick cloth to rest. It will retain its heat for 20 minutes at least.

Strain the liquid and discard the herbs and vegetables (which will have lost most of their flavor). Put the stock back in the pan. Turn the heat up so that the liquid is boiling strongly and add the other half of the carrots and leeks. Boil for 5 minutes, until the stock has reduced and the vegetables are just tender.

To make the salsa verde, whiz all the ingredients together in a food processor with some seasoning. Do this only briefly, or chop by hand to give a coarse texture.

Carve the chicken and serve it with a few carrots and leeks, a dollop of mashed potato, and a good spoonful of salsa verde on each plate.

Pomegranates and cranberries

Make the most of pomegranates and cranberries over the Christmas season. They don't just look festive and beautiful: They can be used in all sorts of wonderful recipes.

There are few stronger contenders for the fruit beauty parade than a pomegranate cut in half. If you just want to admire them, smear the cut surfaces in Vaseline, and they'll look good for twice as long as they would if left open to the air. Make a jumble of them all over your Christmas table.

To extract the seeds, whack the pomegranates against the table, or hit them hard on all sides with a rolling pin or meat mallet. Then slice the fruit and the seeds will tumble out. Or cut the fruit in half and bang the back with a wooden spoon until the seeds fall into a bowl.

The tart flavor and crunchy texture of pomegranates are lovely in salads and with couscous and rice, and they make a good contrast to creamy desserts. Eat them scattered over vanilla ice cream or try them with Panna cotta (see page 416) or Frozen mocha and ginger meringue cake (see page 415).

Cranberries have a versatile and sharp taste. They make a good smoothie with bananas, an excellent uncooked relish, and, of course, good old cranberry sauce.

It's worth remembering that both pomegranates and cranberries are superfoods. Pomegranates are packed with vitamins and antioxidants. They're said to be the most antiaging food you can eat, and the juice, used as a mouthwash, is brilliant for healing mouth ulcers. Also, current research is focusing on a study that suggests that a glass of pomegranate juice a day improves the function of blood vessels, reduces hardening of the arteries, and improves heart health. Cranberry juice should be the drink of choice for those prone to urinary tract infections: The juice is said to be the best thing for mild urinary tract disease—both bacterial and viral.

Jeweled couscous

You can eat this to accompany anything and it looks beautiful. It's delicious on its own with a salad and is perfect for stuffing quail (see right).

Serves 6
- 1½ cups couscous
- ½ cup chopped dried apricots
- ½ cup raisins
- 1 to 1½ cups pomegranate seeds
- 3 shallots, finely chopped
- 2 level tablespoons ground cumin seeds
- 1½ teaspoons ground coriander
- Juice and grated zest of 2 oranges
- ⅓ cup pine kernels, toasted
- ⅓ cup pistachios
- Plenty of flat-leaf parsley, chopped
- Salt and pepper

Put the couscous in a bowl with the fruit (except the pomegranate seeds), the shallots, and the spices. Add enough boiling water to make up the orange juice to 2½ cups of liquid and pour over the couscous, stirring in the orange zest. Cover and leave for 10 to 15 minutes.

Add the nuts, pomegranate seeds, and parsley. Season well, stir, and serve.

Stuffed roast quail with jeweled couscous and spiced citrus sauce

This is wonderful for a party, easy to do for large numbers, and not too filling, so you'll have room for dessert.

Serves 6 to 8
- 8 quail, boned
- Jeweled couscous (see left)
- 8 thin slices Parma ham or pancetta

For the spiced citrus sauce:
- ¾ cup honey
- ½ cup lemon juice
- ½ cup orange juice
- 3 cups good chicken or vegetable stock
- Freshly grated nutmeg
- 2 to 3 cloves
- 4 star anise
- ½ teaspoon ground ginger
- 6 tablespoons butter
- Salt and pepper

Preheat the oven to 350°F.

Stuff the quail with the jeweled couscous. Wrap the whole stuffed quail with a slice of Parma ham or pancetta and secure with a toothpick. Roast the quail in the preheated oven for 25 minutes.

Remove the quail and wrap in foil to rest. Then make the sauce: Place the honey in a medium-sized saucepan and caramelize. Deglaze the roasting pan with the lemon and orange juices, pour them into the saucepan, and cook gently for 10 minutes. Add the stock and spices and reduce by a third. Whisk in the butter, season, and set aside.

Either pour the warm sauce over the birds or serve separately.

Game salad with pomegranate

If you've had game over Christmas, this salad is ideal for Boxing Day, and it's always handy to have some good-looking salads up your sleeve for the winter. You can use a pheasant, as here, or the remains of partridge, grouse, duck, or any game bird. This is the recipe of a friend of mine, Lucy Boyd, who is a wonderful cook.

Serves 6
- 1 whole cooked pheasant
- 1 fennel bulb
- Handful of mixed winter leaves, such as dandelion, the small young tips of cavolo nero, mizuna, and mâche, leaves separated
- 1 head radicchio or Belgian or Treviso endive
- 3 ounces Parmesan cheese, cut into rough slivers
- 12 whole fresh chestnuts, roasted
- Seeds of 1 pomegranate
- 3 tablespoons aged balsamic vinegar

For the dressing:
- 6 tablespoons extra virgin olive oil
- Juice of 1 lemon
- Salt and pepper

Pull the meat off the bird's bones in rough pieces.

Thinly slice the fennel (this is easiest done on a mandoline). Cut the larger salad leaves and the chicory lengthwise down their spine.

Make a simple dressing by mixing the olive oil and lemon juice, salt, and pepper. Toss the salad leaves in the dressing, then add the pheasant pieces. Add some Parmesan slivers and roasted chestnuts and scatter over a few pomegranate seeds.

Drizzle a little of the aged balsamic over and season.

Frozen mocha and ginger meringue cake with pomegranate sauce

I love this dessert and it's very easy to make. Serve it with pomegranates in winter and raspberries in summer. To save time, you can buy the meringues—it doesn't matter if they are powdery and dry.

Serves 8 to 10
For the meringues:
   6 egg whites
   ¾ cup granulated sugar
   ¾ cup superfine sugar
   Sunflower oil

   2 tablespoons strong instant coffee
   1 tablespoon boiling water
   3 cups heavy cream
   1 tablespoon superfine sugar
   1 tablespoon coffee liqueur, such as Tia Maria or Kahlúa
   3 pieces of candied ginger, thinly sliced
   1 tablespoon corn syrup

For the pomegranate sauce:
   3 tablespoons redcurrant jelly
   1 cup pomegranate juice (bought or fresh)
   Juice of 1 lime
   1 heaping tablespoon arrowroot powder
   Seeds of 2 pomegranates

Preheat the oven to 225°F.
   To make the meringues, whisk the egg whites until very stiff and dry, and slowly add the granulated sugar bit by bit, whisking until the egg whites regain their former stiffness. Fold in the superfine sugar with a large metal spoon. Spoon onto parchment paper rubbed with a trace of sunflower oil or use a silicone mat, and bake in the preheated oven for about 3 hours, until crisp. Remove and break the meringues into pieces.
   Mix the instant coffee with the boiling water, then chill it well. Whip the cream to the soft-peak stage and mix

in the sugar, Tia Maria or Kahlúa, and half the coffee. Fold the mixture with the ginger, corn syrup, and meringue pieces. Spoon the mixture into a 3-inch deep straight-sided round cake pan, 8 inches in diameter, or a loaf pan, lined with parchment paper, and marble the top with the remaining coffee. Freeze for at least 24 hours.
   To make the sauce, melt the redcurrant jelly in the pomegranate juice over low heat until dissolved. Add the lime juice. Bring to a boil, remove from the heat, and add the arrowroot (which thickens clear), already mixed with a little cold water. Put back on the heat and simmer gently, while whisking, for a couple of minutes. Then let the sauce cool. When it's completely cold, add the pomegranate seeds.
   Serve the cake straight from the freezer, drizzled with the sauce.

Panna cotta with marinated pomegranate

This is quite alcoholic, so it may be better for dinner than lunch!

Serves 4
For the marinated pomegranate:
   3 ripe pomegranates
   Juice of 1 lemon
   ⅓ cup superfine sugar
   ⅓ cup Grand Marnier or brandy

For the panna cotta:
   1½ teaspoons unflavored gelatin
   1 cup heavy cream
   ¾ cup milk
   ¼ cup superfine sugar, plus
      2 extra teaspoons
   1 vanilla pod
   1 long piece of lemon zest (pared
      with a potato peeler)

Cut the pomegranates in half and knock out the seeds. Place in a bowl and add the lemon juice, sugar, and liqueur and mix carefully. Cover and chill for at least an hour in the fridge.

Dissolve the gelatin in a little water for a few minutes. Heat the cream and the milk with the sugar, vanilla pod, and lemon zest in a heavy saucepan over medium heat.

When the cream and milk reach a boil, remove the vanilla pod and zest. Add the gelatin. Stir well to combine the gelatin and strain into 4 lightly oiled ramekin dishes.

Tap them to release any air bubbles and chill until set. To serve, dip the molds quickly into very hot water and tip out. Surround the panna cotta with a good spoonful of the marinated pomegranate seeds.

Cranberry tart with hot toffee sauce

An excellent Christmas dessert for eating at any time when you have lots of people to feed. It has a good balance of sweet and sour.

Serve 6
   1 pound cranberries, fresh
      or frozen
   Juice and grated zest of 1 orange
   1 cup superfine sugar
   2 cups shelled pecans, chopped
   1 to 2 eggs, beaten well
   ½ cup all-purpose flour, sifted
   5 tablespoons butter, melted
   Crème fraîche, to serve

For the toffee sauce:
   1½ cups dark brown sugar
   ½ cup (1 stick) butter
   ½ cup heavy cream
   Crème fraîche, for serving

Preheat the oven to 350°F. Grease an 8-inch springform cake pan.

Put the cranberries in a non-stick pan with the orange juice and zest and mix well. Cook on the stovetop for about 3 to 4 minutes, until the cranberries pop.

Put the just-cooked cranberries into the prepared springform cake pan. Sprinkle with half the sugar and the pecans, and mix well.

In a bowl, beat the remaining sugar with the egg until well mixed. Add the flour and melted butter to make a smooth batter. Pour this over the cranberries in the pan and bake for 40 to 45 minutes.

To make the toffee sauce, heat the sugar, butter, and cream together until the sugar has dissolved and the sauce is bubbling. Take off the heat and serve warm. This makes generous quantities of sauce and you may have some left over for ice cream the following day.

Serve the tart warm with the hot toffee sauce and crème fraîche.

Orange and cranberry pies

Make these as a refreshing change from mince pies.

Yield: 36 small pies or tartlets
For the orange pastry:
  2½ cups all-purpose flour
  1 cup confectioners' sugar
  Grated zest and juice of ½ orange
  Pinch of salt
  1½ cups (3 sticks) butter

  2 cups soft brown sugar
  ¾ pound cranberries
  Juice of 1 orange
  4 cloves, crushed
  Milk

To make the crust, sift the flour with the confectioners' sugar, orange zest, and salt, and rub in the butter (or pulse in a processor) until the mixture resembles breadcrumbs. Add just enough orange juice to bring the mixture together in a ball and chill for 30 minutes.

Meanwhile, mix the filling ingredients together in a pan and cook over low heat for 10 minutes.

Roll out the pastry and cut out equal numbers of circles and slightly smaller circles. Grease and line a muffin tin with the circles, and spoon the filling into them. Top each pie with a smaller pastry circle. Brush the edge with a little water. Pinch the bottoms and tops together. Chill for about 10 minutes to firm up the pastry.

Preheat the oven to 350°F. Brush the pies with milk and cook in the preheated oven until brown. This should take about 20 minutes.

Cranberry vodka

An excellent drink for a shot or two at Christmas, this vodka is fantastic with blinis and smoked salmon and eel.

Yield: 20 small glasses
  ½ cup fresh cranberries
  l bottle vodka
  1 tablespoon honey

Crush the cranberries and add them to the bottle of vodka with the honey. Infuse at room temperature for 24 hours and then strain.

Cranberry cocktail

A sharp, limey cranberry cocktail that is good for Christmas.

Yield: 1 glass
  4 tablespoons cranberry juice
  1½ tablespoons Grand Marnier
  2½ tablespoons tequila
  ½-inch piece of ginger, crushed
  Dash of lime juice
  Dash of sugar syrup
  (see page 225)
  Crushed ice

Shake all the ingredients with crushed ice and strain into cocktail glasses.

Venison, cranberry, and chestnut casserole

The taste of this dish is much improved if made at least a day in advance and carefully reheated, as this allows the flavors to deepen. Serve with Nutmeg mashed potatoes (see page 336) and Quick braised red cabbage (see page 21).

Serves 6
- **2 pounds lean shoulder of venison**
- **2 tablespoons all-purpose flour**
- **Salt and pepper**
- **18 shallots**
- **4 ounces bacon**
- **1 tablespoon olive oil**
- **¾ bottle red wine**
- **2 bay leaves**
- **3 sprigs of fresh rosemary**
- **3 sprigs of fresh thyme**
- **1 tablespoon dried wild mushrooms (any type or a mixture), soaked in hot water or warm milk for 10 minutes, then drained and chopped**
- **1 tablespoon redcurrant jelly**
- **2 tablespoons tomato paste**
- **½ teaspoon ground juniper berries**
- **½ teaspoon ground coriander seeds**
- **½ teaspoon freshly grated nutmeg**
- **1 cup fresh or frozen cranberries**
- **1 cup peeled chestnuts**

Preheat the oven to 325°F.

Cut the venison into large chunks and toss in the seasoned flour to coat lightly. Peel the shallots and cut the bacon into pieces.

Fry the bacon and shallots until golden and put into a casserole dish. Sear the venison, in batches, in the hot pan in a little oil and add to the casserole dish. Deglaze the pan with the red wine and add with all the other ingredients, except the cranberries and chestnuts, to the dish. Taste and adjust the seasoning if necessary. Cover with a lid and put in the oven.

After an hour, add the cranberries and chestnuts to the casserole. After another half hour, start testing to see if the meat is really tender: the cooking time will vary, depending on the age of the animal and how long it has been hung.

Kate's cranberry and macadamia flapjacks

This was a chance invention of Kate Dawson, my assistant Tam's daughter, who had lots of leftover cranberries after one Christmas. They're so good you'll eat them all year round. Fresh cranberries give a sharper taste than dried, delicious in contrast to the sweetness of the other ingredients.

Yield: 12 flapjacks
- **1 cup (2 sticks) butter, plus more to grease the pan**
- **¾ cup Demerara or soft brown sugar**
- **2 tablespoons corn syrup**
- **½ teaspoon ground ginger**
- **1 cup rolled oats**
- **⅓ cup macadamia nuts, some cut in half**
- **⅓ cup dried or fresh cranberries**

Preheat the oven to 350°F. Butter a shallow baking pan. Put the butter, sugar, and syrup into a heavy-bottomed saucepan and stir over low heat until the sugar has completely dissolved. Add the ground ginger and take the pan off the heat. Stir in the oats, nuts, and cranberries, and press the mixture into the greased pan.

Cook in the preheated oven for 15 minutes. The mixture will still be soft at this stage but it will harden as it cools.

When it has cooled a little, cut it into squares.

Winter
root vegetables

Winter roots are enjoying a renaissance, with great restaurants such as the River Cafe and De Kas in Amsterdam putting parsnips, celeriac, rutabagas, and turnips center stage. We're all familiar with the common roots, but some people are wary of celeriac, Jerusalem artichoke, salsify, and kohlrabi. What do we do with these?

Celeriac has a slightly aniseedy, nutty flavor and it stores well, lasting for over two weeks in the vegetable basket. It's good raw in salads such as Celeriac rémoulade (see page 434) and makes an excellent winter mashed vegetable or soup (see page 432). Try it in a soufflé, cooking it in the scraped-out root (see page 432). On my heavy soil, celeriac is tricky to grow; it needs so much space—eighteen inches between each root to maximize its health and growth—from spring until winter that I tend to buy mine. If you do grow it, don't harvest the roots until after a mild frost, which will improve their flavor. On the other hand, don't leave them in the ground too long, as they will not stand hard frost.

Jerusalem artichokes are sweeter than celeriac, but share the nuttiness. They're a cinch to grow—almost too much so. If you leave a few undug from one winter to the next, they'll start to invade your vegetable patch. Jerusalem artichokes are tubers; spread by runners, and left to romp, they can become a pest. I love them, and they're always there when you're running out of other things to eat from the garden. Don't peel your artichokes: just scrub them. This makes them easier to prepare and the flavor is better. If they are encrusted with soil, leave them to soak in cold water for a while before you scrub.

Kohlrabis aren't strictly speaking a root but a swollen stem base. They have a gentle turnipy flavor and are good raw, thinly sliced, or cooked. I love them as a first course with hollandaise sauce (see page 440). They are easy to grow and, like many brassicas, extremely hardy.

My mother is very keen on salsify and scorzonera—twin sisters with thong-like taproots that are coming back into fashion. Salsify has pale skin and pink-purple flowers, scorzonera black skin and yellow flowers. The flowers of both are edible and good to scatter over a salad. People divide sharply as to whether they think these two roots are deliciously unique or deadly boring. I like the flavor, which is not unlike a sweeter Jerusalem artichoke, but the roots feel a bit measly for the amount of preparation involved.

Winter bagna cauda

There are lots of different versions of this recipe, but many of them are a hassle, with the milk curdling at the drop of a hat. With this one, the cooking of the garlic is easy and works every time. You can make bagna cauda (garlic and anchovy dip) in the summer using eggplant, peppers, fennel, and carrots to dip. In winter, use lots of different roots. I like eating them raw, but sometimes you may prefer to have them warm and lightly steamed.

Serves 6 to 8
For the bagna cauda:
> **16 garlic cloves, peeled**
> **Milk, to cover**
> **10 ounces anchovy fillets (preferably salted and rinsed; if in oil, drained)**
> **¾ cup extra virgin olive oil**
> **1 cup (2 sticks) butter, cut into pieces**
> **½ cup heavy cream**
>
> **1 celeriac, peeled and cut into julienne strips (then doused in lemon juice to keep them from discoloring)**
> **3 Jerusalem artichokes, sliced**
> **½ cauliflower, broken into small florets**
> **2 carrots, cut into sticks**
> **2 fennel bulbs, cut into chunks**
> **1 celery head, broken into sticks**
> **Selection of crunchy-stemmed salad leaves, such as Red Giant mustard, rocket, komatsuna (Japanese mustard spinach)**

First, make the bagna cauda. Preheat the oven to 300°F.

Put the garlic cloves into a small loaf pan. Cover with milk and then with a layer of parchment paper and a layer of foil. Cook in the oven for about 30 to 40 minutes, until the garlic is soft. Make sure that the garlic remains covered by the milk and doesn't dry out. Lift out the garlic and discard the milk.

Put the anchovies into a bowl over a pan of simmering water and add the soft garlic cloves. Mash them together with a fork to a paste. Using a hand whisk, gradually add the oil and butter, whisking to combine. Finally add the cream.

Pour the bagna cauda into a bowl or, even better, into a fondue dish to keep it warm. Then dip the vegetable pieces into it.

Vegetable stock

It's winter roots that give much of the flavor to a good vegetable stock. Use leftovers and the clean peel or tops and bottoms of any of these roots—whatever you have. Homemade stock is really worth having; leave bought stock for emergencies.

For about 6 cups:
- **1 onion, unpeeled and cut in half**
- **2 carrots**
- **1 small celeriac, rutabaga, or turnip—whichever you have around**
- **Bunch of parsley, including the stems**
- **6 celery sticks**
- **2 bay leaves**
- **6 black peppercorns**

Coarsely chop all the vegetables and simmer them gently in 2 quarts of water with the bay and peppercorns for 40 minutes. Strain the liquid and use, or boil for a further 30 minutes until it's reduced right down, pour into ice trays, and freeze. Use for soup, risotto, sauces, and stews.

Slow-roasted winter roots and herb couscous

This makes an excellent vegetarian dish, and you can also serve it with harissa or Cucumber raita (see page 196) as well as the couscous.

Serves 6
For the roasted vegetables:
- **2 beets**
- **2 carrots**
- **1 sweet potato**
- **2 parsnips**
- **2 onions or shallots**
- **2 whole heads garlic**
- **2 tablespoons olive oil**
- **Bunch of thyme**
- **Sprinkling of balsamic vinegar**
- **⅔ cup good vegetable stock**
- **Salt and pepper**

For the herb couscous:
- **1½ cups couscous**
- **2 cups good vegetable stock, brought to a boil**
- **Salt and pepper**
- **Handful of mint or cilantro, chopped**
- **Handful of parsley, chopped**
- **Juice and grated zest of ½ lemon or lime**
- **Extra virgin olive oil (optional)**

Preheat the oven to 325°F.

Scrub the beets, removing any blemishes, but leave the skin on. Cut in half if they're large. Peel the carrots, sweet potato, and parsnips, and cut into wedges. Quarter the onions (unless using shallots) and leave the heads of garlic whole. Lightly oil a baking tray and put in all the vegetables, except the onions, together with the thyme. Turn them so that they are covered with the oil and sprinkle with balsamic vinegar.

Put the vegetables in the preheated oven for about 40 minutes and then add the onion, together with the stock (if you add only this amount, it stops them from burning on the bottom, but still allows them to crisp up). Roast for a further 35 to 40 minutes, until they are crisp and golden, and all the liquid has been absorbed.

Fifteen minutes before the vegetables come out of the oven, make the couscous. Put the couscous into a deep bowl, pour over the boiling stock, stir, cover, and then leave for 5 to 10 minutes for the grains to soften.

Season well and stir in the chopped herbs, lemon zest and juice, and a dash of olive oil if you wish. Season the roasted vegetables with salt and pepper before serving.

Venison fillet with root vegetable chips

I love fillet of venison with root vegetable chips, and the gamier and stronger the venison, the better. The vegetable chips go well with any red meat or game. A mix of beets, sweet potatoes, and parsnips looks wonderfully colorful.

Serves 6
For the root vegetable chips:
   3 parsnips
   3 beets (ideally 2 stripy, 1 purple)
   1 sweet potato
   Salt
   Peanut oil, for frying

For the venison:
   2 garlic cloves, crushed with salt
   15 juniper berries, crushed
   Salt and pepper
   1 venison fillet (about 2 pounds)
   2 tablespoons butter
   1 tablespoon olive oil

   Rowan or redcurrant jelly (see page 324)

First, prepare the vegetables for the root vegetable chips. Peel and slice them into thin slices or chips (use a mandoline if you have one) and soak them in cold water for about an hour.

Next, prepare the venison. Mix the garlic with the crushed juniper berries and black pepper. Roll the venison fillet in the mixture. Leave for at least half an hour to allow the juniper flavor to penetrate.

Preheat the oven to 350°F. Fry the fillet in a mix of butter and olive oil for 5 minutes over high heat, turning it every so often, until all sides of the meat are browned.

Cover the venison with foil and put it in the preheated oven for 15 minutes. With a small fillet this will be sufficient to cook it through. If you have a larger one, then it will need a longer spell in the oven. Remove from the oven and leave to rest for at least 10 minutes, still wrapped in its foil. Turn up the oven to 450°F.

While the venison is cooking and resting, cook the vegetable chips. Preheat the oil for deep-frying to 325°F. Drain the vegetable slices and dry them carefully, then deep-fry them in the very hot oil in small batches, not more than a handful at a time, until they just begin to brown.

If you don't have a deep-fryer, shallow-fry them until golden, taking care not to fill the pan more than a third full with oil. To test the temperature, throw one chip in the oil and it should cook within a minute if the oil is hot enough.

Whether deep- or shallow-fried, as you cook the chips batch by batch, once they begin to brown take them out and put them aside.

Once you've fried all of them, spread them out on a baking tray and blast them in the hot oven for 5 minutes, until they are crisp. Keep an eye on them, as they can burn quickly.

Take the rested venison out of its foil and serve with the chips as soon as they are all cooked, accompanied by the jelly.

Roasted parsnips rolled in Parmesan

These are crunchy and sweet, and great with any meat or stew, to eat with an aperitif, or as a first course dipped into crème fraîche flavored with dill and/or Chili jam (see page 318).

Serves 6
- Olive oil, for the pan
- 1 pound parsnips
- ¾ cup fresh brown or white breadcrumbs
- 4 ounces Parmesan cheese, grated
- Seasoned all-purpose flour
- 2 eggs, beaten

Preheat the oven to 375°F and put an oiled baking tin in it to get really hot.

Peel the parsnips and cut them into wedges, then steam them for 10 minutes.

Mix the breadcrumbs with the Parmesan. Dip the hot parsnips in the seasoned flour, then into the beaten eggs, and lastly roll them in the breadcrumb mixture.

Put the parsnips into the preheated oven in the oiled baking tin and roast for about 35 minutes, until tender and golden brown.

Spiced parsnip soup

A deservedly well-known recipe here. You'll need only a bowl of it—with some bread—for a filling and delicious lunch.

Serves 6
- 2 tablespoons butter
- 1 tablespoon sunflower oil
- 1 onion, chopped
- 1½ pounds parsnips, chopped
- 1 teaspoon ground coriander
- 1 teaspoon ground cumin seeds
- ½ teaspoon ground turmeric
- ¼ teaspoon chili powder
- 5 cups good vegetable stock
- Salt and pepper
- A little milk (optional)
- ⅔ cup light cream
- Yogurt, to serve
- Chopped cilantro, as a garnish

Melt the butter with the oil in a large heavy-bottomed pan and add the chopped onion and parsnips. Sweat them for 5 minutes, without allowing them to color. Stir in the spices and cook gently for another 2 minutes.

Add the stock and bring to a boil. Reduce the heat, cover, and simmer for about 30 minutes, or until the parsnips are quite tender. Allow to cool slightly, season carefully, and puree in a food processor.

Return the soup to a clean pan, adding a little milk if necessary, depending on how thick you would like the soup.

Add the cream and warm through gently without allowing the soup to boil. Serve with a dollop of yogurt and some chopped cilantro.

Parsnip puree with bourbon

A very rich puree, so you'll need only a little. It's wonderful under a piece of rare roast beef and very good with venison or goose.

Serves 6
- 3 pounds parsnips
- Salt and pepper
- 2 tablespoons butter
- ⅓ cup heavy cream
- Freshly grated nutmeg
- 2 tablespoons bourbon or Irish whiskey
- Breadcrumbs (optional)

Peel the parsnips and cut them into wedges. Boil or steam with salt until they are tender. Drain well.

Add the butter to the parsnips and mash well or pulse carefully in a food processor, but don't overblend or the puree will be too smooth.

Stir in the cream and nutmeg to taste, followed by the whiskey. Season.

Serve right away or put the puree into an ovenproof dish, cover with a layer of breadcrumbs, and bake in an oven preheated to 350°F for 20 minutes.

Smoked fish cakes with parsnip

These parsnip fish cakes are delicious—sweet and smoky—and very good with a sharp tartar sauce or mustard mayonnaise. They freeze well, so you can make lots at once.

Yield: 8 fish cakes
- ½ onion, chopped
- 3 ounces bacon or pancetta, thinly cut and chopped
- 10 ounces smoked fish (I use smoked haddock)
- 1 bay leaf
- 6 cloves
- 1 cup milk
- ⅓ pound parsnips, chopped
- ⅓ pound potatoes, chopped
- 1 tablespoon butter
- Salt and pepper
- Chopped parsley
- 1 red chili, finely chopped (optional)
- Seasoned all-purpose flour
- 1 egg, beaten
- ¾ cup white breadcrumbs
- Olive oil, for frying

Cook the onion with the bacon or pancetta over moderate heat for 10 minutes and put to one side.

Put the smoked fish into a pan together with the bay leaf and cloves. Pour over the milk, cover, and bring to a boil. As soon as the milk boils, remove from the heat and allow the fish to cool in the liquid.

Boil or steam the parsnips and potatoes together until they are tender. Mash them with the butter and a dash of the boiled milk and season well.

Combine the onion, bacon, mashed potatoes and parsnips, parsley, and chili, if using. Barely flake the fish, and fold carefully into the vegetable mixture. The fish cakes are far nicer if the flakes of fish are intact. Adjust the seasoning.

Dust your hands with seasoned flour and shape balls of the mixture into cakes. Dip these into the beaten egg and coat with the breadcrumbs.

Shallow-fry in the olive oil until golden or bake for 15 to 20 minutes in an oven preheated to 350°F. They can be made in advance and kept on a baking tray in the fridge until you want to cook them.

Vichy carrots

This is very good for cooking winter carrots, which have less taste than summer-harvested ones. Lengthy cooking intensifies the flavor.

Serves 6
- 2 pounds carrots
- 4 tablespoons butter
- Pinch of salt and pepper
- 1 teaspoon sugar
- Plenty of chopped parsley
- Juice of 1 lemon

Peel the carrots and slice them. Put them in a saucepan with the butter, salt, pepper, and sugar. Just cover with cold water and let them boil until the water has evaporated and they are tender and glazed.

Stir in masses of chopped parsley and the lemon juice to taste.

Grated carrot and poppy seed salad

A good salad for when you've got a few maincrop carrots that are a bit on the old side in midwinter. It has a delicious sharp and nutty taste. Make it a few hours in advance so that the carrot gets a chance to marinate in the lime and oil. The texture of grated carrot is quite dense, so a little of this salad goes a long way.

Serves 6
   3 large carrots
   1 tablespoon extra virgin olive oil
   Juice and grated zest of 1 lime
   Salt and pepper
   1 tablespoon poppy seeds

Peel the carrots and grate on a medium-grade grater.
   Mix the oil with the lime juice and zest, and salt and pepper in a large salad bowl. Put the carrot in on top.
   Toast the poppy seeds and mix them while still hot with the carrots.
   Stir everything together and leave for a couple of hours. Actually, this is surprisingly good the next day.

Bejuja carrots

This robust carrot dish is from Jude Maynard, who cooked here in the school for several years. It is good for a vegetarian lunch, eaten with a dollop of yogurt and rice, and also as a side vegetable.

Serves 4
   4 tablespoons vegetable oil
   1½ pounds carrots, sliced
   4 garlic cloves, chopped
   2-inch piece of ginger
   1 teaspoon poppy seeds
   1 teaspoon ground turmeric
   2 teaspoons ground cumin seeds
   2 teaspoons ground coriander
   1 chili, deseeded and chopped
   1 teaspoon salt
   Large handful of chopped cilantro
   Plain yogurt

Heat the oil in a frying pan and gently fry the carrots for 10 minutes. Stir in the garlic, ginger, and poppy seeds, and fry for a couple of minutes.
   Stir in the turmeric, cumin, coriander, chili, and salt, and cook until the carrots are tender. Cook them very slowly so that they don't catch.
   Finally, stir in the chopped cilantro and serve the carrots with a bowl of yogurt.

Carrot cake with grapes and honey

The good thing about any carrot cake is that it lasts well and, in this recipe, the grapes make a lovely addition. It makes a good dessert, and can also be served with a good vanilla ice cream.

Serves 6 to 8
   2 cups all-purpose flour
   1 teaspoon baking soda
   2 teaspoons baking powder
   1 cup grated carrot
   4 tablespoons honey
   ½ cup orange juice
   3 eggs, beaten
   ¾ cup sunflower oil
   1 teaspoon poppy seeds
   ½ teaspoon ground cinnamon
   ½ teaspoon salt
   Small bunch (about ¼ pound) of seedless green grapes, halved if large

For the mascarpone cream:
   1 cup mascarpone cheese
   1 tablespoon confectioners' sugar
   A few drops of vanilla extract

Preheat the oven to 350°F. Line the bottom and sides of an 8-inch springform cake pan with parchment paper.
   Sift the flour, baking soda, and baking powder into a large bowl. Then add all the remaining ingredients, except for the grapes, and mix thoroughly. Fold in the grapes and pour the mixture into the prepared pan.
   Cook in the preheated oven for about 1½ hours, covering the top with foil after 1 hour. The cake is ready when a skewer inserted into the middle comes out clean.
   To make the mascarpone cream, sweeten the mascarpone with sifted confectioners' sugar. Add the vanilla and beat together. Serve each slice of cake with a generous dollop of the cream.

Carrot and Jerusalem artichoke soup

The problem with Jerusalem artichoke soup is that it's one of the most wind-producing things that you can eat. If you mix artichokes with the same amount of carrot, you still enjoy the artichoke's lovely sweet flavor, but without the same effect. This is a recipe from *Gardener Cook* by Christopher Lloyd.

Serves 6 to 8
   1 small onion, chopped
   1 tablespoon olive oil
   2 tablespoons butter
   1½ pounds Jerusalem artichokes
   1 pound carrots
   ½ pound celeriac
   6 cups vegetable stock
   Salt and pepper
   Bunch of parsley, finely chopped
   Dollop of crème fraîche
   or natural yogurt

Fry the onion in the oil and the butter until soft.

Peel the Jerusalem artichokes (this is not essential), discarding the hard knobbles, and chop them. Peel the carrots and celeriac and cut them into slices. Sweat all the vegetables together with the onion for 5 minutes. Add the stock and simmer for 20 minutes.

Puree in a blender or with an immersion blender and season carefully.

Add plenty of finely chopped parsley and a dollop of crème fraîche or plain yogurt.

Jerusalem artichoke gratin

I prefer this gratin to one made only with potato. It has a richer, more interesting taste. You could add cheese—any grated hard cheese—on the top.

Serves 4
   ½ pound Jerusalem artichokes
   ½ pound potatoes
   Butter, to grease the dish and to
   dot the top
   3 ounces pancetta or prosciutto
   Freshly grated nutmeg
   Salt and pepper
   Grated pecorino romano cheese
   (optional)
   2½ cups vegetable stock

Preheat the oven to 350°F.

Peel the artichokes and potatoes, and slice them thinly (the slicing disc of a food processor is ideal for this).

Butter an ovenproof dish and put a layer of mixed artichokes and potatoes at the bottom. Snip over some strips of pancetta or prosciutto, then some grated nutmeg and season.

Crumble over some of the cheese, if you are using it, and dot with a little butter.

Repeat the layers, pour in the stock, and finish with a layer of cheese. Cover and bake in the preheated oven for 1 hour. Remove the cover, dot with butter if you omitted the cheese, and increase the temperature to 400°F to brown the top for about 10 minutes.

Allow to cool for 10 to 15 minutes before serving.

Grated celeriac with lime

As with carrot, celeriac with lime is a good combination. This is an excellent way of serving celeriac as a vegetable or side salad (preparation for both is shown below).

Serves 6
- **1 pound celeriac**
- **1 teaspoon caraway seeds**
- **½ pound carrots**
- **3 tablespoons butter**
- **Juice of 1 lime**
- **1 tablespoon honey**
- **2 tablespoons sour cream**
- **Salt and pepper**
- **1 teaspoon Dijon mustard (optional)**

Peel the celeriac and use it immediately to keep it from discoloring. Toast the caraway seeds.

To prepare as a vegetable side dish, grate the celeriac and carrots on the largest grating, or julienne, disc of a food processor. Heat the butter in a sauté pan and toss the celeriac and carrots in it for 2 minutes. Add the lime juice, honey, and caraway seeds, and take the pan off the heat. Stir in the sour cream, season, and serve immediately. This is delicious with grilled chicken.

If you want instead to prepare this as a salad, once you have grated the celeriac and carrots (or use celeriac on its own, if you prefer), pour over the lime juice, mixed with the honey. Stir in the sour cream, Dijon mustard (if you like), and caraway seeds, and season with sea salt and pepper.

Celeriac and apple soup

I love the sweetness of the celeriac, the sharpness of the apple, and the richness of the cheese in this recipe. Celeriac as a soup on its own is, I think, too soft a flavor.

Serves 6 to 8
- **1 quart good chicken or vegetable stock, hot**
- **1 celeriac**
- **2 onions**
- **2 celery stalks**
- **1 tablespoon butter**
- **2 garlic cloves, crushed or chopped**
- **1 tart apple, peeled and chopped**
- **1 sweet dessert apple, peeled and chopped**
- **Salt and pepper**
- **3 ounces blue cheese, such as Stilton or Cashel Blue, crumbled**
- **2 tablespoons light cream (optional)**

Warm the stock, and peel and chop the vegetables.

Melt the butter in a large pan. Add the vegetables and sweat them for several minutes without allowing them to color. Add the garlic and pour over the hot stock. Bring to a simmer.

Simmer for 10 minutes, then add the peeled chopped apples. Season, then cover and simmer for another 20 minutes.

Puree with an immersion blender or in a food processor, and season with salt and pepper.

Just before serving, stir in the crumbled cheese and the cream if you are using it.

Celeriac soufflé

I first saw this in a pretentious French cookbook, and I loved the idea—the contrast of a frothy soufflé in a knobby old root. A soufflé dish is fine if you can't face scraping out the root.

Serves 4 as a starter,
2 as a main course
- **1 large celeriac**
- **3 tablespoons butter**
- **2 egg yolks and 5 egg whites**
- **1 tablespoon Dijon mustard**
- **Plenty of freshly grated nutmeg**
- **Salt and pepper**
- **Chopped parsley**

Preheat the oven to 350°F.

Take a slice off the bottom of the celeriac so that it stands upright, and cut off the top. Scoop out the flesh with a strong pointed spoon (or melon baller), leaving about ¼ inch of shell.

Steam the flesh until tender and put it into a food processor. Process while adding the butter, chopped into small cubes, egg yolks, mustard, nutmeg, and salt and pepper.

Beat the egg whites into stiff peaks and carefully fold them into the celeriac mixture.

Spoon the mixture back into the celeriac shell and bake in the preheated oven for 35 to 40 minutes.

Scatter with chopped parsley and serve immediately.

Apple and celeriac salad

A good sharp-tasting and crunchy winter salad.

Serves 4 as a starter, 6 as a side dish
For the dressing:
   1 tablespoon cider vinegar
   1 shallot, finely chopped
   2 teaspoons Dijon mustard
   Juice and grated zest of ½ lemon
   1 tablespoon honey
   ⅓ cup walnut oil
   Salt and pepper

   ½ cup walnuts
   2 crisp eating apples
   ½ medium celeriac root
   Plenty of flat-leaf parsley

Make the dressing by mixing together the vinegar, shallot, mustard, lemon juice, and honey in a food processor. Add the oil in a stream while processing and check the seasoning. Toast the walnuts.

Peel, core, and slice the apples. Grate the celeriac, using a food processor fitted with a large grating disc, or cut into fine matchsticks. You must dress the apples and celeriac immediately before they start to turn brown. Toss the apples and celeriac together and pour over just enough dressing to coat.

Garnish with the toasted walnuts, lemon zest, and plenty of flat-leaf parsley.

Celeriac rémoulade

I like the texture of raw celeriac. There are recipes for this dish that tell you to blanch it briefly first, but I think that's unnecessary. Eat this as a first course on its own, or serve it with a plate of ham.

Serves 6
For the homemade mayonnaise:
   1 whole egg and 1 extra yolk
   1 level teaspoon mustard powder
   1 garlic clove (optional)
   Good pinch of salt and pepper
   ¾ cup good sunflower oil
   ½ cup olive oil
   Lemon juice or white wine vinegar, to taste
   ⅔ cup whipped cream (optional)

   1 medium-sized celeriac
   Lemon juice, for acidulation
   1 (2-ounce) can anchovies in oil, drained and chopped
   3 tablespoons capers
   Large bunch of parsley, coarsely chopped

To make the mayonnaise, put the egg and yolk, mustard powder, garlic (if using), salt, and pepper into a blender or bowl. Process or whisk until the mixture becomes frothy. Add the oils in a stream while processing or whisking, until it thickens. Add the lemon juice or vinegar to taste and then season. If you prefer a milder taste, you can add some whipped cream.

If the mayonnaise curdles at any point, start the whole process again with a third egg yolk, whisking it in a clean bowl and adding the curdled mixture in a slow stream while processing or whisking. This makes about 1½ cups and the extra can be stored in the fridge for a few days.

Peel the celeriac root and slice it as thinly as you can into big round discs. Then slice these into julienne (matchsticks). You can use a food processor for this, but I like the mix of shapes and sizes that you get when doing it by hand. As you cut them, put the matchsticks into a bowl of water acidulated with a good squeeze of lemon juice to stop them from turning brown.

Drain them, pat them dry with a kitchen towel, and put into a bowl. Stir in just enough mayonnaise to coat them. Mix in the chopped anchovies, capers, and parsley. This adds to the texture and gives some strong taste highlights.

Caramelized celeriac with pancetta

I had this when I went to the wonderful Amsterdam restaurant De Kas. The sugars caramelize and the taste, mixed with the smoky saltiness of the pancetta, is fantastic.

Serves 4 to 5
- **1 large celeriac, peeled and sliced into 10 pieces**
- **Salt and pepper**
- **½ tablespoon chopped lemon thyme**
- **½ tablespoon chopped rosemary**
- **2 garlic cloves, chopped**
- **2 tablespoons olive oil**
- **20 slices pancetta**

Preheat the oven to 325°F.

Steam the raw chunks of celeriac for 10 minutes. Dry them and put them into a large bowl. Season with salt, pepper, chopped herbs, garlic, and olive oil, and mix well. Leave for at least 10 minutes.

Wrap each chunk in 2 slices of pancetta and then roast them in the preheated oven until the pancetta is crisp and the celeriac is soft in the middle.

Puree of rutabaga

A deluxe version of that Scottish classic, mashed neeps.

Serves 4
- **2 pounds rutabaga**
- **Salt and pepper**
- **¼ cup (½ stick) butter**
- **4 garlic cloves, crushed and chopped**
- **2 heaping teaspoons finely chopped ginger**
- **4 tablespoons heavy cream**
- **A little cinnamon, to taste**

Peel and chop the rutabaga into large chunks and steam or boil in salted water until tender.

Melt the butter in a small saucepan and cook the garlic and ginger gently for 3 to 4 minutes, without allowing them to brown.

Puree the rutabaga in a food processor, adding the garlic and ginger, then pour in the cream.

Season with salt, cinnamon, and black pepper.

Roast rutabaga with maple syrup

You can roast rutabaga as you would celeriac, wrapped in pancetta (see left), or douse it with maple syrup, as here, for a lovely caramelized taste. Serve this with any roasted meat.

Serves 4
- **1½ pounds rutabaga**
- **2 tablespoons olive oil**
- **3 tablespoons maple syrup**
- **Salt and pepper**

Preheat the oven to 400°F.

Peel and cut the rutabaga into large pieces, about the size of a new potato. Heat the olive oil in a baking pan and, when it is hot, add the pieces of rutabaga and toss them in the oil.

Using a pastry brush, coat the rutabaga with the maple syrup and season with salt and pepper. This prevents a pool of maple syrup forming in the tray, which would burn easily.

Bake in the preheated oven, turning from time to time, for 45 minutes, until crisp and golden.

Braised turnips

I'm not a massive fan of the turnip. They can be good when small, grated or finely sliced in a salad—but this is probably my favorite way of eating them cooked.

Serves 6 to 8

1¼ pounds small to medium-sized turnips
3 tablespoons butter
Salt and pepper
1 teaspoon sugar
4 teaspoons white wine vinegar

Peel and cut the turnips into segments, then heat the butter and sweat these in it over very low heat for 5 minutes. Season with salt and pepper and add the sugar.

Pour in the vinegar and turn up the heat to reduce the liquid by about two-thirds. Add ½ cup water, cover with parchment paper, and cook gently for 10 minutes.

Scotch broth

When you're in Scotland, you'll see neeps (rutabaga) in even the smallest shop. The Scots often use them as a mashed vegetable with haggis and in soup. Rutabaga is one of the essential tastes in a good Scotch broth.

Serves 8 to 10

Leftover roast leg of lamb and vegetables
1 onion, thinly sliced
1 leek, thinly sliced
2 tablespoons olive oil
1 cup pearl barley
1 small rutabaga, diced
2 small turnips, diced
1 carrot, diced
3 celery stalks, thinly sliced
½ pound cabbage, cut into strips
Large bunch of parsley, coarsely chopped
Plenty of salt and pepper

If you've had a leg of lamb for supper, boil up the bone with any leftover vegetables. Drain, reserving the stock, and allow to cool. Cut up the remaining meat.

In a large pot, sweat the onion and leek in the oil. Pour in the stock, add the pearl barley and the chopped meat, and cook gently for half an hour.

Then add the rutabaga, turnips, carrot, and celery, and cook in the pot for a further half hour.

Throw in the cabbage for the last 2 minutes and finally the parsley. Season generously and serve.

Roasted salsify

Salsify used to be more widely available, but today it isn't around so much. However, many chefs are now seeking it out. It has an unusual rich taste to which many become addicted after just one tasting. Cook the roots and simply turn them in crème fraîche with nutmeg, or add them to a lemon béchamel. This roast salsify with thyme is quick, simple, and delicious, and particularly good with lamb or beef.

Serves 3 to 4
1 pound salsify
Lemon juice or vinegar, for
**   acidulation**
2 tablespoons extra virgin olive oil
1 tablespoon chopped thyme
Salt and pepper

Preheat the oven to 375°F.

Scrub and scrape the salsify (a stiff vegetable brush will get rid of all the whiskery roots), and cut it at an angle into 2-inch lengths. Put the roots straight into a bowl of water acidulated with a good squeeze of lemon juice to keep them from going brown. When you are ready to cook the salsify, dry the roots on paper towels and place them into a roasting pan.

Turn the roots over in a little olive oil, scatter with the thyme, and season.

Roast for about half an hour, until the salsify is tender.

Fried salsify in breadcrumbs

Fried salsify is good served as a first course, with melted butter, a wedge of lemon, and some chopped parsley. Serve this dish as a first course or a side vegetable.

Serves 4
1½ pounds salsify
Lemon juice, for acidulation
Seasoned all-purpose flour
1 egg, beaten
1 cup fresh white breadcrumbs
Sunflower oil, for deep- or
**   shallow-frying**

Scrub the salsify and scrape or peel the roots, then immediately put them into cold water with a good squeeze of lemon juice to stop them from turning brown. Steam the roots, or boil until they are just tender but still have a bite. Dip the roots first in well-seasoned flour, then into the beaten egg, and lastly into the breadcrumbs. Either heat oil in a pan and deep- or shallow-fry until the roots are golden and crisp, or roast in an oiled baking pan in an oven preheated to 325°F until tender and golden.

Marni's salsify

This is my godmother Marni Hodgkin's favorite recipe for salsify, which came originally from Rosamund Richardson's book *Definitely Different*. Small chunks of the cooked root are tossed in a mix of garlic and parsley, and served sizzling hot.

Serves 4
1½ pounds salsify or scorzonera
Salt and pepper
¼ cup (½ stick) butter
4 tablespoons good olive oil
2 garlic cloves, crushed
2 tablespoons finely chopped flat-
**   leaf parsley**

Clean and scrub the salsify and cut into chunks. Cook them unpeeled in a little boiling salted water in a covered pan for about 10 minutes, until just tender. Salsify has a waxy bite and is better soft than al dente. Rinse the salsify under cold running water, as this makes peeling easier, and peel.

Melt the butter with the olive oil and gently fry the garlic for a couple of minutes.

Add the salsify roots and toss them in the garlic butter mix. Sprinkle with lots of parsley and serve.

Scorzonera salad

Scorzonera, sometimes called black or Spanish salsify, was much more widely eaten in our parents' generation. The dressing peps it up nicely.

Serves 4
- **1½ pounds scorzonera**
- **Lemon juice, for acidulation**
- **1 teaspoon salt**
- **Bunch of flat-leaf parsley, finely chopped, as a garnish**

For the dressing:
- **1 shallot, finely chopped**
- **1 teaspoon Dijon mustard**
- **1 egg yolk**
- **1 tablespoon lemon juice**
- **1 teaspoon superfine sugar, or to taste**
- **3 tablespoons extra virgin olive oil**
- **3 tablespoons sunflower oil**

Scrape or peel the scorzonera and cut at an angle into large pieces. Immediately put the roots into a pan with cold water (enough to cover), a squeeze of lemon, and a teaspoon of salt. Bring to a boil, reduce the heat, and simmer until just tender.

While the roots are cooking, combine all the ingredients for the dressing, except the oil, and whisk with an immersion blender or in a processor. Add the oil in a stream while you are whisking. Season carefully.

When the scorzonera is ready, drain and let it cool slightly. When it is lukewarm, pour over the dressing.

Serve with plenty of chopped flat-leaf parsley.

Kohlrabi and hollandaise

The simple, earthy, cabbage-tasting vegetable is lovely in contrast to the creamy richness of hollandaise sauce. The combination makes an excellent winter first course.

Serves 6
- **5 to 6 kohlrabi**

For the hollandaise sauce:
- **3 tablespoons white wine vinegar**
- **6 black peppercorns**
- **1 bay leaf**
- **2 egg yolks**
- **6 tablespoons unsalted butter, cut into small chunks**
- **Salt and pepper**

Cut the kohlrabi into chunks. Steam them for about 10 minutes, until tender. Keep warm.

To make the sauce, boil the vinegar and 1 tablespoon of water with the peppercorns and bay leaf until reduced to 1 tablespoon.

Fill a wide shallow pan halfway with water and bring to a simmer. Put the yolks in a heatproof bowl, sit this in the pan of water, and whisk well. Add the butter, bit by bit, whisking all the time. As it warms, the mixture will gradually become thick and shiny. Remove from the heat and stir in the cooled reduced vinegar, salt, and pepper. (See page 233 for more hollandaise tips.)

Serve with the hollandaise in a bowl in the middle of a large plate of the kohlrabi chunks.

Horseradish sauce

Horseradish sauce is, of course, the best thing to eat with roast beef, and it's also lovely with smoked fish—such as trout, eel, and mackerel—and other root vegetables, such as potatoes, celeriac, and beets.

You can't be precise about quantities for this recipe, as the root varies hugely in strength according to when you dig it. It's at its strongest in October and November, and best when freshly dug, but will keep without drying out too much for 2 to 3 months. Scrub it and wrap it in very slightly dampened paper towels, then store it in a plastic bag in the fridge until it is needed.

You need:

Grated horseradish
Heavy cream or crème fraîche
A little mustard powder
Pinch of white pepper
Salt
Lemon juice, to taste

Peel and grate the horseradish. If you want it very strong, grate it right before you use it. It has highly volatile essential oils and so its strength will fade quickly—which is why you never want to cook it. It also discolors quickly, so mix it with the other ingredients immediately.

Add enough cream (or crème fraîche) to the grated horseradish to give you a creamy consistency. Add a little mustard powder, white pepper, and salt, and finish by adding lemon juice to taste.

Horseradish cheese on toast

A tasty twist on grilled cheese.

Serves 4
2 ounces grated Gruyère cheese
2 ounces grated Parmesan cheese
1 tablespoon heavy cream
2 teaspoons freshly grated horseradish
Few drops of tarragon vinegar
Pinch of paprika
4 slices toast or fried bread

Preheat the broiler or an oven to 450°F. Mix all the ingredients together and pile on to the fried or toasted bread.

Put in the preheated oven or under the broiler for a few minutes until the cheese is melting and brown.

Horseradish dumplings

These are excellent in any beef or game stew and they're lovely with pork chops. This recipe comes from Lynda Brown's book *The Cook's Garden.*

Yield: 12 dumplings
½ teaspoon baking powder
½ cup all-purpose flour
1 egg, beaten
5 tablespoons butter
¾ cup breadcrumbs
1 heaping tablespoon freshly grated horseradish
Salt and pepper

Sift the baking powder and flour into a bowl, and then mix in the egg. Then add all the other ingredients and mix together.

Using wet hands, pinch off the dough into 12 portions and roll each one into a ball. Add these to a casserole—if you're eating them with one—for the last 20 minutes of the cooking time. Make sure they sit on top of the stew and are not submerged.

Continue to cook your casserole, covered. About 10 minutes before the end, if cooking in the oven, remove the lid and allow the dumplings to brown a little on top. If cooking on the stovetop, take the lid off and place the casserole in a 400°F oven for the final 10 minutes.

If you're eating the dumplings with pork chops, poach them in barely simmering salted water for 15 minutes. They should double in size and be light and cooked through.

A

aioli 137

Allen, Darina

    Pears poached in saffron syrup 361

    Tuscan plum tart 257

almonds

    Almond meringues 173

    Damson plum and almond pudding 323

    orange and almond cake, Tunisian 34

    Pear and almond tart 362

alpine strawberries 144

    Alpine strawberry gratin 150

    French strawberry jam 150

Amber marmalade 33

anchovies

    Bagna cauda 422

    Caesar salad 112

    Crisp zucchini wedges with anchovy mayonnaise 187

    Niçoise salad 210

    Potato salad with capers and anchovies 124

Andalusian soup-salad 272

apples 288

    Apple and celeriac salad 434

    Apple and plum chutney 295

    apple and quince cake, Windfall 380

    apple cake, Kentish 295

    apple hotpot, Jane's 291

    Apple juice 294

    Baked apples 291

    Celeriac and apple soup 432

    Chestnut pavlova with caramelized apples 353

    Mint and apple compote 231

    Mint and apple jelly 231

    Pear, apple, and quince Charlotte 365

    Pheasant with Calvados, apple, and chestnut 292

    Plum, apple, and chili jelly 319

    Sloe and apple jelly 324

    Toffee apples 294

    Uncooked autumn chutney 295

apricots 154

    Apricot tart 157

    French apricot jam 157

artichokes see globe artichokes; Jerusalem artichokes

arugula 50, 55

    Arugula, beet, and feta salad 55

    Fillet of beef with arugula 55

    Melon, pear, and arugula salad 237

    Peppery-leaf salad 53

    Salad of asparagus, fava beans, arugula, and peas 102

    Squash and arugula salad with pears and rosemary 376

asparagus 98

    Asparagus omelette 101

    Asparagus pasta with lemon 101

    Asparagus with almonds 101

    Primavera risotto 102

    Salad of asparagus, fava beans, arugula, and peas 102

avocado

    Penne with preserved lemon and avocado 36

B

Baba ghanouj with naan bread 299

bacon

    Bea's stuffed cabbage leaves 18

    see also pancetta

bagna cauda, Winter 422

Baked apples 291

Baked blackberries and mascarpone 325

Baked cream with gooseberries 217

Baked eggplant with mozzarella 301

Baked potatoes with pesto, Stuffed 339

Baked quinces in orange syrup 380

Baked tomatoes with cream 268

bananas

    Pears, bananas, and grapes with fudge sauce 361

basil 218

    Basil custards 221

    Basil ice cream 221

    Basil oil 224

    Marcella's homemade pesto 225

bass see sea bass

bay 40

beans see cranberry beans; fava beans; cannellini; green beans

Bea's stuffed cabbage leaves 18

béchamel sauce 29, 40, 165, 301, 346

beef

    Bea's stuffed cabbage leaves 18

    Fillet of beef with arugula 55

    Green beans in truffle oil with fillet steak and hollandaise 208

    see also Horseradish sauce

beets 160

    Arugula, beet, and feta salad 55

    Beet relish 164

    Beets and mini onions in béchamel 165

    Grated beet salad with toasted mustard seeds and orange 163

    Lebanese beet salad, Nadah Saleh's 163

    Pantzarosalata 163

    Risotto of beet, dill, and fennel 165

    Roasted beet soup 164

    Roasted beets with lentils and goat cheese 162

    Root vegetable chips 425

    Slow-roasted winter roots and herb couscous 424

    Stir-fried beet tops with chili and ginger 165

Bejuja carrots 430

Belgian endive 22 see chicories

Bellinis 154

blackberries 320

    Baked blackberries and mascarpone 325

    Bramble jelly 325

    Cranachan 327

    melon with blackberries, Teresa's 237

blackcurrants 166

    Blackcurrant and almond cake 169

    Blackcurrant cupcakes 169

    Blackcurrant jam 170

    blackcurrant leaf sorbet, Philippa's 169

    Cassis 170

blinis, Corn 385

borage flowers 198

Bramble jelly 325

bread

    crostini 109

croutons 79
garlic bread (Pizza bianca) 250
naan bread 299
Roasted plums with bread and
    butter pudding 256
see also bruschetta; flat bread;
    pita bread
bream see sea bream
broccoli 62
Broccoli soup with Gorgonzola 64
Double pepper broccoli 65
Purple sprouting broccoli pasta 64
Purple sprouting broccoli with
    lemon and hazelnuts 64
bruschetta
Kale bruschetta 403
Tomato bruschetta 278
brussels sprouts 388
Professor Van Mons's Brussels
    sprouts 391
Pureed Brussels sprouts in nutmeg
    cream 391
Sauté of red Brussels sprouts with
    almonds 391
Bubble and squeak cakes 340
Buckwheat pancakes 222
burgers
Lamb burgers with thyme and
    rosemary 49
butter beans
White butter bean soup 305
butternut squashes see squashes
butters, herb 80

C
cabbages 14
Fried cabbage with juniper 17
Quick braised red cabbage 21
Savoy cabbage and cilantro soup
    17
Stuffed cabbage leaves, Bea's 18
Sweet-and-sour marinated
    cabbage 18
The ultimate minestrone 21
Caesar salad 112
cakes
apple and quince cake, Windfall
    380
apple cake, Kentish 295
Blackcurrant and almond cake 169

Blackcurrant cupcakes 169
Carrot cake with grapes and honey
    430
mocha and ginger meringue cake
    with pomegranate sauce, Frozen
    415
orange and almond cake, Tunisian
    34
Rhubarb upside-down cake 69
calabrese see broccoli
cannellini
Cannellini soup 305
The ultimate minestrone 21
White beans with garlic and thyme
    250
Caponata 300
Caroline's cherry tart 178
carrots 238, 420
Bejuja 430
Carrot and Jerusalem artichoke
    soup 431
Carrot cake with grapes and honey
    430
carrots and peas, Sally Clarke's 240
Glazed summer vegetables 137
Grated carrot and poppy seed
    salad 430
Grilled new carrots 241
New carrots and potatoes roasted
    with garlic and thyme 241
Riverford new summer carrots and
    turnips 240
Vichy carrots 428
Cassis 170
cauliflower 58
Cauliflower cheese with Lord
    Dalrymple's top 61
Cauliflower soup 61
Vegetable korma 61
celeriac 420
Apple and celeriac salad 434
Caramelized celeriac with pancetta
    435
Celeriac and apple soup 432
Celeriac rémoulade 434
Celeriac soufflé 432
Grated celeriac with lime 432
Vegetable stock 424
Winter bagna cauda 422
celery 312

Bottled celery 315
Braised beans and celery 314
Braised celery 314
Celery and cucumber salad in
    mustard dressing 315
Ceviche 39
Champagne cocktail with alpine
    strawberries 150
chanterelles 342
Jane's chanterelles 345
Chantilly cream 173
chard 72, 392
Chard and coconut soup 395
Chard and feta parcels 395
Chard and nutmeg farfalle 396
Chard and risotto balls 396
Chard gratin 397
Chard stems in a mustardy
    dressing 397
Horta 395
Ithaca pie 74
Ribollita 402
see also Spinach with split peas or
    lentils; Spring vegetable soup
Charentais melons 234
Charlotte
Pear, apple, and quince Charlotte
    365
cheese
Arugula, beet, and feta salad 55
Baked eggplant with mozzarella 301
Broccoli soup with Gorgonzola 64
Cauliflower cheese with Lord
    Dalrymple's top 61
Chard and feta parcels 395
Eggplant and feta salad 300
Endive and blue cheese salad 25
Grilled goat cheese salad 54
Halloumi, mint, cilantro, and dill
    pitas 228
Horseradish cheese on toast 441
Leek and goat cheese tart 407
Parmesan and walnut crisps 354
Pea and ricotta tart with thyme
    pastry 131
Ricotta al forno 224
Roasted beets with lentils and goat
    cheese 162
Roasted sweet potato and feta
    salad 341

Roasted stuffed figs with
Gorgonzola and walnuts 331
Saganaki 273
Spinach and Gruyère tart 77
see also Pizza
cherries 174
Cherry clafoutis 177
Cherry compote for ice cream 177
cherry tart, Caroline's 178
Sour cherry jam 177
chervil 50, 55, 80
Chervil butter 84
Smoked salmon pâté with chervil 85
see also herbs, mixed
chestnuts 348
Chestnut pavlova with caramelized
apples 353
Chestnut-stuffed pork fillet 350
Venison, cranberry, and chestnut
casserole 419
chicken
Boiled chicken with leeks and
salsa verde 409
Chicken in tarragon cream 233
confit of chicken, Matthew's 48
Jambalaya 370
Penne with preserved lemon and
avocado 36
Rosemary, olive, and lemon
chicken 44
stuffed chicken with cilantro pesto,
Alastair Little's 87
Thai chicken curry, Jane's 88
chickpeas
Hummus with cilantro 85
Kale and chickpea curry 401
Patmos chickpeas 44
Warm chickpea and parsley salad
90
chicory 22, 198
Braised endive 25
Endive and blood orange salad 26
Endive and blue cheese salad 25
Treviso al forno with grilled polenta
28
Treviso lasagne 29
chilis 316
Barbecued stuffed chilis 319
Chili chocolate 319
Chili dipping sauce 318

Chili jam 318
Pickled chilis 318
Plum, apple, and chili jelly 319
chives 80
Herb dumplings 83
see also herbs, mixed
chocolate, Chili 319
chorizo
Chorizo with potatoes 125
Squid, pea, and chorizo stew 133
chowder
Smoked haddock and corn
chowder 384
chutneys
Apple and plum chutney 295
Damson plum chutney 322
Green tomato chutney 285
Uncooked autumn chutney 295
Zucchini chutney 190
citrus fruits 30
see grapefruits; lemons; oranges
clafoutis, Cherry 177
Clarke, Sally
Carrots and peas 240
clementines 30
Cleopatra's tomato soup 269
Clove and onion pasta 245
coconut milk
Chard and coconut soup 395
Zucchini and coconut soup 190
compotes
Cherry compote for ice cream 177
Damson plum compote 322
Mint and apple compote 231
Sweet onion compote 249
confits
confit of chicken, Matthew's 48
Fig confit 333
Cookies
Hazelnut biscotti 357
Lemon and cumin cookies 38
cordials
Elderflower cordial 142
Lemon cordial 35
Lemongrass cordial 228
cilantro 80
Cilantro pesto 87
Halloumi, mint, cilantro, and dill
pitas 228
Hummus with cilantro 85

Pork fillet with cilantro 85
Savoy cabbage and cilantro soup
17
see also herbs, mixed
corn 382
Barbecued corn with thyme butter
or chili jam 384
Corn blinis 385
Smoked haddock and corn
chowder 384
Smoked haddock and corn soufflé
385
corn on the cob 382
corn salad 50
coulis, raspberry 158
couscous
Jeweled couscous 412
Slow-roasted winter roots and herb
couscous 424
crabapples 288
Crabapple and herb jelly 292
Plum, apple, and chili jelly 319
Cranachan 327
cranberries 410
cranberry and macadamia
flapjacks, Kate's 419
Cranberry cocktail 418
Cranberry tart with hot toffee
sauce 416
Cranberry vodka 418
Orange and cranberry pies 418
Venison, cranberry, and chestnut
casserole 419
cranberry beans 302
Braised beans and celery 314
Cranberry bean brandade 307
Cranberry bean hummus 305
Cranberry bean ratatouille 304
Cranberry bean soup 305
Cranberry beans with sage 307
Ribollita 402
Sweet-and-sour cranberry beans
304
The ultimate minestrone 21
Creamed spinach 78
crème brûlée, Lavender 202
crostini
Fava bean crostini 109
see also Tomato bruschetta
croutons 79

crudités
    cauliflower 58
    Early summer crudités on ice with aioli 137
crumble
    Best ever plum crumble 257
cucumbers 192
    Celery and cucumber salad in mustard dressing 315
    Cucumber and garlic soup with chives 195
    Cucumber raita 196
    Dill-pickled cornichons 197
    Fresh horseradish and cucumber sauce 196
    Marinated cucumber and dill salad 195
    Mint and cucumber soup 195
    Peas with cucumber and mint 130
    Surinam pickled cucumber 197
    Sweet cucumber pickle 197
currants, black-, red-, and white 166
    see also blackcurrants; redcurrants
curries
    Kale and chickpea curry 401
    Thai chicken curry, Jane's 88
    Vegetable korma 61
    see also naan bread; Sag aloo
custard, homemade 256

D

Damson plums 320
    Damson plum and almond pudding 323
    Damson plum chutney 322
    Damson plum compote 322
    Damson plum ice cream 322
    Damson plum vodka or gin 323
dandelions 84, 198
De Kas tomato jam 282
desserts
    Alpine strawberry gratin 150
    apple hotpot, Jane's 291
    Apricot tart 157
    Baked apples 291
    Baked blackberries and mascarpone 325
    Baked cream with gooseberries 217

Baked quinces in orange syrup 380
Basil ice cream 221
blackcurrant leaf sorbet, Philippa's 169
Cherry clafoutis 177
Cherry compote for ice cream 177
cherry tart, Caroline's 178
Chestnut pavlova with caramelized apples 353
Cranberry tart with hot toffee sauce 416
Damson plum and almond pudding 323
Damson plum compote 322
Damson plum ice cream 322
Elderflower and gooseberry ice cream 143
Elderflower fritters 142
fig tart, Fresh 333
Frosted redcurrants with Chantilly cream 173
Gooseberry and elderflower sorbet 215
Gooseberry tart 214
grapefruit and Pimm's granita, Pink 39
Grapes with caramel 330
Greengage sorbet 259
Hazelnut ice cream and praline 357
lavender crème brûlée 202
lavender ice cream, Quick 201
Lemon and mint ice cream 38
Lemon posset 38
lemon soufflé, Mrs Root's 36
Mandarin sorbet 39
Marmalade ice cream with fresh oranges 33
Melon and ginger sorbet 237
melon with blackberries, Teresa's 237
Meringue roulade with raspberries 263
Nectarine zabaglione 158
Orange and cranberry pies 418
Panna cotta with marinated pomegranate 416
Peach melba 158
Peach zabaglione 158
Peaches with bourbon 158
Pear and almond tart 362

Pear, apple, and quince Charlotte 365
Pears, bananas, and grapes with fudge sauce 361
pears, Poached 361
pears poached in saffron syrup, Darina Allen's 361
plum crumble, Best ever 257
plum tart, Darina Allen's Tuscan 257
plums with bread and butter pudding, Roasted 256
plums with homemade custard, Roasted 256
Pumpkin pie 377
redcurrant steamed pudding, Emma's 171
redcurrants with Chantilly cream, Frosted 173
Rhubarb sorbet 69
Rhubarb syllabub 69
Rhubarb tart 70
rhubarb with ginger ice cream, Poached 70
rice pudding with raspberry and redcurrant jam, Spectacular 265
Russian redcurrant and raspberry pudding 171
strawberries, Marinated 148
Strawberries Romanoff 149
Strawberries with meringues 148
Strawberries with rosé wine 149
Strawberry and black pepper ice cream 147
strawberry and shortbread tart, Fresh 149
summer pudding, Juicy 263
Tiramisu with red berries 265
Toffee pear tart 362
Verveine sorbet 225
Walnut tart 355
dill 218
    Dill and mustard sauce 222
    Dill-pickled cornichons 197
    Halloumi, mint, cilantro, and dill pitas 228
Double pepper broccoli 65
drinks
    Apple juice 294
    Cassis 170

Champagne cocktail with alpine
    strawberries 150
Cranberry cocktail 418
Cranberry vodka 418
Damson plum vodka or gin 323
Elderflower cordial 142
Homemade lemonade 35
Lemon cordial 35
Lemongrass cordial 228
Mint-and-gingerade 230
Mint julep 230
Sloe vodka or gin 323
Duck breast and peppery-leaf salad 53
dumplings, Horseradish 441

E

eggplant 296
    Baba ghanouj with naan bread 299
    Baked eggplant with mozzarella 301
    Caponata 300
    eggplant and feta salad 300
    Moussaka 301
    Roasted squash, eggplant, and
        onion with balsamic sauce 191
    Spiced eggplant salad 299
elderberries 320
elderflowers 138
    Elderflower and gooseberry ice
        cream 143
    Elderflower and gooseberry jam
        142
    Elderflower and gooseberry sauce
        143
    Elderflower cordial 142
    Elderflower fritters 142
    Jane's gooseberry and elderflower
        sorbet 215
Emma's redcurrant steamed pudding
    171
endive 22

F

farfalle
    Chard and nutmeg farfalle 396
    Pea and pancetta farfalle 133
    Rosemary and pork farfalle 43
    Zucchini and dill farfalle 182
Fattoush 273
fava beans 104
    Fava bean crostini 109

Fava beans with olive tapenade 107
Salad of asparagus, fava beans,
    arugula, and peas 102
Samphire with fresh peas and
    young fava beans 141
Tagliolini with fava beans and
    beurre blanc 109
Warm fava bean salad 107
Young fava beans in cream 109
fave e foglie see Spinach with split
    peas or lentils
fennel 80, 218, 308
    Braised fennel 310
    Fennel and grape salad 310
    Fennel and prawn risotto 311
    Risotto of beets, dill, and fennel 165
    Sage, fennel, and Pernod pasta 311
    Whole fish stuffed with fennel 227
feta cheese
    Arugula, beet, and feta salad 55
    Chard and feta parcels 395
    Eggplant and feta salad 300
    Roasted sweet potato and feta
        salad 341
    Saganaki 273
figs 328
    Fig confit 333
    Fresh fig tart 333
    Quail with figs 333
    Roasted stuffed figs with
        Gorgonzola and walnuts 331
fish
    Ceviche 39
    Creamed leek and haddock 406
    Gravlax 222
    Jane Grigson's sorrel sauce with
        fish 91
    Niçoise salad 210
    Smoked fish and nasturtium cakes
        202
    Smoked fish cakes with parsnip 428
    Smoked haddock and corn
        chowder 384
    Smoked haddock and corn soufflé
        385
    Smoked salmon pâté with chervil
        85
    Watercress and smoked trout salad
        with horseradish 95
    Whole fish stuffed with fennel 227

see also anchovies
flageolet beans
    White beans with garlic and thyme
        250
flapjacks
    Kate's cranberry and macadamia
        flapjacks 419
flat bread
    Rosemary flat bread 46
    Sungold tomato focaccia 271
Florence fennel see fennel
flowers, edible 180, 198
    Romano bean flower salad 211
    stuffed zucchini flowers, Matthew's
        189
    stuffed zucchini flowers, Tam's 189
    Winter flower and toasted seed
        salad 55
focaccia see flat bread
fool, Gooseberry 214
French onion soup 245
frisée 22
frittate
    Red pepper frittata with prosciutto
        371
    Spinach and sorrel frittata 77
fritters
    Elderflower 142
    see also blinis, Corn
Frosted redcurrants with Chantilly
    cream 173
Frozen mocha and ginger meringue
    cake with pomegranate sauce
    415
fudge sauce 361

G

Game salad with pomegranate 412
garlic 242
    aioli 137
    Bagna cauda 422
    Microwave roasted garlic 253
    Pizza bianca (garlic bread) 250
    Roasted garlic 253
    see also garlic, wild
garlic, wild 92
    Wild garlic pesto 95
    Wild garlic soup 95
Gazpacho 269
    White gazpacho with grapes 330

gin
    Damson plum gin 323
    Sloe gin 323
globe artichokes 116
    Braised globe artichokes 121
    Globe artichoke heart tempura 119
    Globe artichokes with Angelica's
        sauce 118
    Globe artichoke tart 121
    Grilled mini globe artichokes 118
    Raw globe artichoke heart salad
        119
    see also Spring vegetable soup
goat cheese
    Grilled goat cheese salad 54
    Leek and goat cheese tart 407
    Roast beets with lentils and goat
        cheese 162
gooseberries 212
    Baked cream with gooseberries
        217
    Elderflower and gooseberry ice
        cream 143
    Elderflower and gooseberry jam
        142
    Elderflower and gooseberry sauce
        143
    gooseberry and elderflower sorbet,
        Jane's 215
    Gooseberry and thyme jelly 215
    Gooseberry fool 214
    Gooseberry tart 214
goulash with lovage, Hungarian 88
granita
    Pink grapefruit and Pimm's granita
        39
granola 327
grapefruit 30
    Pink grapefruit and Pimm's granita
        39
grapes 328
    Black and white grape salad 330
    Fennel and grape salad 310
    Grape jelly 331
    Grapes with caramel 330
    Pears, bananas, and grapes with
        fudge sauce 361
    White gazpacho with grapes 330
gratins
    Alpine strawberry gratin 150

Chard gratin 397
Jerusalem artichoke gratin 431
Potato and sage gratin 48
Potato gratin with sorrel 91
Sweet potato gratin 341
Gravlax 222
Greek zucchini pie 186
Green beans 204
    Green beans in truffle oil with fillet
        steak and hollandaise 208
    Green beans with new potatoes
        125
    Lemon bean salad 210
    Spaghetti with beans and tomatoes
        207
    Summer garden tempura 207
    Trofie with potatoes, beans, and
        pesto 208
greengages 254
    Greengage sorbet 259
Green mayonnaise 83
Green tomato chutney 285
Grilled corn with thyme butter or chili
    jam 384
Grilled mini globe artichokes 118
Grilled new carrots 241
Grilled stuffed chilis 319
Grilled sweet potato with ginger, chili,
    and lime 341
Grigson, Jane
    Sorrel sauce with fish 91

H
haddock
    Creamed leek and haddock 406
haddock, smoked
    Smoked haddock and nasturtium
        fish cakes 202
    Smoked fish cakes with parsnip
        428
    Smoked haddock and corn
        chowder 384
    Smoked haddock and corn soufflé
        385
Halloumi, mint, cilantro, and dill pitas
    228
haricots verts see Green beans
hazelnuts 348
    Hazelnut biscotti 357
    Hazelnut ice cream and praline 357

herbs
    Herb butters 80
    spring herbs 80
    summer herbs 218
    see also herbs, mixed and specific
herbs, mixed
    Green mayonnaise 83
    Spring herb and wild greens pasta
        84
    Spring salsa verde 83
Hollandaise sauce 440
    Kohlrabi and hollandaise 440
    Tarragon hollandaise 233
    Watercress hollandaise 94
horseradish
    Beet relish 164
    Fresh horseradish and cucumber
        sauce 196
    Horseradish cheese on toast 441
    Horseradish dumplings 441
    Horseradish sauce 441
Horta 395
hummus
    Cranberry bean hummus 305
    Hummus with cilantro 85
Hungarian goulash with lovage 88

I
ice cream
    Basil ice cream 221
    Cherry compote for ice cream 177
    Damson plum ice cream 322
    Elderflower and gooseberry ice
        cream 143
    Hazelnut ice cream and praline 357
    lavender ice cream, Quick 201
    Lemon and mint ice cream 38
    Marmalade ice cream with fresh
        oranges 33
    Poached rhubarb with ginger ice
        cream 70
    Strawberry and black pepper ice
        cream 147
    Strawberry sauce for ice cream 147
    see also granita; sorbets
ice cubes, edible flower 198
Ithaca pie 74

J
Jambalaya 370

jams
Blackcurrant jam 170
cherry jam, Sour 177
Chili jam 318
Elderflower and gooseberry jam 142
French apricot jam 157
French strawberry jam 150
Raspberry and redcurrant jam 265
tomato jam, De Kas 282
Zucchini and ginger jam 191
see also compotes; jellies
Jane's apple hotpot 291
Jane's chanterelles 345
Jane's gooseberry and elderflower sorbet 215
Jane's Thai chicken curry 88
jellies
Bramble jelly 325
Crabapple and herb jelly 292
Gooseberry and thyme jelly 215
Grape jelly 331
Medlar jelly 381
Mint and apple jelly 231
Plum, apple, and chili jelly 319
Quince jelly 381
Redcurrant jelly 171
Rowan jelly 324
Sloe and apple jelly 324
Jerusalem artichokes 420
Carrot and Jerusalem artichoke soup 431
Jerusalem artichoke gratin 431
Winter bagna cauda 422
Jude's stuffed grapevine leaves 331

K

kale 398
Ithaca pie 74
Kale and chickpea curry 401
Kale bruschetta 403
Kale seaweed 403
Quick-fried kale 402
Ribollita 402
Kate's cranberry and macadamia flapjacks 419
Kentish apple cake 295
kohlrabi 420
Kohlrabi and hollandaise 440
korma, Vegetable 61

L

lamb
Lamb burgers with thyme and rosemary 49
Lamb fricassée with Cos lettuce and lemon juice 115
Rosemary and anchovy crusted lamb 43
Stuffed lamb with lavender 201
lasagne, Treviso 29
lavender 198
Lavender crème brûlée 202
Quick lavender ice cream 201
Stuffed lamb with lavender 201
Lebanese beet salad 163
leeks 404
Boiled chicken with leeks and salsa verde 409
Creamed leek and haddock 406
Leek and goat cheese tart 407
pheasant and leek pie, Ray Smith's 407
Potato and leek soup 406
lemon 30
Homemade lemonade 35
Lemon and cumin biscuits 38
Lemon and mint ice cream 38
Lemon bean salad 210
Lemon cordial 35
Lemon posset 38
lemon soufflé, Mrs. Root's 36
Penne with preserved lemon and avocado 36
Preserved lemons 35
lemongrass 218
Lemongrass cordial 228
Lemongrass rice 227
lemon verbena 218
Verveine sorbet 225
lentils
Roast beets with lentils and goat cheese 162
Spinach and lentil soup 74
Spinach with split peas or lentils 78
Warm potato and lentil salad 340
lettuces 50, 110
Caesar salad 112

Lamb fricassee with romaine lettuce and lemon juice 115
Lettuce and lovage soup 87
Lettuce hearts with hot butter dressing 112
Sauté of peas and lettuce 115
limes 30
loganberries 260
Juicy summer pudding 263
Tiramisu with red berries 265
lovage 80
Herb dumplings 83
Hungarian goulash with lovage 88
Lettuce and lovage soup 87

M

Mandarin sorbet 39
Marcella's homemade pesto 225
marigolds (calendula) 198
marjoram see oregano
marmalade
Amber marmalade 33
Marmalade ice cream with fresh oranges 33
Red onion marmalade 249
Seville marmalade 30, 33
Marni's salsify 438
Masai mara 369
Matthew's confit of chicken 48
Matthew's stuffed zucchini flowers 189
mayonnaise
Anchovy mayonnaise 187
Green mayonnaise 83
homemade mayonnaise 124
meat dishes see chicken; beef; lamb; pork
medlars 378
Medlar jelly 381
melons 234
Melon and ginger sorbet 237
Melon, pear, and arugula salad 237
melon with blackberries, Teresa's 237
Membrillo 380
meringues
Almond meringues 173
Chestnut pavlova with caramelized apples 353
Frozen mocha and ginger meringue

cake with pomegranate sauce
415

Meringue roulade with raspberries
263

Strawberries with meringues 148

mibuna 50

Microwave roasted garlic 253

minestrone, The ultimate 21

mint 218

Halloumi, mint, cilantro, and dill
pitas 228

Mint and apple compote 231

Mint and apple jelly 231

Mint and cucumber soup 195

Mint-and-gingerade 230

Mint and pea tip risotto 131

Mint julep 230

Mint potato cakes 230

mizuna 50

peppery-leaf salad 53

mocha and ginger meringue cake
with pomegranate sauce, Frozen
415

Moussaka 301

Mrs. Root's lemon soufflé 36

mulberries 320

Sweet black mulberry vinegar
324

mushrooms 342

Jane's chanterelles 345

Mushroom pasta 347

Mushroom soup 345

Mushrooms with polenta 347

Porcini and prosciutto pasticcio
346

Raw mushroom salad 345

mussels see Chard gratin

mustard, 'Red Giant' 50

peppery-leaf salad 53

N

naan bread 299

nasturtiums 198

Smoked fish and nasturtium cakes
202

nectarines 154

Peach or nectarine zabaglione 158

Nutmeg mashed potatoes 336

nuts

Almond meringues 173

cranberry and macadamia
flapjacks, Kate's 419

Damson plum and almond pudding
323

Hazelnut biscotti 357

Hazelnut ice cream and praline 357

orange and almond cake, Tunisian
34

Pappardelle with walnuts 354

Parmesan and walnut crisps 354

Pear and almond tart 362

Pickled walnuts 353

Roast stuffed figs with Gorgonzola
and walnuts 331

Walnut tart 355

O

olives

Fava beans with olive tapenade 107

Pork scallops with thyme tapenade
49

omelette, Asparagus 101

onions 242

Clove and onion pasta 245

French onion soup 245

Onion tart from Beamish and
McGlue 247

Onions baked whole in parchment
paper parcels 248

Pissaladière 246

Red onion marmalade 249

Sweet onion compote 249

see also Shallot tatin

oranges 30

Amber marmalade 33

Endive and blood orange salad
26

Marmalade ice cream with fresh
oranges 33

orange and almond cake, Tunisian
34

Orange and cranberry pies 418

orange and lemon salad, Sicilian 34

Orange pasta 34

Seville marmalade 33

see also Mandarin sorbet

oregano 218

see also Rosemary, olive, and
lemon chicken

P

pancakes, buckwheat 222

pancetta

Caramelized celeriac with pancetta
435

Grilled goat cheese salad 54

Pea and pancetta farfalle 133

Quick-fried kale 402

Radicchio and lemon pasta 29

Spinach, pancetta, and roasted
almond salad 79

Panna cotta with marinated
pomegranate 416

Pantzarosalata 163

Panzanella 274

Pappardelle with walnuts 354

Parmesan and walnut crisps 354

parsley 50, 80

Deep-fried parsley 90

Herb dumplings 83

Parsley sauce 89

Parsley soup 89

Spring salsa verde 83

Warm chickpea and parsley salad
90

see also herbs, mixed

parsnips 420

Parsnip purée with bourbon 427

Roasted parsnips rolled in
Parmesan 427

Root vegetable chips 425

Slow-roasted winter roots and herb
couscous 424

Smoked fish cakes with parsnips
428

Spiced parsnip soup 427

pasta

Asparagus pasta with lemon 101

Chard and nutmeg farfalle 396

Clove and onion pasta 245

Mushroom pasta 347

Orange pasta 34

Pappardelle with walnuts 354

Pasta with roasted tomatoes and
garlic 278

Pea and pancetta farfalle 133

Penne with preserved lemon and
avocado 36

Purple sprouting broccoli pasta 64

Radicchio and lemon pasta 29
Radish top pasta 137
Rosemary and pork farfalle 43
Sage, fennel, and Pernod pasta 311
Spaghetti with beans and tomatoes
    207
Spring herb and wild greens pasta
    84
Tagliolini with fava beans and
    beurre blanc 109
tomato pasta, Raw 277
Treviso lasagne 29
Trofie with potatoes, beans, and
    pesto 208
Zucchini and dill farfalle 182
pastry, shortcrust 70, 74
    orange 178
Patmos chickpeas 44
pavlova
    Chestnut pavlova with caramelized
        apples 353
peaches 154
    Bellinis 154
    Peach melba 158
    Peach zabaglione 158
    Peaches with bourbon 158
pears 358
    Melon, pear, and arugula salad 237
    Pear and almond tart 362
    Pear, apple, and quince Charlotte
        365
    Pears, bananas, and grapes with
        fudge sauce 361
    pears poached in saffron syrup,
        Darina Allen's 361
    Poached pears 361
    Spiced preserved pears 365
    Toffee pear tart 362
peas 128
    carrots and peas, Sally Clarke's
        240
    Chilled pea soup with roasted
        garlic 133
    Crushed peas 130
    Mint and pea tip risotto 131
    Pea and pancetta farfalle 133
    Pea and ricotta tart with thyme
        pastry 131
    Pea puree 130
    Peas with cucumber and mint 130

Samphire with fresh peas and
    young fava beans 141
Sauté of peas and lettuce 115
Penne with preserved lemon and
    avocado 36
Peperonata 371
peppers 366
    Double pepper broccoli 65
    Masai mara 369
    Peperonata 371
    Red pepper frittata with prosciutto
        371
    Roasted pepper soup 369
    Roasted red peppers with
        mozzarella 370
pesto
    Cilantro pesto 87
    Marcella's homemade pesto
        225
    Stuffed baked potatoes with pesto
        339
    Wild garlic pesto 95
pheasant
    Game salad with pomegranate 412
    pheasant and leek pie, Ray Smith's
        407
    Pheasant soup 369
    Pheasant with Calvados, apple, and
        chestnut 292
Philippa's blackcurrant leaf sorbet
    169
pickles
    Pickled chilis 318
    Pickled cucumber, Surinam 197
    Pickled walnuts 353
    Sweet cucumber pickle 197
pies
    zucchini pie, Greek 186
    Ithaca pie 74
    Orange and cranberry pies 418
    pheasant and leek pie, Ray Smith's
        407
    Pumpkin pie 377
Pissaladière 246
pita bread
    Fattoush 273
    Halloumi, mint, cilantro, and dill
        pitas 228
Pizza 281
Pizza bianca 250

plums 254
    Apple and plum chutney 295
    Best ever plum crumble 257
    Plum, apple, and chili jelly 319
    Plum sauce 257
    Roasted plums with bread and
        butter pudding 256
    Roasted plums with homemade
        custard 256
    Savory plum jam 259
    tuscan plum tart, Darina Allen's 257
polenta
    Mushrooms with polenta 347
    Treviso al forno with grilled polenta
        28
pomegranates 410
    Frozen mocha and ginger meringue
        cake with pomegranate sauce
        415
    Game salad with pomegranate
        412
    Jeweled couscous 412
    Panna cotta with marinated
        pomegranate 416
porcini 342
    Porcini and prosciutto pasticcio
        346
pork
    Chestnut-stuffed pork fillet 350
    Pork scallops with thyme tapenade
        49
    Greek pork with quince 381
    Hungarian goulash with lovage 88
    Jambalaya 370
    Pork fillet with cilantro 85
    Rosemary and pork farfalle 43
    stuffed cabbage leaves, Bea's 18
Potatoes, maincrop/floury 334
    Bubble and squeak cakes 340
    Mint potato cakes 230
    Nutmeg mashed potatoes 336
    Potato and leek soup 406
    Potato and sage gratin 48
    Potato gratin with sorrel 91
    Rosemary saddleback potatoes
        336
    Rösti potatoes 336
    Sag aloo 78
    Stuffed baked potatoes with pesto
        339

Stuffed tomatoes with roast
potatoes 284
Warm potato and lentil salad 340
see also potatoes, new; potatoes,
sweet
potatoes, new/waxy 122
Chorizo with potatoes 125
Glazed summer vegetables 137
Green beans with new potatoes
125
New carrots and potatoes roasted
with garlic and thyme 241
New potato salad with quail eggs
and black pudding 127
New potatoes in saffron dressing
124
Potato salad with capers and
anchovies 124
Smashed roasted new potatoes
with garlic and rosemary 127
see also Spring vegetable soup
potatoes, sweet 334
Grilled sweet potato with ginger,
chili, and lime 341
Roasted sweet potato and feta
salad 341
Root vegetable chips 425
Sweet potato gratin 341
praline
Hazelnut ice cream and praline 357
prawns
Fennel and prawn risotto 311
puddings see desserts
pumpkins 372
Pumpkin pie 377
Pumpkin, sage, and pecorino
tortellini 377
see also squashes
purple sprouting broccoli see broccoli
purslane 50, 84

Q

quail
Quail with figs 333
Stuffed roasted quail with jeweled
couscous and spiced citrus
sauce 412
quail eggs
New potato salad with quail eggs
and black pudding 127

Niçoise salad 210
Quick braised red cabbage 21
Quick-fried kale 402
Quick lavender ice cream 201
Quick tomato tart 279
quinces 378
apple and quince cake, Windfall
380
Baked quinces in orange syrup 380
Greek pork with quince 381
Membrillo 380
Pear, apple, and quince Charlotte
365
Quince jelly 381

R

radicchio 22
Radicchio and lemon pasta 29
see also Treviso lasagne
radishes 134
Early summer crudités on ice with
aioli 137
Glazed summer vegetables137
Radish top pasta 137
raita, Cucumber 196
raspberries 260
Cranachan 327
Juicy summer pudding 263
Meringue roulade with raspberries
263
Peach melba 158
Raspberry and redcurrant jam 265
Russian redcurrant and raspberry
pudding 171
Spectacular rice pudding with
raspberry and redcurrant jam
265
see also loganberries
ratatouille, Cranberry bean 304
redcurrants 166
Frosted redcurrants with Chantilly
cream 173
Juicy summer pudding 263
Raspberry and redcurrant jam 265
Redcurrant jelly 171
redcurrant steamed pudding,
Emma's 171
Russian redcurrant and raspberry
pudding 171
rhubarb 66

Poached rhubarb with ginger ice
cream 70
Rhubarb sorbet 69
Rhubarb syllabub 69
Rhubarb tart 70
Rhubarb upside-down cake 69
Ribollita 402
rice
Lemongrass rice 227
Spectacular rice pudding with rasp-
berry and redcurrant jam 265
see also risotti
ricotta cheese
Pea and ricotta tart with thyme
pastry 131
Ricotta al forno 224
risotti
Chard and risotto balls 396
Fennel and prawn risotto 311
Mint and pea tip risotto 131
Primavera risotto 102
Risotto of beets, dill, and fennel 165
Spring greens risotto 65
Zucchini risotto 182
Riverford new summer carrots and
turnips 240
romano beans 204
Romano bean flower salad 211
Romano beans with cream and
savory 211
Root vegetable chips 425
rose flowers 198
rosemary 40
Rosemary and anchovy crusted
lamb 43
Rosemary and pork farfalle 43
Rosemary flat bread 46
Rosemary, olive, and lemon
chicken 44
Rosemary saddleback potatoes
336
Rösti potatoes 336
rowan berries 320
Rowan jelly 324
Russian redcurrant and raspberry
pudding 171
rutabagas 420
Puree of rutabaga 435
Roast rutabaga with maple syrup
435

Scotch broth 437
Vegetable stock 424

S

saffron
  saffron dressing 124
  saffron syrup 361
Sag aloo 78
Saganaki 273
sage 40
  Cranberry beans with sage 307
  Potato and sage gratin 48
  Sage and squash soufflé 374
  Sage, fennel, and Pernod pasta 311
  Sage leaf tempura 46
salads 50
  Apple and celeriac salad 434
  Arugula, beet, and feta salad 55
  Asparagus, fava beans, arugula,
    and pea salad 102
  beet salad, Nadah Saleh's
    Lebanese 163
  beet salad with toasted mustard
    seeds and orange, Grated 163
  Black and white grape salad 330
  Caesar salad 112
  Celery and cucumber salad in
    mustard dressing 315
  chickpea and parsley salad, Warm
    90
  Cucumber and dill salad, Marinated
    195
  Duck breast and peppery-leaf
    salad 53
  Eggplant and feta salad 300
  eggplant salad, Spiced 299
  Endive and blood orange salad 26
  Endive and blue cheese salad 25
  fava bean salad, Warm 107
  Fennel and grape salad, 310
  Game salad with pomegranate 412
  globe artichoke heart salad, Raw
    119
  Grilled goat cheese salad 54
  Lemon bean salad 210
  Melon, pear, and arugula salad 237
  mushroom salad, Raw 345
  New potato salad with quail eggs
    and black pudding 127
  Niçoise salad 210

orange and lemon salad, Sicilian 34
Panzanella 274
potato and lentil salad, Warm 340
Romano bean flower salad 211
Scorzonera salad 440
spinach, pancetta, and roasted
  almond salad, Baby 79
Squash and arugula salad with
  pears and rosemary 376
sweet potato and feta salad,
  Roasted 341
Watercress and smoked trout salad
  with horseradish 95
Winter flower and toasted seed salad
  55
Zucchini and lemon salad 184
salmon
  Ceviche 39
  Gravlax 222
  Whole fish stuffed with fennel 227
salmon, smoked
  Smoked salmon pâté with chervil
    85
Salsa verde 227, 409
  Spring salsa verde 83
salsify 420
  Fried salsify in breadcrumbs 438
  Marni's salsify 438
  Roasted salsify 438
samphire 138
  Samphire sauce 141
  Samphire with fresh peas and
    young fava beans 141
sauces
  aioli 137
  Angelica's sauce (for globe
    artichokes) 118
  béchamel sauce 29, 165, 346
  Chili dipping sauce 318
  citrus sauce, Spiced 412
  Dill and mustard sauce 222
  Elderflower and gooseberry sauce
    143
  fudge sauce 361
  hollandaise sauce 440
  horseradish and cucumber sauce,
    Fresh 196
  Horseradish sauce 441
  Orange pasta sauce 34
  Parsley sauce 89

Plum sauce 257
pomegranate sauce 415
Samphire sauce 141
sorrel sauce with fish, Jane
  Grigson's 91
Strawberry sauce for ice cream 147
Tarragon hollandaise sauce 233
toffee sauce, hot 416
tomato sauce, Really rich 277
Watercress hollandaise sauce 94
see also pasta; Salsa verde
savory
  Romano beans with cream and
    savory 211
savoy cabbages 14
  Savoy cabbage and cilantro soup 17
scorzonera 420
  Scorzonera salad 440
Scotch broth 437
sea bass
  Whole fish stuffed with fennel 227
sea bream
  Whole fish stuffed with fennel 227
sea kale 50
Seville marmalade 33
Seville oranges 30
shallots 242
  Shallot dressing 248
  Shallot tatin 247
Sicilian orange and lemon salad 34
sloes 320
  Sloe and apple jelly 324
  Sloe vodka or gin 323
Smashed roasted new potatoes with
  garlic and rosemary 127
smoked haddock see haddock,
  smoked
smoked salmon see salmon, smoked
snacks
  Parmesan and walnut crisps 354
  see also tapenades; tempura
snow peas 128
sole
  Ceviche 39
sorbets
  blackcurrant leaf sorbet, Philippa's
    169
  gooseberry and elderflower sorbet,
    Jane's 215
  Greengage sorbet 259

Mandarin sorbet 39
Melon and ginger sorbet 237
Orange sorbet see Mandarin
    sorbet
Rhubarb sorbet 69
Verveine (lemon verbena) sorbet 225
sorrel 80
    Potato gratin with sorrel 91
    sorrel sauce with fish, Jane
        Grigson's 91
    Sorrel soup 91
    Spinach and sorrel frittata 77
    see also herbs, mixed
soufflés
    Celeriac soufflé 432
    Zucchini soufflé 183
    Mrs. Root's lemon soufflé 36
    Sage and squash soufflé 374
    Smoked haddock and corn soufflé
        385
soups
    Andalusian soup-salad 272
    beet soup, Roasted 164
    Broccoli soup with Gorgonzola 64
    cabbage and cilantro soup, Savoy
        17
    Cannellini, borlotti, or white butter
        bean soup 305
    Carrot and Jerusalem artichoke
        soup 431
    Cauliflower soup 61
    Celeriac and apple soup 432
    Chard and coconut soup 395
    Cucumber and garlic soup with
        chives 195
    garlic soup, Wild 95
    Gazpacho 269
    gazpacho with grapes, White 330
    Lettuce and lovage soup 87
    Minestrone 21
    Mint and cucumber soup 195
    Mushroom soup 345
    onion soup, French 45
    Parsley soup 89
    parsnip soup, Spiced 427
    pea soup with roasted garlic,
        Chilled 133
    pepper soup, Roasted 369
    Pheasant soup 369
    Potato and leek soup 406

Ribollita 402
Scotch broth 437
Smoked haddock and corn
    chowder 384
Sorrel soup 91
Spinach and lentil soup 74
spring onion and cilantro
    vichyssoise, Ingrid Marsh's 248
Spring vegetable soup 107
Squash and cumin soup 376
Tomato soup 268
tomato soup, Cleopatra's 269
Watercress soup 94
Zucchini and coconut soup 190
Sour cherry jam 177
spaghetti
    Spaghetti with beans and tomatoes
        207
spearmint 218
Spectacular rice pudding with
        raspberry and redcurrant jam
        265
spinach 72
    Baby spinach, pancetta, and
        roasted almond salad 79
    Creamed spinach 78
    Horta 395
    Ithaca pie 74
    Sag aloo 78
    Spinach and Gruyère tart 77
    Spinach and lentil soup 74
    Spinach and sorrel frittata 77
    Spinach malfatta 79
    Spinach with split peas or lentils
        78
spinach, 'perpetual' 72
Spring greens risotto 65
Spring herb and wild greens pasta 84
spring onions 242
    Ingrid Marsh's spring onion and
        cilantro vichyssoise 248
Spring vegetable soup 107
squashes 372
    Sage and squash soufflé 374
    Stuffed butternut squash 374
    Winter squash and arugula salad
        with pears and rosemary 376
    Winter squash and cumin soup
        with squash chips 376
Squid, pea, and chorizo stew 133

Stir-fried beet tops with chili and
    ginger 165
stock, Vegetable 424
strawberries 144
    Alpine strawberry gratin 150
    Champagne cocktail with alpine
        strawberries 150
    French strawberry jam 150
    Fresh strawberry and shortbread
        tart 149
    Marinated strawberries 148
    Strawberries Romanoff 149
    Strawberries with meringues 148
    Strawberries with rosé wine 149
    Strawberry and black pepper ice
        cream 147
    Strawberry sauce for ice cream
        147
sugar snap peas 128
Summer garden tempura 207
summer pudding, Juicy 263
Sun-blushed tomatoes 285
Surinam pickled cucumber 197
Sweet-and-sour borlotti beans 304
Sweet-and-sour marinated cabbage
    18
sweet potato see potatoes, sweet

T
Tabbouleh 272
Tagliolini with fava beans and beurre
    blanc 109
Tam's stuffed zucchini flowers 189
tapenades
    Fava beans with olive tapenade 107
    Pork scallops with thyme tapenade
        49
tarragon 218
    Chicken in tarragon cream 233
    Tarragon hollandaise 233
    Tarragon vinegar 233
tarts
    Apricot tart 157
    cherry tart, Caroline's 178
    Cranberry tart with hot toffee
        sauce 416
    Fresh fig tart 333
    Globe artichoke tart 121
    Gooseberry tart 214
    Leek and goat cheese tart 407

Onion tart from Beamish and McGlue 247
Pea and ricotta tart with thyme pastry 131
Pear and almond tart 362
plum tart, Darina Allen's Tuscan 257
Rhubarb tart 70
Shallot tatin 247
Spinach and Gruyère tart 77
strawberry and shortbread tart, Fresh 149
Toffee pear tart 362
tomato tart, Quick 279
Walnut tart 355
Zucchini soufflé tart 183
tayberries 260
Tiramisu with red berries 265
tempura
Globe artichoke heart tempura 119
Sage leaf tempura 46
Summer garden tempura 207
Teresa's melon with blackberries 237
thyme 40
Pork scallops with thyme tapenade 49
Lamb burgers with thyme and rosemary 49
Pea and ricotta tart with thyme pastry 131
Tiramisu with red berries 265
Toffee apples 294
Toffee pear tart 362
Toffee sauce 416
tomatoes 266
Andalusian soup-salad 272
Baked tomatoes with cream 268
Cranberry bean ratatouille 304
Fattoush 273
Gazpacho 269
Green tomato chutney 285
Panzanella 274
Pasta with roasted tomatoes and garlic 278
Raw tomato pasta 277
Saganaki 273
Spaghetti with beans and tomatoes 207
Stuffed tomatoes with roasted potatoes 284
Sun-blushed tomatoes 285

Sungold tomato focaccia 271
Tabbouleh 272
Tomato bruschetta 278
tomato jam, De Kas 282
tomato sauce, Really rich 277
Tomato soup 268
tomato soup, Cleopatra's 269
tomato tart, Quick 279
Treviso chicory 22
Treviso al forno with grilled polenta 28
Treviso lasagne 29
Trofie with potatoes, beans, and pesto 208
trout, smoked
Watercress and smoked trout salad with horseradish 95
Tunisian orange and almond cake 34
turnips 420
Braised turnips 437
Glazed summer vegetables 137
Riverford new summer carrots and turnips 240
Vegetable stock 424

U
upside-down cake, Rhubarb 69

V
vegetables, mixed
Primavera risotto 102
Slow roasted winter roots and herb couscous 424
Spring vegetable soup 107
Summer garden tempura 207
Vegetable korma 61
Vegetable stock 424
Winter bagna cauda 422
see also specific vegetables
Venison, cranberry, and chestnut casserole 419
Venison fillet with root vegetable chips 425
Verveine sorbet 225
Vichy carrots 428
vichyssoise, Ingrid Marsh's spring onion and cilantro 248
vine leaves, Jude's stuffed 331
vinegars
Sweet black mulberry vinegar 324

Tarragon vinegar 233
vodka
Cranberry vodka 418
Damson plum vodka 323
Sloe vodka 323

W
walnuts 348
Pappardelle with walnuts 354
Parmesan and walnut crisps 354
Pickled walnuts 353
Roasted stuffed figs with Gorgonzola and walnuts 331
Walnut tart 355
Warm fava bean salad 107
Warm chickpea and parsley salad 90
Warm potato and lentil salad 340
watercress 50, 92
Fried watercress 94
peppery-leaf salad 53
Watercress and smoked trout salad with horseradish 95
Watercress hollandaise 94
Watercress soup 94
watermelons 234
white currants 166
Windfall apple and quince cake 380
Winter bagna cauda 422
Winter flower and toasted seed salad 55

Z
zabaglione, Peach or nectarine 158
zucchini 180
Crisp zucchini wedges with anchovy mayonnaise 187
Greek zucchini pie 186
Roasted zucchini, eggplant, and onion with balsamic sauce 191
stuffed zucchini flowers, Matthew's 189
stuffed zucchini flowers, Tam's 189
Zucchini and coconut soup 190
Zucchini and dill farfalle 182
Zucchini and ginger jam 191
Zucchini and lemon salad 184
Zucchini chutney 190
Zucchini risotto 182
Zucchini soufflé 183
Zuccini soufflé tart 183

Acknowledgements

This book was long in the making and Adam, Rosie, and Molly have lived with it as much as I have, trying all the recipes and being immensely supportive. My friend and colleague Louise Farman has also put up with my long-term distraction.

Warm thanks go to my agent Caroline Michel, who has always been hugely enthusiastic about the idea, and to Richard Atkinson, my commissioning editor at Bloomsbury, who from the word go understood the concept of such a large book on this simple subject and, like me, wanted to make it beautiful. That absolute support and mutuality has been invaluable. I would like to thank Natalie Hunt who coordinated the whole project, Lisa Fiske in the production department, and everyone at Bloomsbury who has been involved with the book. As soon as I met Karl Shanahan, the designer, I knew he would create the book I hoped for—and he did. And thanks too, to Lewis Esson and Anne Askwith, who did wonderful work neatening up the text.

There have been many different inspirations for this book. The first was from my childhood, when holidays at Asolo in the Veneto introduced me to the colorful spectrum of Mediterranean vegetables and to the practice of shopping and cooking every day according to what the market could provide. I think this more than anything has made me love the food I do. I owe enormous thanks to my mother for introducing me to that world.

I greatly value the real and direct way of cooking that Nigel Slater has championed for so long. Rose Gray and Ruth Rogers, Antonio Carluccio, the Clarks from Moro and the chefs from the great Dutch restaurant in Amsterdam, De Kas, have all been sources of enthusiasm and inspiration. I am indebted to them all.

I've always had fun cooking and, of course, eating with friends. Many of the recipes here have been taught to me by my friends: Ivan and Pots Samarine, Aurea Carpenter and Andrew Palmer, Hugh Fearnley-Whittingstall, Kate and Charlie Boxer, Flora McDonnell, Kate Hubbard, Sarah and Montagu Don, Caroline Owen-Lloyd, Pip Morrison, John Keeling, Jane Sackville West, Jude Maynard, Jo Clark, Tessa and Simon Bishop, and Sofka Zinovieff. I have loved cooking with Matthew Rice, a man who is as committed to beautiful vegetables as I am, and learning from my sister, Jane Raven, who now has an allotment, and from her mother-in-law, Teresa Wallace. Clare Smith, Pip Morrison, Jane Raven, Teresa Wallace, Kate Hubbard, and Matthew Rice have been a terrific help with the unwieldy manuscript. All thanks to them!

I am very grateful for the meticulous work done by the recipe testers: Debbie Staples, Liz Wood, and Caroline Davenport Thomas.

Bea Burke and Colin Pilbeam have grown all the vegetables at Perch Hill. Warm, heartfelt thanks goes to them. They make the whole process of cooking from the garden a joy, with a harvesting walk one of the greatest pleasures in my life.

I have worked with Jonathan Buckley photographing plants and gardens for ten years, but this was the first time we photographed food together, and I love the results. We often had very long days, starting at dawn and having to keep going until long into the evening, but Jonathan was always extremely patient. At the end of one day in May I ran over his camera case in the Land Rover! It still contained two cameras and all but one of his lenses—I think he wanted to cry, but he laughed instead. I hope that we continue doing gardening books together, and that this is the first of many on food.

The person who has influenced me most in recent years is Tam Lawson. She has taught me that it is sometimes best to follow a plan. She is a wonderful cook, light on her feet, ocean-like in her knowledge, and vastly generous in sharing her expertise. Many of the recipes included here are originally hers. We've spent days, months, years chatting about food, and it's to her that I dedicate this book.

Many thanks for specific recipes also go to: Carolyn Agius (Double pepper broccoli, page 65); Emma Ainslie (Onions baked whole, page 248); Lucy Baring (orange firelighters, page 30); Caroline Beamish (Onion tart from Beamish and McGlue, page 247); Cathy Bevan (Strawberry and black pepper ice cream, page 147); Lucy Boyd (Chard gratin, page 397); Ruth Bradley (Pumpkin pie, page 377); Lynda Brown (Spring greens risotto, page 65); William Buckingham (Naan bread, page 299); Virginia Chapman (Pureed brussels sprouts in nutmeg cream, page 391); Jo Clark (Quick tomato tart, page 279, Stuffed baked potatoes with pesto, page 339, and Stuffed butternut squash, page 374); Harold Costello (Braised beans and celery, page 314); Sue Culley (Cranberry tart with hot toffee sauce, page 416); Adrian and Michael Daniel, *The Gate Vegetarian* (adaptation of their Spinach and tomato dhal, page 74); Caroline Davenport Thomas (Smoked salmon pâté with chervil, page 85); Kate Dawson (Watercress and smoked trout salad with horseradish, page 95); Jane Dunn (Grilled mini globe artichokes, page 118); Hugh Van Dusen (Parsnip puree with bourbon, page 427); Kate Gattaker (Baked cream with gooseberries, page 217); Laurie Graizeau (French onion soup, page 245); Annie de la Grange Sury (Roasted beet soup, page 164); Michael Hobbs (Grated carrot and poppy seed salad, page 430); Sue Kennedy (Baked quinces in orange syrup, page 380); Michael Lawson or "Judge

Jam" (French strawberry jam, page 150, French apricot jam, page 157, Peach zabaglione, page 158, Savory plum jam, page 259, Mushroom soup, page 345, and Fried salsify in breadcrumbs, page 438); Sophia Lawson (White gazpacho with grapes, page 330, and Panna cotta with marinated pomegranate, page 416); Ingrid Marsh (Tunisian orange and almond cake, page 34); Fiona Mates (onion cutting technique, page 242); Rebecca Nicolson (Cranberry bean ratatouille, page 304); Andrew Palmer (Smashed roasted new potatoes with garlic and rosemary, page 127); Emmanuela Palú (Tiramisu with red berries, page 265, and Pumpkin, sage, and pecorino tortellini, page 377); Daniela Piccolotto (Sweet-and-sour cranberry beans, page 304, Bottled celery, page 315, and Peperonata, page 371); Efi Pollis (Greek zucchini pie, page 186); Anna Raven (Rosemary saddleback potatoes, page 336); Faith Raven (Celeriac rémoulade, page 434); Jane Raven (Sun-blushed tomatoes, page 285); Anne Revell (Chili jam, page 318); Matthew Rice (Chard and risotto balls, page 396, and Quick-fried kale, page 402); Mary Samarine (orange slices, page 33); South Devon Chilli Farm (Pickled chilis, page 318, Chili dipping sauce, page 318, and Chili chocolate, page 319); Debbie Staples (Grated beet salad with toasted mustard seeds and orange, page 163, Warm potato and lentil salad, page 340, and Chard and feta parcels, page 395); Alice Stobart (Roasted sweet potato and feta salad, page 341); Josie Stow and Jan Baldwin, *The African Kitchen* (Grilled sweet potato with ginger, chili, and lime, page 341, and Masai mara, page 369); Teresa Wallace (adaptation of her Lemon soufflé, page 36); Janet Wilson (Sloe and apple jelly, page 324); Wendy Wolf (Peaches with bourbon, page 158); Liz Wood (Toffee apples, page 294); Sofka Zinovieff (Spinach with split peas or lentils, page 78).

About the author

Sarah Raven is the expert on all things to grow, cut, and eat from your garden. She is an inspirational and passionate teacher, running cooking, flower arranging, and gardening courses at the school she set up in 1999 at her farm in East Sussex, England. Her mail order company, Sarah Raven's Kitchen and Garden, sells seeds, bulbs, books, and her favorite things for the kitchen and garden. She has also written for *Domino, House & Garden,* and *Country Living*. A host on BBC's *Gardeners' World,* Raven is also the author of the books *The Great Vegetable Plot, The Cutting Garden,* and *The Bold and Brilliant Garden.* Raven is married to the writer Adam Nicolson and has two daughters and three stepsons.

About the photographer

Jonathan Buckley specializes in garden and plant photography and his work has been widely published in books, magazines, and newspapers worldwide. He has been collaborating with Sarah Raven, taking photographs at Perch Hill, for ten years. He was named Photographer of the Year and Features Photographer of the Year by the Garden Writers' Guild in 2006.

To Tam, with love and thanks

First published in the United States of America in 2008
by Universe Publishing, A Division of
Rizzoli International Publications, Inc.
300 Park Avenue South
New York, NY 10010
www.rizzoliusa.com

First published in the United Kingdom as
The Garden Cookbook by Bloomsbury Publishing Plc
36 Soho Square
London W1D 3QY

2008 2009 2010 2011 / 10 9 8 7 6 5 4 3 2 1

Text adapted for the United States by Stephen Orr

Printed by Tien Wah Press, Singapore

ISBN-10: 0-7893-1811-4
ISBN-13: 978-0-7893-1811-3

Library of Congress Control Number: 2008923453